SUPERMAN BATMAN
NIGHT AND DAY

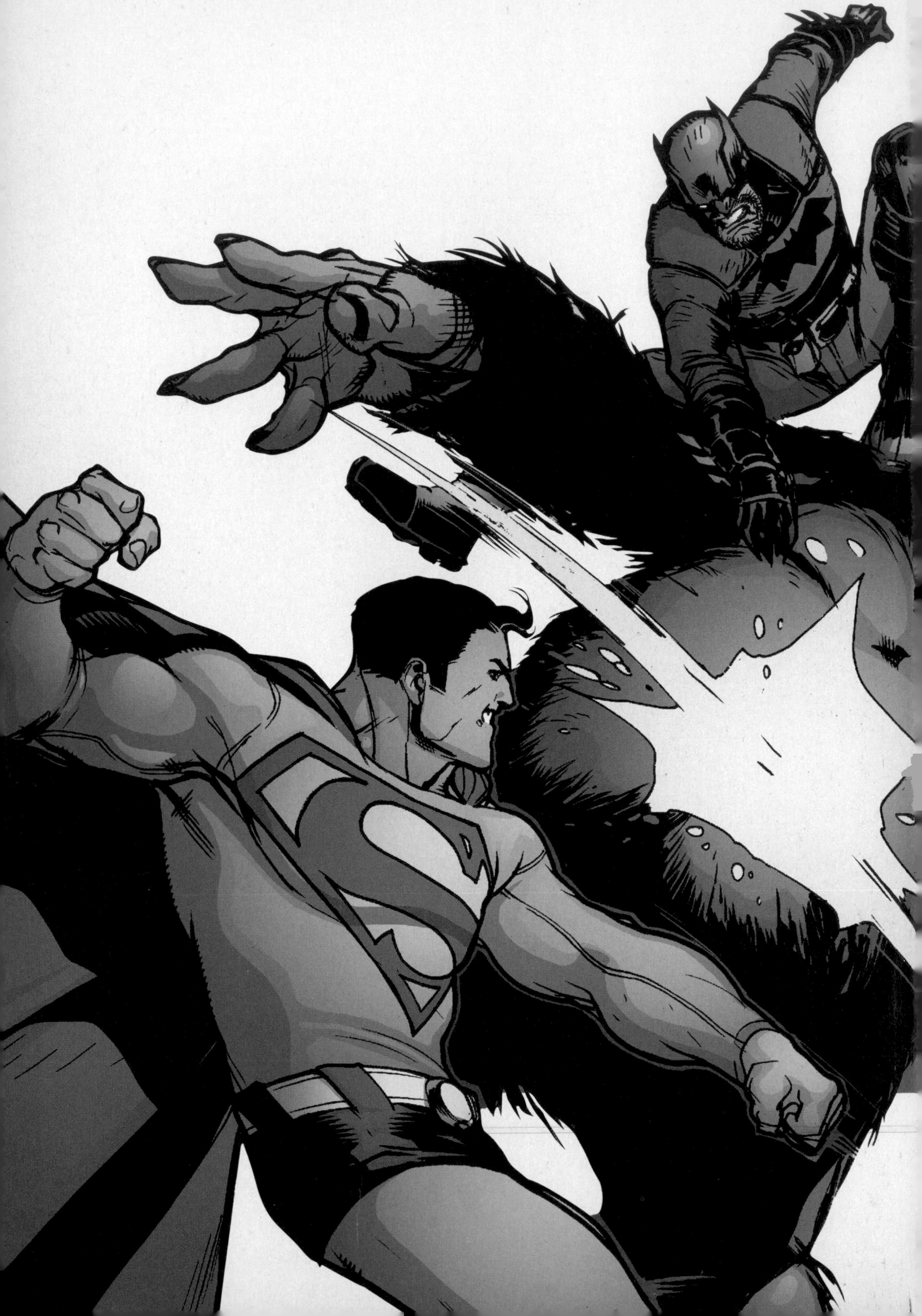

Michael Green
Mike Johnson
Peter Johnson
Matt Cherniss
Scott Kolins
Writers

Francis Manapul
Rafael Albuquerque
Brian Stelfreeze
Brian Haberlin
Kelley Jones
Joe Quinones
Federico Dallocchio
Scott Kolins
Artists

Brian Buccellato
David Baron
Joe Quinones
Michael Atiyeh
Colorists

Rob Leigh
Sal Cipriano
Letterers

SUPERMAN BATMAN

NIGHT AND DAY

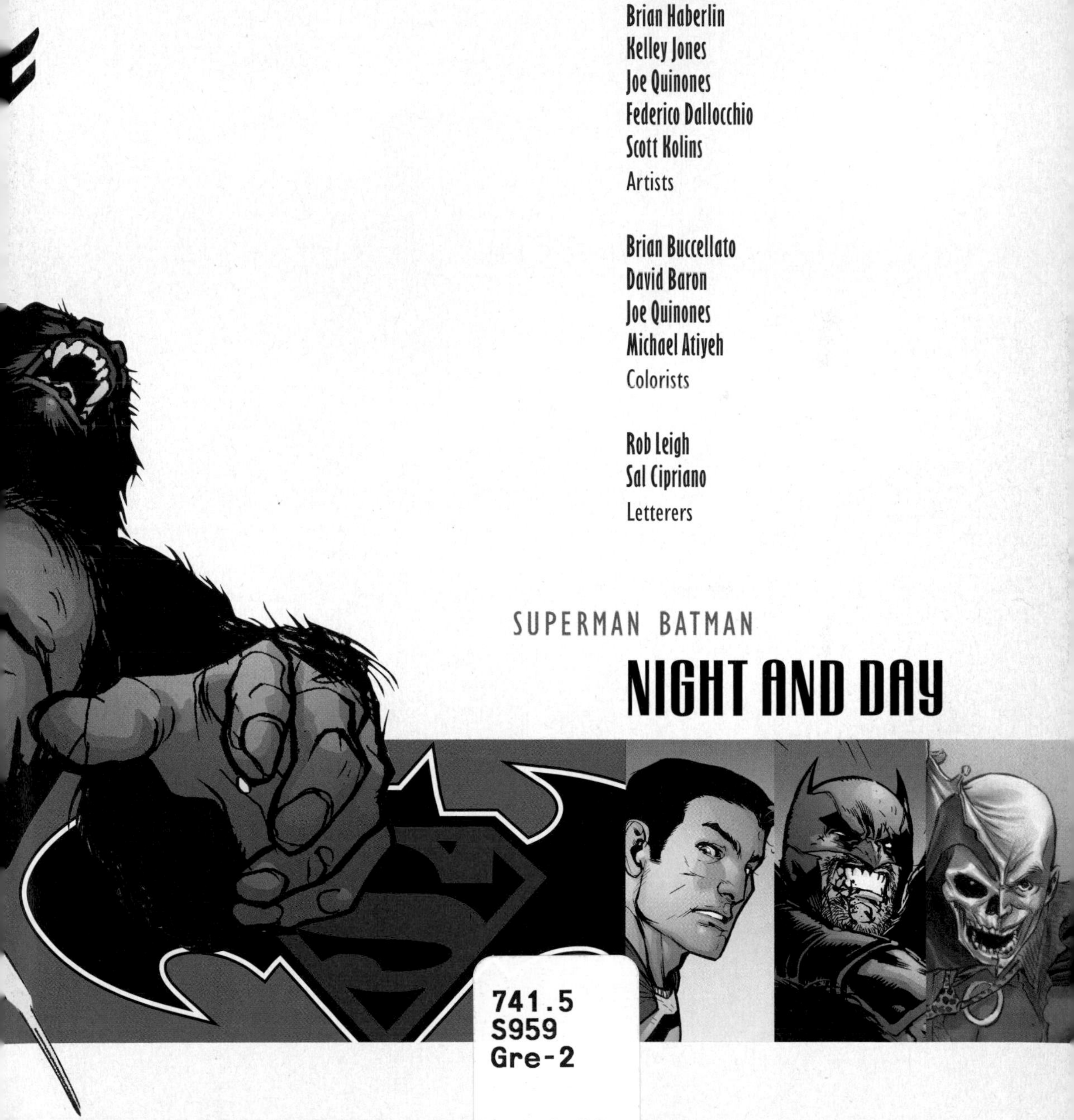

Superman created by Jerry Siegel and Joe Shuster
Batman created by Bob Kane

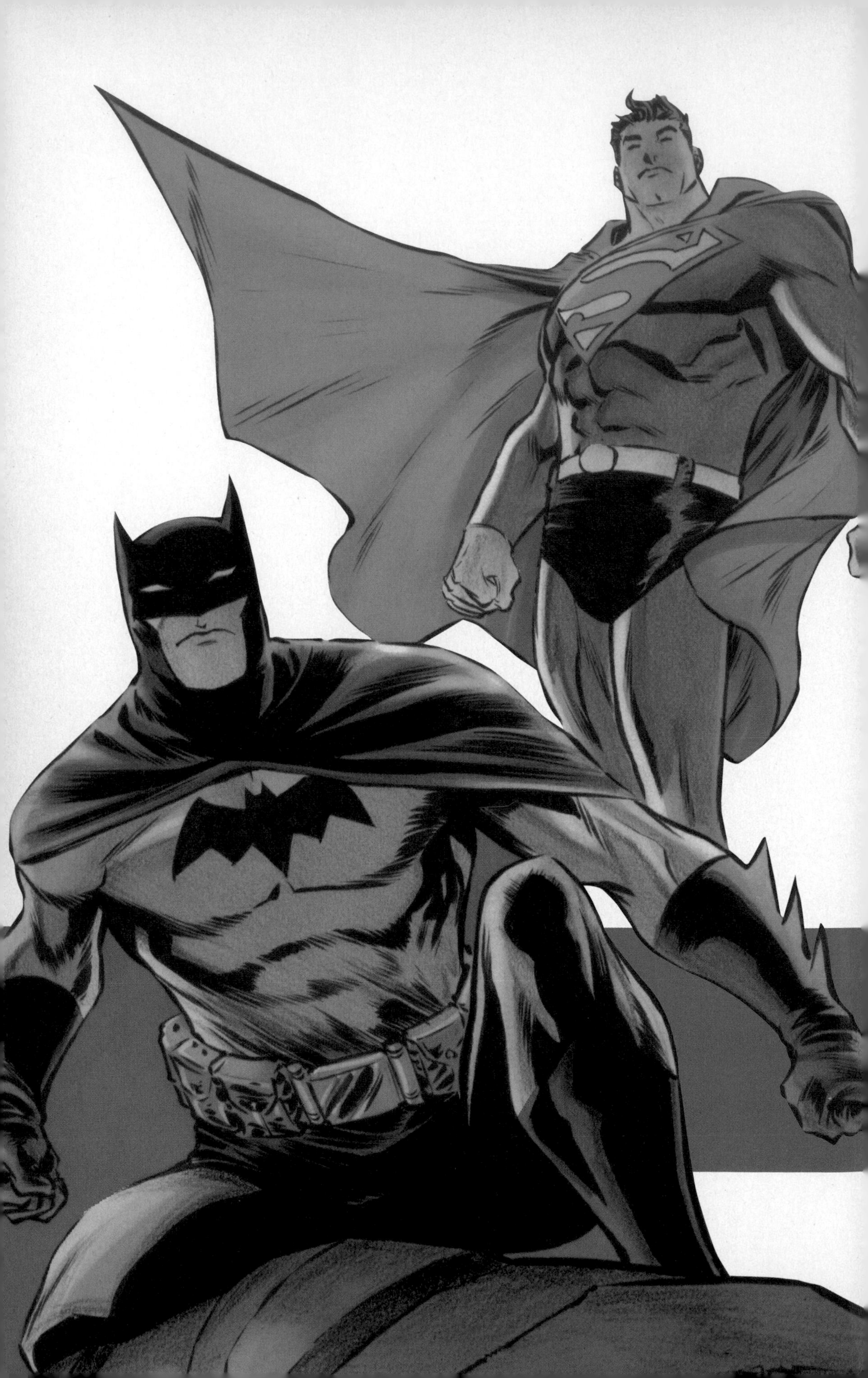

EDDIE BERGANZA Editor-Original Series ADAM SCHLAGMAN Associate Editor-Original Series BOB HARRAS Group Editor-Collected Editions
BOB JOY Editor ROBBIN BROSTERMAN Design Director-Books

DC COMICS
DIANE NELSON President DAN DIDIO and JIM LEE Co-Publishers GEOFF JOHNS Chief Creative Officer PATRICK CALDON EVP-Finance and Administration
JOHN ROOD EVP-Sales, Marketing and Business Development AMY GENKINS SVP-Business and Legal Affairs STEVE ROTTERDAM SVP-Sales and Marketing
JOHN CUNNINGHAM VP-Marketing TERRI CUNNINGHAM VP-Managing Editor ALISON GILL VP-Manufacturing DAVID HYDE VP-Publicity
SUE POHJA VP-Book Trade Sales ALYSSE SOLL VP-Advertising and Custom Publishing BOB WAYNE VP-Sales MARK CHIARELLO Art Director

SUPERMAN/BATMAN: NIGHT AND DAY. Published by DC Comics. Cover and compilation Copyright © 2010 DC Comics. All Rights Reserved.
Originally published in single magazine form as SUPERMAN/BATMAN 60-63, 65-67 Copyright © 2009, 2010 DC Comics. All Rights Reserved.
All characters, their distinctive likenesses and related elements featured in this publication are trademarks of DC Comics. The stories,
characters and incidents featured in this publication are entirely fictional. DC Comics does not read or accept unsolicited submissions
of ideas, stories or artwork.

DC Comics, 1700 Broadway, New York, NY 10019. A Warner Bros. Entertainment Company
Printed by RR Donnelley, Salem, VA, USA. 7/28/10. First Printing.
HC ISBN: 978-1-4012-2792-0 SC ISBN: 978-1-4012-2808-8 Cover art by Francis Manapul

SUSTAINABLE
FORESTRY
INITIATIVE
Certified Chain of Custody
Promoting Sustainable
Forest Management
www.sfiprogram.org

Fiber used in this product line meets the
sourcing requirements of the SFI program.
www.sfiprogram.org NFS-SPIC0C-C0001801

MASH-UP

PART ONE

Plot: Michael Green and Mike Johnson

Dialogue: Mike Johnson

Artist: Francis Manapul

SUPERMAN/BATMAN No. 60
Francis Manapul with Brian Buccellato

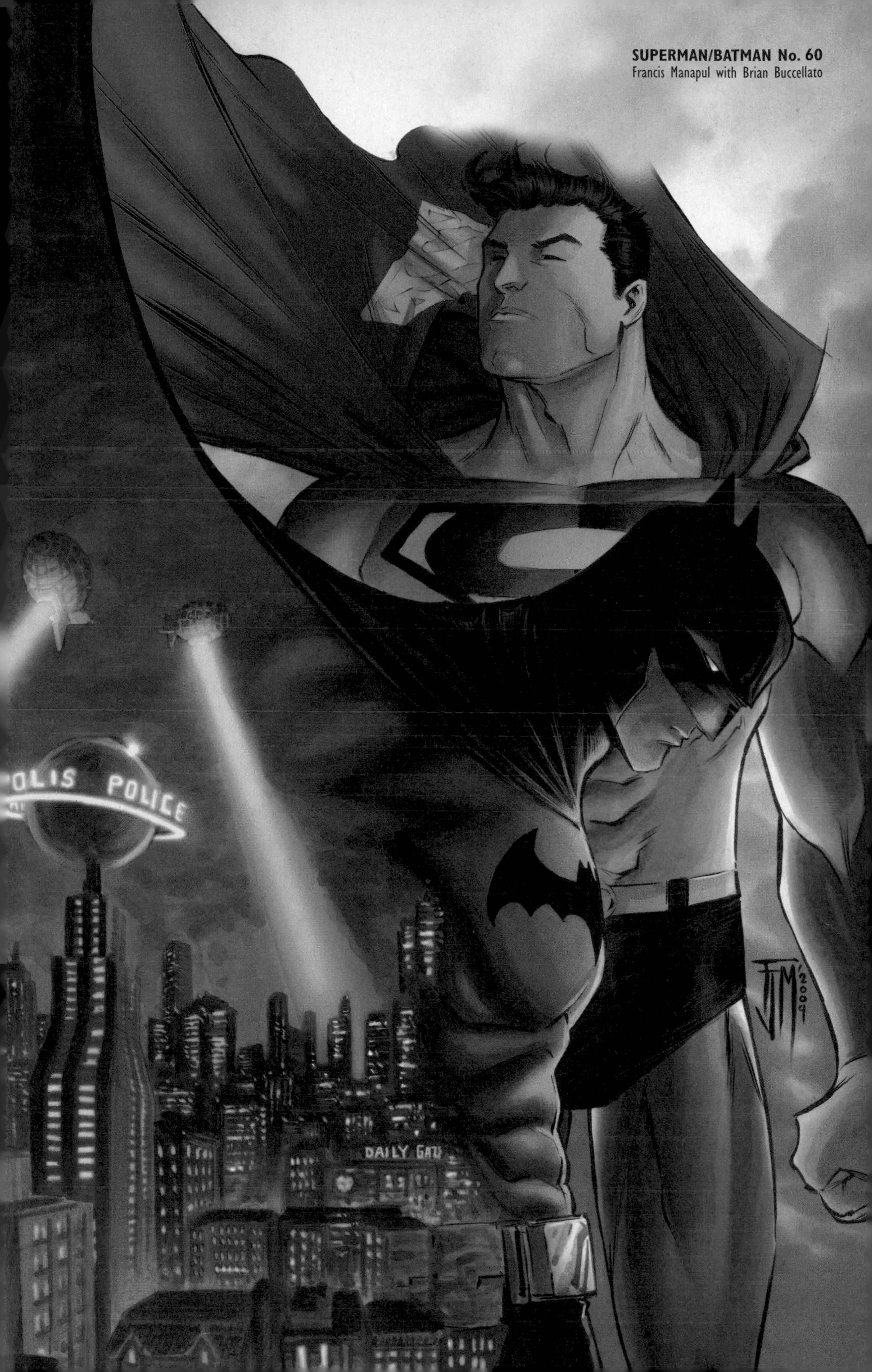
OLIS POLICE
DAILY GAZ
FJM'2009

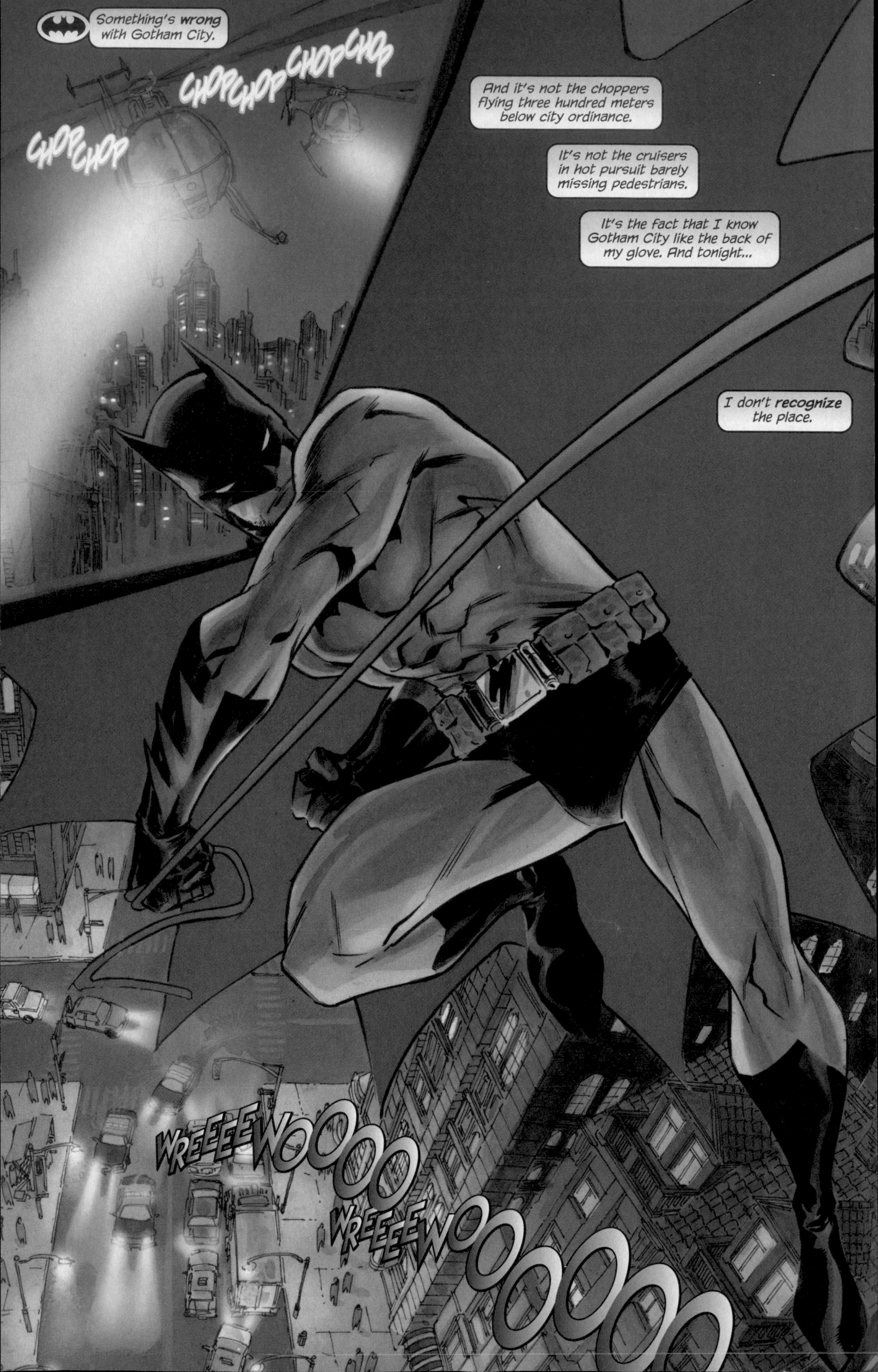
Something's wrong with Gotham City.
CHOP CHOP
CHOP CHOP CHOP CHOP
And it's not the choppers flying three hundred meters below city ordinance.
It's not the cruisers in hot pursuit barely missing pedestrians.
It's the fact that I know Gotham City like the back of my glove. And tonight...
I don't recognize the place.
WREEEEWOOOOO
WREEEEWOOOOOOO

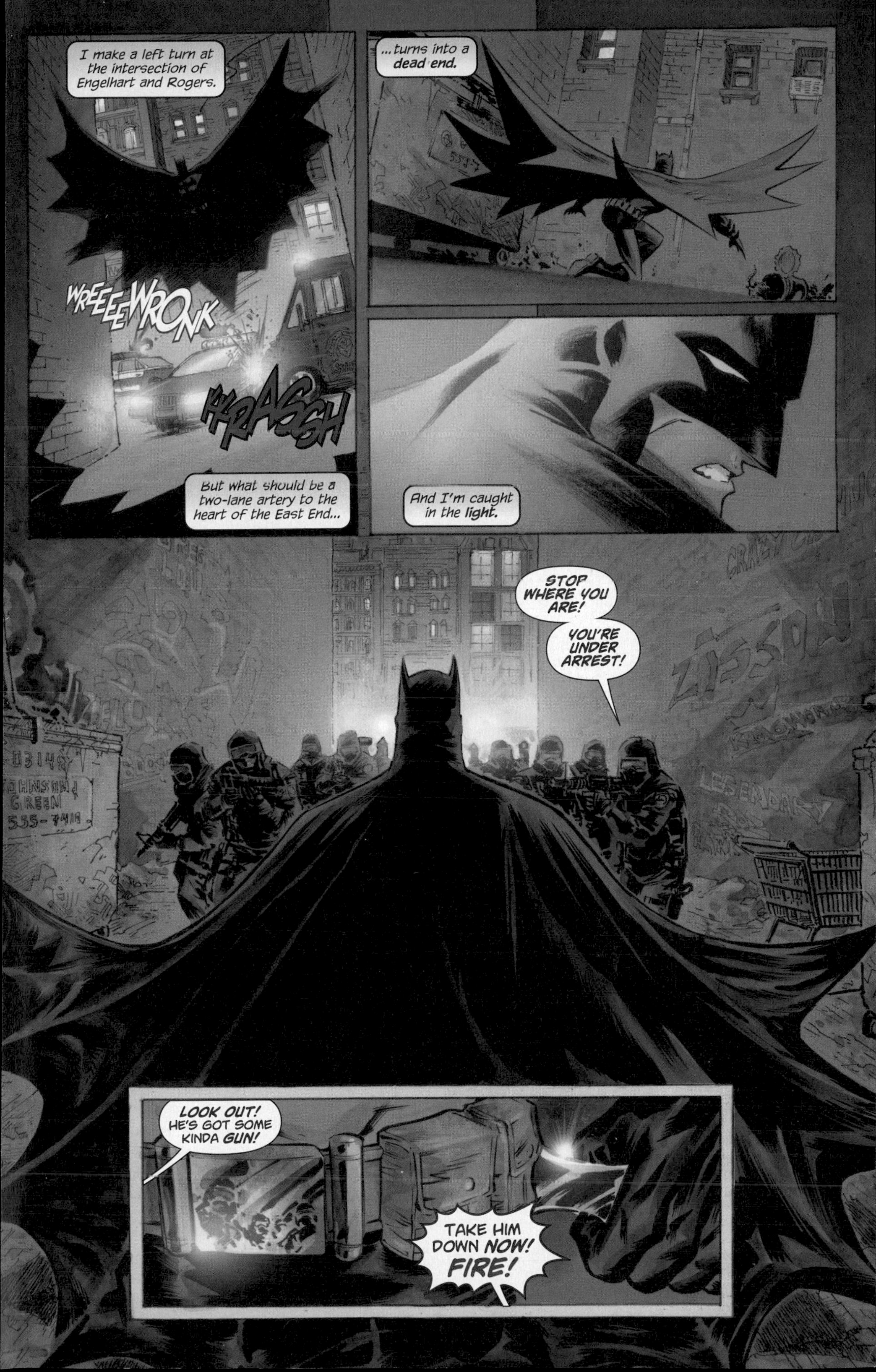

I make a left turn at the intersection of Engelhart and Rogers.
WREEEEWRONK
KKRASSGH
But what should be a two-lane artery to the heart of the East End...
...turns into a dead end.
And I'm caught in the light.
STOP WHERE YOU ARE!
YOU'RE UNDER ARREST!
LOOK OUT! HE'S GOT SOME KINDA GUN!
TAKE HIM DOWN NOW! FIRE!

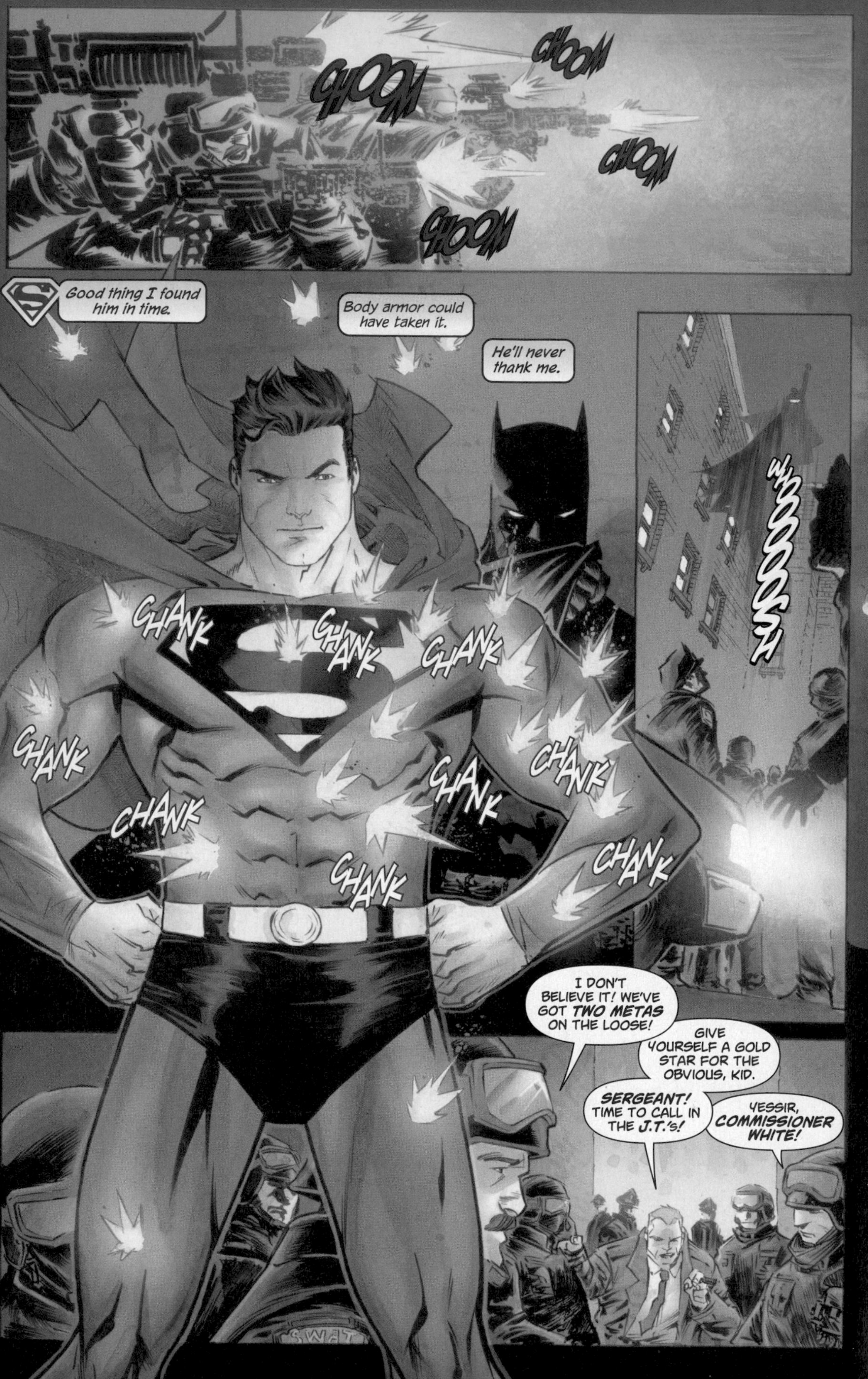
CHOOM
CHOOM
CHOOM
CHOOM
Good thing I found him in time.
Body armor could have taken it.
He'll never thank me.
WHOOOOOSH
CHANK
CHANK
CHANK
CHANK
CHANK
CHANK
CHANK
CHANK
CHANK
I DON'T BELIEVE IT! WE'VE GOT TWO METAS ON THE LOOSE!
GIVE YOURSELF A GOLD STAR FOR THE OBVIOUS, KID.
SERGEANT! TIME TO CALL IN THE J.T.'s!
YESSIR, COMMISSIONER WHITE!

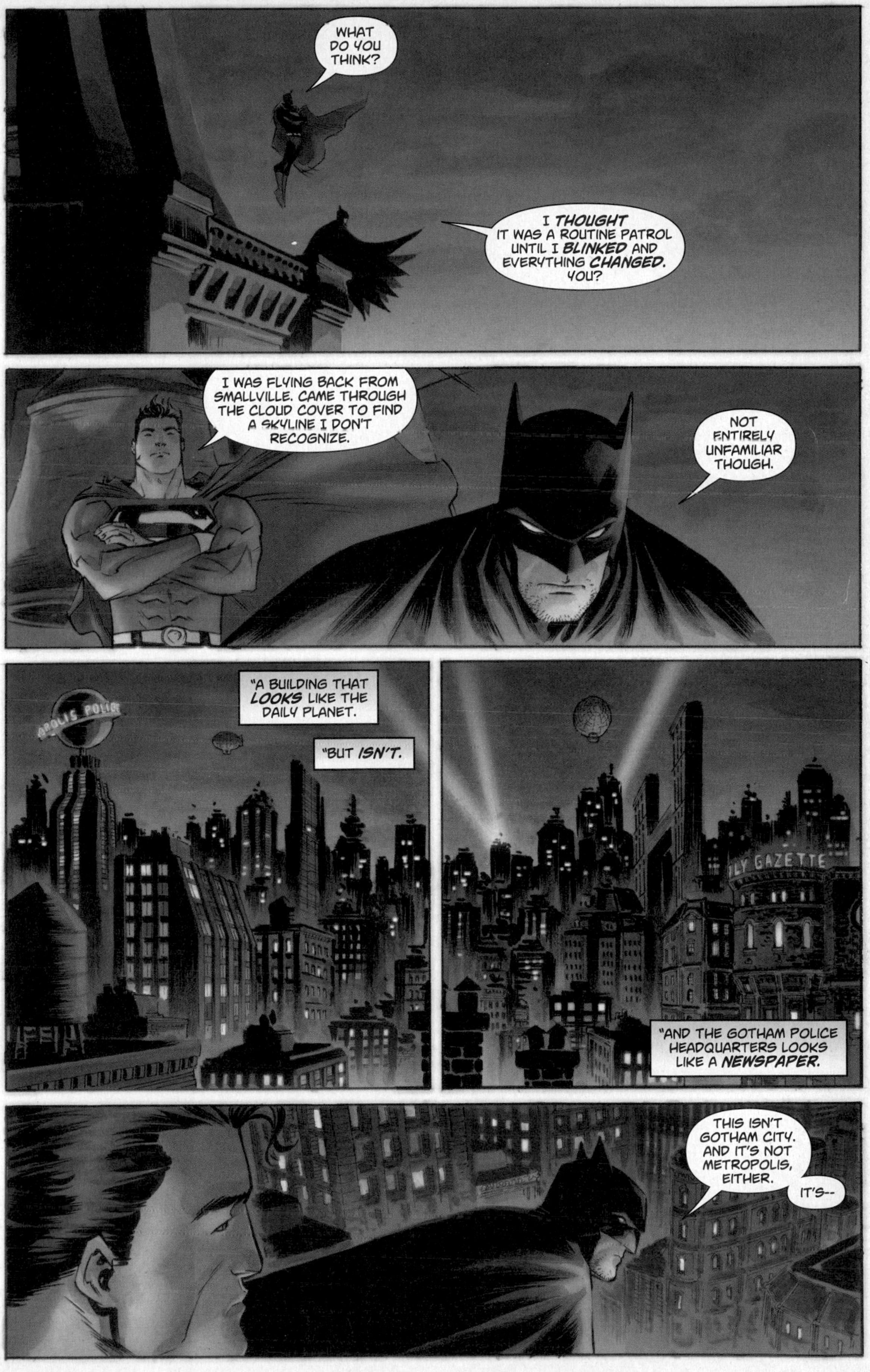
WHAT DO YOU THINK?
I *THOUGHT* IT WAS A ROUTINE PATROL UNTIL I *BLINKED* AND EVERYTHING *CHANGED.* YOU?
I WAS FLYING BACK FROM SMALLVILLE. CAME THROUGH THE CLOUD COVER TO FIND A SKYLINE I DON'T RECOGNIZE.
NOT ENTIRELY UNFAMILIAR THOUGH.
"A BUILDING THAT *LOOKS* LIKE THE DAILY PLANET.
"BUT *ISN'T.*
"AND THE GOTHAM POLICE HEADQUARTERS LOOKS LIKE A *NEWSPAPER.*
THIS ISN'T GOTHAM CITY. AND IT'S NOT METROPOLIS, EITHER.
IT'S--

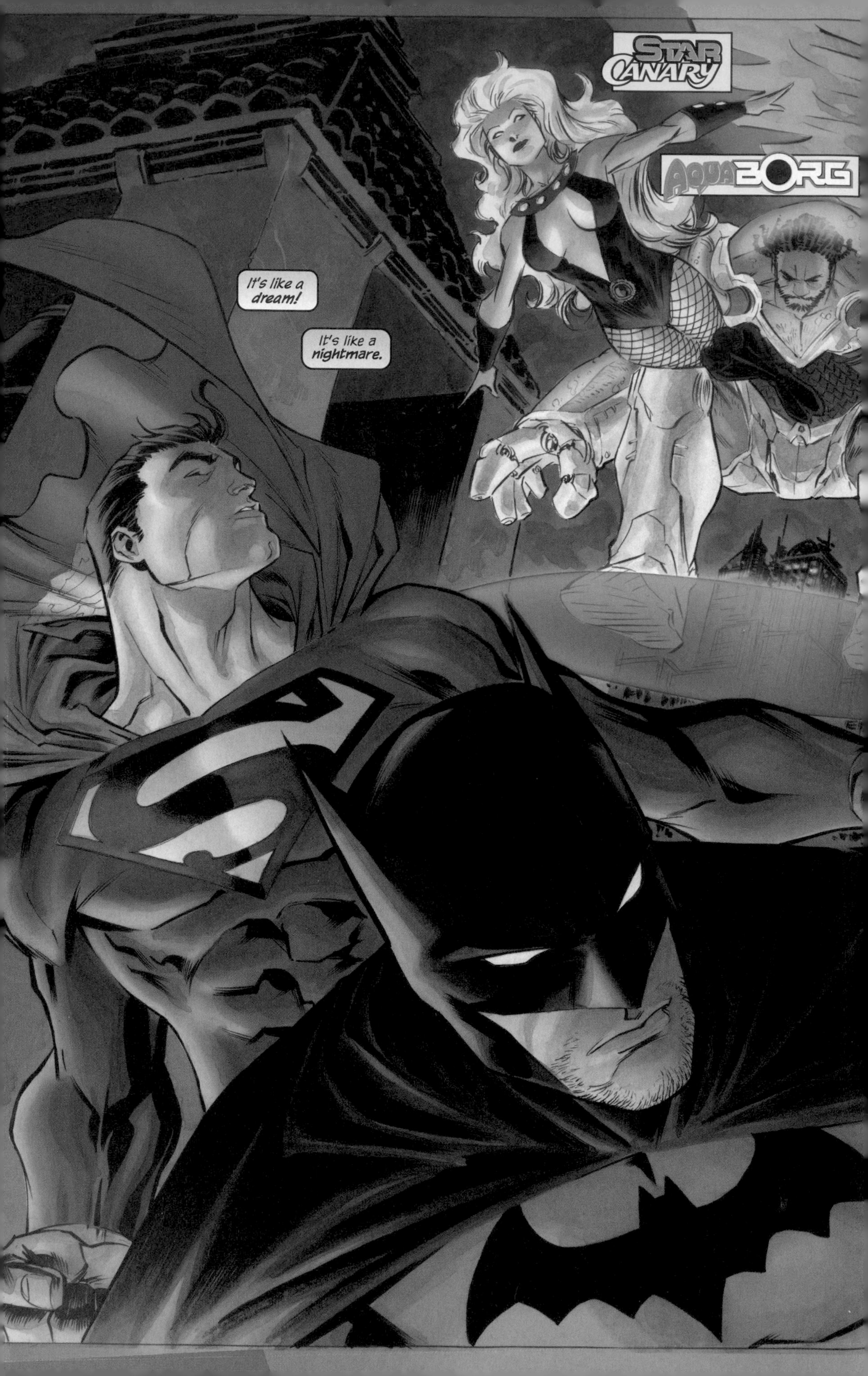
STAR CANARY
AQUABORG
It's like a dream!
It's like a nightmare.

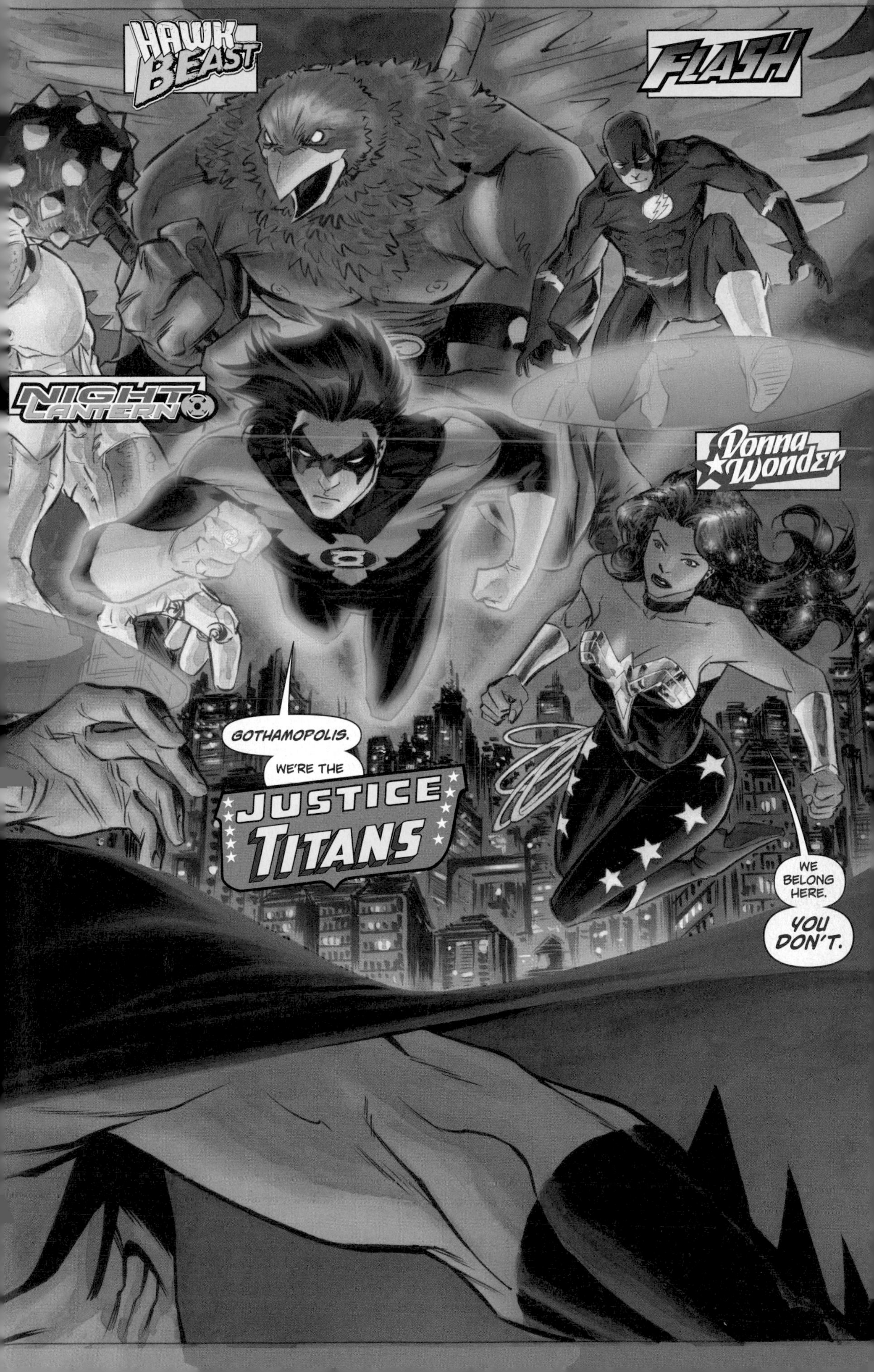
HAWK BEAST
FLASH
NIGHT LANTERN
DONNA WONDER
GOTHAMOPOLIS.
WE'RE THE
JUSTICE TITANS
WE BELONG HERE.
YOU DON'T.

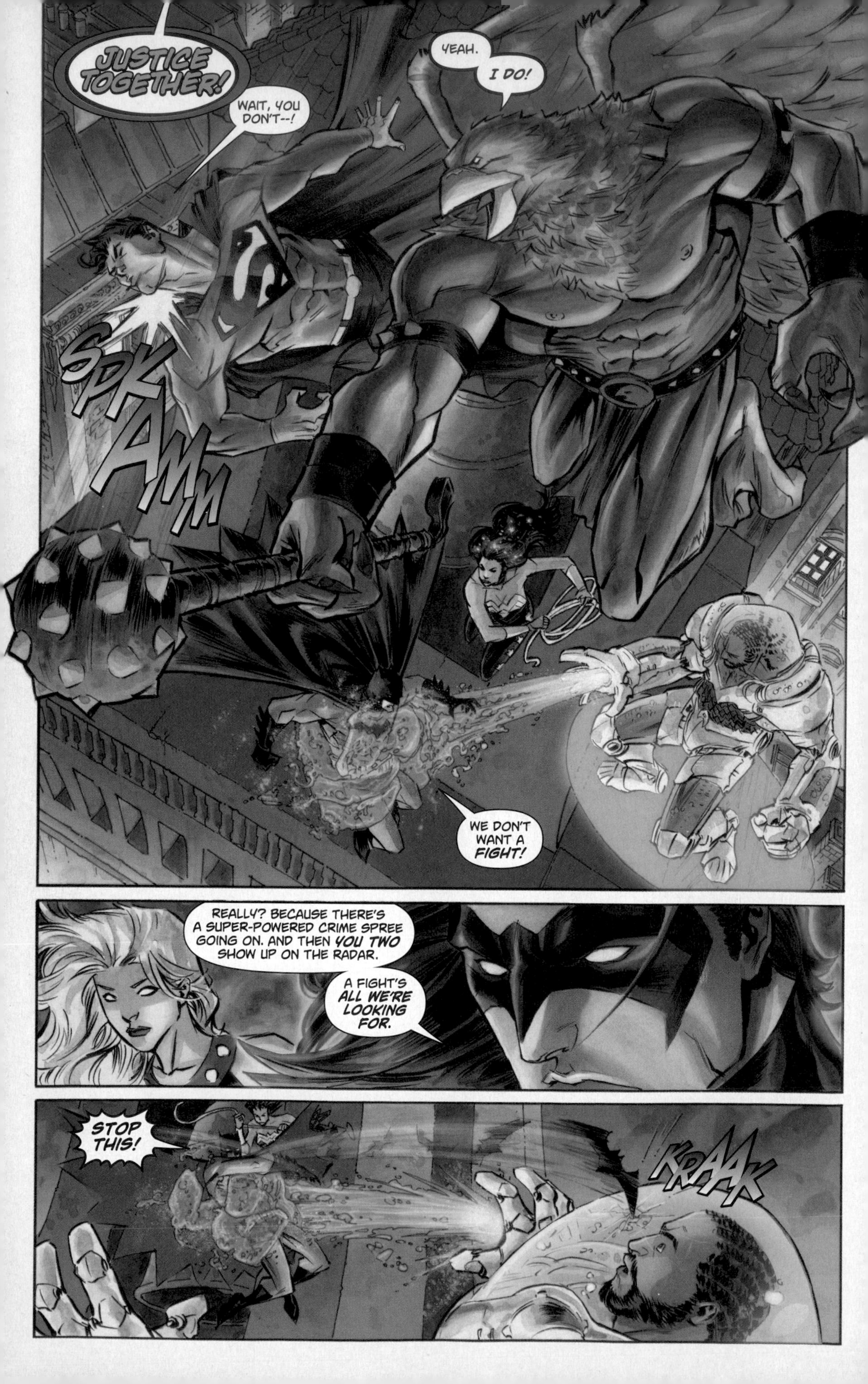

JUSTICE TOGETHER!
WAIT, YOU DON'T--!
YEAH.
I DO!
SPKAMM
WE DON'T WANT A FIGHT!
REALLY? BECAUSE THERE'S A SUPER-POWERED CRIME SPREE GOING ON. AND THEN YOU TWO SHOW UP ON THE RADAR.
A FIGHT'S ALL WE'RE LOOKING FOR.
STOP THIS!
KRAAK

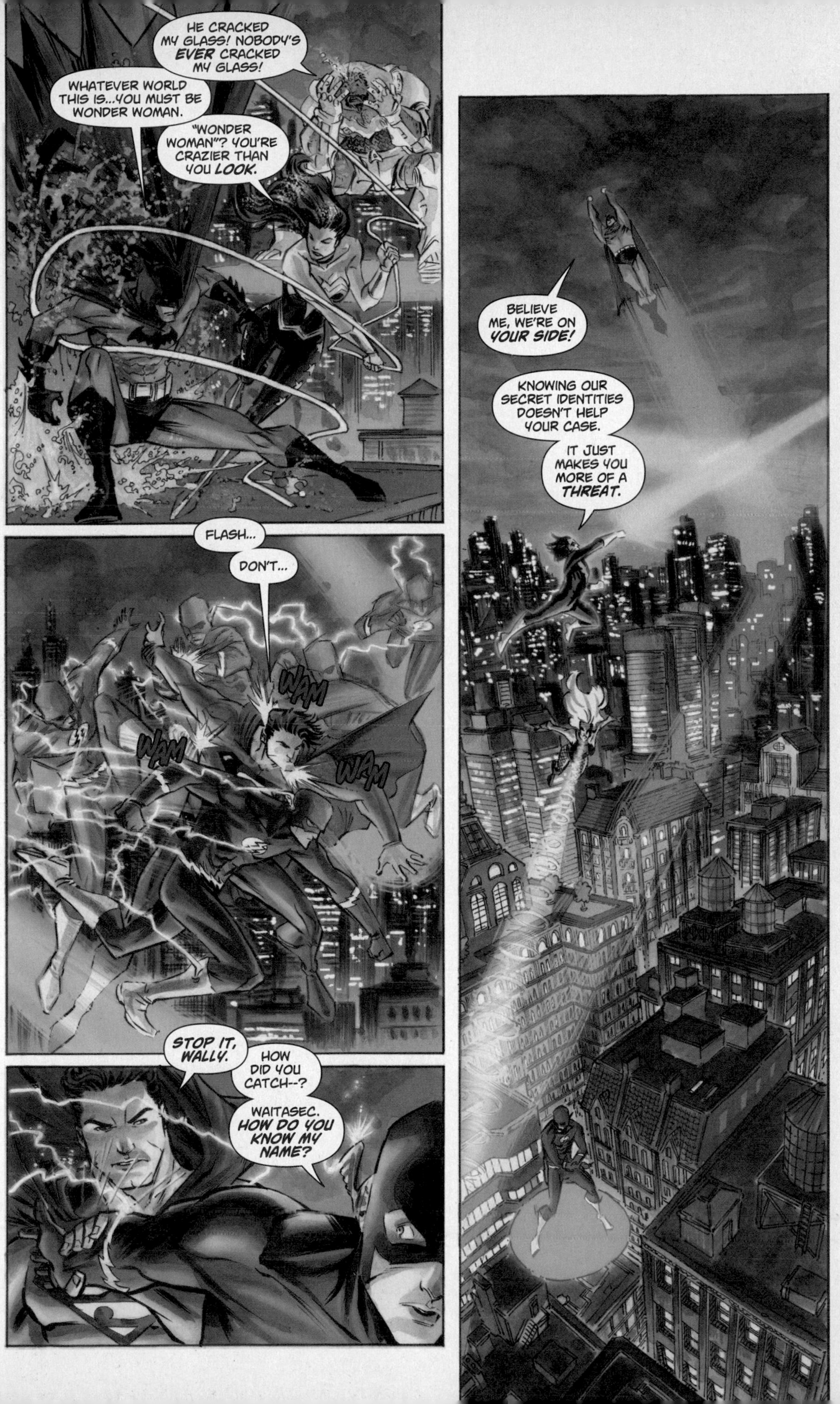

HE CRACKED MY GLASS! NOBODY'S EVER CRACKED MY GLASS!
WHATEVER WORLD THIS IS...YOU MUST BE WONDER WOMAN.
"WONDER WOMAN"? YOU'RE CRAZIER THAN YOU LOOK.
FLASH...
DON'T...
WAM
WAM
WAM
STOP IT, WALLY.
HOW DID YOU CATCH--?
WAITASEC. HOW DO YOU KNOW MY NAME?
BELIEVE ME, WE'RE ON YOUR SIDE!
KNOWING OUR SECRET IDENTITIES DOESN'T HELP YOUR CASE.
IT JUST MAKES YOU MORE OF A THREAT.

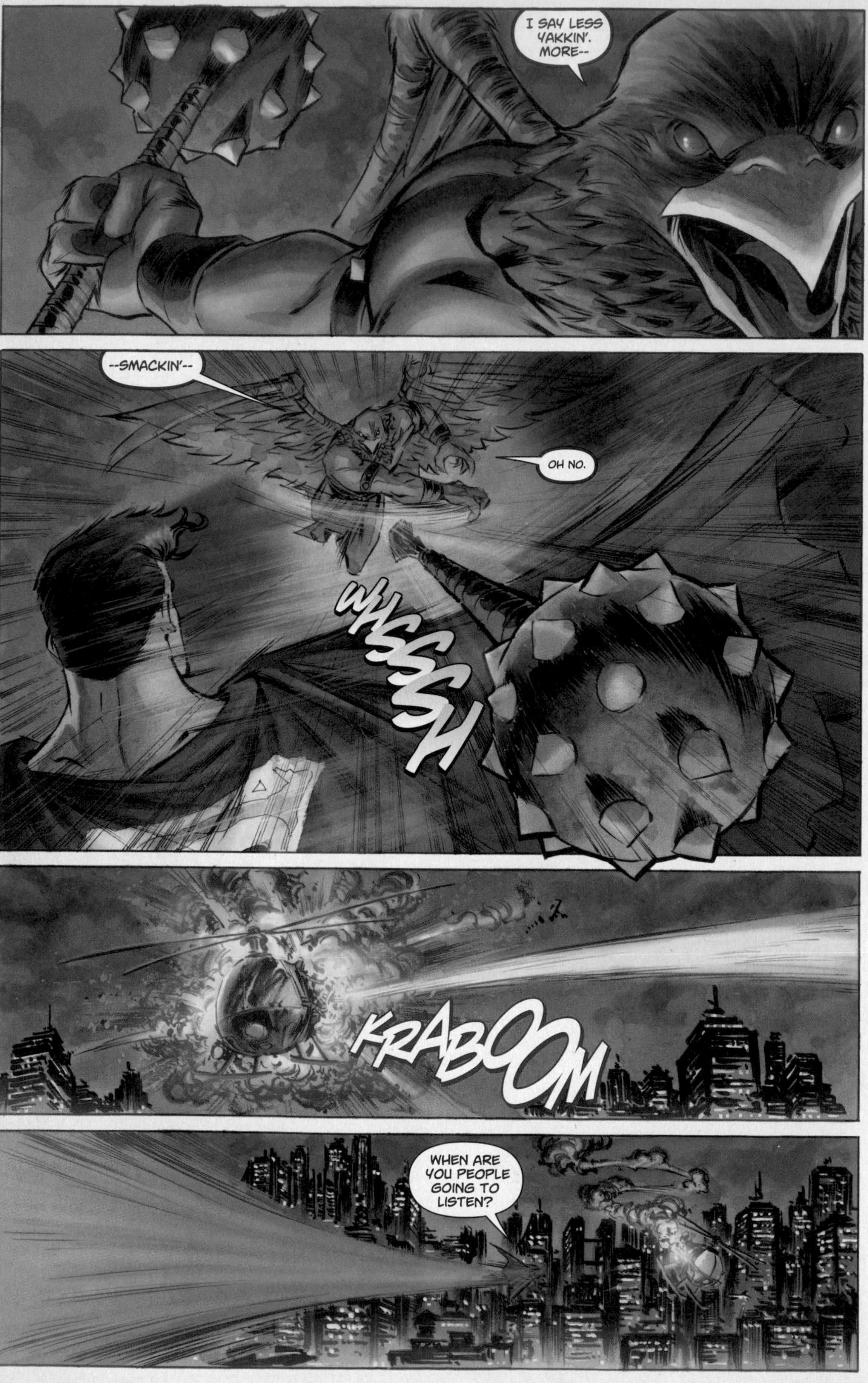
I SAY LESS YAKKIN'. MORE--
--SMACKIN'--
OH NO.
WHSSSH
KRABOOOM
WHEN ARE YOU PEOPLE GOING TO LISTEN?

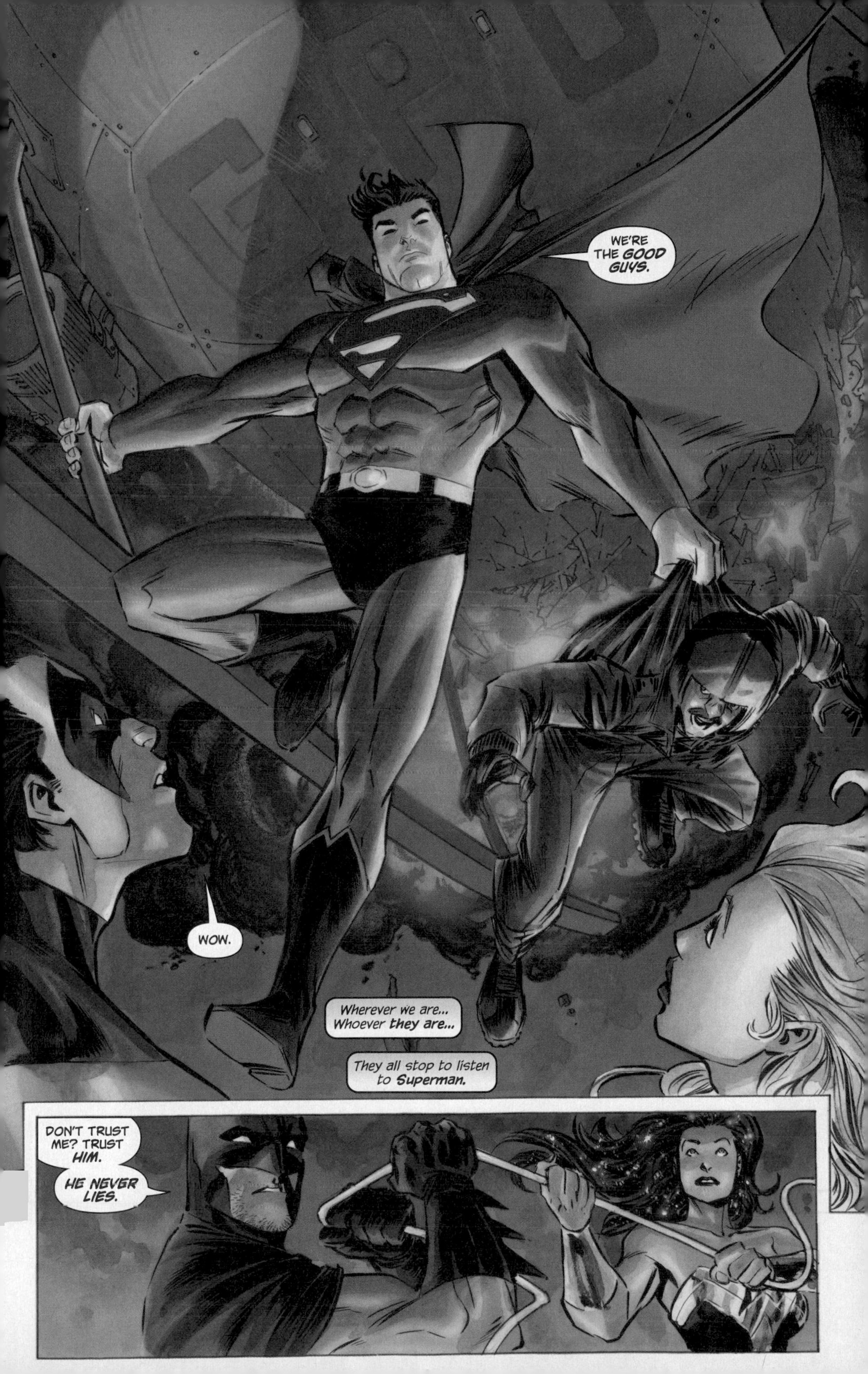
WE'RE THE GOOD GUYS.
WOW.
Wherever we are... Whoever they are...
They all stop to listen to Superman.
DON'T TRUST ME? TRUST HIM.
HE NEVER LIES.

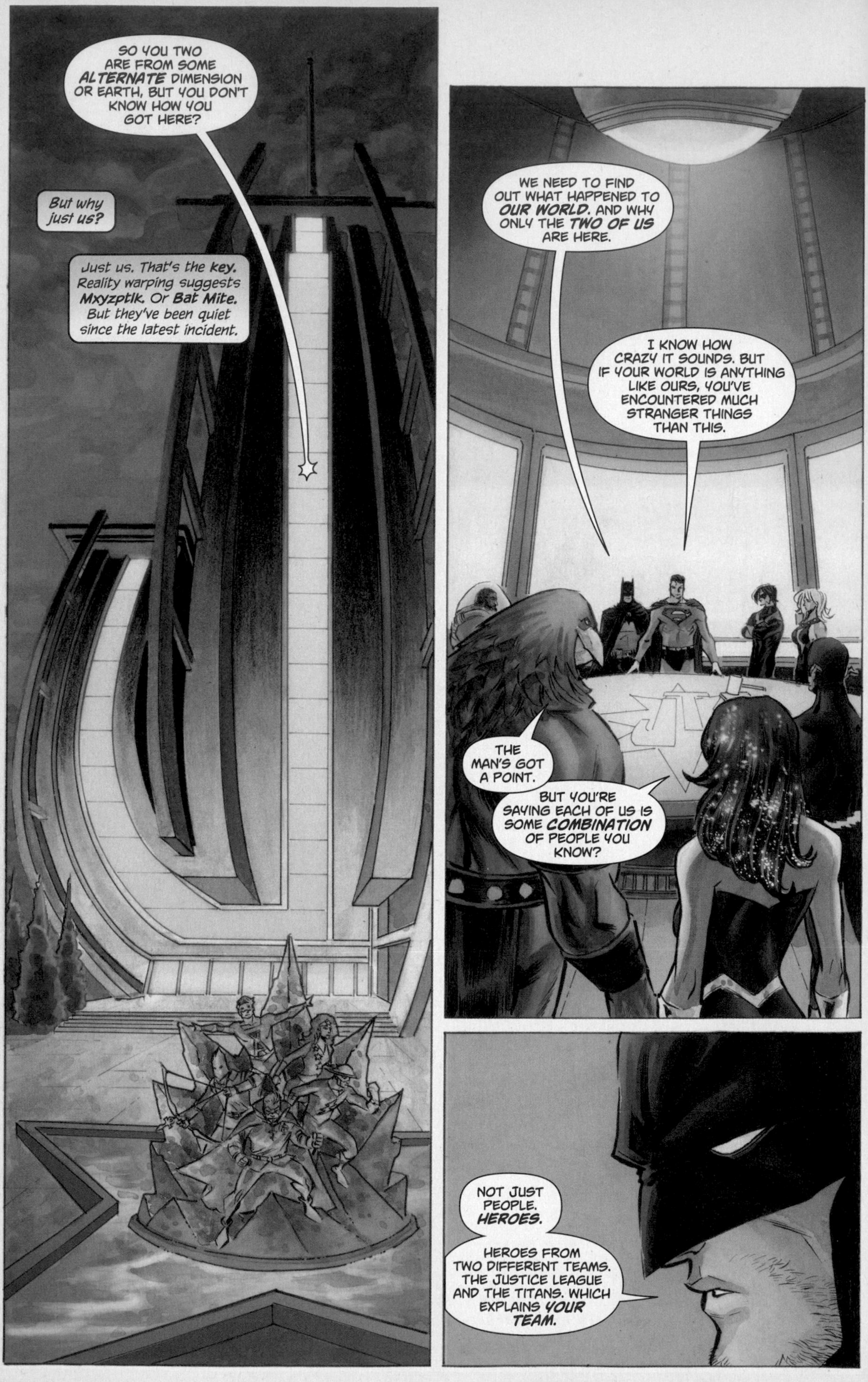
SO YOU TWO ARE FROM SOME ALTERNATE DIMENSION OR EARTH, BUT YOU DON'T KNOW HOW YOU GOT HERE?
But why just us?
Just us. That's the key. Reality warping suggests Mxyzptlk. Or Bat Mite. But they've been quiet since the latest incident.
WE NEED TO FIND OUT WHAT HAPPENED TO OUR WORLD. AND WHY ONLY THE TWO OF US ARE HERE.
I KNOW HOW CRAZY IT SOUNDS. BUT IF YOUR WORLD IS ANYTHING LIKE OURS, YOU'VE ENCOUNTERED MUCH STRANGER THINGS THAN THIS.
THE MAN'S GOT A POINT.
BUT YOU'RE SAYING EACH OF US IS SOME COMBINATION OF PEOPLE YOU KNOW?
NOT JUST PEOPLE. HEROES.
HEROES FROM TWO DIFFERENT TEAMS. THE JUSTICE LEAGUE AND THE TITANS. WHICH EXPLAINS YOUR TEAM.

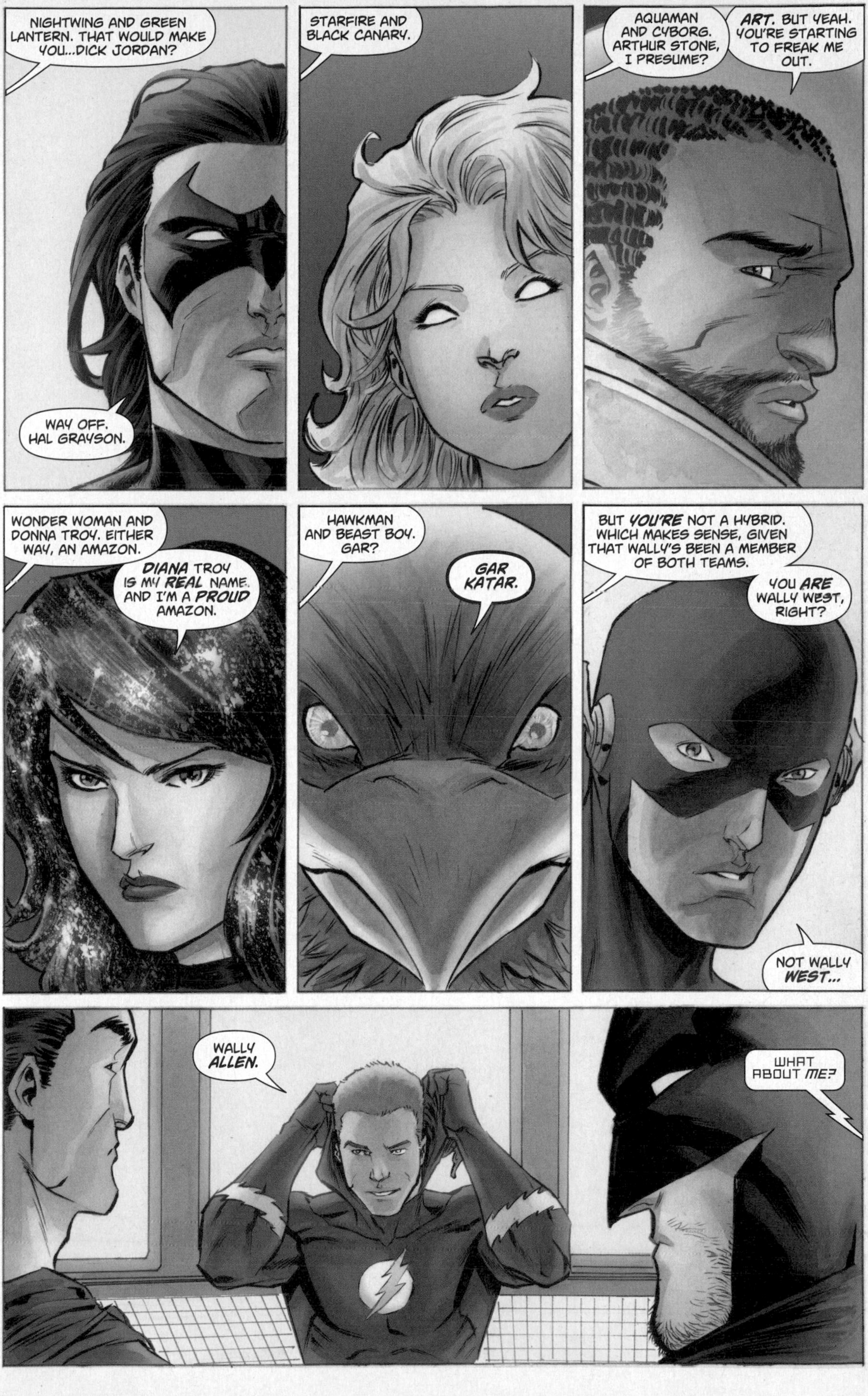
NIGHTWING AND GREEN LANTERN. THAT WOULD MAKE YOU...DICK JORDAN?
WAY OFF. HAL GRAYSON.
STARFIRE AND BLACK CANARY.
AQUAMAN AND CYBORG. ARTHUR STONE, I PRESUME?
ART. BUT YEAH. YOU'RE STARTING TO FREAK ME OUT.
WONDER WOMAN AND DONNA TROY. EITHER WAY, AN AMAZON.
DIANA TROY IS MY REAL NAME. AND I'M A PROUD AMAZON.
HAWKMAN AND BEAST BOY. GAR?
GAR KATAR.
BUT YOU'RE NOT A HYBRID. WHICH MAKES SENSE, GIVEN THAT WALLY'S BEEN A MEMBER OF BOTH TEAMS.
YOU ARE WALLY WEST, RIGHT?
NOT WALLY WEST...
WALLY ALLEN.
WHAT ABOUT ME?

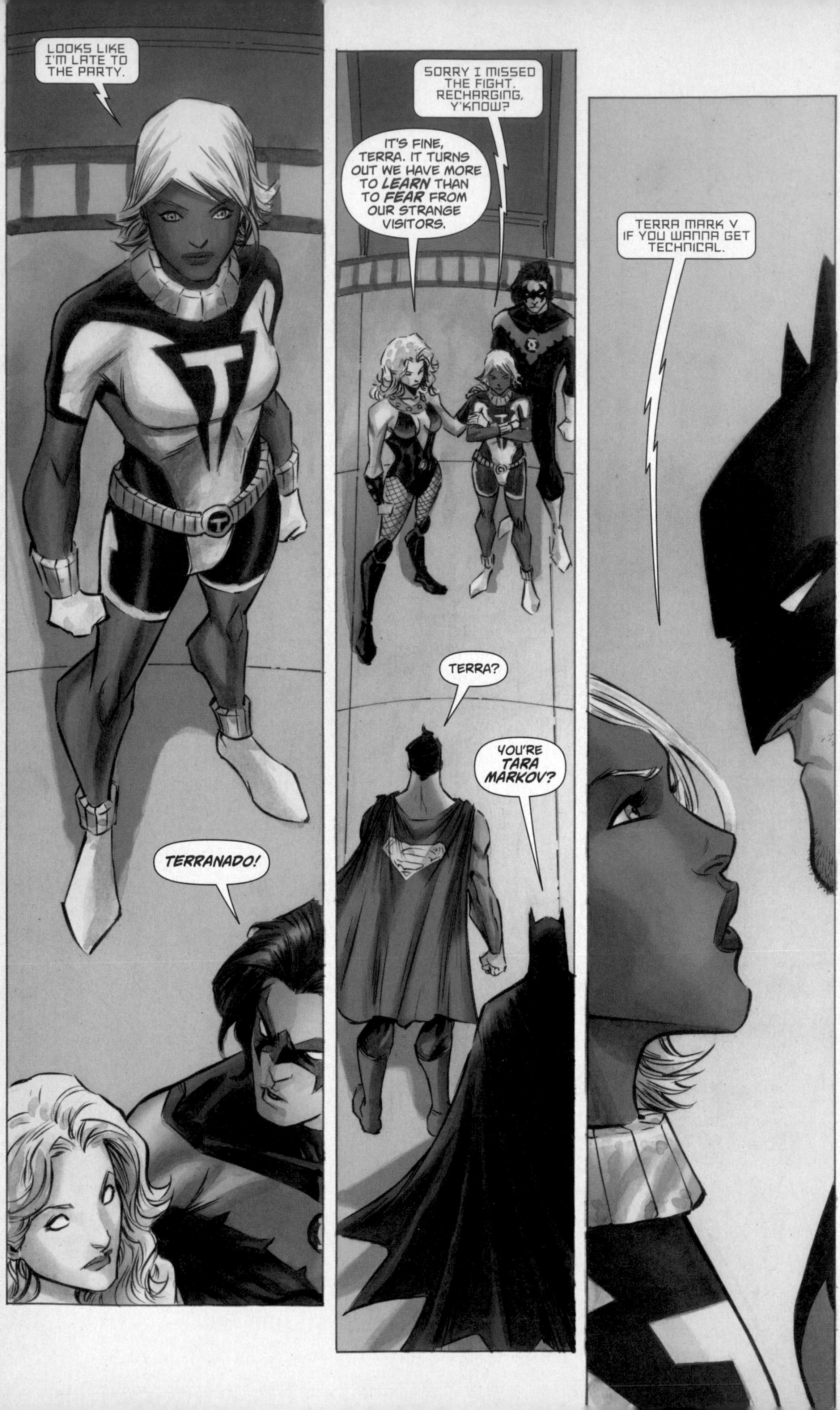
LOOKS LIKE I'M LATE TO THE PARTY.
TERRANADO!
SORRY I MISSED THE FIGHT. RECHARGING, Y'KNOW?
IT'S FINE, TERRA. IT TURNS OUT WE HAVE MORE TO *LEARN* THAN TO *FEAR* FROM OUR STRANGE VISITORS.
TERRA?
YOU'RE *TARA MARKOV?*
TERRA MARK V IF YOU WANNA GET TECHNICAL.

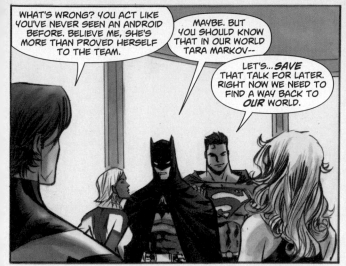

WHAT'S WRONG? YOU ACT LIKE YOU'VE NEVER SEEN AN ANDROID BEFORE. BELIEVE ME, SHE'S MORE THAN PROVED HERSELF TO THE TEAM.

MAYBE. BUT YOU SHOULD KNOW THAT IN OUR WORLD TARA MARKOV--

LET'S... *SAVE* THAT TALK FOR LATER. RIGHT NOW WE NEED TO FIND A WAY BACK TO *OUR* WORLD.

REET REET

CODE ALPHA

THAT WILL HAVE TO WAIT! WE'VE GOT AN ALPHA IN PROGRESS DOWNTOWN! SOMEONE'S BROKEN INTO *S.T.A.RKHAM!*

FIRE UP THE *J.JET!*

THE *JUSTICE JET*, huh? YOU ALWAYS THE PILOT?

YEAH, AIR FORCE VET. BORN TO FLY.

Hmm.

WHAT?

THE TWO PEOPLE YOU REMIND ME OF... WHERE I'M FROM, I HAVE A VERY DIFFERENT RELATIONSHIP WITH EACH OF THEM.

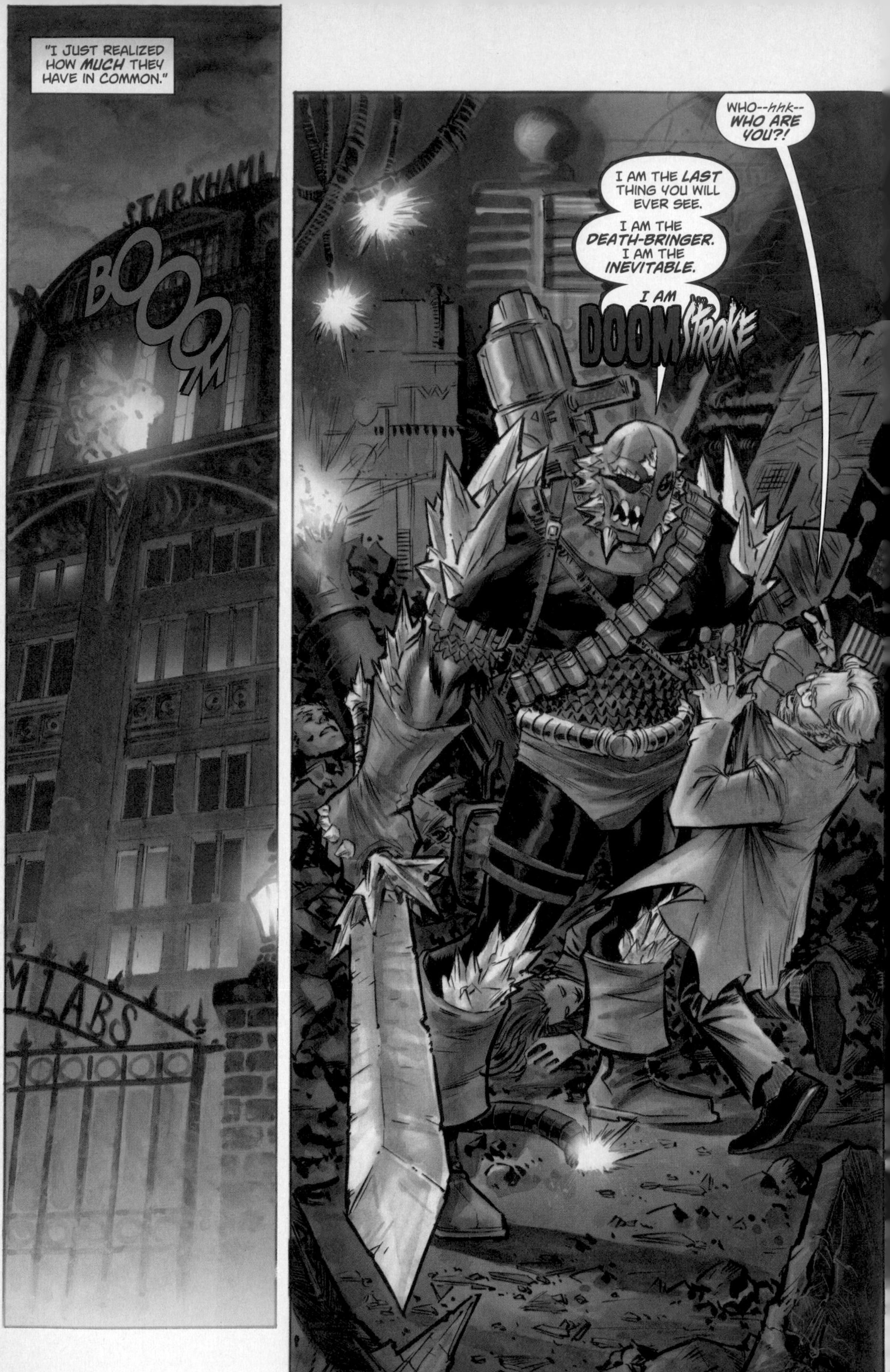
"I JUST REALIZED HOW *MUCH* THEY HAVE IN COMMON."
STAR.KHAML
BOOOM
M.LABS
WHO--*hhk*-- *WHO ARE YOU?!*
I AM THE *LAST* THING YOU WILL EVER SEE.
I AM THE *DEATH-BRINGER*. I AM THE *INEVITABLE*.
I AM
DOOMSTROKE

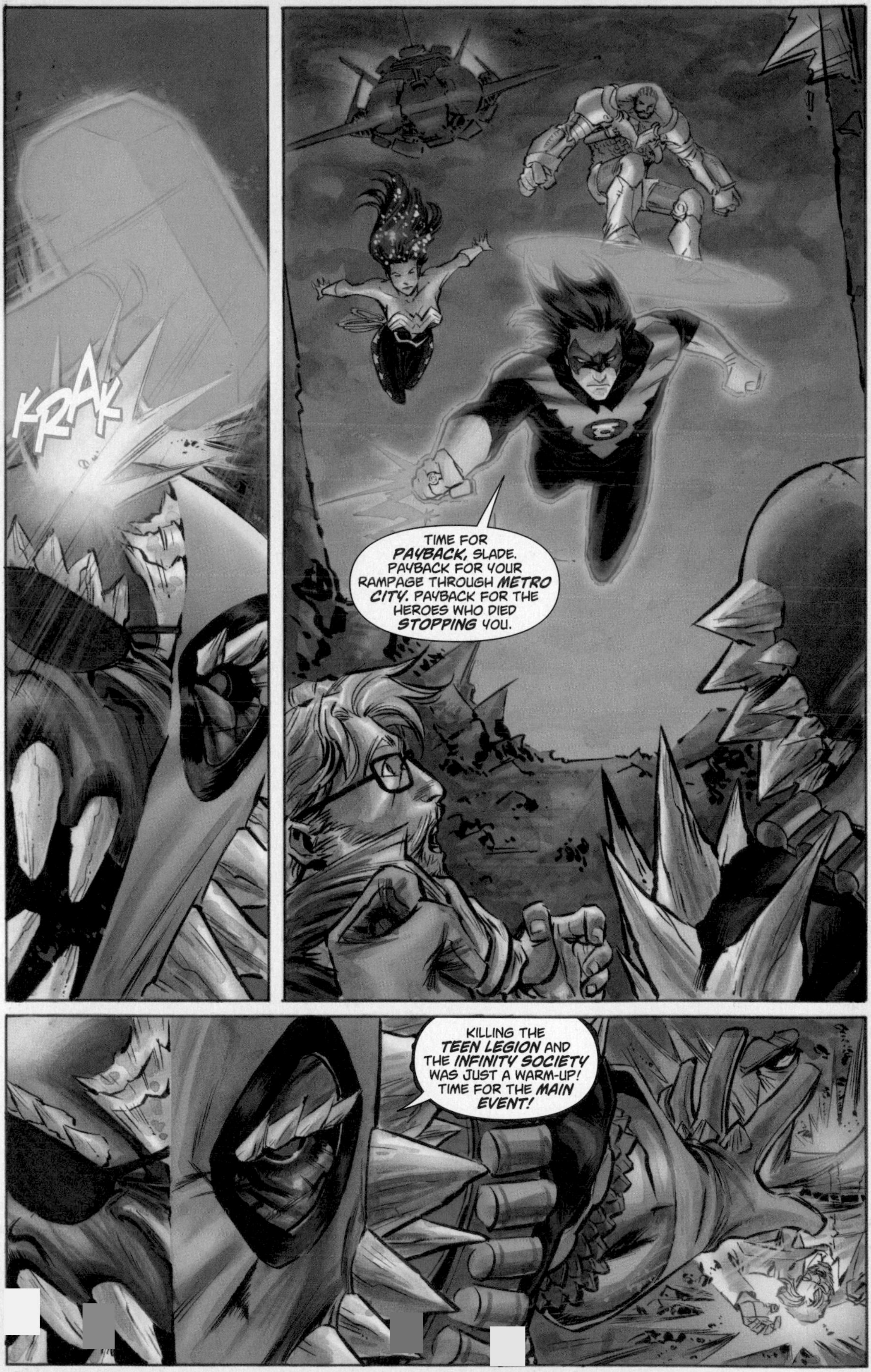
KRAK
TIME FOR PAYBACK, SLADE. PAYBACK FOR YOUR RAMPAGE THROUGH METRO CITY. PAYBACK FOR THE HEROES WHO DIED STOPPING YOU.
KILLING THE TEEN LEGION AND THE INFINITY SOCIETY WAS JUST A WARM-UP! TIME FOR THE MAIN EVENT!

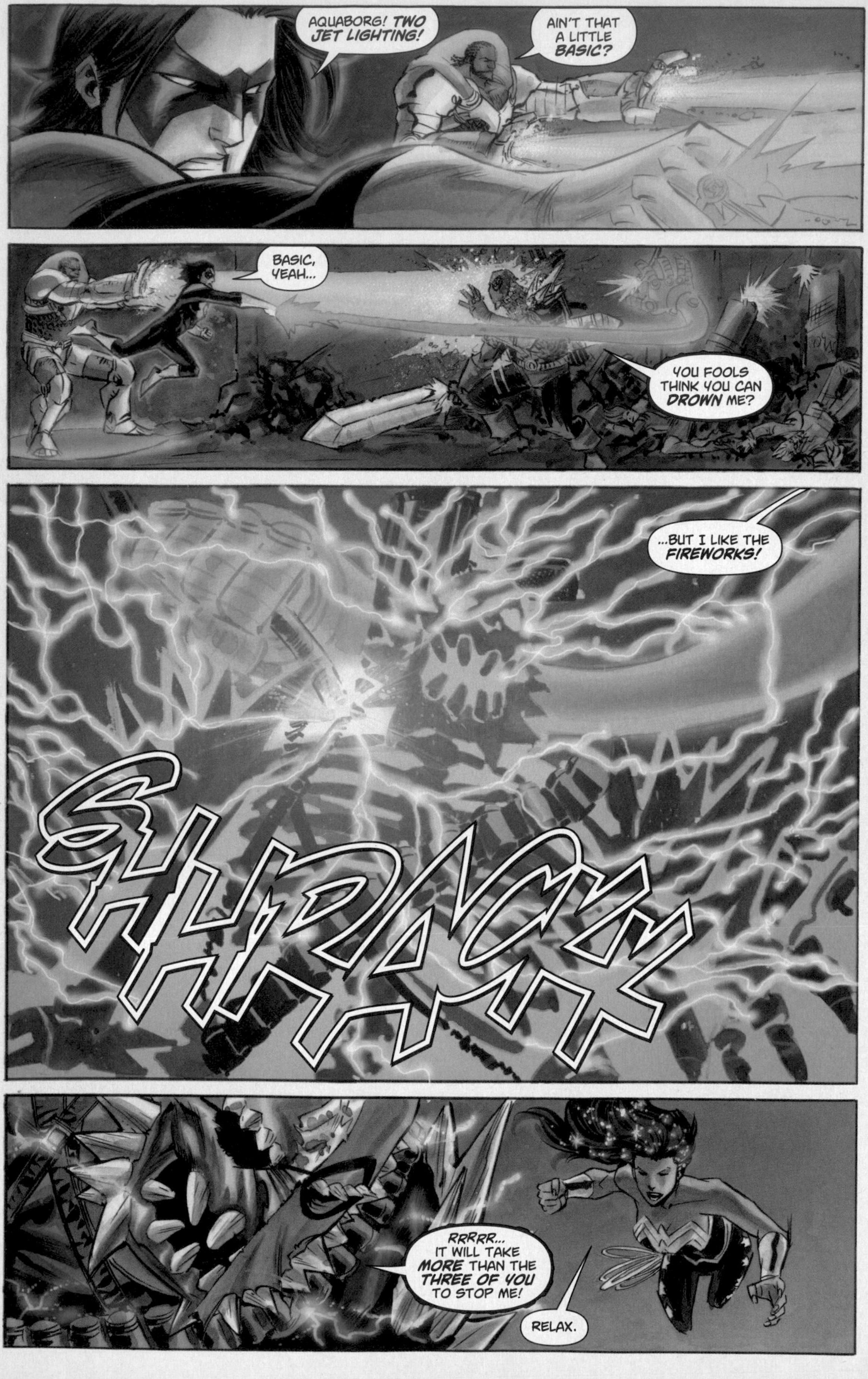
AQUABORG! TWO JET LIGHTING!
AIN'T THAT A LITTLE BASIC?
BASIC, YEAH...
YOU FOOLS THINK YOU CAN DROWN ME?
...BUT I LIKE THE FIREWORKS!
RRRRR... IT WILL TAKE MORE THAN THE THREE OF YOU TO STOP ME!
RELAX.

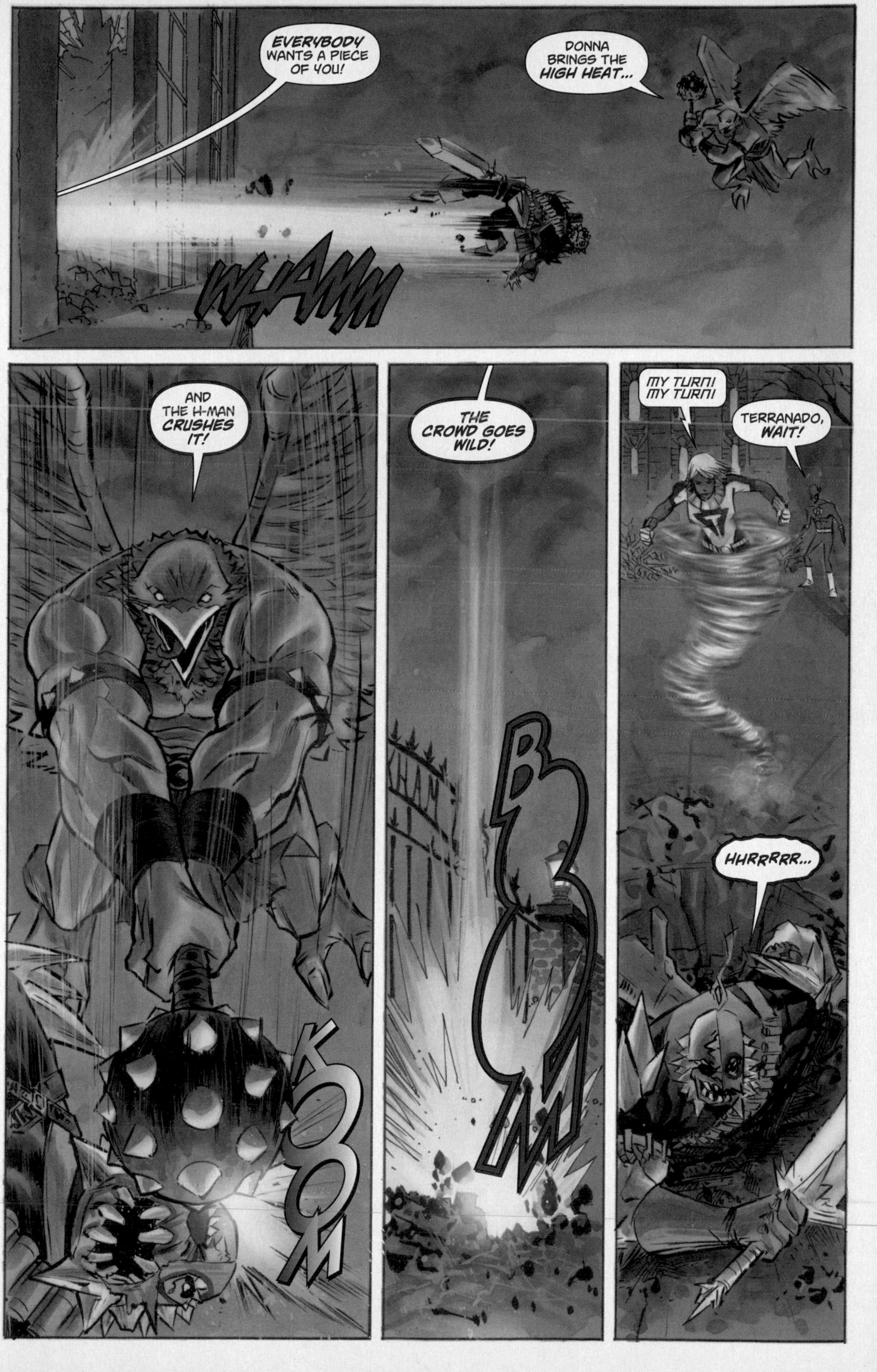
EVERYBODY WANTS A PIECE OF YOU!
DONNA BRINGS THE HIGH HEAT...
WHAMM
AND THE H-MAN CRUSHES IT!
KROOM
THE CROWD GOES WILD!
BOOM
MY TURN! MY TURN!
TERRANADO, WAIT!
HHRRRRR...

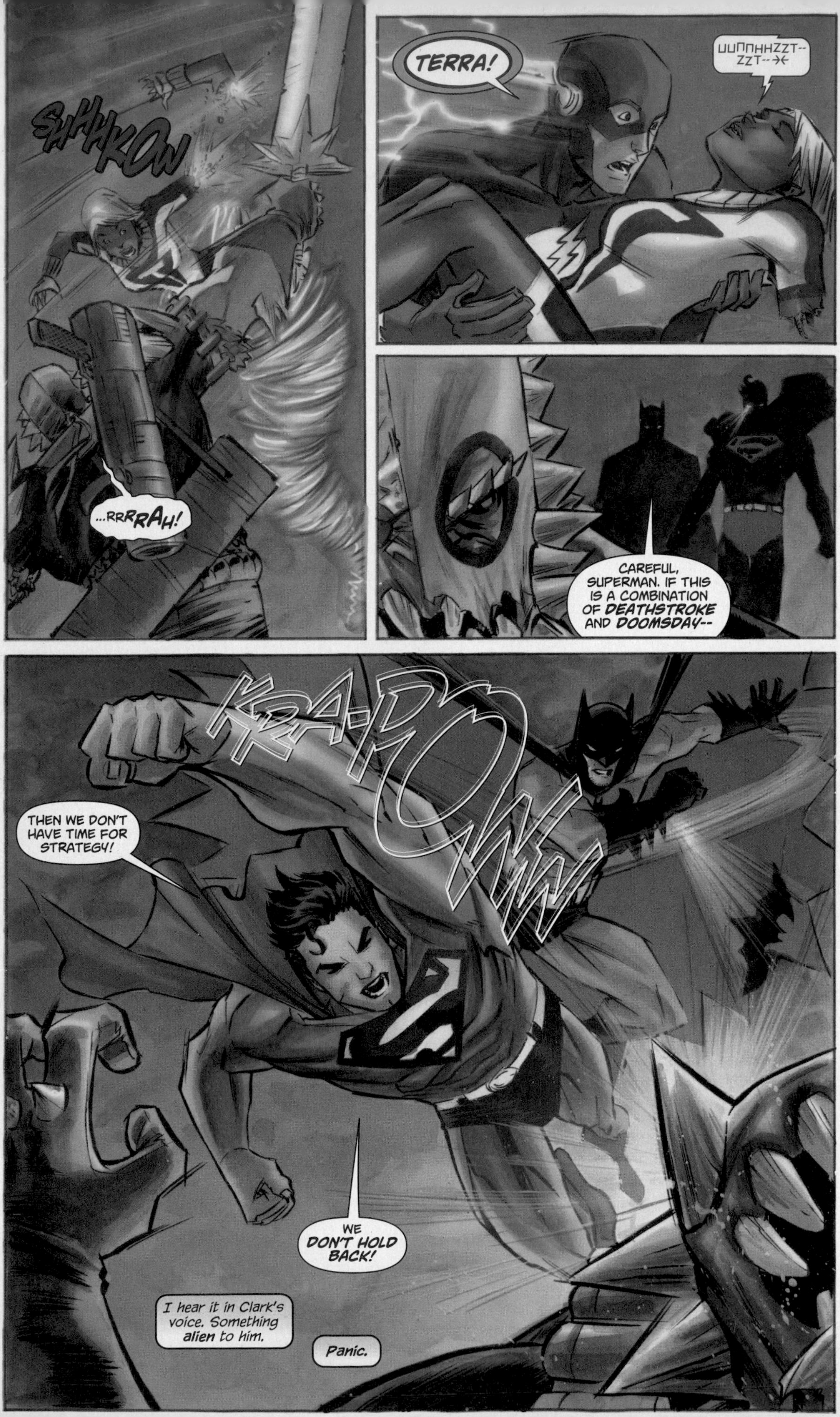
SHHHKOW
...RRRRAH!
TERRA!
UUNNHHZZT-- ZZT--
CAREFUL, SUPERMAN. IF THIS IS A COMBINATION OF DEATHSTROKE AND DOOMSDAY--
KRA-POWW
THEN WE DON'T HAVE TIME FOR STRATEGY!
WE DON'T HOLD BACK!
I hear it in Clark's voice. Something alien to him.
Panic.

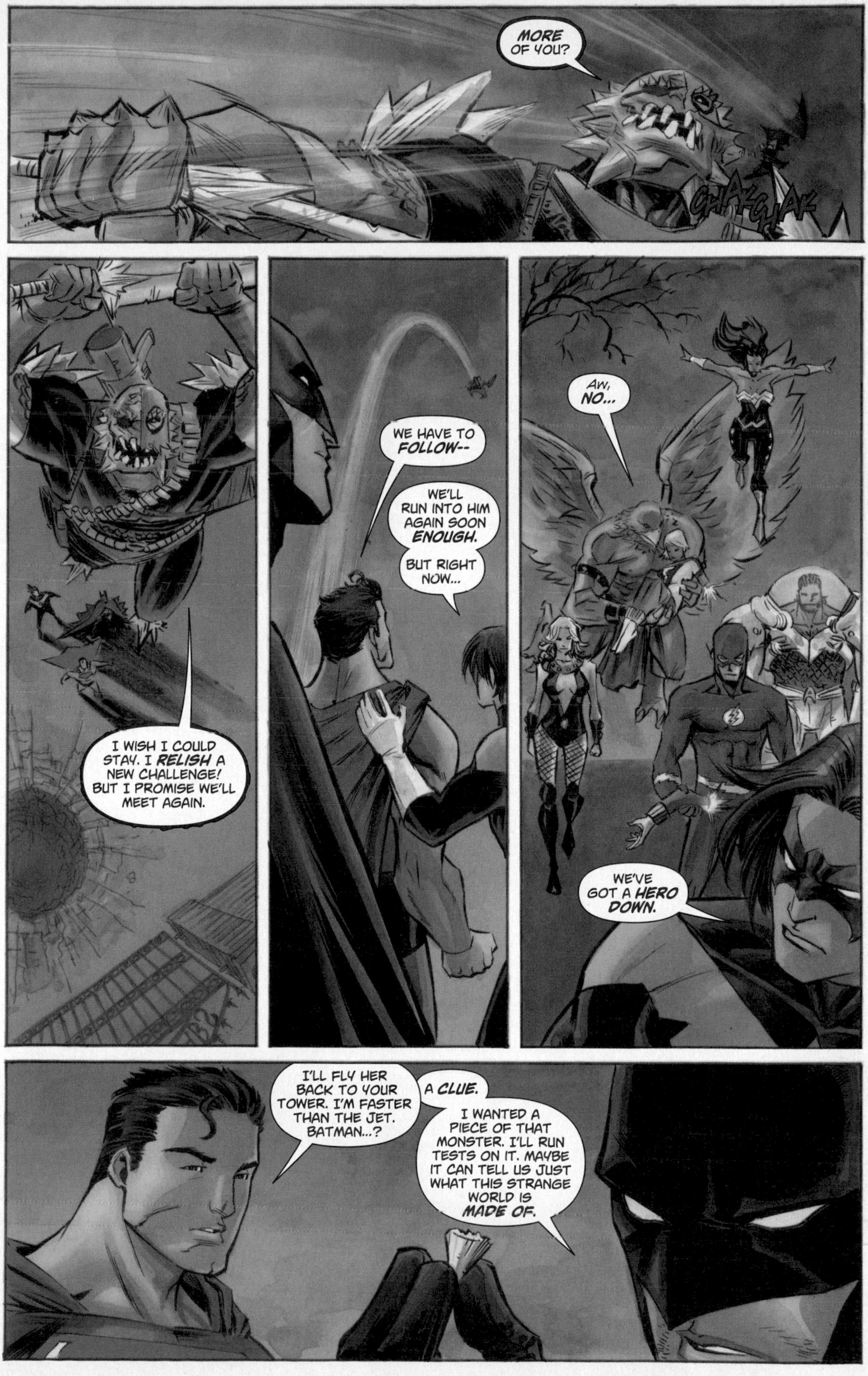
MORE OF YOU?
CHAKGAK
I WISH I COULD STAY. I RELISH A NEW CHALLENGE! BUT I PROMISE WE'LL MEET AGAIN.
WE HAVE TO FOLLOW--
WE'LL RUN INTO HIM AGAIN SOON ENOUGH.
BUT RIGHT NOW...
AW, NO...
WE'VE GOT A HERO DOWN.
I'LL FLY HER BACK TO YOUR TOWER. I'M FASTER THAN THE JET. BATMAN...?
A CLUE.
I WANTED A PIECE OF THAT MONSTER. I'LL RUN TESTS ON IT. MAYBE IT CAN TELL US JUST WHAT THIS STRANGE WORLD IS MADE OF.

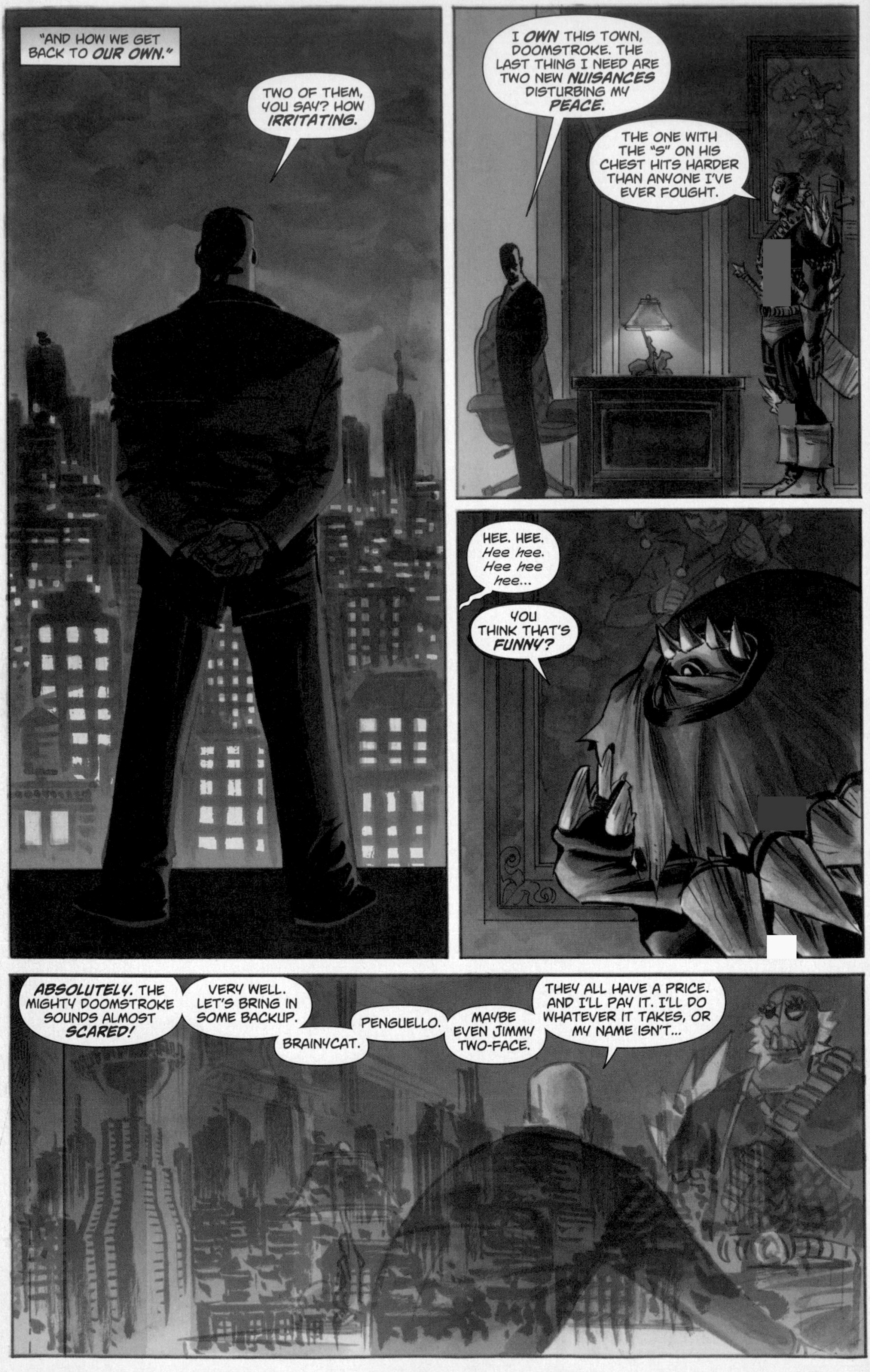
"AND HOW WE GET BACK TO OUR OWN."
TWO OF THEM, YOU SAY? HOW IRRITATING.
I OWN THIS TOWN, DOOMSTROKE. THE LAST THING I NEED ARE TWO NEW NUISANCES DISTURBING MY PEACE.
THE ONE WITH THE "S" ON HIS CHEST HITS HARDER THAN ANYONE I'VE EVER FOUGHT.
HEE. HEE. Hee hee. Hee hee hee...
YOU THINK THAT'S FUNNY?
ABSOLUTELY. THE MIGHTY DOOMSTROKE SOUNDS ALMOST SCARED!
VERY WELL. LET'S BRING IN SOME BACKUP.
BRAINYCAT.
PENGUELLO.
MAYBE EVEN JIMMY TWO-FACE.
THEY ALL HAVE A PRICE. AND I'LL PAY IT. I'LL DO WHATEVER IT TAKES, OR MY NAME ISN'T...

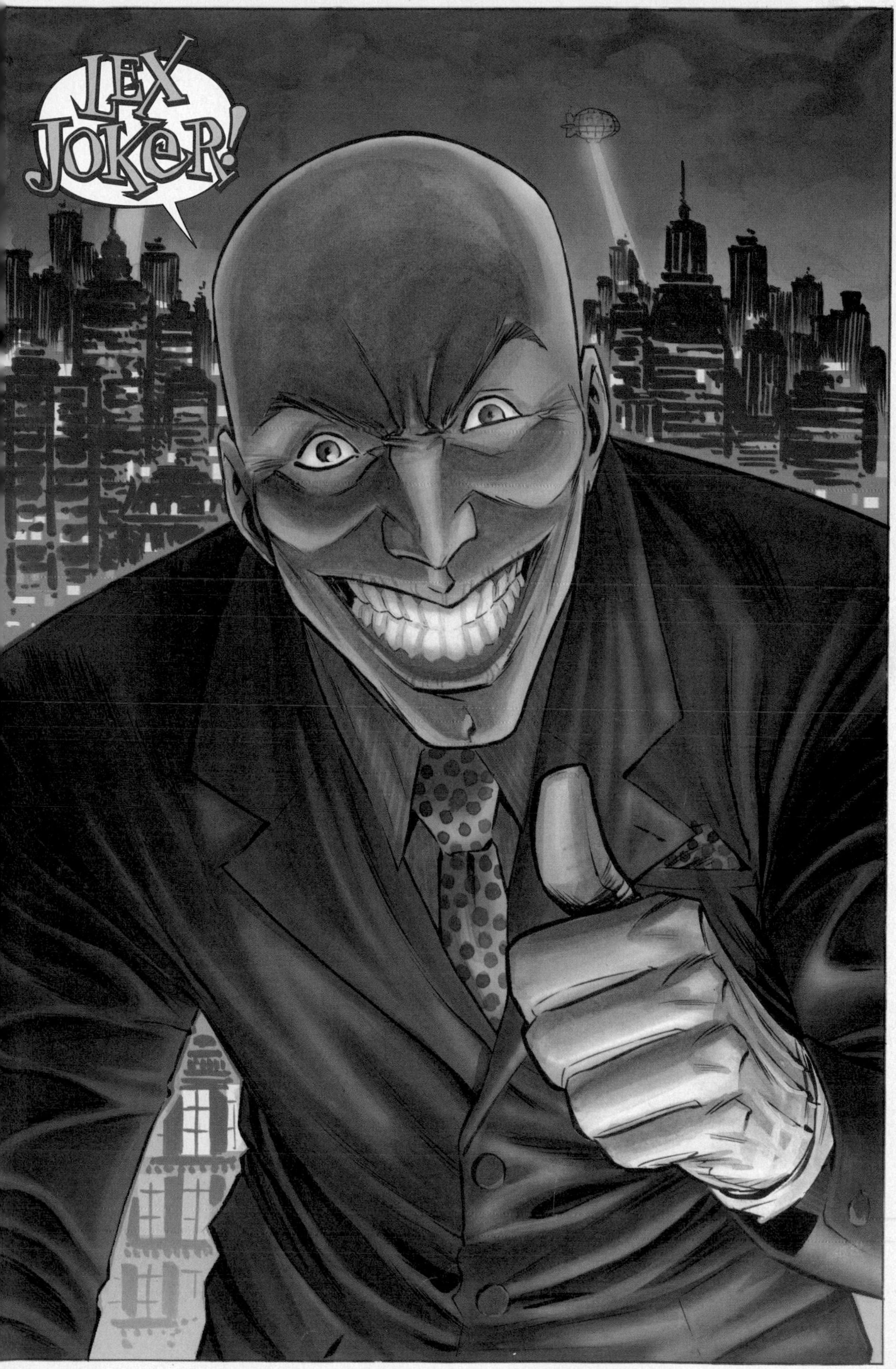
LEX JOKER!

MASH-UP
PART TWO
Plot: Michael Green and Mike Johnson

Dialogue: Mike Johnson

Artist: Francis Manapul

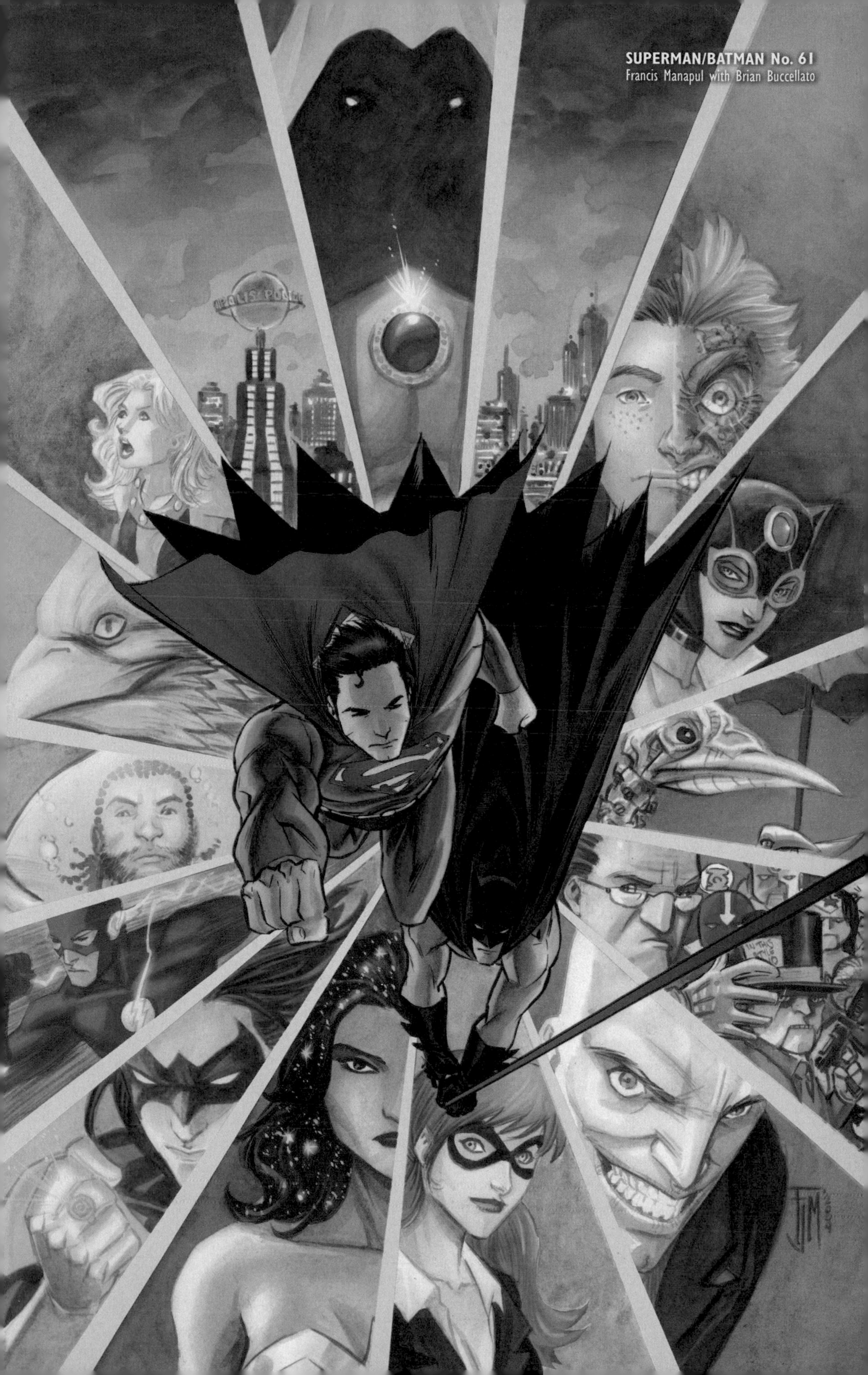

SUPERMAN/BATMAN No. 61
Francis Manapul with Brian Buccellato

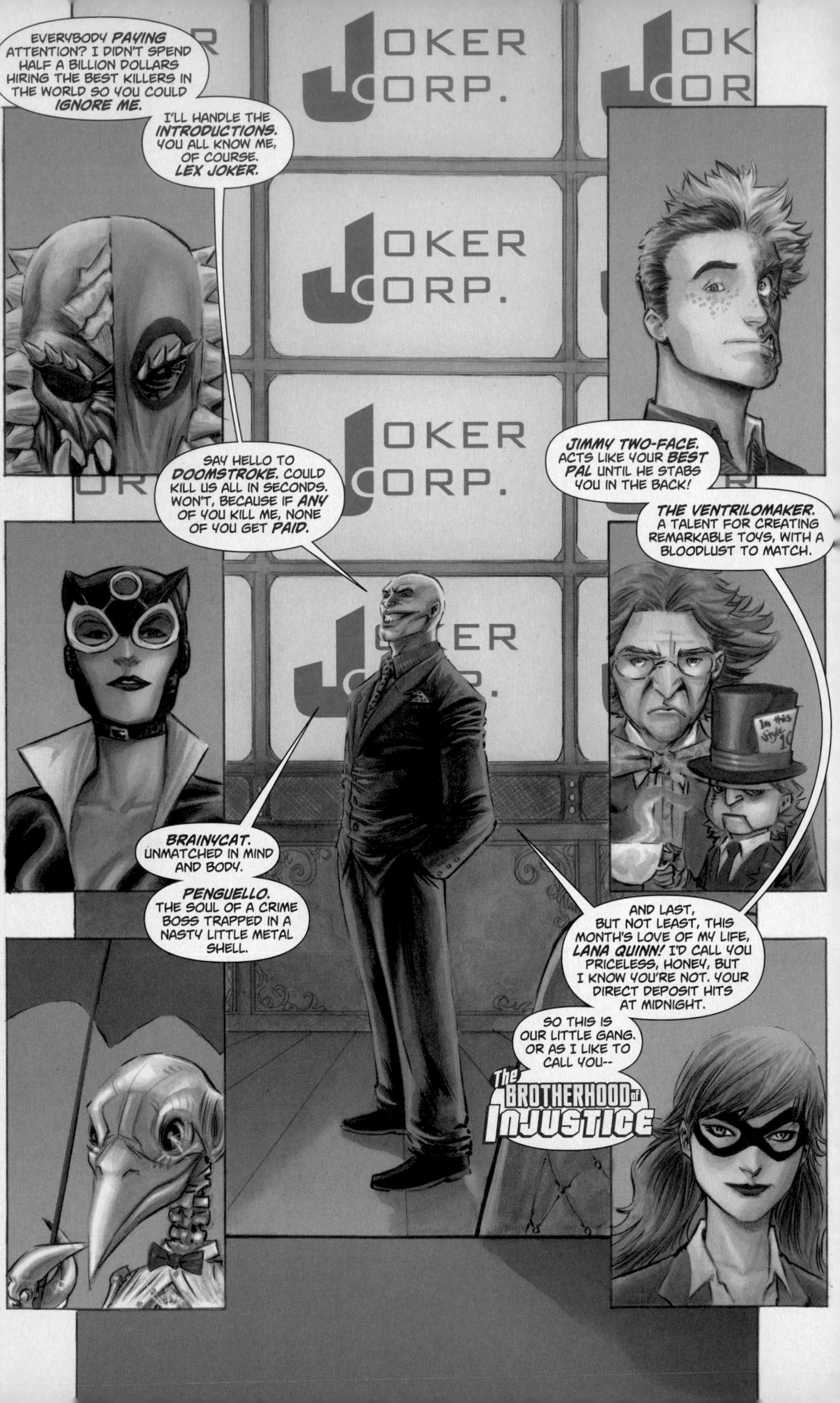
JOKER CORP.
EVERYBODY PAYING ATTENTION? I DIDN'T SPEND HALF A BILLION DOLLARS HIRING THE BEST KILLERS IN THE WORLD SO YOU COULD IGNORE ME.
I'LL HANDLE THE INTRODUCTIONS. YOU ALL KNOW ME, OF COURSE. LEX JOKER.
SAY HELLO TO DOOMSTROKE. COULD KILL US ALL IN SECONDS. WON'T, BECAUSE IF ANY OF YOU KILL ME, NONE OF YOU GET PAID.
BRAINYCAT. UNMATCHED IN MIND AND BODY.
PENGUELLO. THE SOUL OF A CRIME BOSS TRAPPED IN A NASTY LITTLE METAL SHELL.
JIMMY TWO-FACE. ACTS LIKE YOUR BEST PAL UNTIL HE STABS YOU IN THE BACK!
THE VENTRILOMAKER. A TALENT FOR CREATING REMARKABLE TOYS, WITH A BLOODLUST TO MATCH.
AND LAST, BUT NOT LEAST, THIS MONTH'S LOVE OF MY LIFE, LANA QUINN! I'D CALL YOU PRICELESS, HONEY, BUT I KNOW YOU'RE NOT. YOUR DIRECT DEPOSIT HITS AT MIDNIGHT.
SO THIS IS OUR LITTLE GANG. OR AS I LIKE TO CALL YOU--
The BROTHERHOOD of INJUSTICE

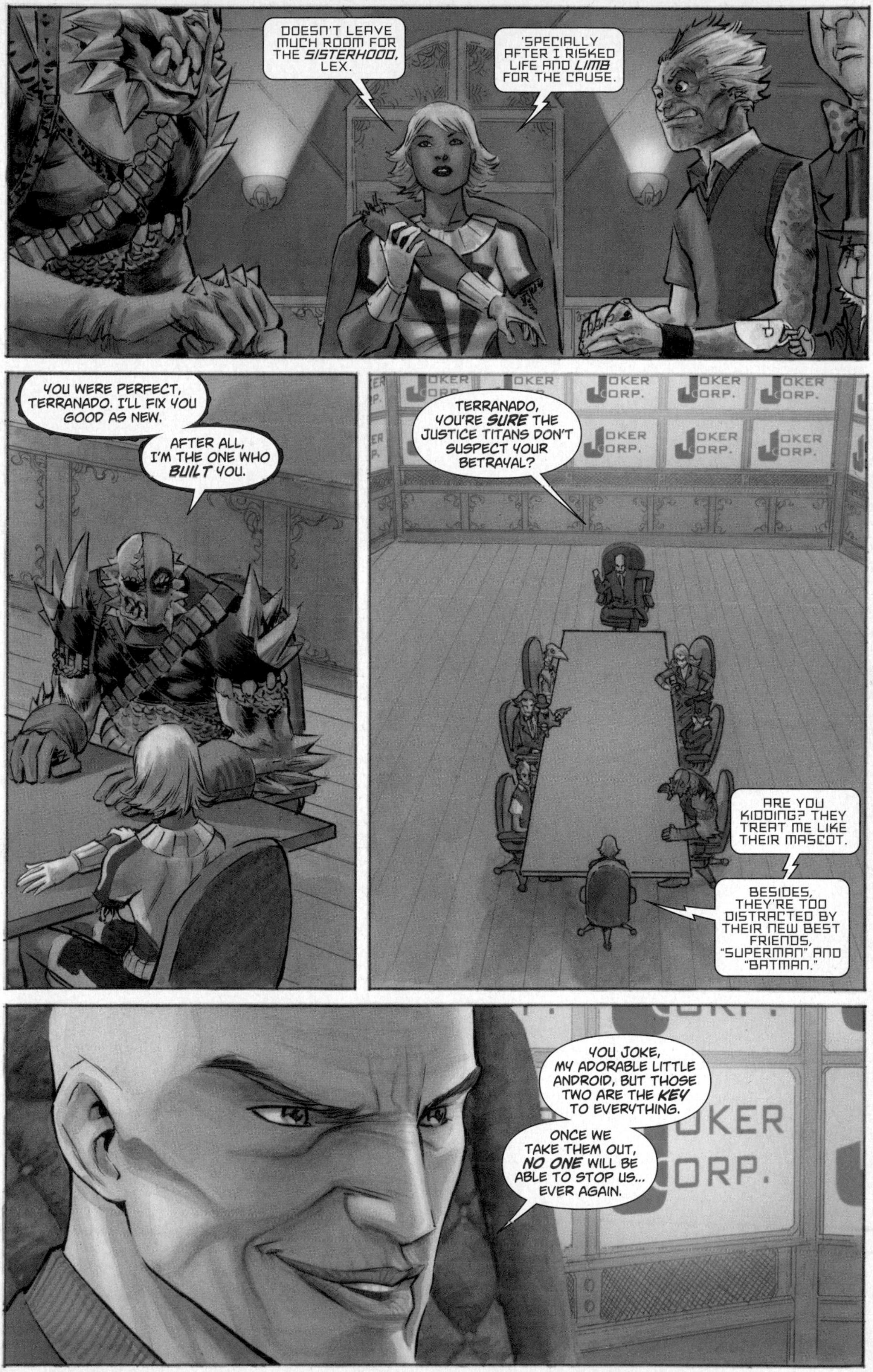
DOESN'T LEAVE MUCH ROOM FOR THE SISTERHOOD, LEX.
'SPECIALLY AFTER I RISKED LIFE AND LIMB FOR THE CAUSE.
YOU WERE PERFECT, TERRANADO. I'LL FIX YOU GOOD AS NEW.
AFTER ALL, I'M THE ONE WHO BUILT YOU.
JOKER CORP.
TERRANADO, YOU'RE SURE THE JUSTICE TITANS DON'T SUSPECT YOUR BETRAYAL?
ARE YOU KIDDING? THEY TREAT ME LIKE THEIR MASCOT.
BESIDES, THEY'RE TOO DISTRACTED BY THEIR NEW BEST FRIENDS, "SUPERMAN" AND "BATMAN."
YOU JOKE, MY ADORABLE LITTLE ANDROID, BUT THOSE TWO ARE THE KEY TO EVERYTHING.
ONCE WE TAKE THEM OUT, NO ONE WILL BE ABLE TO STOP US... EVER AGAIN.
OKER ORP.

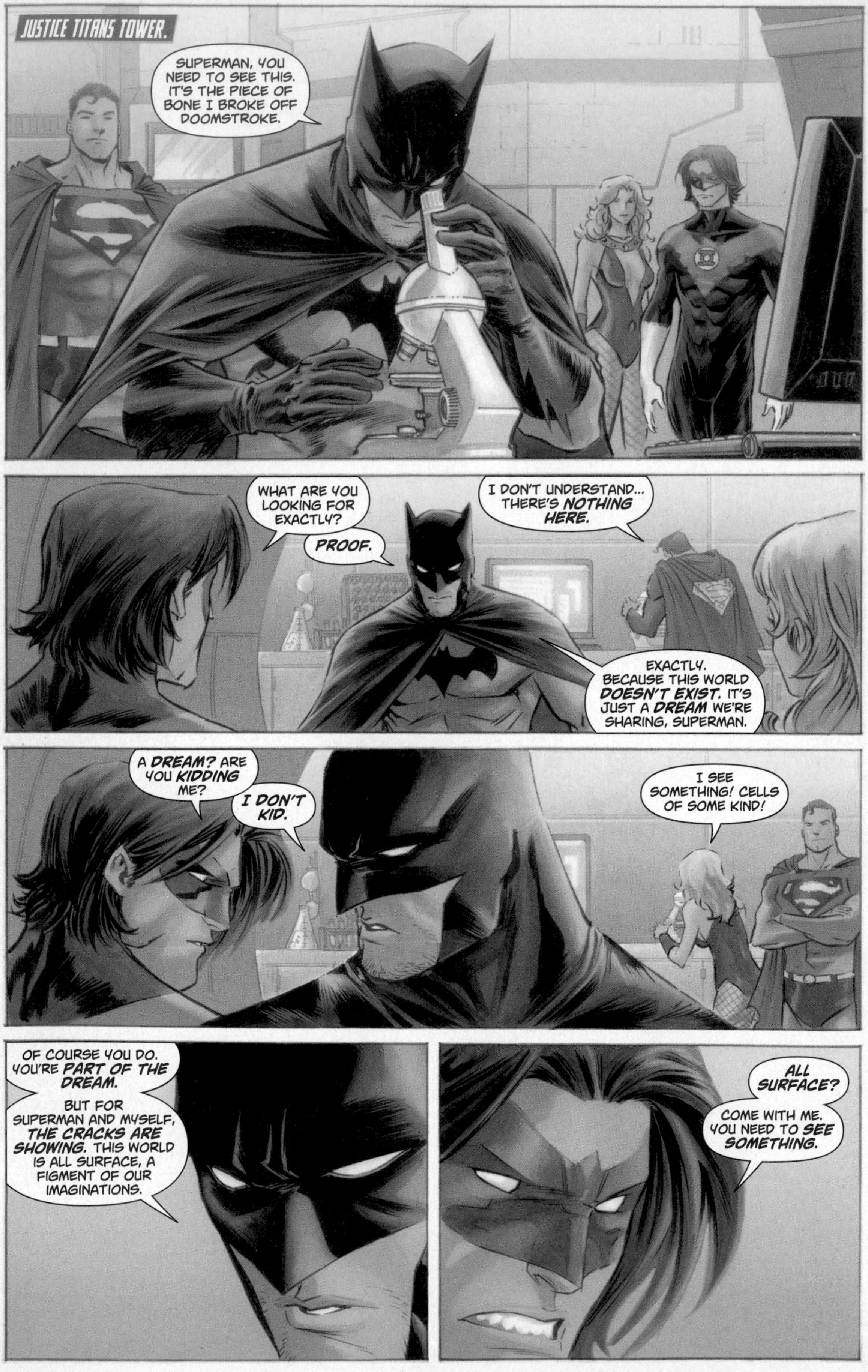
JUSTICE TITANS TOWER.
SUPERMAN, YOU NEED TO SEE THIS. IT'S THE PIECE OF BONE I BROKE OFF DOOMSTROKE.
WHAT ARE YOU LOOKING FOR EXACTLY?
PROOF.
I DON'T UNDERSTAND... THERE'S NOTHING HERE.
EXACTLY. BECAUSE THIS WORLD DOESN'T EXIST. IT'S JUST A DREAM WE'RE SHARING, SUPERMAN.
A DREAM? ARE YOU KIDDING ME?
I DON'T KID.
I SEE SOMETHING! CELLS OF SOME KIND!
OF COURSE YOU DO. YOU'RE PART OF THE DREAM.
BUT FOR SUPERMAN AND MYSELF, THE CRACKS ARE SHOWING. THIS WORLD IS ALL SURFACE, A FIGMENT OF OUR IMAGINATIONS.
ALL SURFACE?
COME WITH ME. YOU NEED TO SEE SOMETHING.

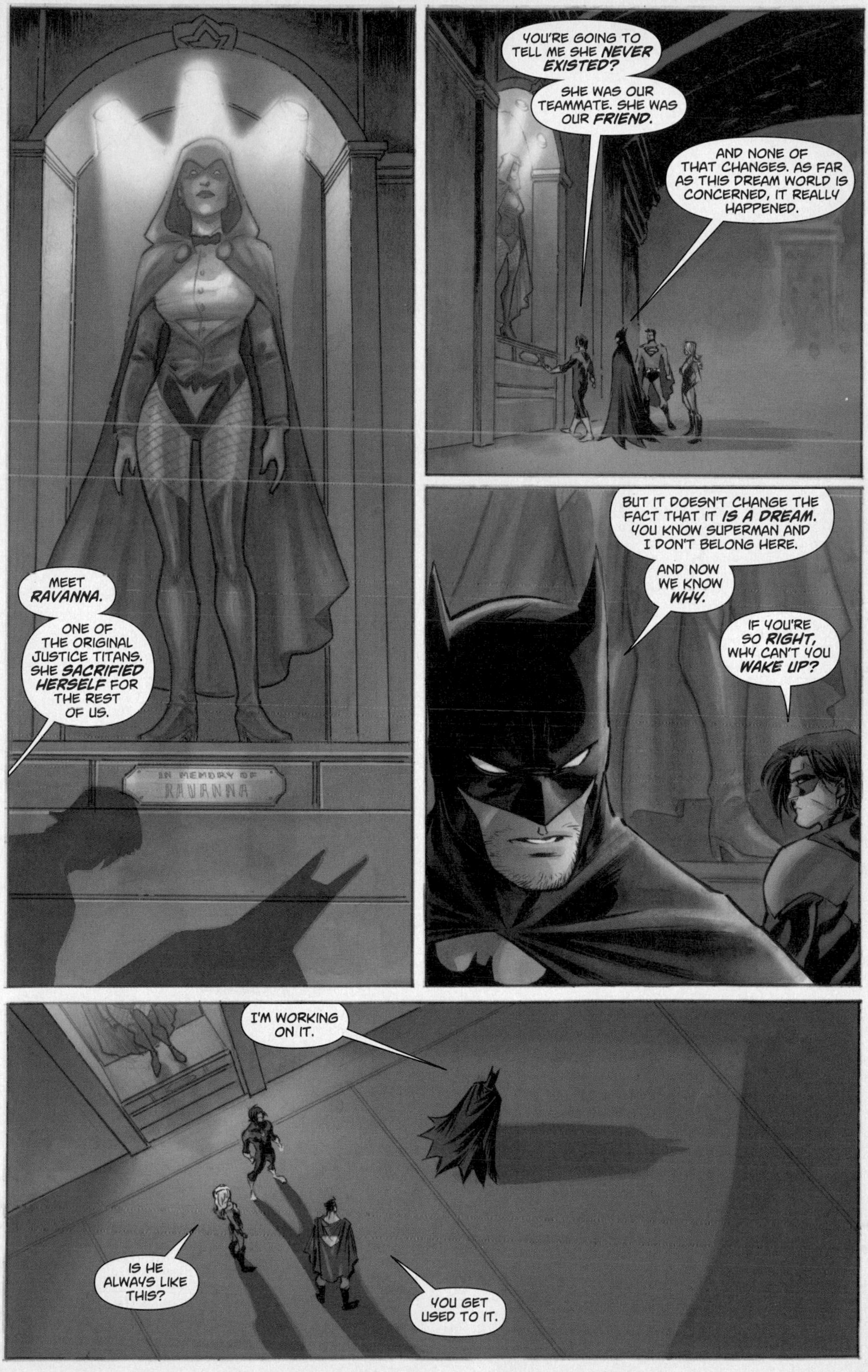
MEET RAVANNA.
ONE OF THE ORIGINAL JUSTICE TITANS. SHE SACRIFIED HERSELF FOR THE REST OF US.
IN MEMORY OF RAVANNA
YOU'RE GOING TO TELL ME SHE NEVER EXISTED?
SHE WAS OUR TEAMMATE. SHE WAS OUR FRIEND.
AND NONE OF THAT CHANGES. AS FAR AS THIS DREAM WORLD IS CONCERNED, IT REALLY HAPPENED.
BUT IT DOESN'T CHANGE THE FACT THAT IT IS A DREAM. YOU KNOW SUPERMAN AND I DON'T BELONG HERE.
AND NOW WE KNOW WHY.
IF YOU'RE SO RIGHT, WHY CAN'T YOU WAKE UP?
I'M WORKING ON IT.
IS HE ALWAYS LIKE THIS?
YOU GET USED TO IT.

COME ON, COME ON...

IT'S ME! OPEN UP, WOULD YA?

SHEESH, THIS PLACE IS *CREEPY* AT NIGHT.

GOTTA BE CAREFUL NOT TO WAKE UP THE CHUMPS.

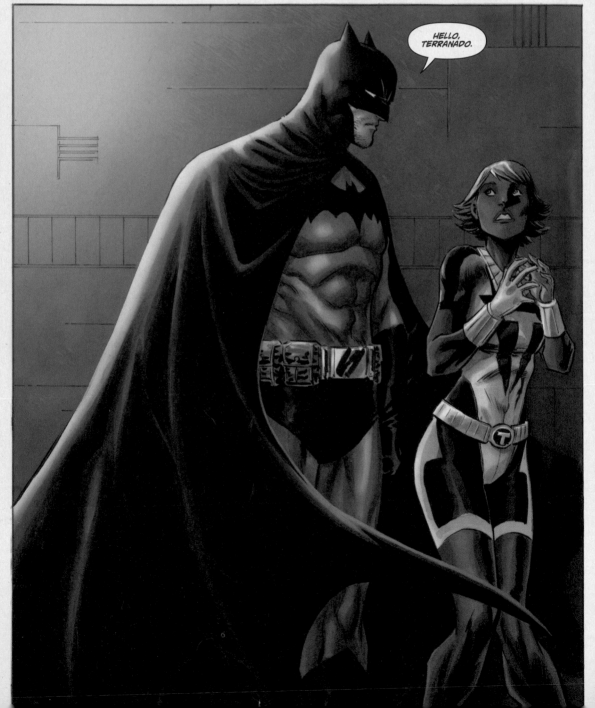

HELLO, TERRANADO.

UH, HEY THERE, BATMAN!

I WAS JUST, UM, CHECKING THE TOWER'S SECURITY SYSTEMS.

LOOKS LIKE YOUR ARM HEALED QUICKLY.

OH, THIS LITTLE THING? ONE OF THE BENEFITS OF BEING A GIRL-BOT, I GUESS. PLUG AND PLAY, Y'KNOW?

WRONG ARM, TERRANADO. DOOMSTROKE CUT OFF YOUR LEFT.

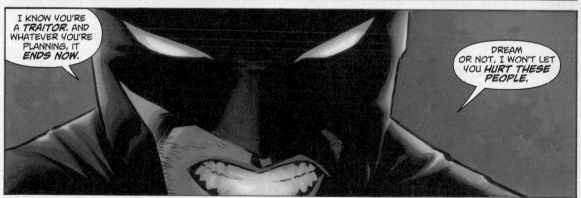

I KNOW YOU'RE A TRAITOR. AND WHATEVER YOU'RE PLANNING, IT ENDS NOW.

DREAM OR NOT, I WON'T LET YOU HURT THESE PEOPLE.

BUT I TOLD YOU THE TRUTH, BATMAN. I WAS CHECKING THE SECURITY SYSTEMS...

...CHECKING THEY WERE ALL OFF!

RRRRRRRUMMMBLE

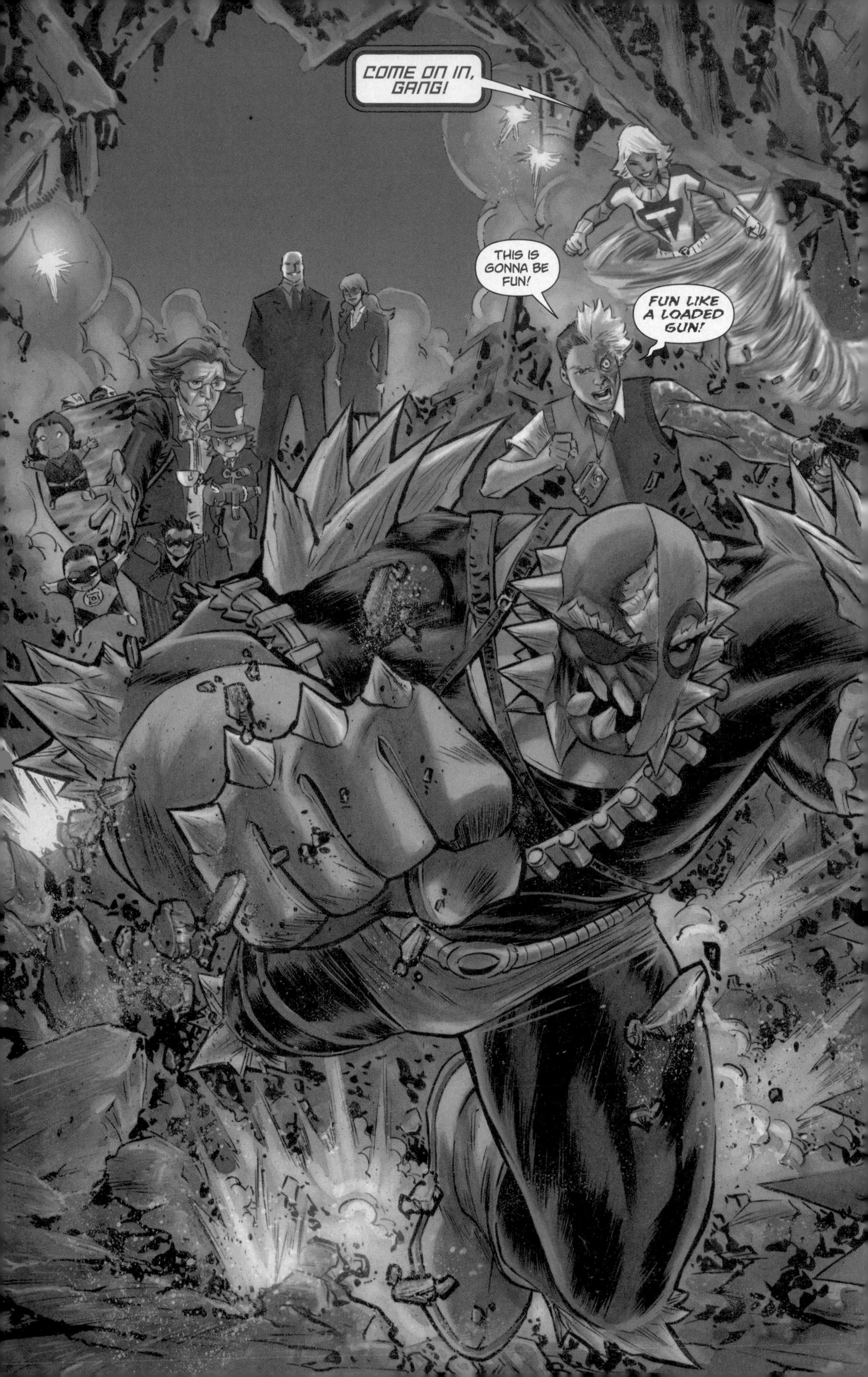
COME ON IN, GANG!
THIS IS GONNA BE FUN!
FUN LIKE A LOADED GUN!

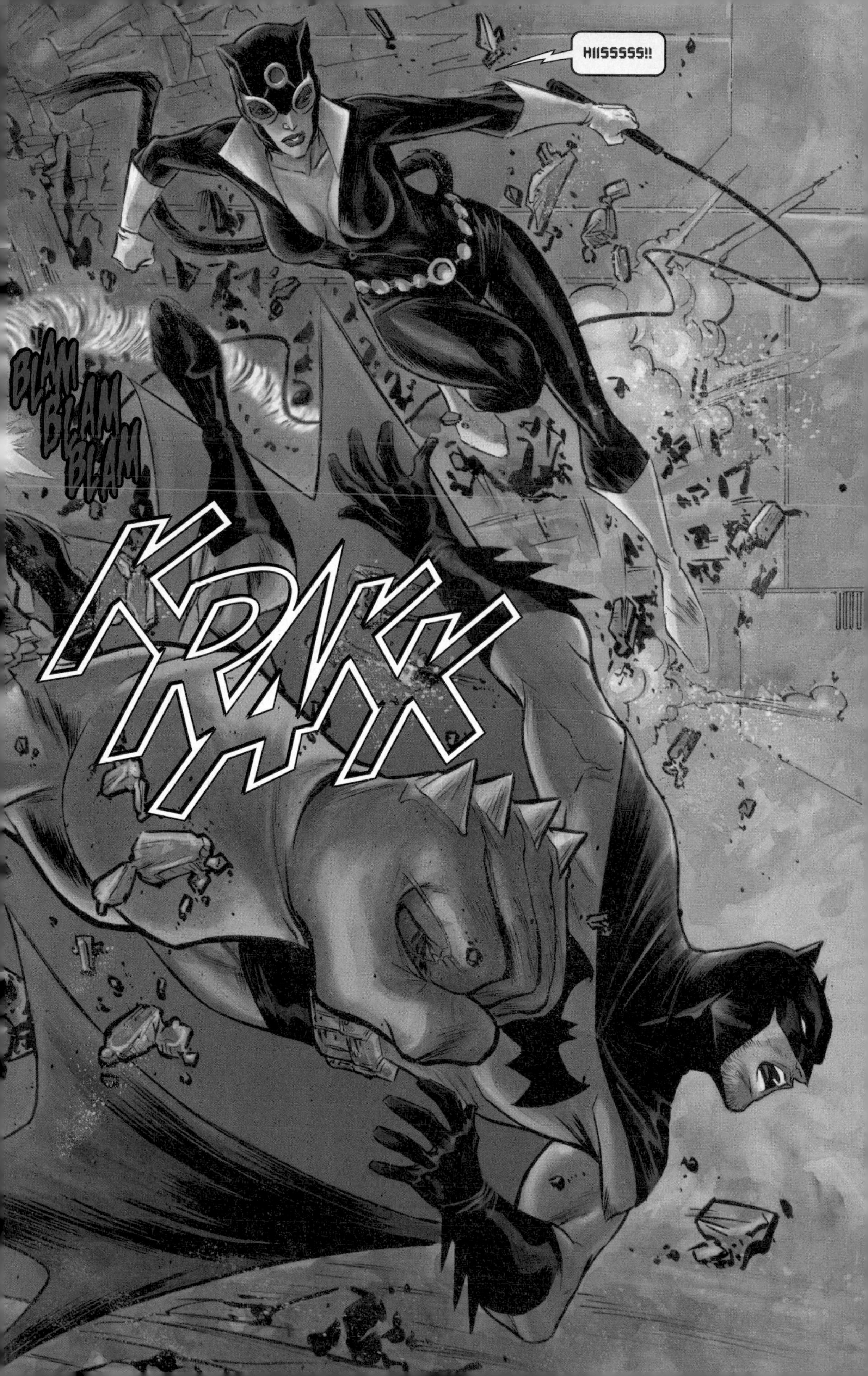
HIISSSSS!!
BLAM BLAM BLAM
KRAKK

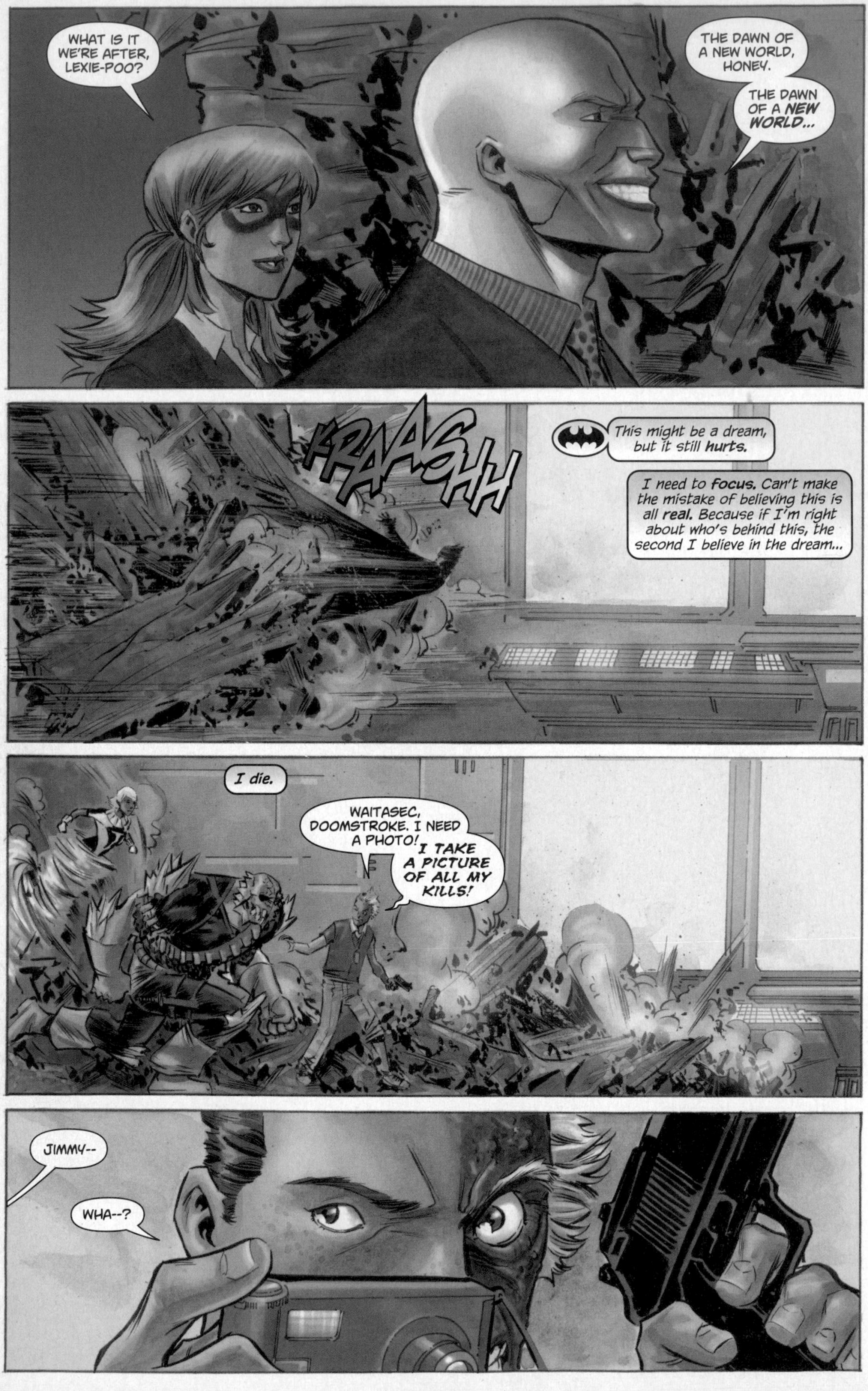
WHAT IS IT WE'RE AFTER, LEXIE-POO?
THE DAWN OF A NEW WORLD, HONEY.
THE DAWN OF A NEW WORLD...
KRAASHH
This might be a dream, but it still hurts.
I need to focus. Can't make the mistake of believing this is all real. Because if I'm right about who's behind this, the second I believe in the dream...
I die.
WAITASEC, DOOMSTROKE. I NEED A PHOTO!
I TAKE A PICTURE OF ALL MY KILLS!
JIMMY--
WHA--?

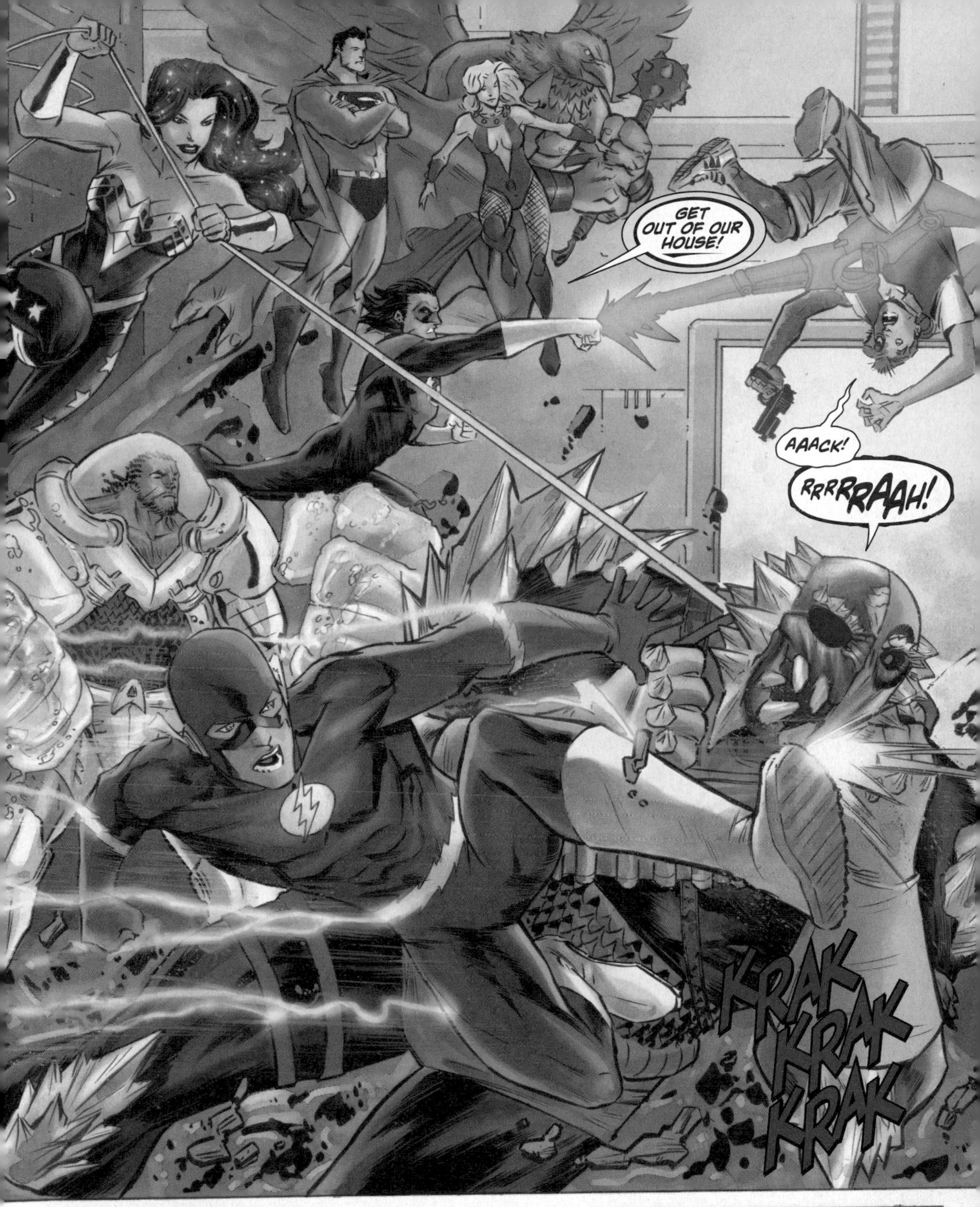
GET OUT OF OUR HOUSE!
AAACK!
RRRRRAAH!
KRAK KRAK KRAK
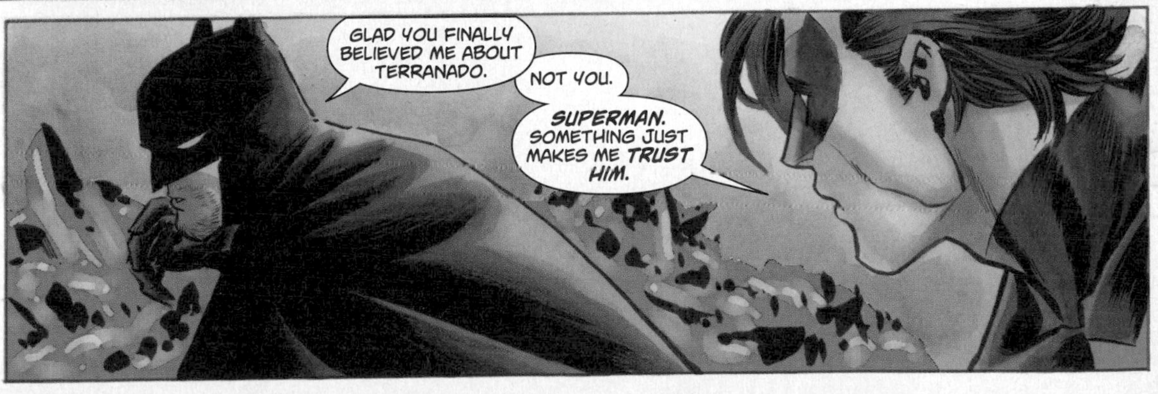
GLAD YOU FINALLY BELIEVED ME ABOUT TERRANADO.
NOT YOU.
SUPERMAN. SOMETHING JUST MAKES ME TRUST HIM.

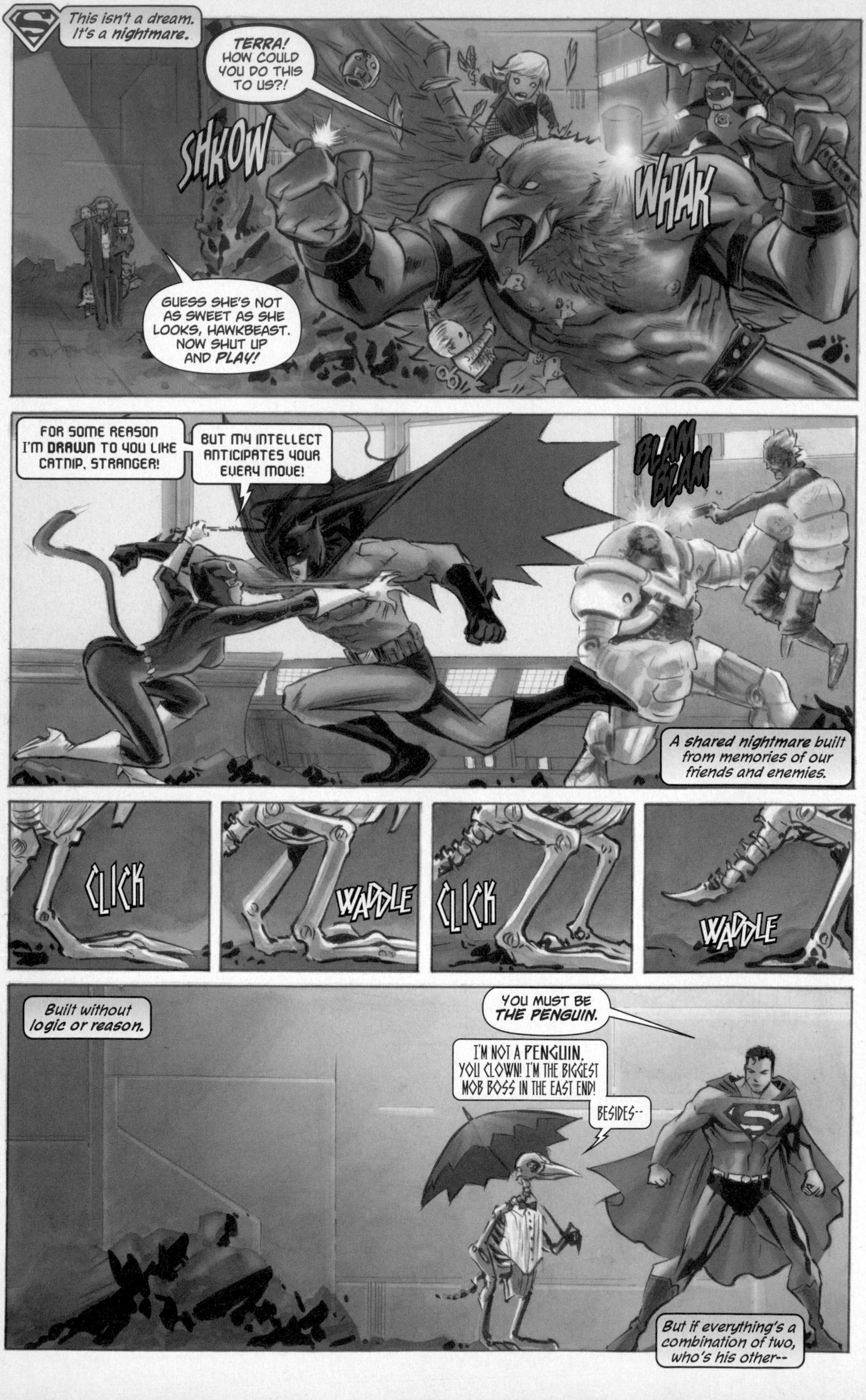
This isn't a dream. It's a nightmare.
TERRA! HOW COULD YOU DO THIS TO US?!
SHKOW
WHAK
GUESS SHE'S NOT AS SWEET AS SHE LOOKS, HAWKBEAST. NOW SHUT UP AND PLAY!
FOR SOME REASON I'M DRAWN TO YOU LIKE CATNIP, STRANGER!
BUT MY INTELLECT ANTICIPATES YOUR EVERY MOVE!
BLAM BLAM
A shared nightmare built from memories of our friends and enemies.
CLICK
WADDLE
CLICK
WADDLE
Built without logic or reason.
YOU MUST BE THE PENGUIN.
I'M NOT A PENGUIN, YOU CLOWN! I'M THE BIGGEST MOB BOSS IN THE EAST END!
BESIDES--
But if everything's a combination of two, who's his other--

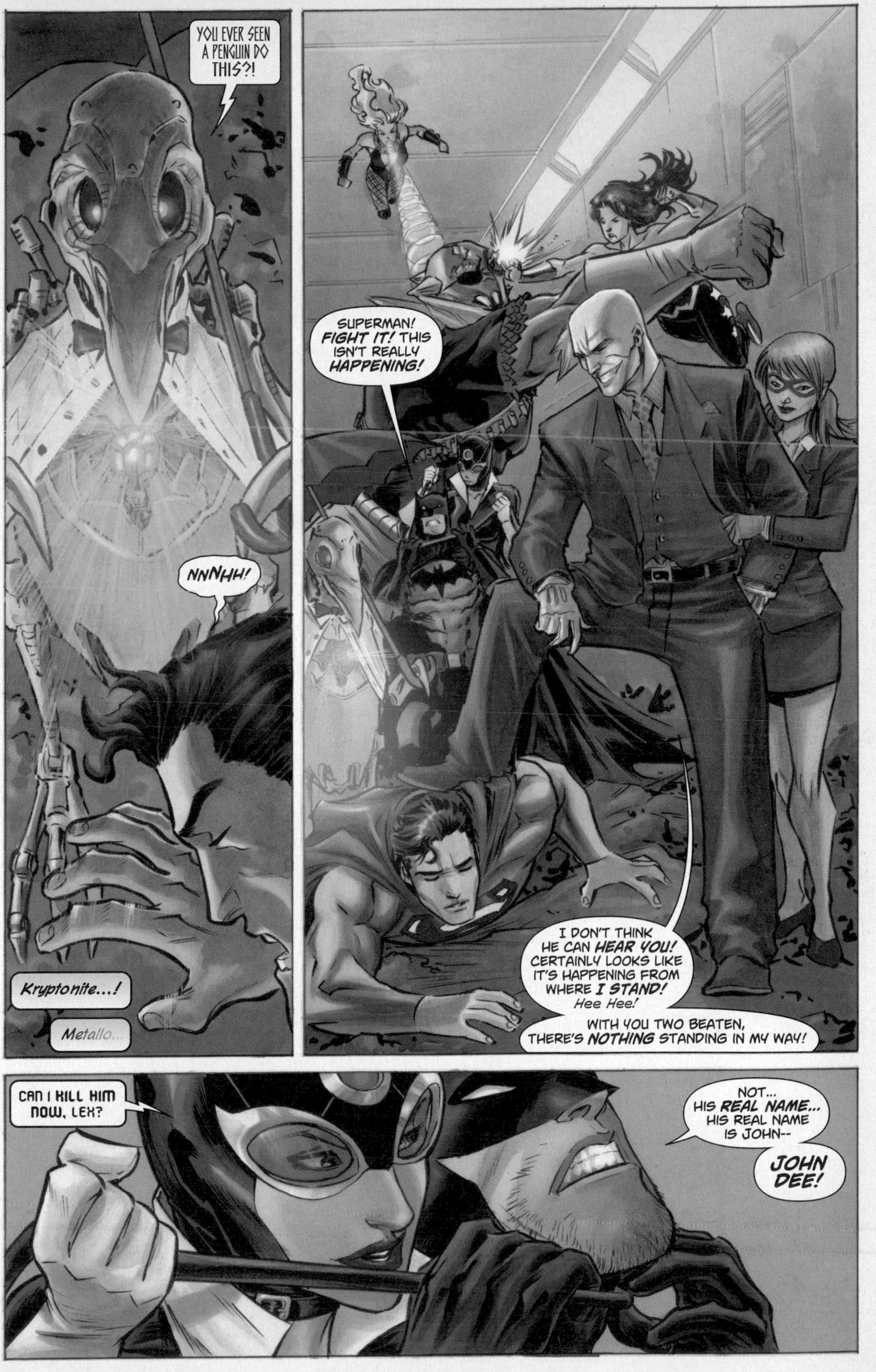
YOU EVER SEEN A PENGUIN DO THIS?!
NNNHH!
Kryptonite...!
Metallo...
SUPERMAN! FIGHT IT! THIS ISN'T REALLY HAPPENING!
I DON'T THINK HE CAN HEAR YOU! CERTAINLY LOOKS LIKE IT'S HAPPENING FROM WHERE I STAND! Hee Hee!
WITH YOU TWO BEATEN, THERE'S NOTHING STANDING IN MY WAY!
CAN I KILL HIM NOW, LEX?
NOT... HIS REAL NAME... HIS REAL NAME IS JOHN--
JOHN DEE!

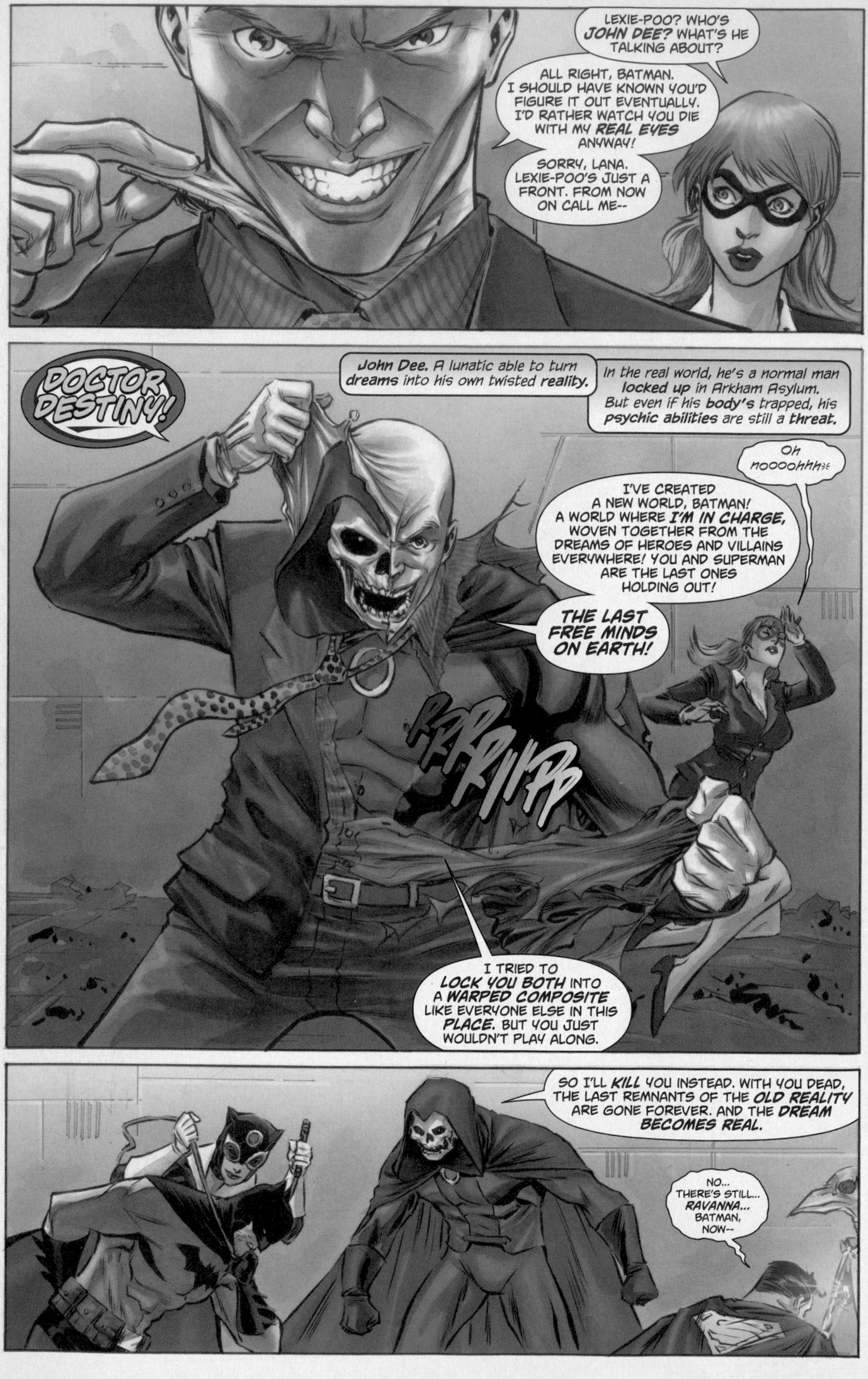
LEXIE-POO? WHO'S JOHN DEE? WHAT'S HE TALKING ABOUT?
ALL RIGHT, BATMAN. I SHOULD HAVE KNOWN YOU'D FIGURE IT OUT EVENTUALLY. I'D RATHER WATCH YOU DIE WITH MY REAL EYES ANYWAY!
SORRY, LANA. LEXIE-POO'S JUST A FRONT. FROM NOW ON CALL ME--
DOCTOR DESTINY!
John Dee. A lunatic able to turn dreams into his own twisted reality.
In the real world, he's a normal man locked up in Arkham Asylum. But even if his body's trapped, his psychic abilities are still a threat.
Oh noooohhh*
I'VE CREATED A NEW WORLD, BATMAN! A WORLD WHERE I'M IN CHARGE, WOVEN TOGETHER FROM THE DREAMS OF HEROES AND VILLAINS EVERYWHERE! YOU AND SUPERMAN ARE THE LAST ONES HOLDING OUT!
THE LAST FREE MINDS ON EARTH!
I TRIED TO LOCK YOU BOTH INTO A WARPED COMPOSITE LIKE EVERYONE ELSE IN THIS PLACE. BUT YOU JUST WOULDN'T PLAY ALONG.
SO I'LL KILL YOU INSTEAD. WITH YOU DEAD, THE LAST REMNANTS OF THE OLD REALITY ARE GONE FOREVER. AND THE DREAM BECOMES REAL.
NO... THERE'S STILL... RAVANNA... BATMAN, NOW--

Yes.

Superman's **right**.

CHK ON

Destiny's powers have a **supernatural** connection.

It can't be a **coincidence** that the only **magic-based** heroes here are **locked in stone**.

WHP

WHP

WHP

NO!

YOU **FOOL!** YOU DON'T KNOW WHAT YOU'VE **DONE!**

K'RAAASH

YOU'VE RUINED **EVERYTHING!**

EVERYTHING...!

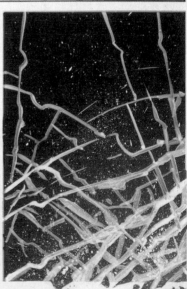

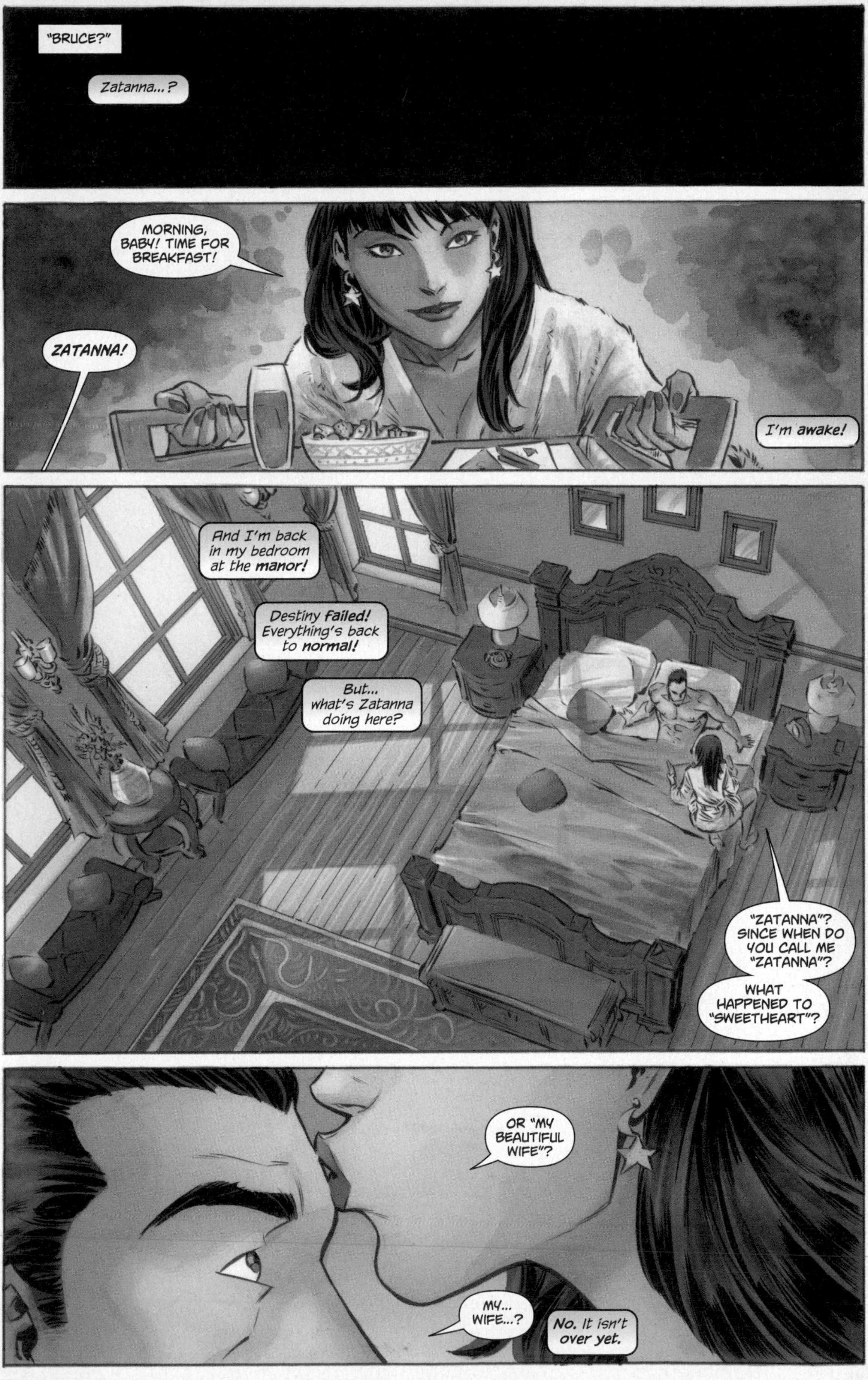
"BRUCE?"
Zatanna...?
MORNING, BABY! TIME FOR BREAKFAST!
ZATANNA!
I'm awake!
And I'm back in my bedroom at the manor!
Destiny failed! Everything's back to normal!
But... what's Zatanna doing here?
"ZATANNA"? SINCE WHEN DO YOU CALL ME "ZATANNA"?
WHAT HAPPENED TO "SWEETHEART"?
OR "MY BEAUTIFUL WIFE"?
MY... WIFE...?
No. It isn't over yet.

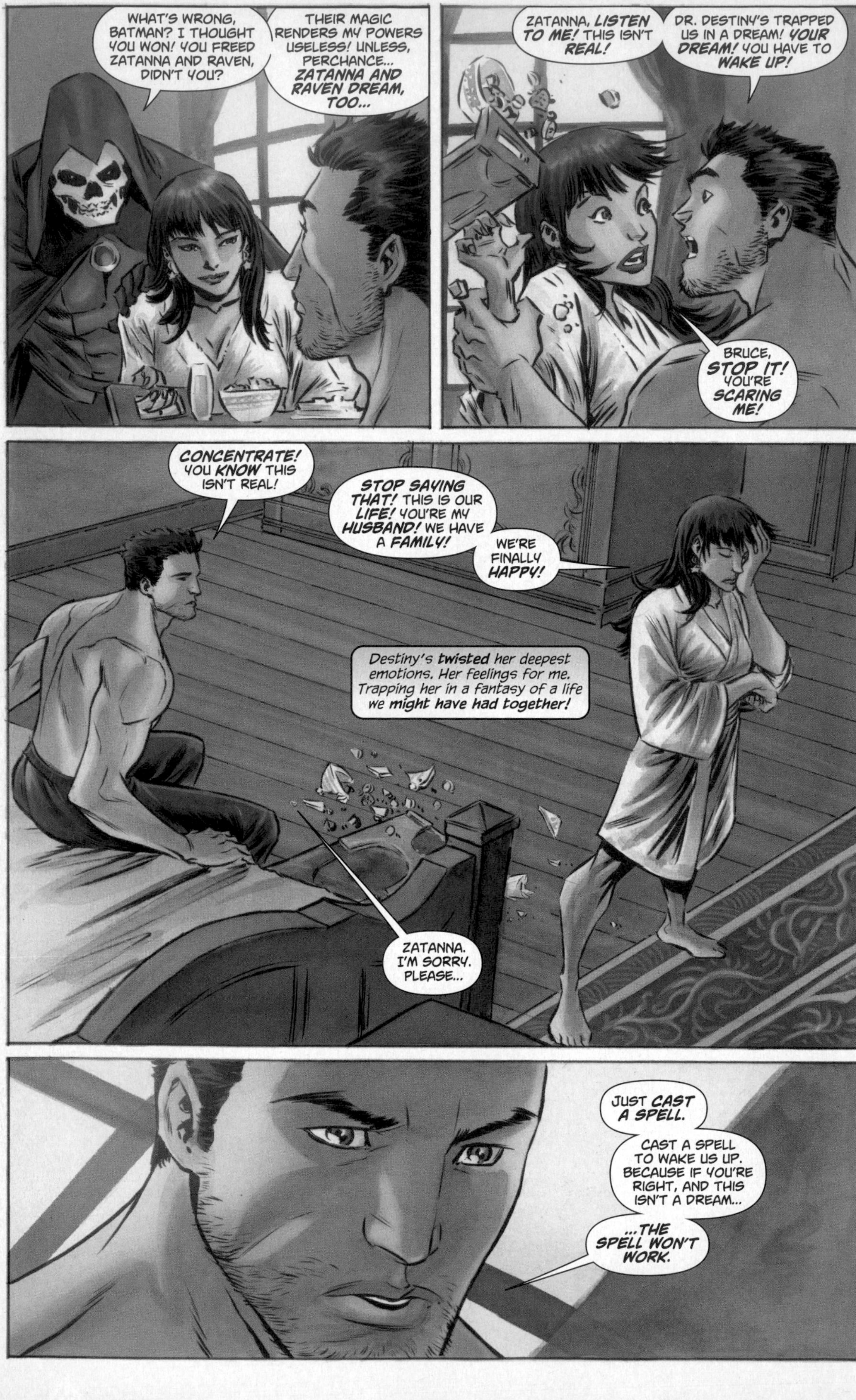
WHAT'S WRONG, BATMAN? I THOUGHT YOU WON! YOU FREED ZATANNA AND RAVEN, DIDN'T YOU?
THEIR MAGIC RENDERS MY POWERS USELESS! UNLESS, PERCHANCE... ZATANNA AND RAVEN DREAM, TOO...
ZATANNA, LISTEN TO ME! THIS ISN'T REAL!
DR. DESTINY'S TRAPPED US IN A DREAM! YOUR DREAM! YOU HAVE TO WAKE UP!
BRUCE, STOP IT! YOU'RE SCARING ME!
CONCENTRATE! YOU KNOW THIS ISN'T REAL!
STOP SAYING THAT! THIS IS OUR LIFE! YOU'RE MY HUSBAND! WE HAVE A FAMILY!
WE'RE FINALLY HAPPY!
Destiny's twisted her deepest emotions. Her feelings for me. Trapping her in a fantasy of a life we might have had together!
ZATANNA. I'M SORRY. PLEASE...
JUST CAST A SPELL.
CAST A SPELL TO WAKE US UP. BECAUSE IF YOU'RE RIGHT, AND THIS ISN'T A DREAM...
...THE SPELL WON'T WORK.

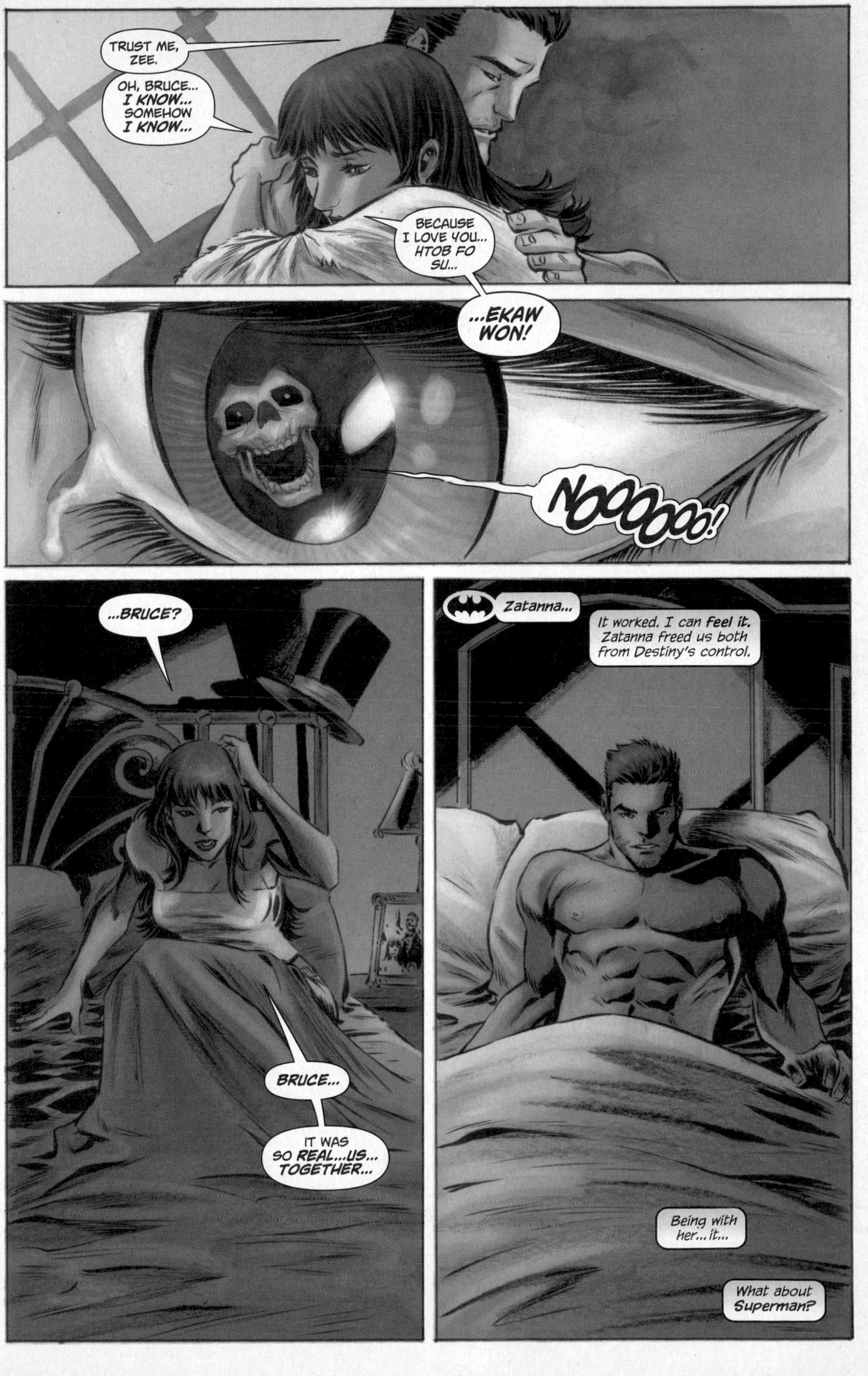
TRUST ME, ZEE.
OH, BRUCE... I KNOW... SOMEHOW I KNOW...
BECAUSE I LOVE YOU... HTOB FO SU...
...EKAW WON!
NOOOOOO!
...BRUCE?
BRUCE...
IT WAS SO REAL...US... TOGETHER...
Zatanna...
It worked. I can feel it. Zatanna freed us both from Destiny's control.
Being with her...it...
What about Superman?

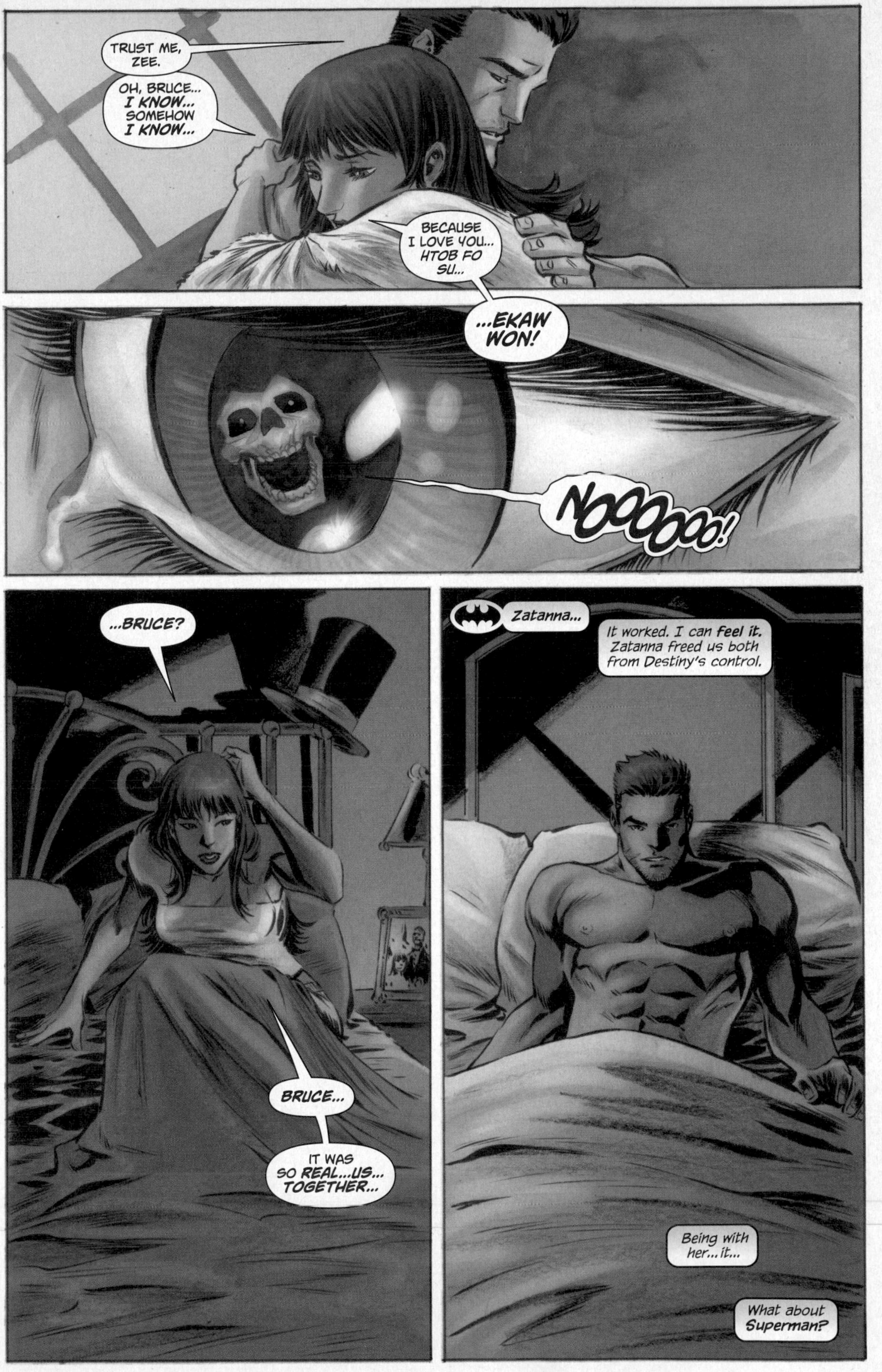
TRUST ME, ZEE.
OH, BRUCE... I KNOW... SOMEHOW I KNOW...
BECAUSE I LOVE YOU... HTOB FO SU...
...EKAW WON!
NOOOOOO!
...BRUCE?
BRUCE...
IT WAS SO REAL...US... TOGETHER...
Zatanna...
It worked. I can feel it. Zatanna freed us both from Destiny's control.
Being with her...it...
What about Superman?

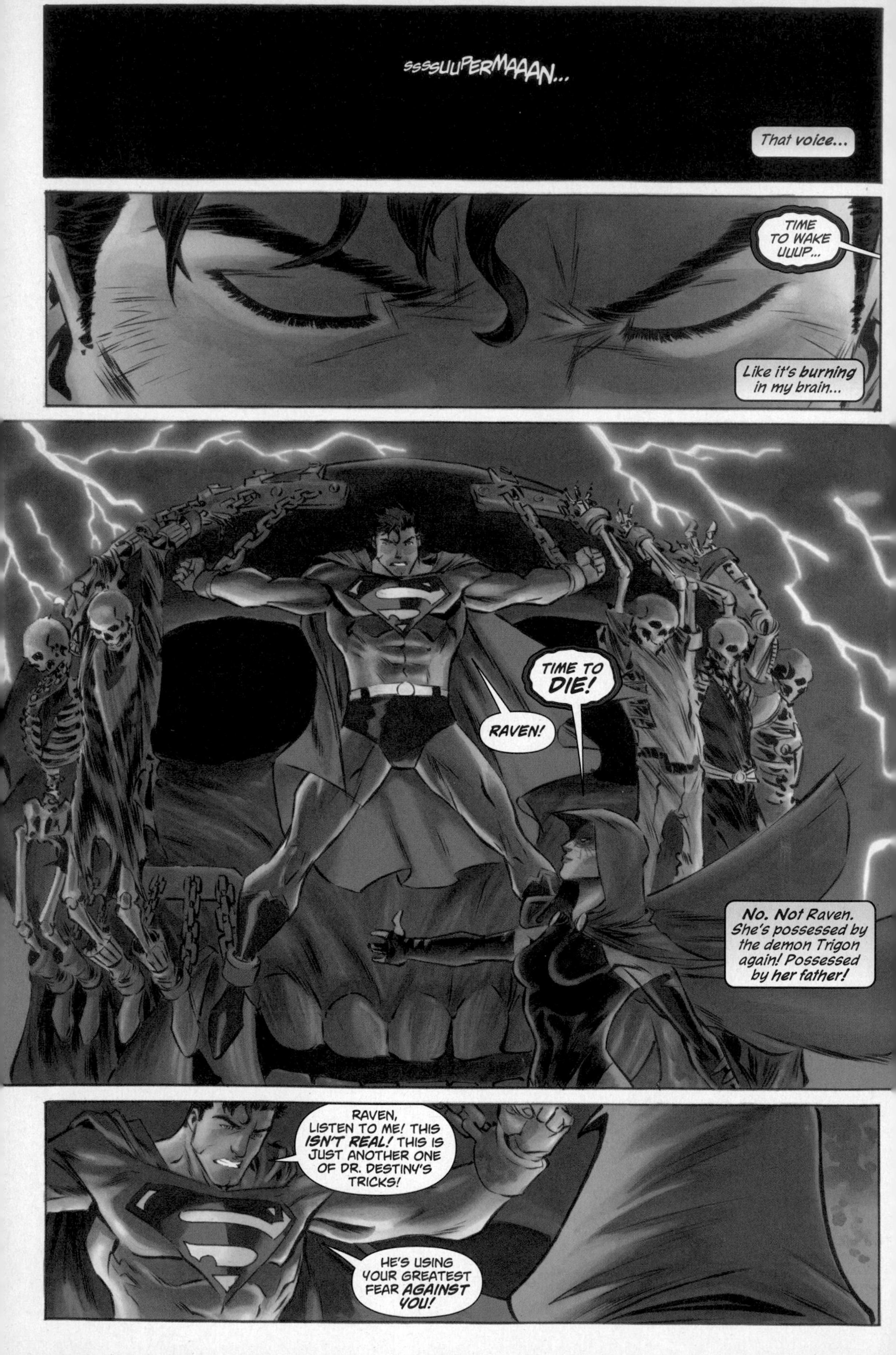
SSSSUUPERMAAAN...
That voice...
TIME TO WAKE UUUP...
Like it's burning in my brain...
RAVEN!
TIME TO DIE!
No. Not Raven. She's possessed by the demon Trigon again! Possessed by her father!
RAVEN, LISTEN TO ME! THIS ISN'T REAL! THIS IS JUST ANOTHER ONE OF DR. DESTINY'S TRICKS!
HE'S USING YOUR GREATEST FEAR AGAINST YOU!

"OKAY, MR. DEE, TIME FOR YOUR NIGHTLY COCKTAIL.
"POOR GUY...
ARKHAM ASYLUM
...THERE'S ENOUGH HERE TO KNOCK OUT A T-REX.
AT LEAST IT KEEPS HIM QUIET. SWEET DREAMS, MR. DEE.
...Buh...
BRUUUCE...
...KENT...
...BRUUUCE...
BRUCE KENT...
THE END?

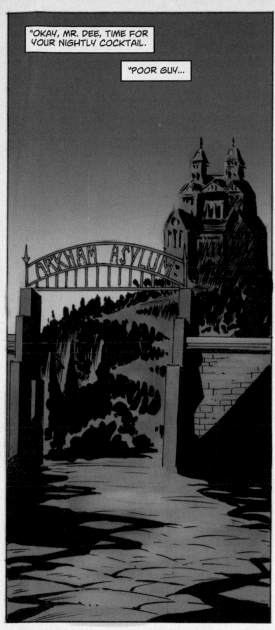

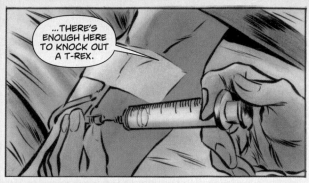

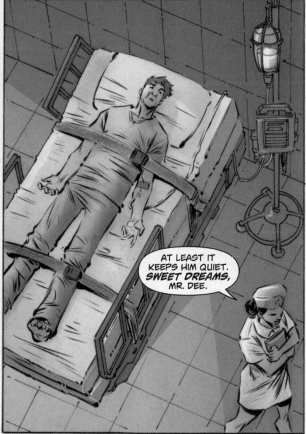

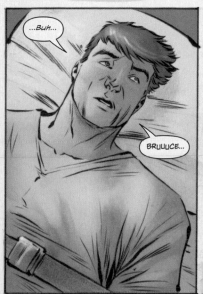

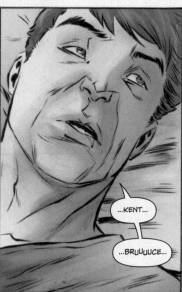

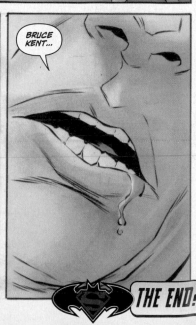

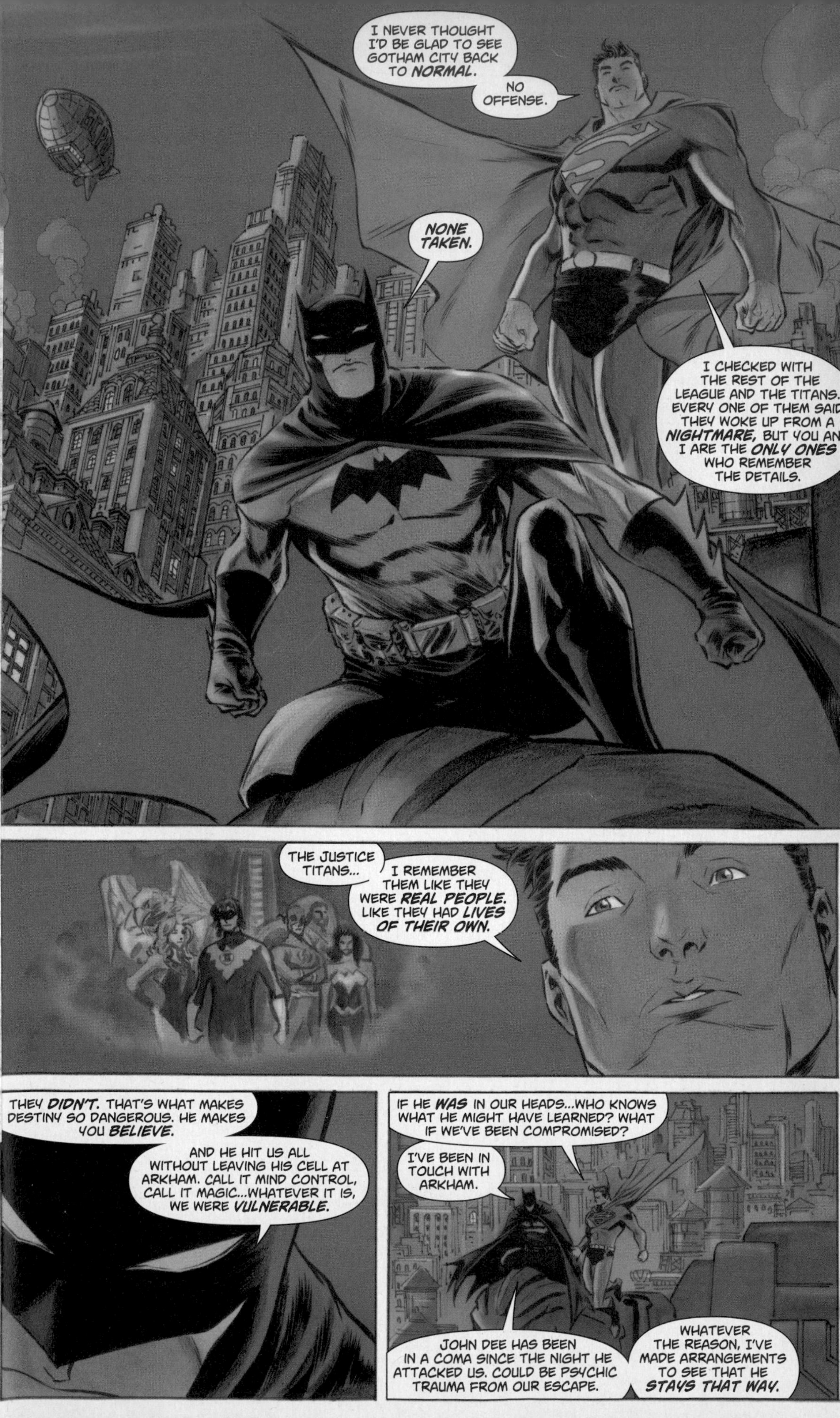

I NEVER THOUGHT I'D BE GLAD TO SEE GOTHAM CITY BACK TO NORMAL.
NO OFFENSE.
NONE TAKEN.
I CHECKED WITH THE REST OF THE LEAGUE AND THE TITANS. EVERY ONE OF THEM SAID THEY WOKE UP FROM A NIGHTMARE, BUT YOU AND I ARE THE ONLY ONES WHO REMEMBER THE DETAILS.
THE JUSTICE TITANS...
I REMEMBER THEM LIKE THEY WERE REAL PEOPLE. LIKE THEY HAD LIVES OF THEIR OWN.
THEY DIDN'T. THAT'S WHAT MAKES DESTINY SO DANGEROUS. HE MAKES YOU BELIEVE.
AND HE HIT US ALL WITHOUT LEAVING HIS CELL AT ARKHAM. CALL IT MIND CONTROL, CALL IT MAGIC...WHATEVER IT IS, WE WERE VULNERABLE.
IF HE WAS IN OUR HEADS...WHO KNOWS WHAT HE MIGHT HAVE LEARNED? WHAT IF WE'VE BEEN COMPROMISED?
I'VE BEEN IN TOUCH WITH ARKHAM.
JOHN DEE HAS BEEN IN A COMA SINCE THE NIGHT HE ATTACKED US. COULD BE PSYCHIC TRAUMA FROM OUR ESCAPE.
WHATEVER THE REASON, I'VE MADE ARRANGEMENTS TO SEE THAT HE STAYS THAT WAY.

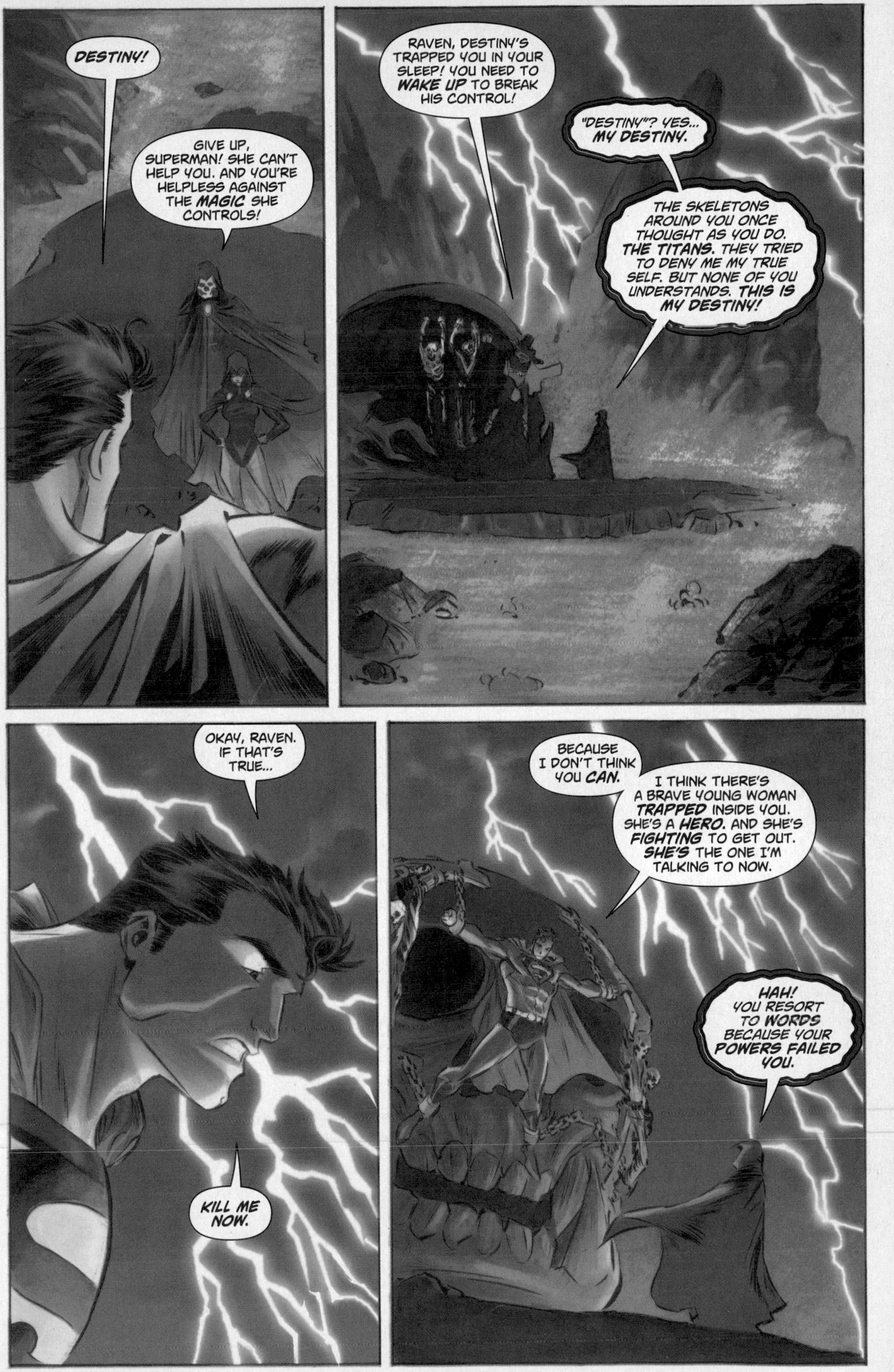
DESTINY!
GIVE UP, SUPERMAN! SHE CAN'T HELP YOU. AND YOU'RE HELPLESS AGAINST THE MAGIC SHE CONTROLS!
RAVEN, DESTINY'S TRAPPED YOU IN YOUR SLEEP! YOU NEED TO WAKE UP TO BREAK HIS CONTROL!
"DESTINY"? YES... MY DESTINY.
THE SKELETONS AROUND YOU ONCE THOUGHT AS YOU DO. THE TITANS. THEY TRIED TO DENY ME MY TRUE SELF. BUT NONE OF YOU UNDERSTANDS. THIS IS MY DESTINY!
OKAY, RAVEN. IF THAT'S TRUE...
KILL ME NOW.
BECAUSE I DON'T THINK YOU CAN.
I THINK THERE'S A BRAVE YOUNG WOMAN TRAPPED INSIDE YOU. SHE'S A HERO. AND SHE'S FIGHTING TO GET OUT. SHE'S THE ONE I'M TALKING TO NOW.
HAH! YOU RESORT TO WORDS BECAUSE YOUR POWERS FAILED YOU.

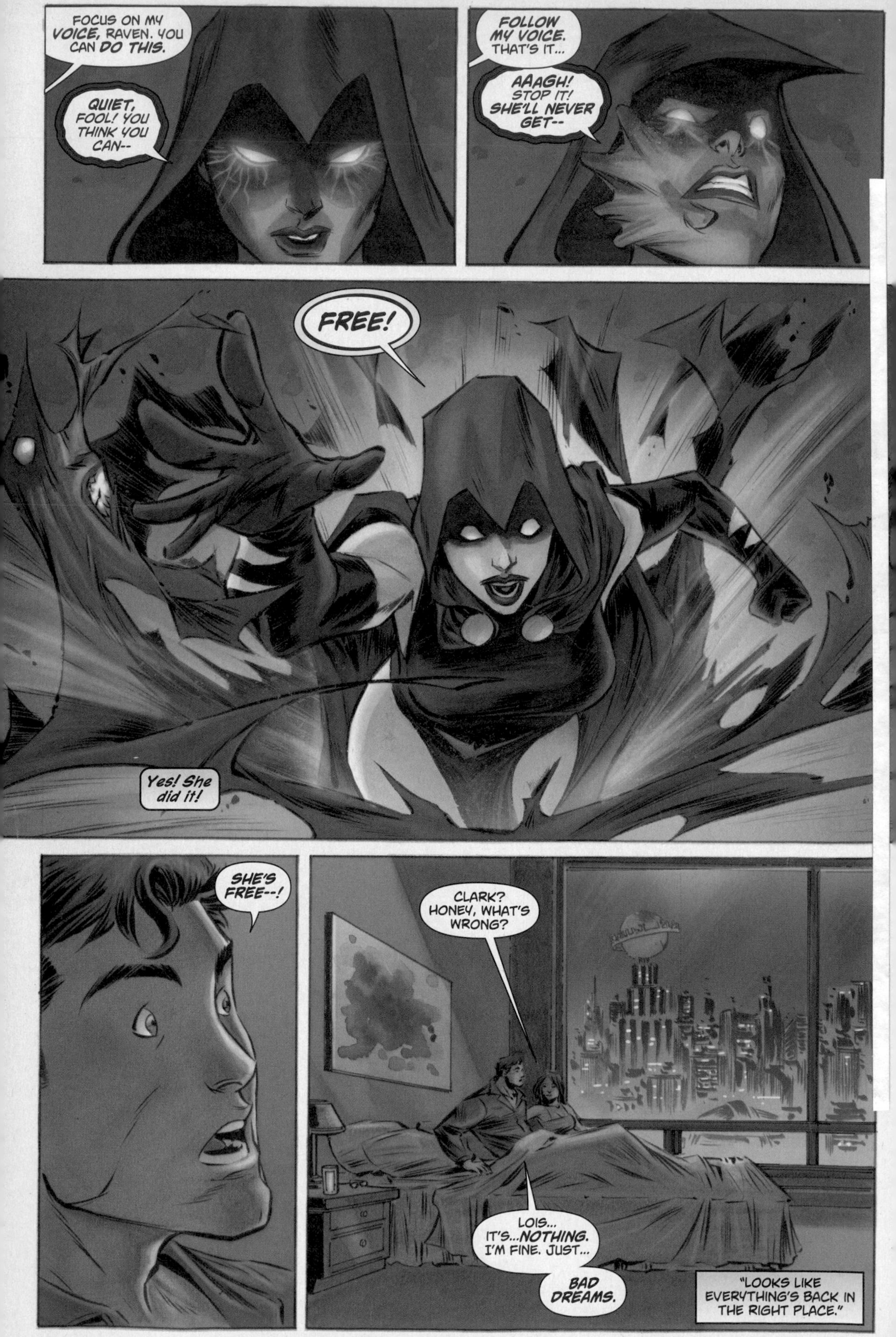
FOCUS ON MY VOICE, RAVEN. YOU CAN DO THIS.
QUIET, FOOL! YOU THINK YOU CAN--
FOLLOW MY VOICE. THAT'S IT...
AAAGH! STOP IT! SHE'LL NEVER GET--
FREE!
Yes! She did it!
SHE'S FREE--!
CLARK? HONEY, WHAT'S WRONG?
LOIS... IT'S...NOTHING. I'M FINE. JUST...
BAD DREAMS.
"LOOKS LIKE EVERYTHING'S BACK IN THE RIGHT PLACE."

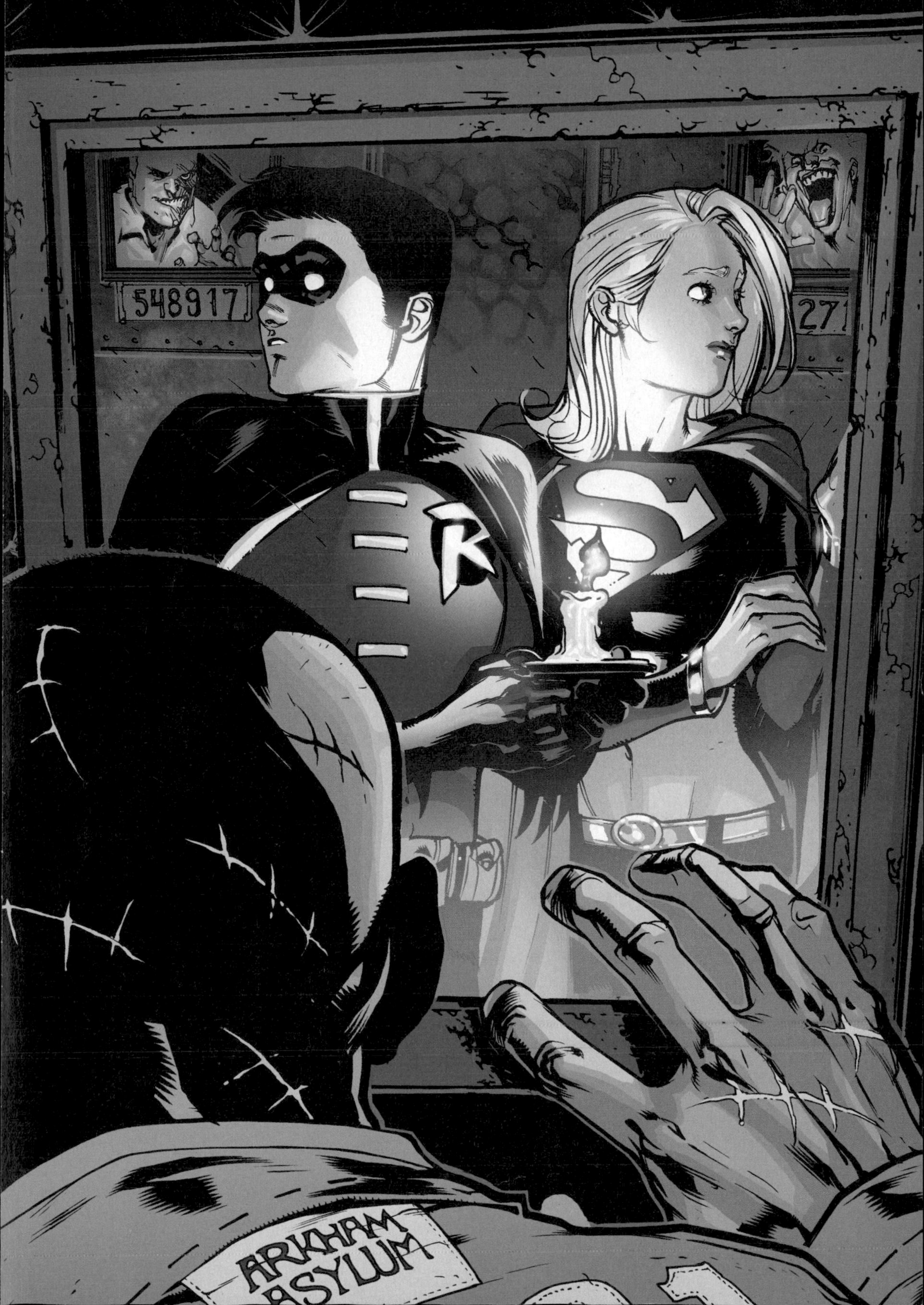

548917
271
ARKHAM ASYLUM

SIDEKICKED

Plot: Michael Green and Mike Johnson

Dialogue: Mike Johnson

Artist: Rafael Albuquerque

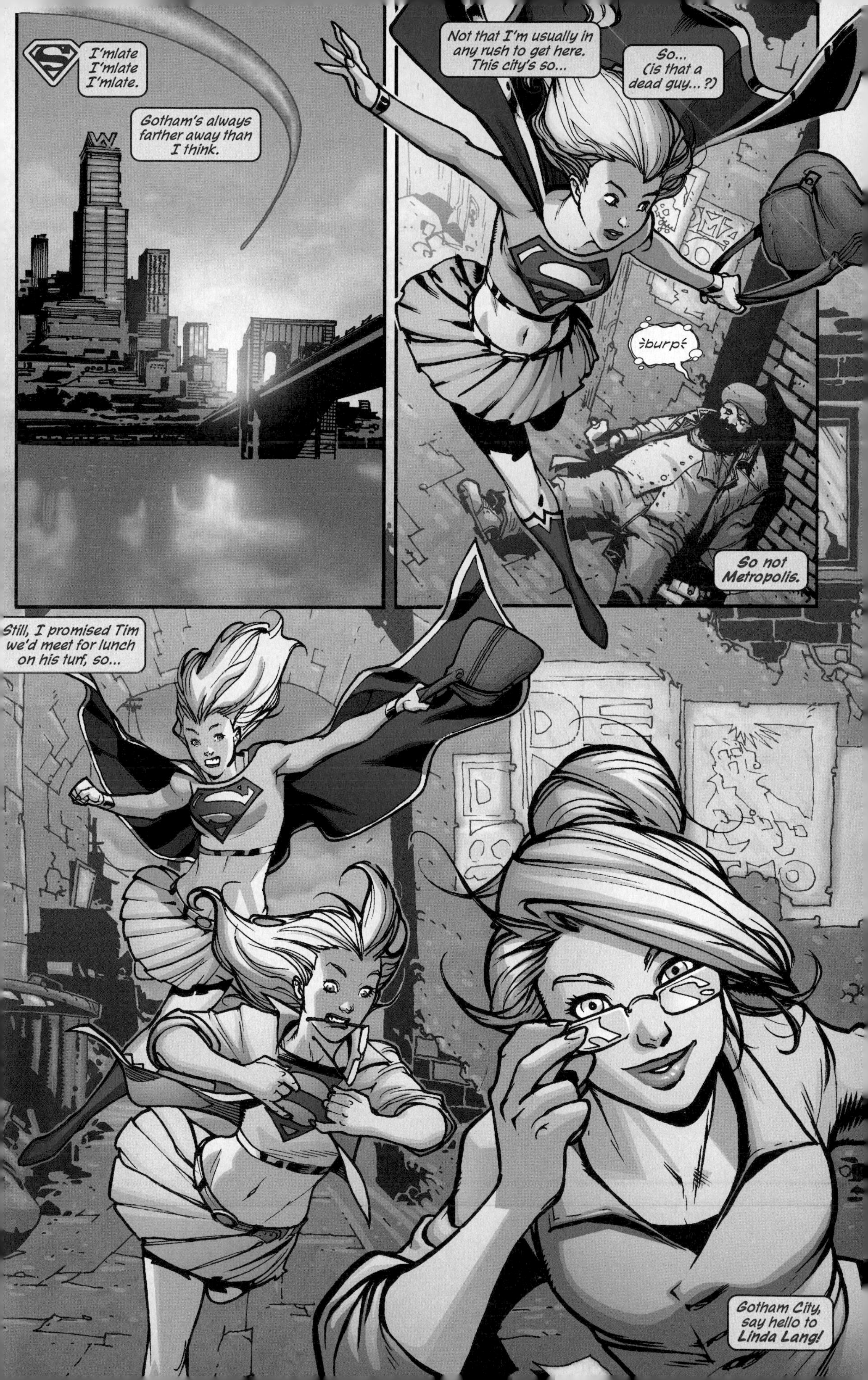
I'mlate I'mlate I'mlate.
Gotham's always farther away than I think.
Not that I'm usually in any rush to get here. This city's so...
So... (is that a dead guy...?)
burp
So not Metropolis.
Still, I promised Tim we'd meet for lunch on his turf, so...
Gotham City, say hello to Linda Lang!

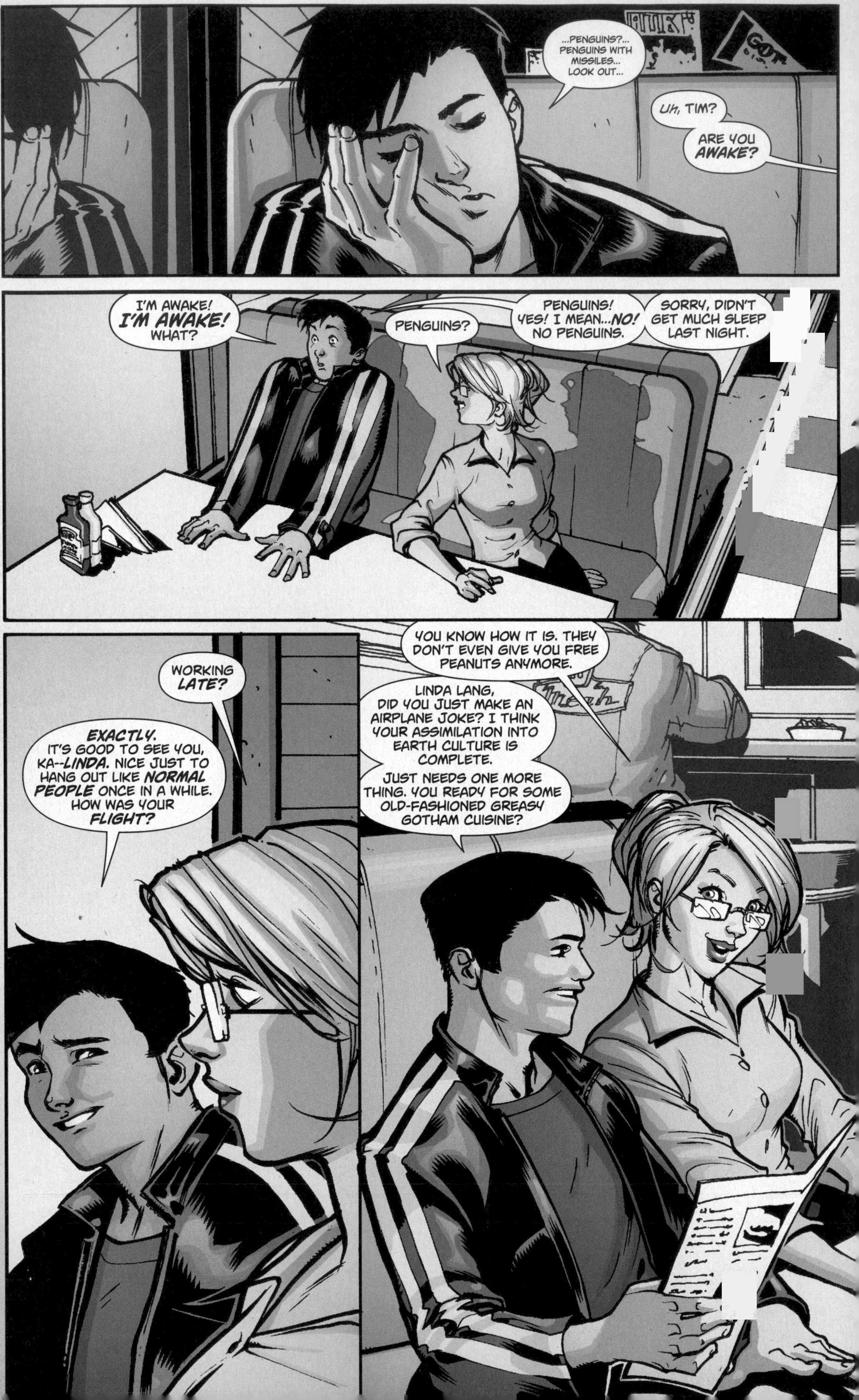
...PENGUINS?... PENGUINS WITH MISSILES... LOOK OUT...
UH, TIM?
ARE YOU AWAKE?
I'M AWAKE! I'M AWAKE! WHAT?
PENGUINS?
PENGUINS! YES! I MEAN...NO! NO PENGUINS.
SORRY, DIDN'T GET MUCH SLEEP LAST NIGHT.
WORKING LATE?
EXACTLY. IT'S GOOD TO SEE YOU, KA--LINDA. NICE JUST TO HANG OUT LIKE NORMAL PEOPLE ONCE IN A WHILE. HOW WAS YOUR FLIGHT?
YOU KNOW HOW IT IS. THEY DON'T EVEN GIVE YOU FREE PEANUTS ANYMORE.
LINDA LANG, DID YOU JUST MAKE AN AIRPLANE JOKE? I THINK YOUR ASSIMILATION INTO EARTH CULTURE IS COMPLETE.
JUST NEEDS ONE MORE THING. YOU READY FOR SOME OLD-FASHIONED GREASY GOTHAM CUISINE?

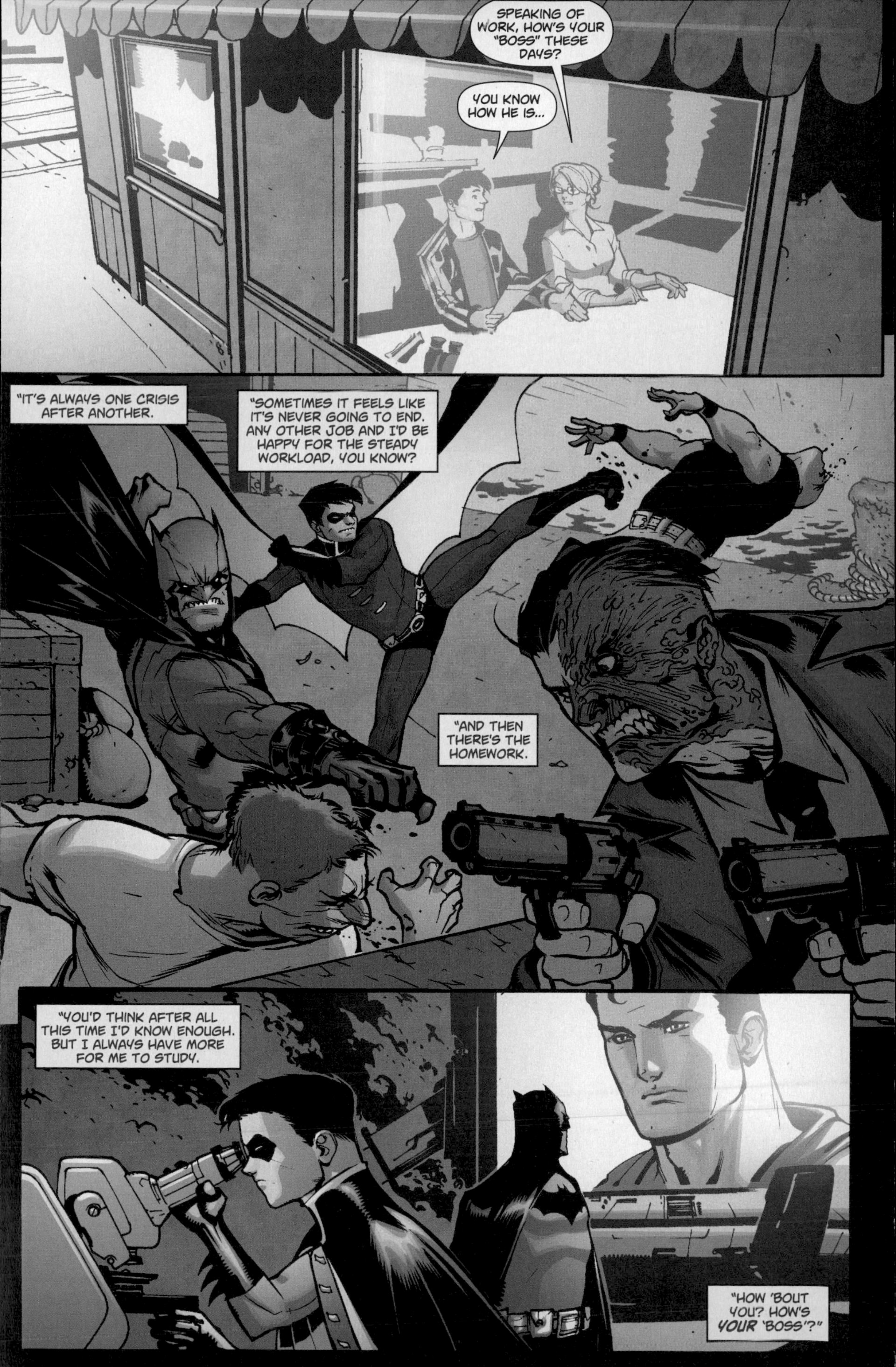
SPEAKING OF WORK, HOW'S YOUR "BOSS" THESE DAYS?
YOU KNOW HOW HE IS...
"IT'S ALWAYS ONE CRISIS AFTER ANOTHER.
"SOMETIMES IT FEELS LIKE IT'S NEVER GOING TO END. ANY OTHER JOB AND I'D BE HAPPY FOR THE STEADY WORKLOAD, YOU KNOW?
"AND THEN THERE'S THE HOMEWORK.
"YOU'D THINK AFTER ALL THIS TIME I'D KNOW ENOUGH. BUT I ALWAYS HAVE MORE FOR ME TO STUDY.
"HOW 'BOUT YOU? HOW'S YOUR 'BOSS'?"

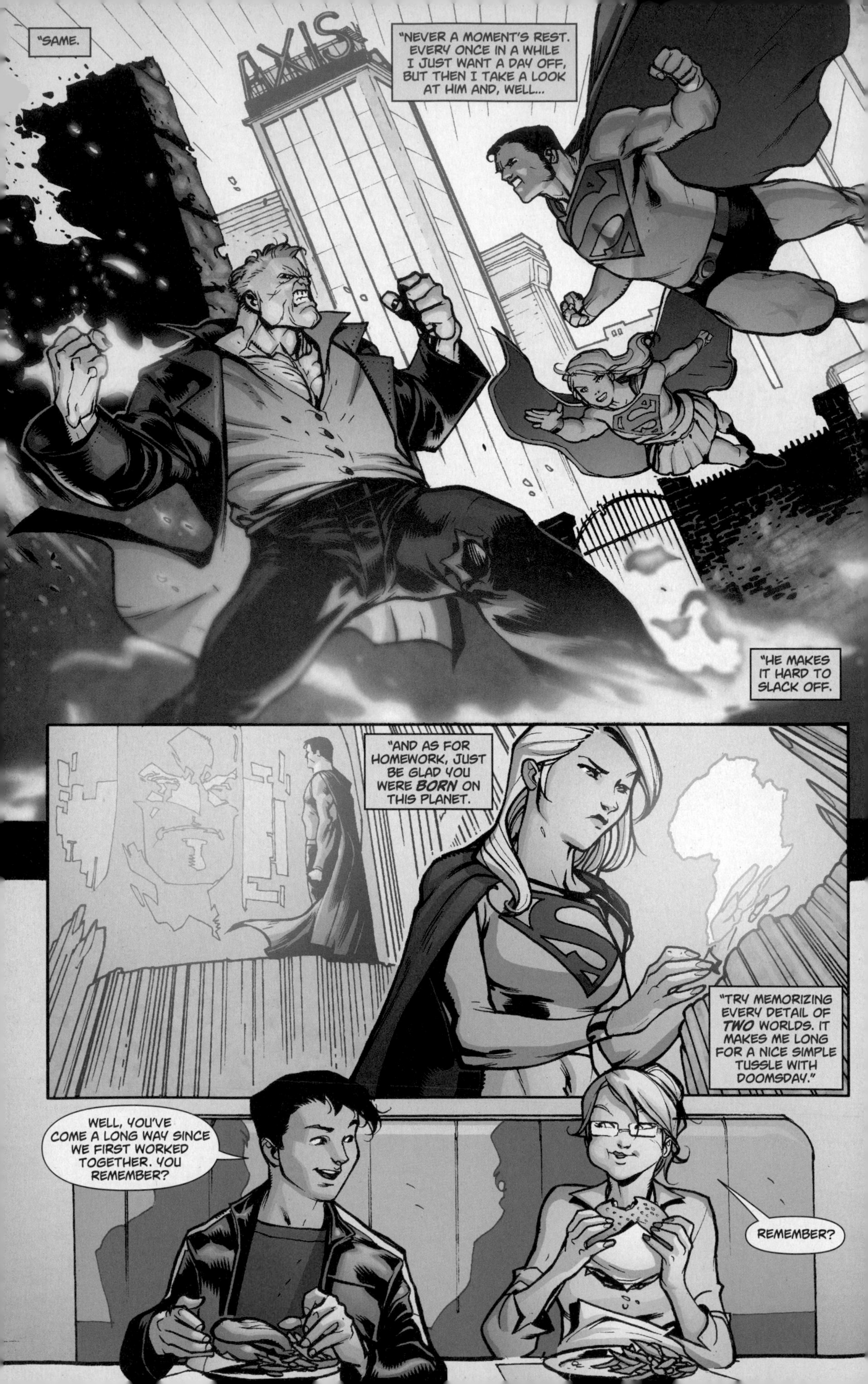
"SAME.
"NEVER A MOMENT'S REST. EVERY ONCE IN A WHILE I JUST WANT A DAY OFF, BUT THEN I TAKE A LOOK AT HIM AND, WELL...
AXIS
"HE MAKES IT HARD TO SLACK OFF.
"AND AS FOR HOMEWORK, JUST BE GLAD YOU WERE BORN ON THIS PLANET.
"TRY MEMORIZING EVERY DETAIL OF TWO WORLDS. IT MAKES ME LONG FOR A NICE SIMPLE TUSSLE WITH DOOMSDAY."
WELL, YOU'VE COME A LONG WAY SINCE WE FIRST WORKED TOGETHER. YOU REMEMBER?
REMEMBER?

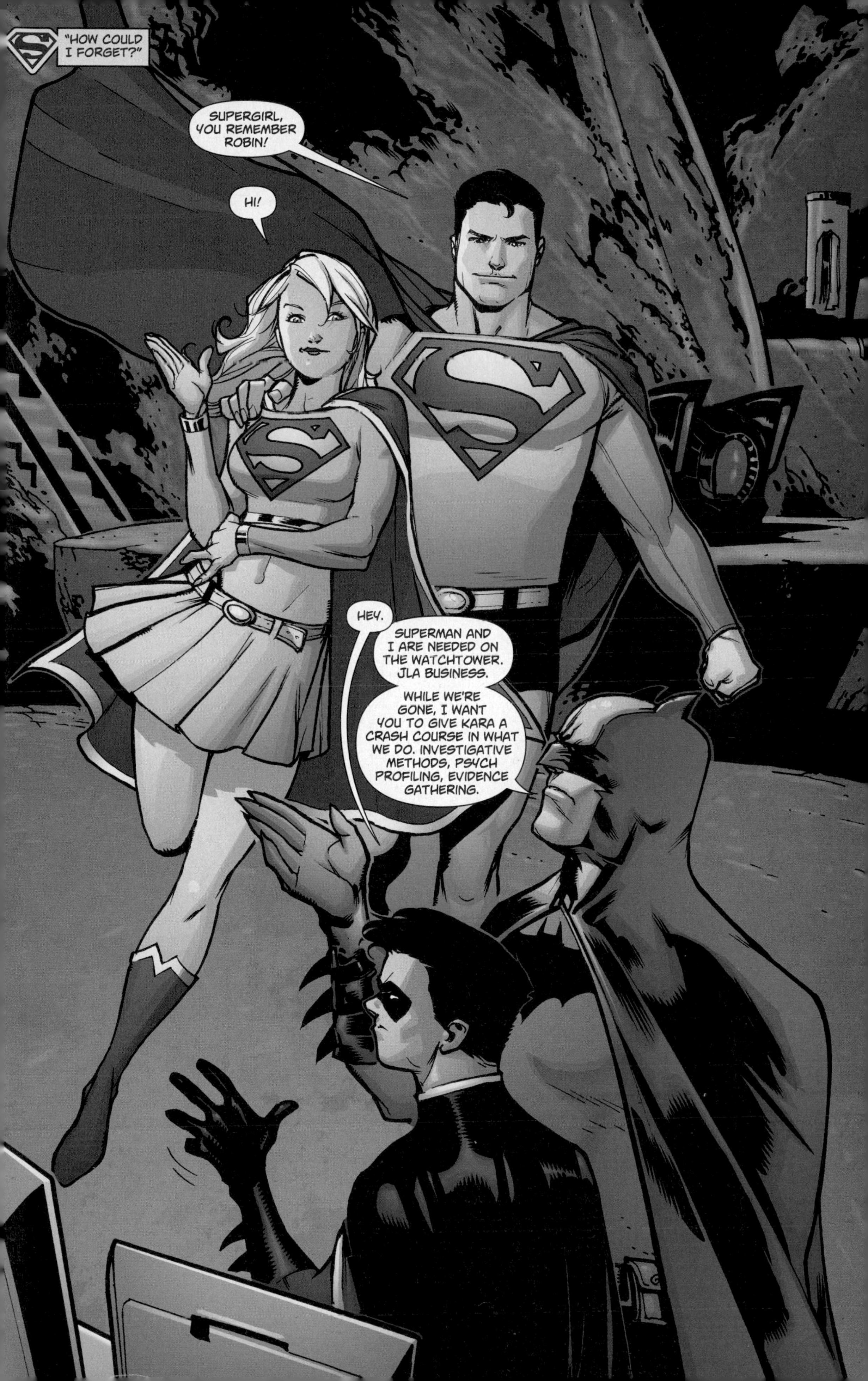
"HOW COULD I FORGET?"
SUPERGIRL, YOU REMEMBER ROBIN!
HI!
HEY.
SUPERMAN AND I ARE NEEDED ON THE WATCHTOWER. JLA BUSINESS.
WHILE WE'RE GONE, I WANT YOU TO GIVE KARA A CRASH COURSE IN WHAT WE DO. INVESTIGATIVE METHODS, PSYCH PROFILING, EVIDENCE GATHERING.

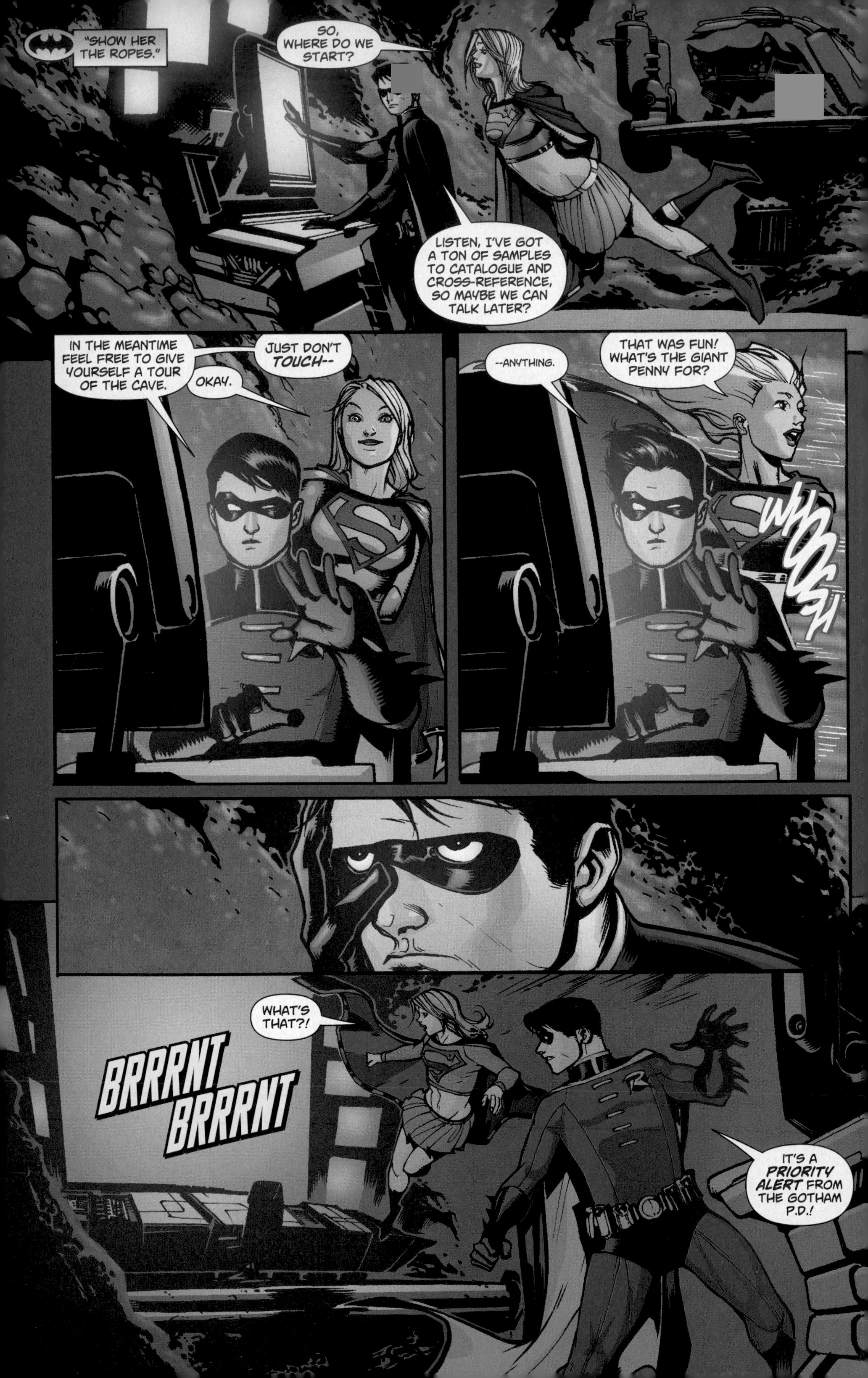

"SHOW HER THE ROPES."
SO, WHERE DO WE START?
LISTEN, I'VE GOT A TON OF SAMPLES TO CATALOGUE AND CROSS-REFERENCE, SO MAYBE WE CAN TALK LATER?
IN THE MEANTIME FEEL FREE TO GIVE YOURSELF A TOUR OF THE CAVE.
OKAY.
JUST DON'T TOUCH--
--ANYTHING.
THAT WAS FUN! WHAT'S THE GIANT PENNY FOR?
WHOOOSH
WHAT'S THAT?!
BRRRNT BRRRNT
IT'S A PRIORITY ALERT FROM THE GOTHAM P.D.!

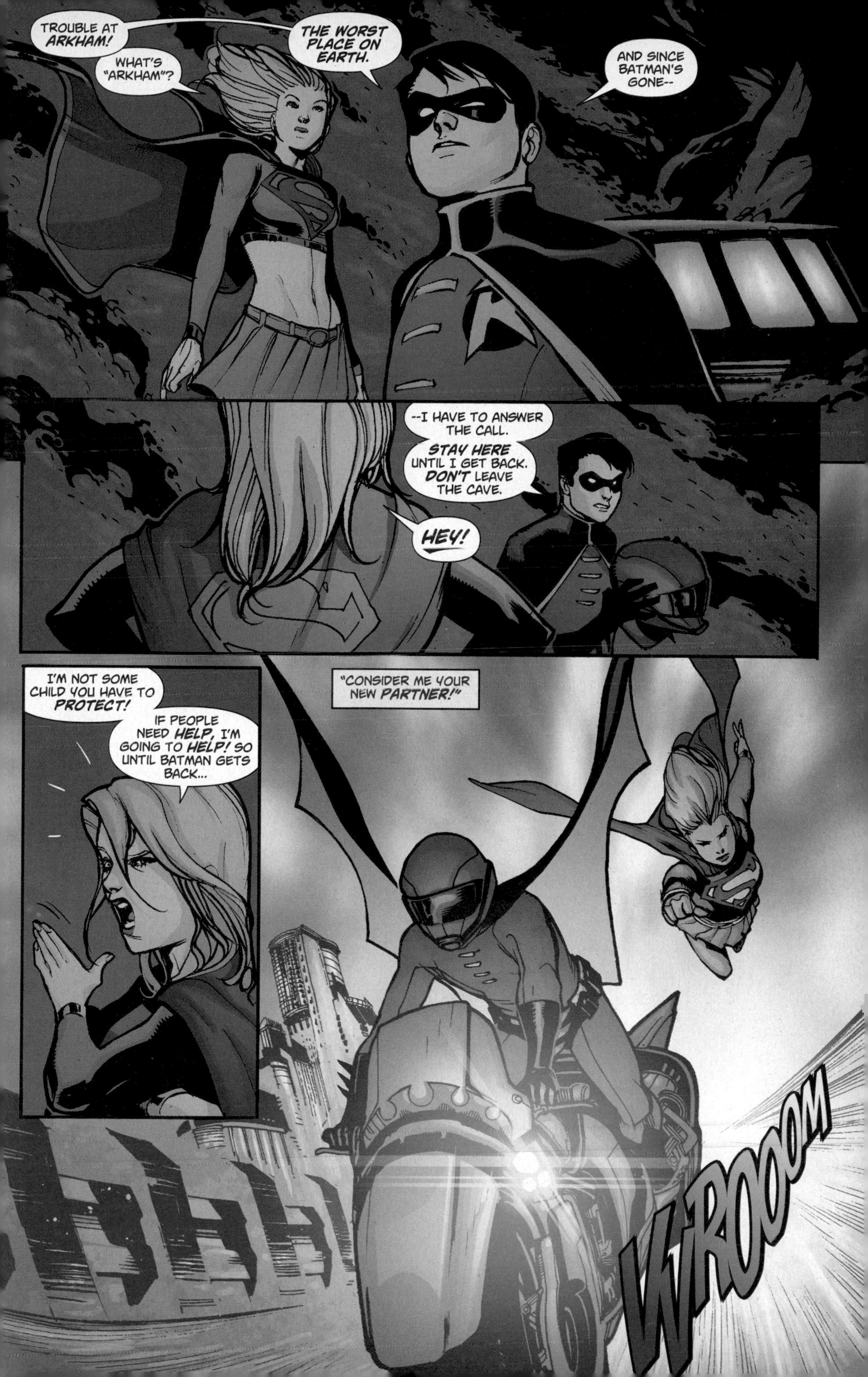
TROUBLE AT ARKHAM!
WHAT'S "ARKHAM"?
THE WORST PLACE ON EARTH.
AND SINCE BATMAN'S GONE--
--I HAVE TO ANSWER THE CALL. STAY HERE UNTIL I GET BACK. DON'T LEAVE THE CAVE.
HEY!
I'M NOT SOME CHILD YOU HAVE TO PROTECT!
IF PEOPLE NEED HELP, I'M GOING TO HELP! SO UNTIL BATMAN GETS BACK...
"CONSIDER ME YOUR NEW PARTNER!"
VVROOOM

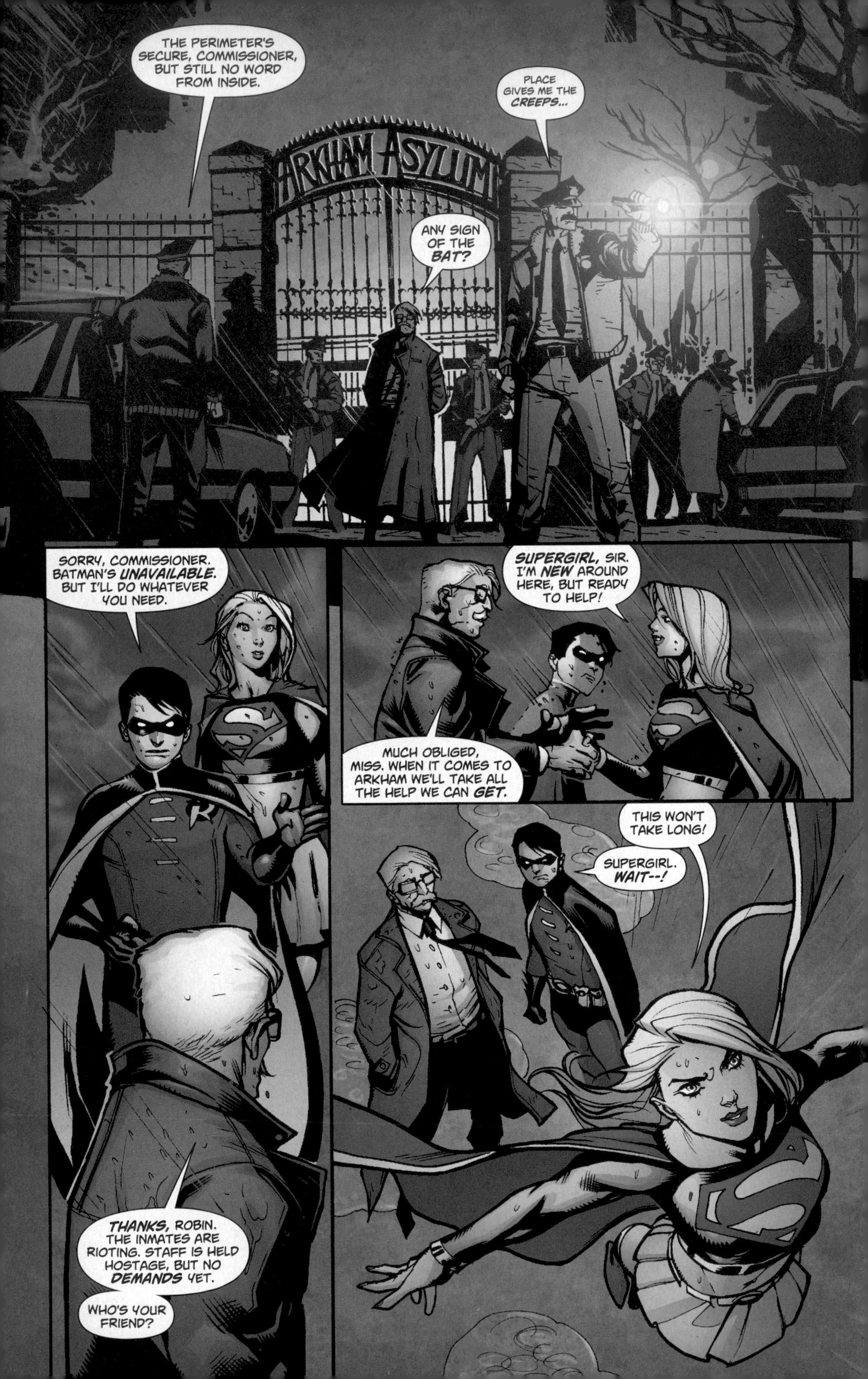
THE PERIMETER'S SECURE, COMMISSIONER, BUT STILL NO WORD FROM INSIDE.
PLACE GIVES ME THE CREEPS...
ARKHAM ASYLUM
ANY SIGN OF THE BAT?
SORRY, COMMISSIONER. BATMAN'S UNAVAILABLE. BUT I'LL DO WHATEVER YOU NEED.
THANKS, ROBIN. THE INMATES ARE RIOTING. STAFF IS HELD HOSTAGE, BUT NO DEMANDS YET.
WHO'S YOUR FRIEND?
SUPERGIRL, SIR. I'M NEW AROUND HERE, BUT READY TO HELP!
MUCH OBLIGED, MISS. WHEN IT COMES TO ARKHAM WE'LL TAKE ALL THE HELP WE CAN GET.
THIS WON'T TAKE LONG!
SUPERGIRL. WAIT--!

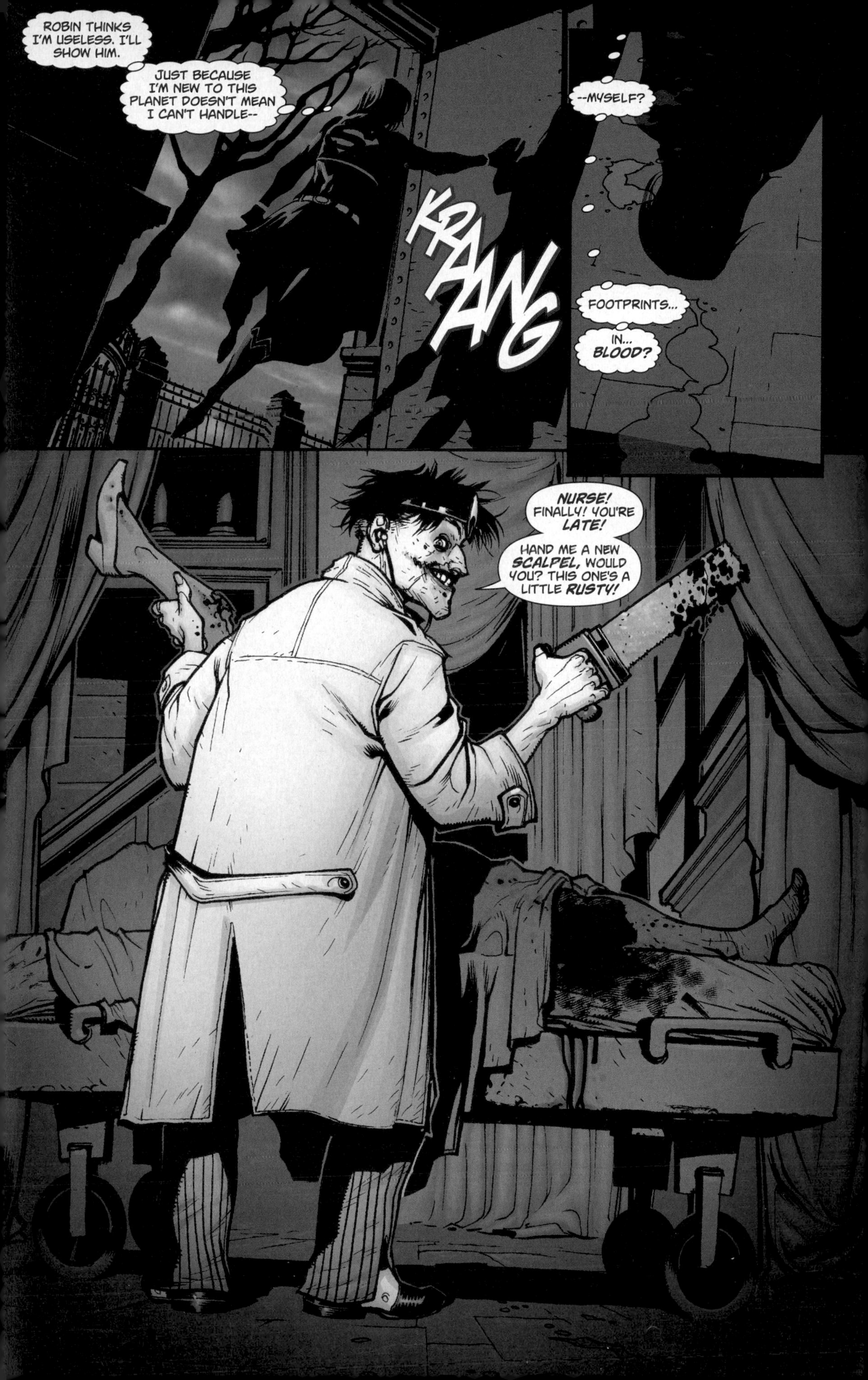
ROBIN THINKS I'M USELESS. I'LL SHOW HIM.
JUST BECAUSE I'M NEW TO THIS PLANET DOESN'T MEAN I CAN'T HANDLE--
--MYSELF?
KRANG
FOOTPRINTS...
IN... BLOOD?
NURSE! FINALLY! YOU'RE LATE!
HAND ME A NEW SCALPEL, WOULD YOU? THIS ONE'S A LITTLE RUSTY!

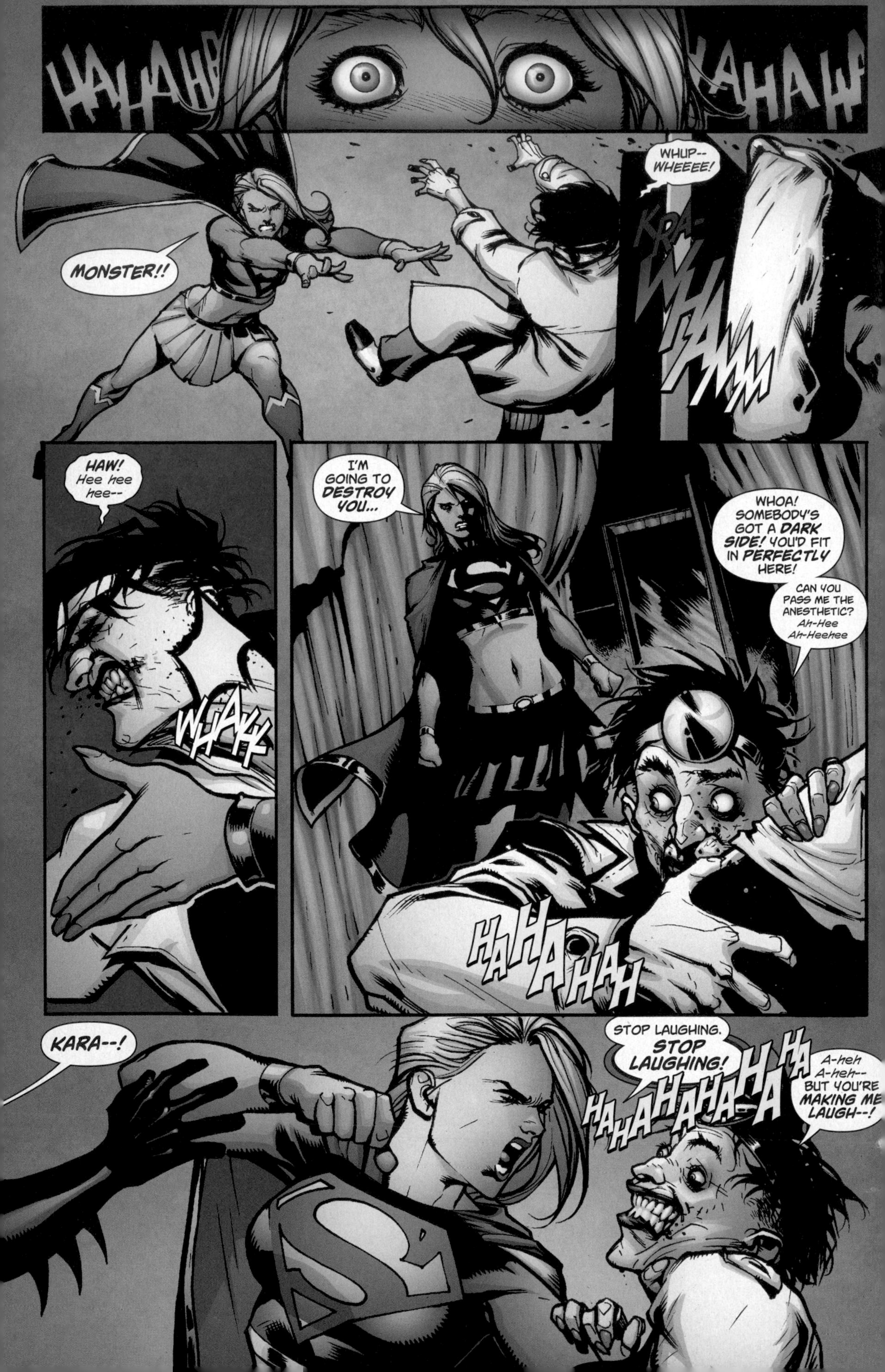
HAHAHA
HAHAHA
WHUP-- WHEEEE!
MONSTER!!
KRA-WHAMM
HAW! Hee hee hee--
WHAKK
I'M GOING TO DESTROY YOU...
WHOA! SOMEBODY'S GOT A DARK SIDE! YOU'D FIT IN PERFECTLY HERE!
CAN YOU PASS ME THE ANESTHETIC? Ah-Hee Ah-Heehee
HAHAHAHAH
KARA--!
STOP LAUGHING. STOP LAUGHING!
HAHAHAHAHAHAHA
A-heh A-heh-- BUT YOU'RE MAKING ME LAUGH--!

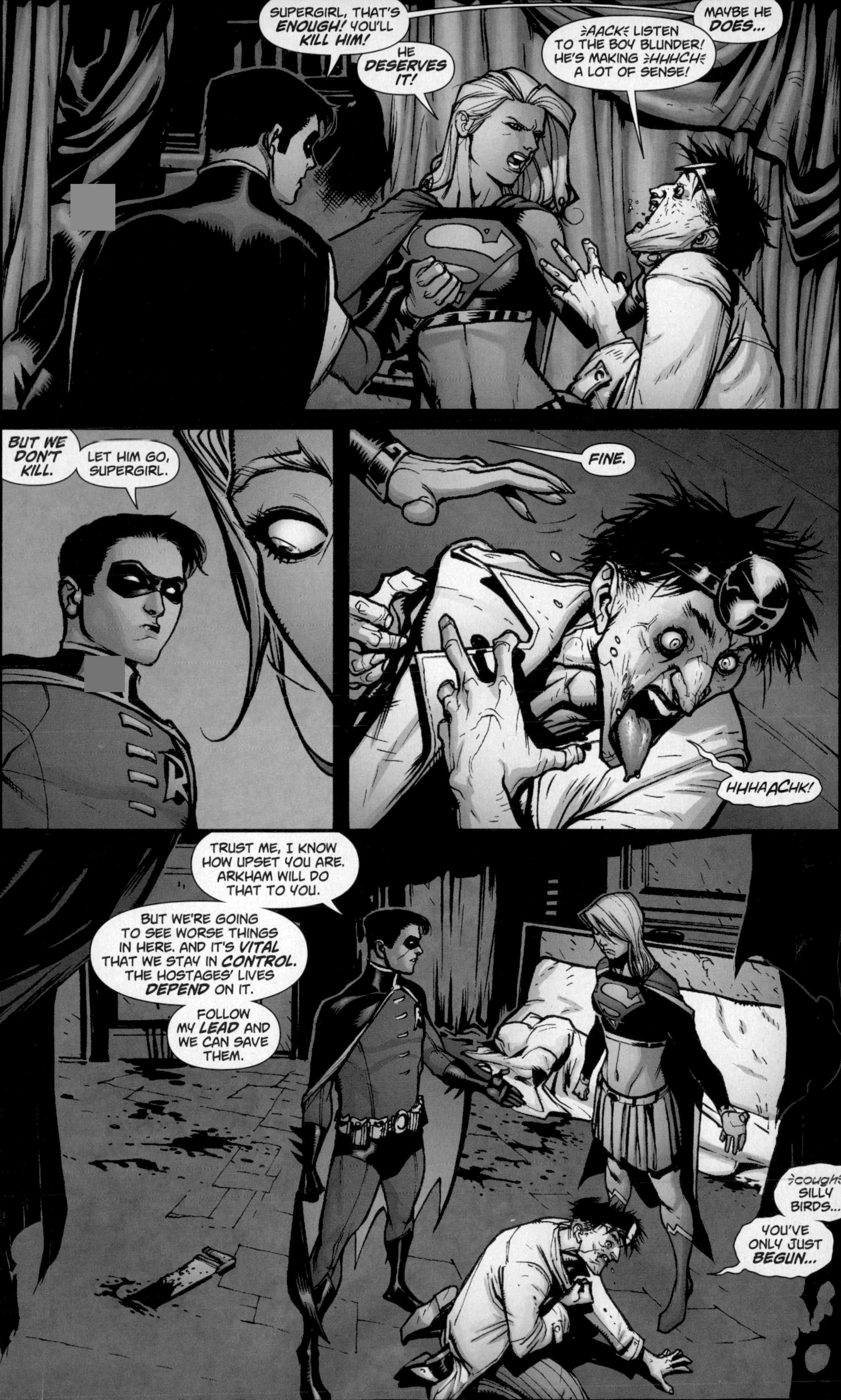
SUPERGIRL, THAT'S ENOUGH! YOU'LL KILL HIM!
HE DESERVES IT!
MAYBE HE DOES...
AACK LISTEN TO THE BOY BLUNDER! HE'S MAKING HHHCH A LOT OF SENSE!
BUT WE DON'T KILL.
LET HIM GO, SUPERGIRL.
FINE.
HHHAACHK!
TRUST ME, I KNOW HOW UPSET YOU ARE. ARKHAM WILL DO THAT TO YOU.
BUT WE'RE GOING TO SEE WORSE THINGS IN HERE. AND IT'S VITAL THAT WE STAY IN CONTROL. THE HOSTAGES' LIVES DEPEND ON IT.
FOLLOW MY LEAD AND WE CAN SAVE THEM.
cough SILLY BIRDS...
YOU'VE ONLY JUST BEGUN...

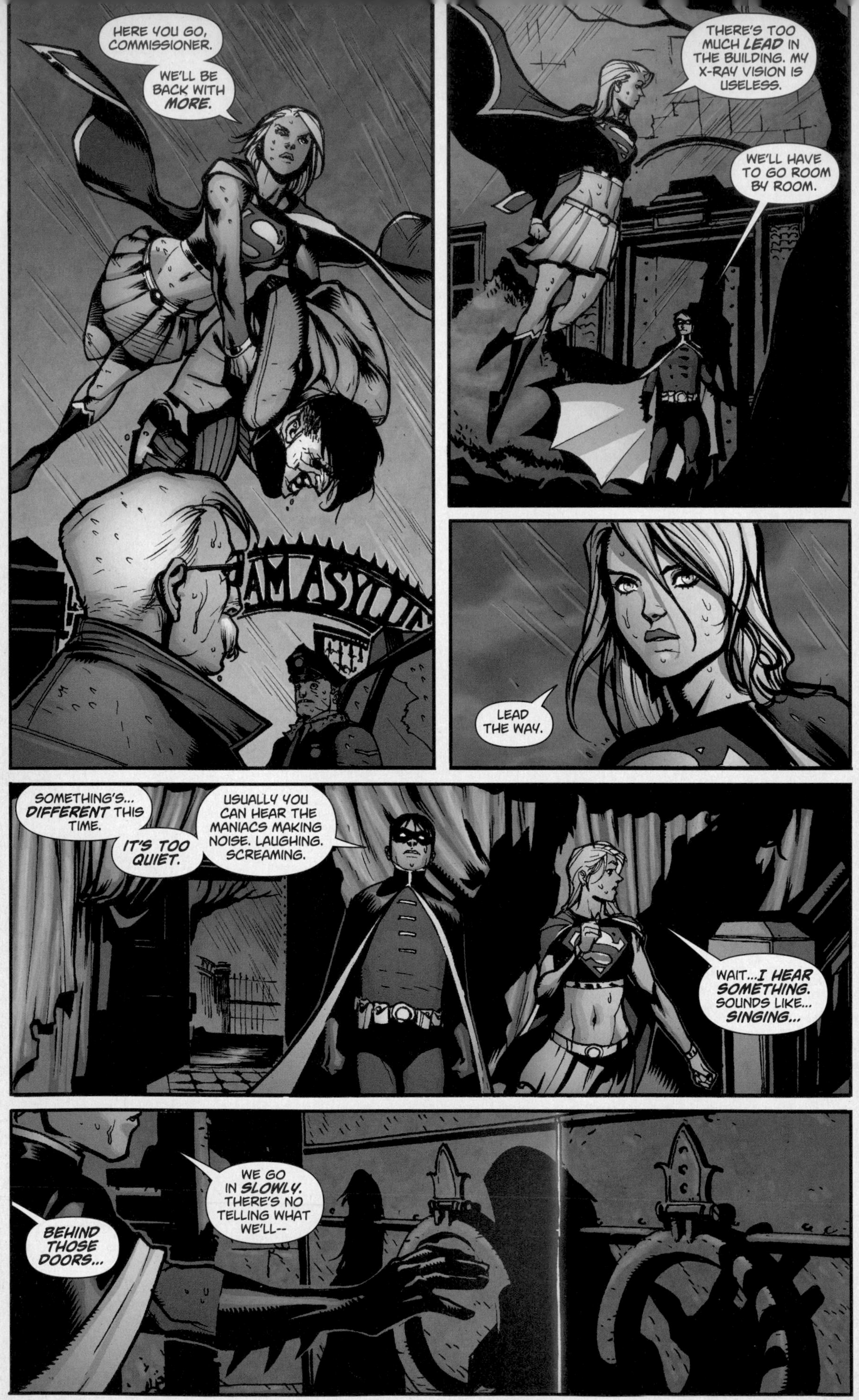
HERE YOU GO, COMMISSIONER.
WE'LL BE BACK WITH MORE.
THERE'S TOO MUCH LEAD IN THE BUILDING. MY X-RAY VISION IS USELESS.
WE'LL HAVE TO GO ROOM BY ROOM.
LEAD THE WAY.
SOMETHING'S... DIFFERENT THIS TIME.
IT'S TOO QUIET.
USUALLY YOU CAN HEAR THE MANIACS MAKING NOISE. LAUGHING. SCREAMING.
WAIT...I HEAR SOMETHING. SOUNDS LIKE... SINGING...
BEHIND THOSE DOORS...
WE GO IN SLOWLY. THERE'S NO TELLING WHAT WE'LL--

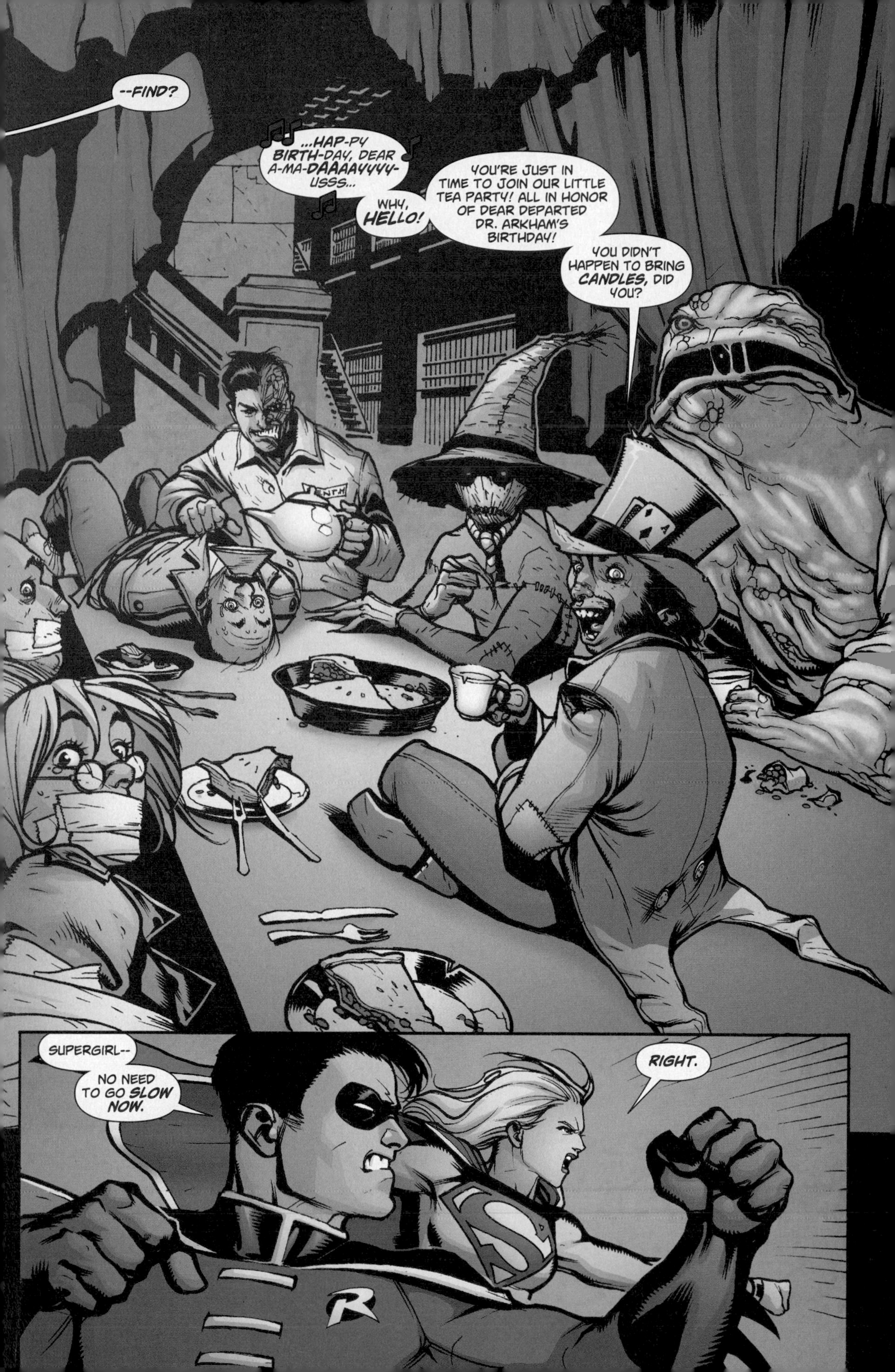
--FIND?
...HAP-PY BIRTH-DAY, DEAR A-MA-DAAAAYYYY-USSS...
WHY, HELLO!
YOU'RE JUST IN TIME TO JOIN OUR LITTLE TEA PARTY! ALL IN HONOR OF DEAR DEPARTED DR. ARKHAM'S BIRTHDAY!
YOU DIDN'T HAPPEN TO BRING CANDLES, DID YOU?
SUPERGIRL--
NO NEED TO GO SLOW NOW.
RIGHT.

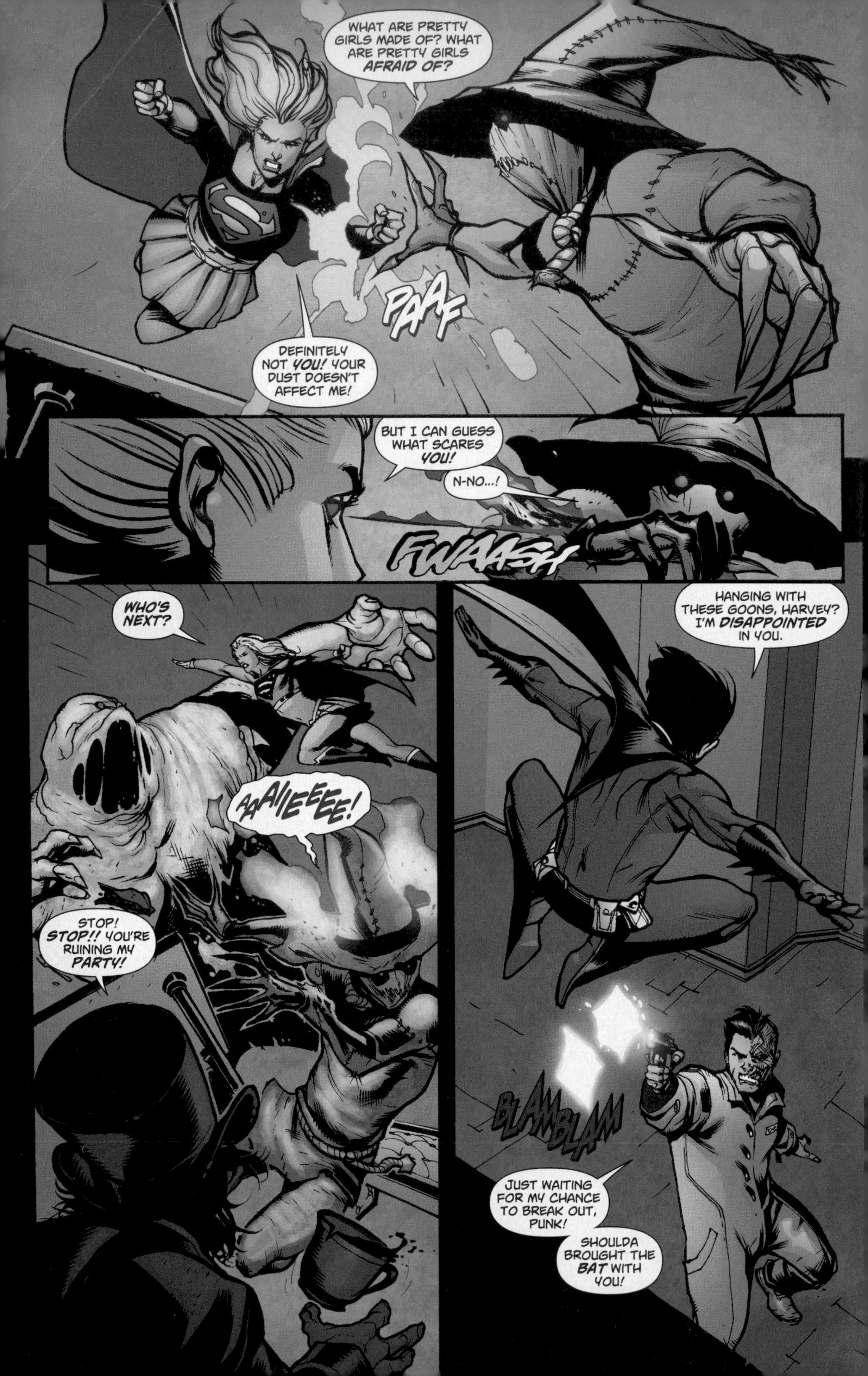
WHAT ARE PRETTY GIRLS MADE OF? WHAT ARE PRETTY GIRLS AFRAID OF?
PAAF
DEFINITELY NOT YOU! YOUR DUST DOESN'T AFFECT ME!
BUT I CAN GUESS WHAT SCARES YOU!
N-NO...!
FWAASH
WHO'S NEXT?
AAAIIEEEEE!
STOP! STOP!! YOU'RE RUINING MY PARTY!
HANGING WITH THESE GOONS, HARVEY? I'M DISAPPOINTED IN YOU.
BLAMBLAM
JUST WAITING FOR MY CHANCE TO BREAK OUT, PUNK!
SHOULDA BROUGHT THE BAT WITH YOU!

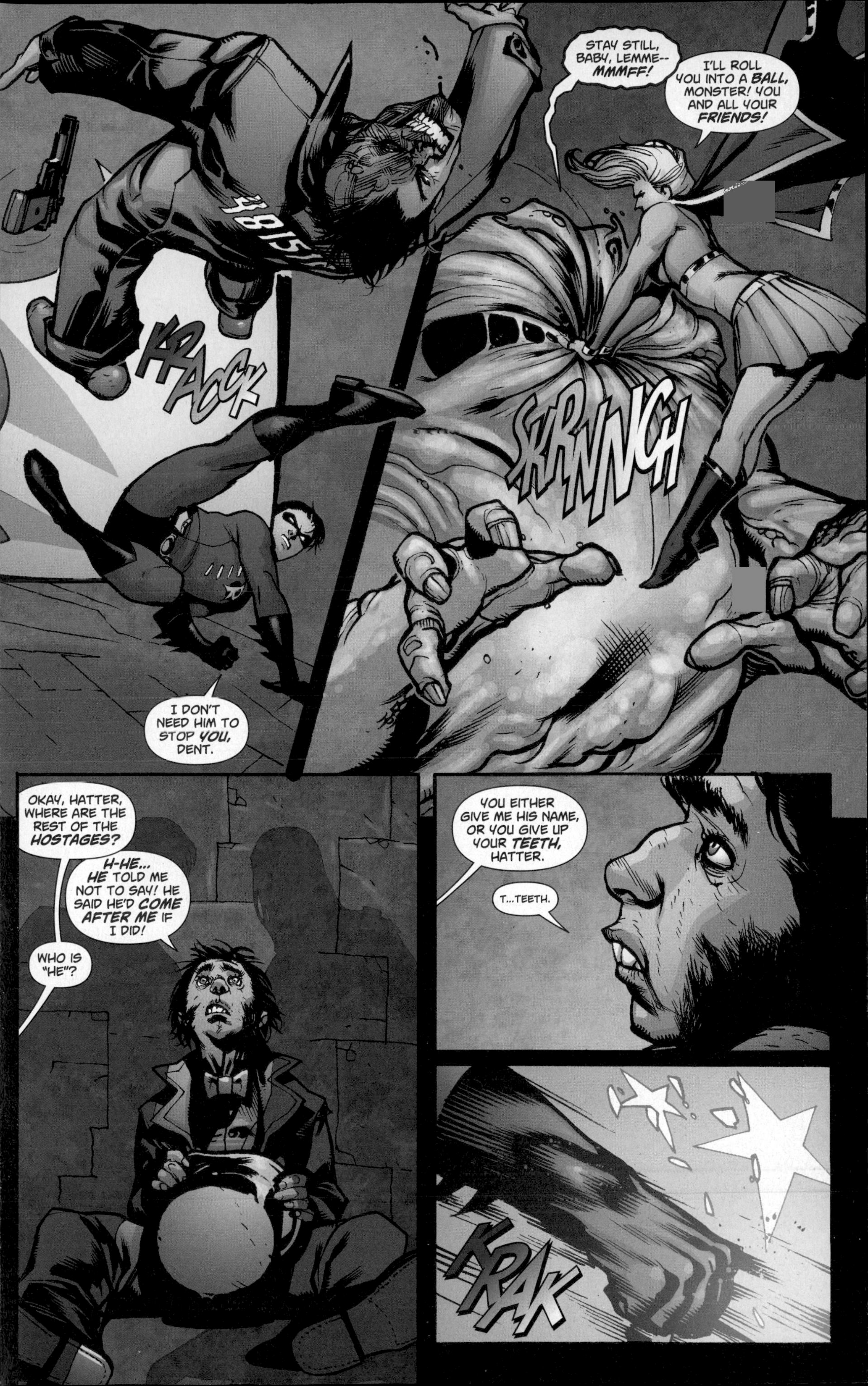
STAY STILL, BABY, LEMME-- MMMFF!
I'LL ROLL YOU INTO A BALL, MONSTER! YOU AND ALL YOUR FRIENDS!
KRACCK
SKRNNCH
I DON'T NEED HIM TO STOP YOU, DENT.
OKAY, HATTER, WHERE ARE THE REST OF THE HOSTAGES?
H-HE... HE TOLD ME NOT TO SAY! HE SAID HE'D COME AFTER ME IF I DID!
WHO IS "HE"?
YOU EITHER GIVE ME HIS NAME, OR YOU GIVE UP YOUR TEETH, HATTER.
T...TEETH.
KRAK

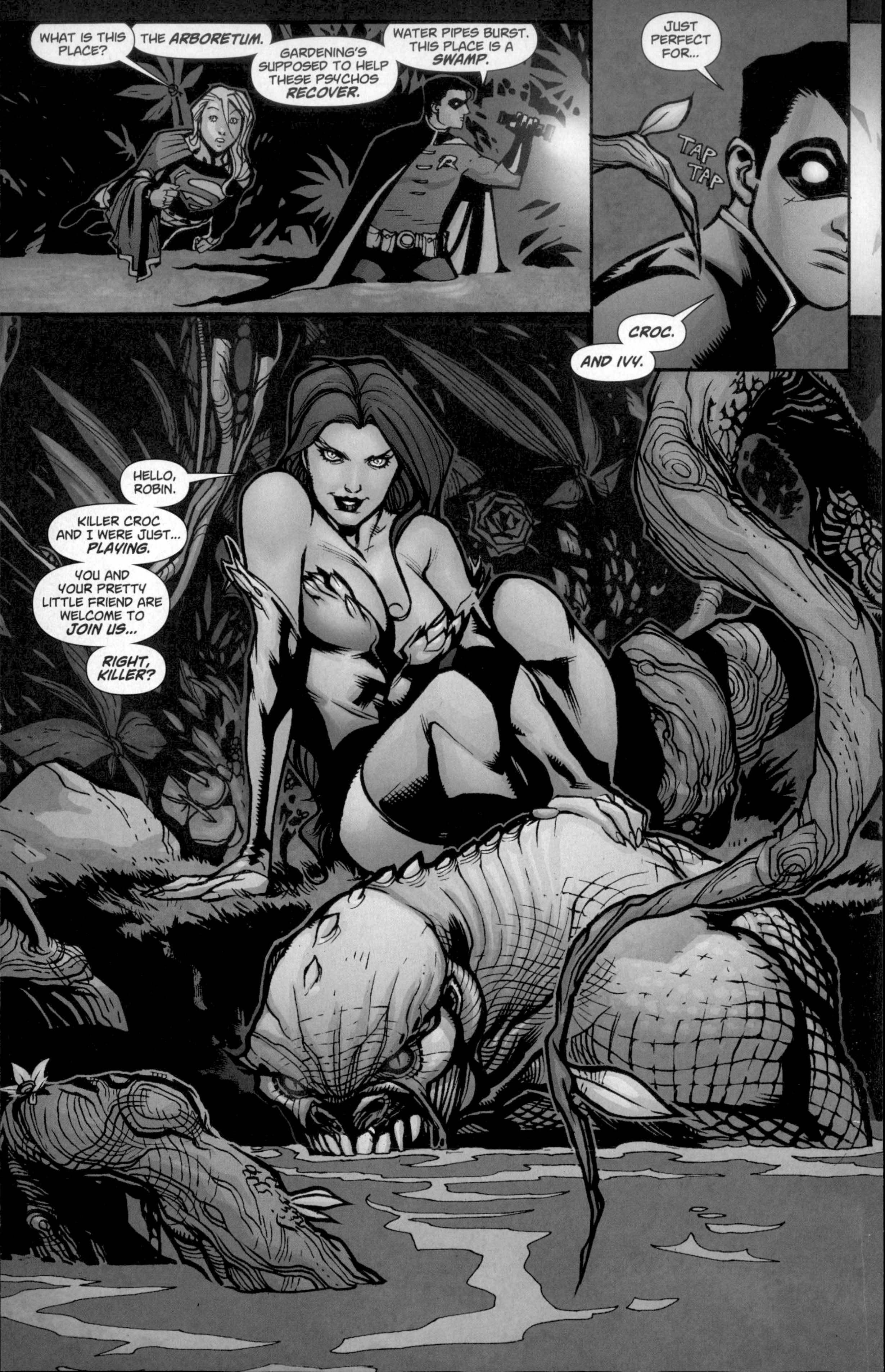
WHAT IS THIS PLACE?
THE ARBORETUM.
GARDENING'S SUPPOSED TO HELP THESE PSYCHOS RECOVER.
WATER PIPES BURST. THIS PLACE IS A SWAMP.
JUST PERFECT FOR...
TAP TAP
CROC.
AND IVY.
HELLO, ROBIN.
KILLER CROC AND I WERE JUST... PLAYING.
YOU AND YOUR PRETTY LITTLE FRIEND ARE WELCOME TO JOIN US...
RIGHT, KILLER?

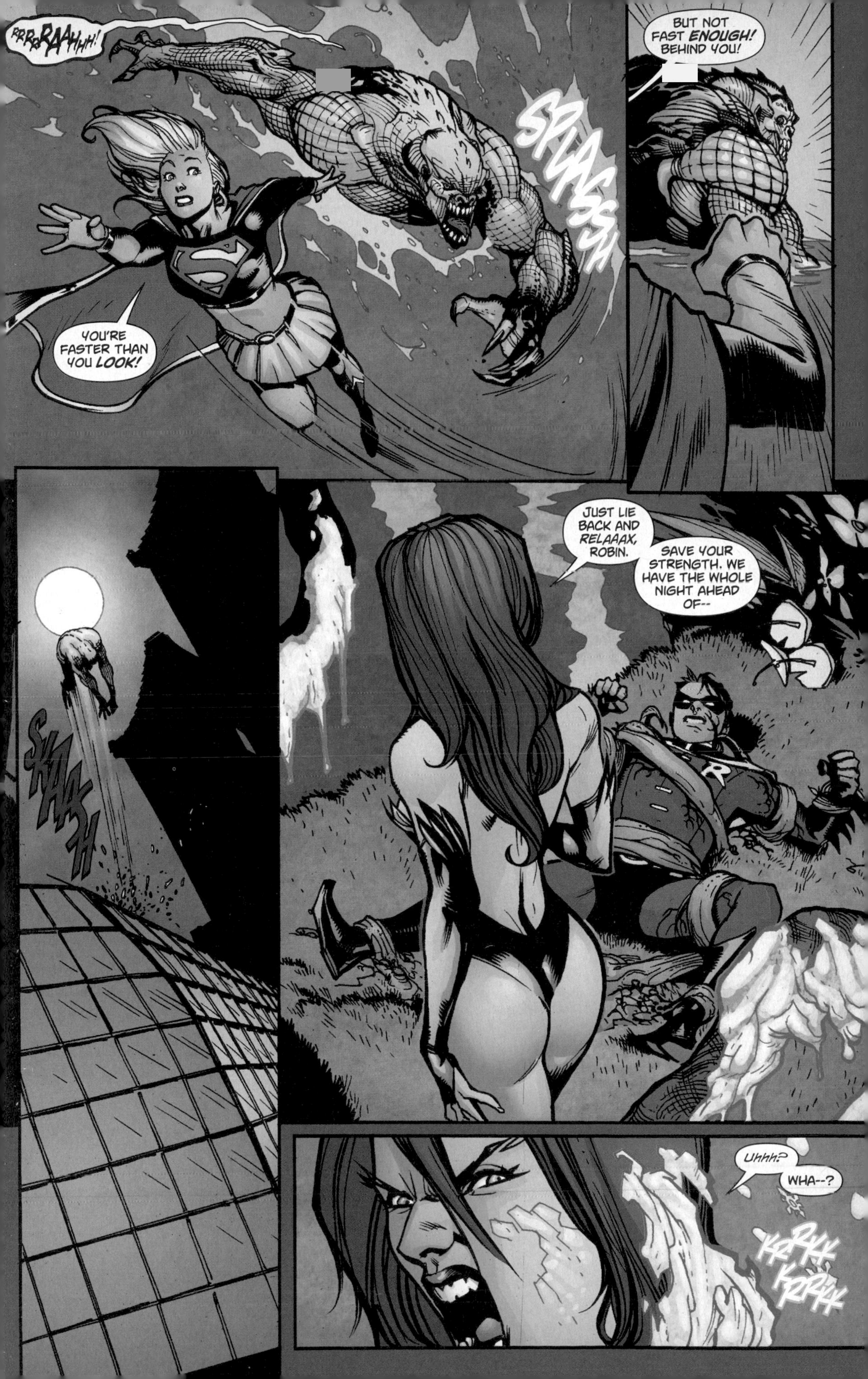
RRRRRAAHHH!
SPLASSSH
YOU'RE FASTER THAN YOU LOOK!
BUT NOT FAST ENOUGH! BEHIND YOU!
SKAAASH
JUST LIE BACK AND RELAAAX, ROBIN.
SAVE YOUR STRENGTH. WE HAVE THE WHOLE NIGHT AHEAD OF--
Uhhh?
WHA--?
KRRKK KRRAK

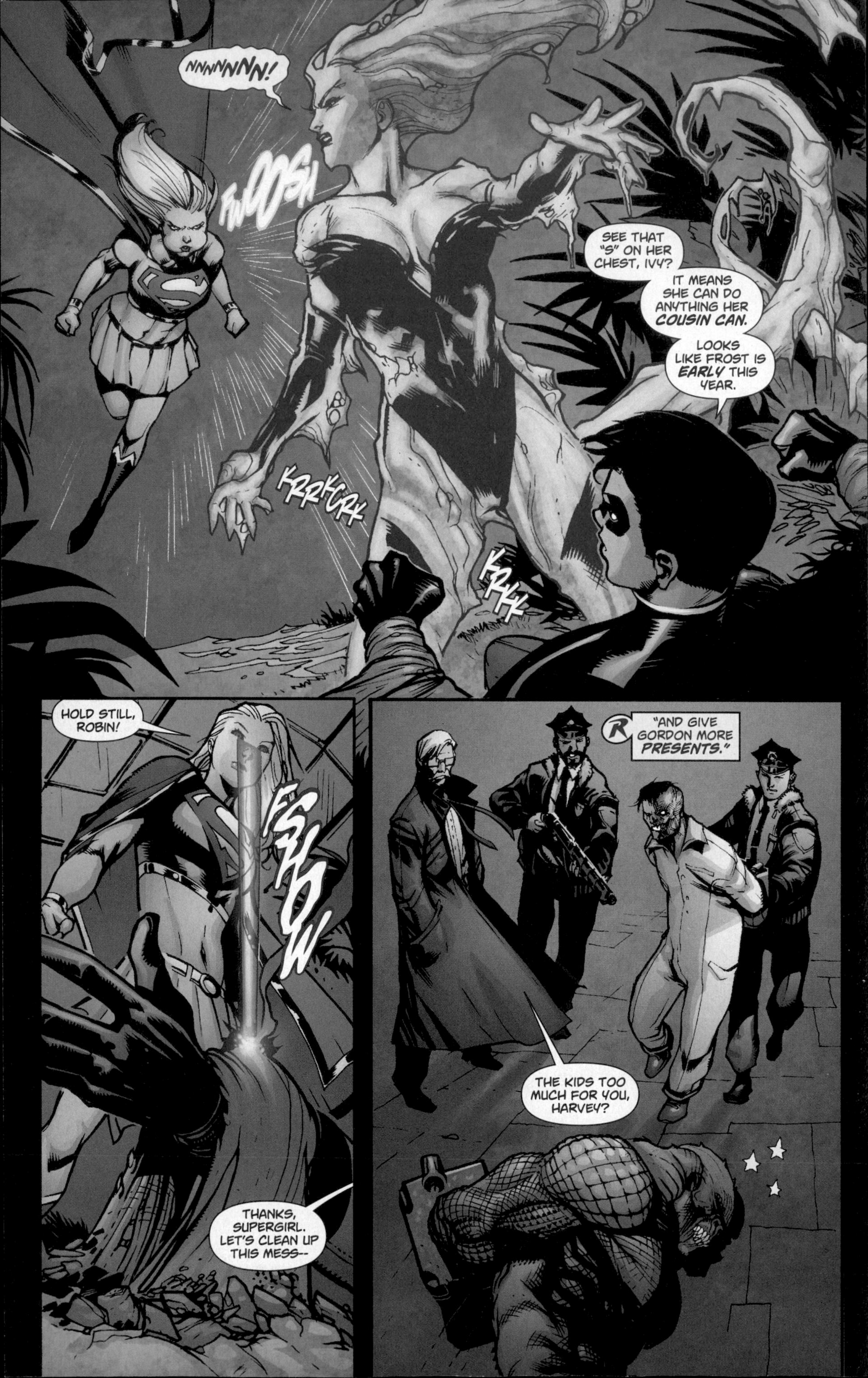
NNNNNNN!
FWOOSH
SEE THAT "S" ON HER CHEST, IVY?
IT MEANS SHE CAN DO ANYTHING HER COUSIN CAN.
LOOKS LIKE FROST IS EARLY THIS YEAR.
KRRKCRK
KRKK
HOLD STILL, ROBIN!
FSHOW
THANKS, SUPERGIRL. LET'S CLEAN UP THIS MESS--
"AND GIVE GORDON MORE PRESENTS."
THE KIDS TOO MUCH FOR YOU, HARVEY?

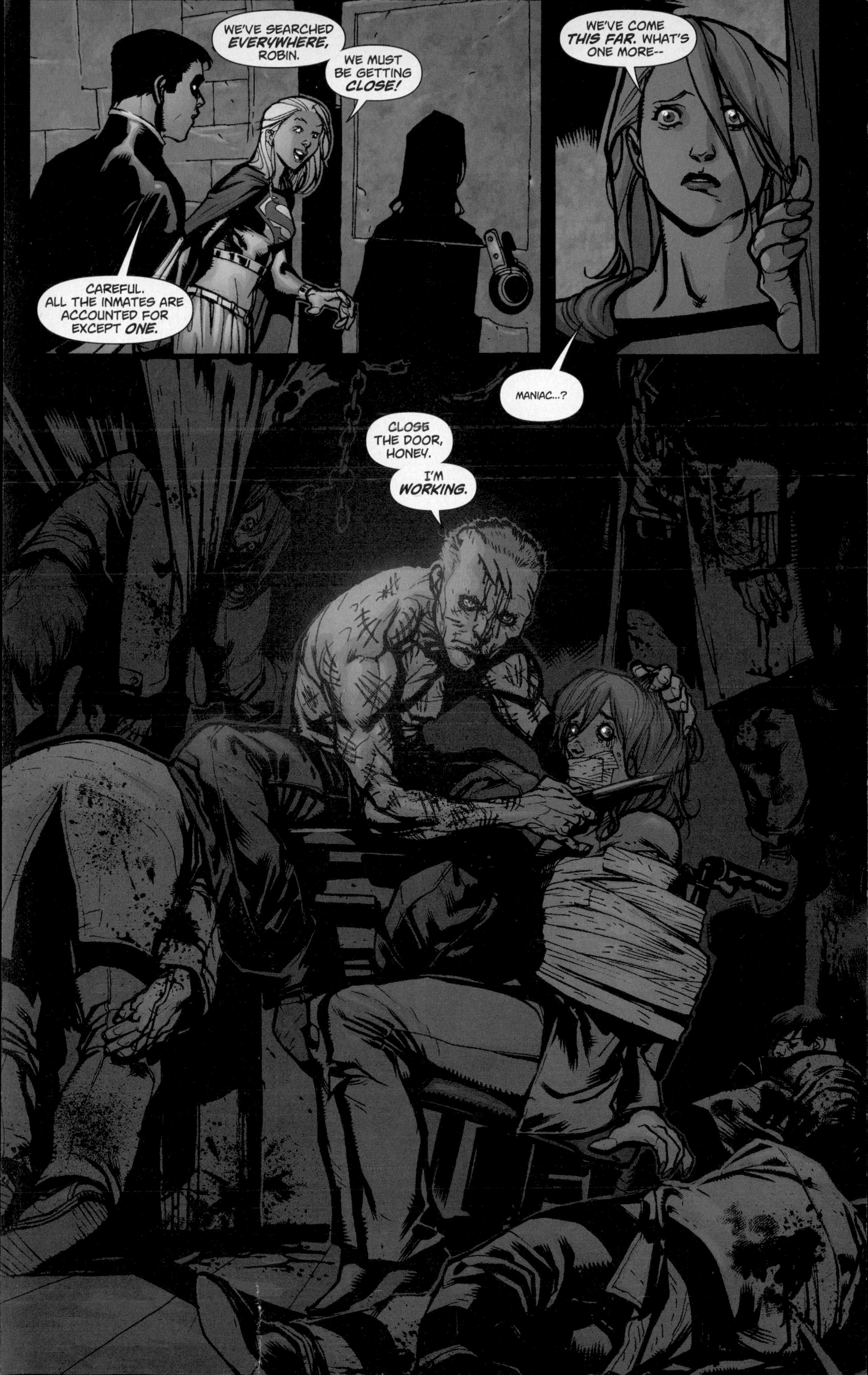
WE'VE SEARCHED EVERYWHERE, ROBIN.
WE MUST BE GETTING CLOSE!
CAREFUL. ALL THE INMATES ARE ACCOUNTED FOR EXCEPT ONE.
WE'VE COME THIS FAR. WHAT'S ONE MORE--
MANIAC...?
CLOSE THE DOOR, HONEY.
I'M WORKING.

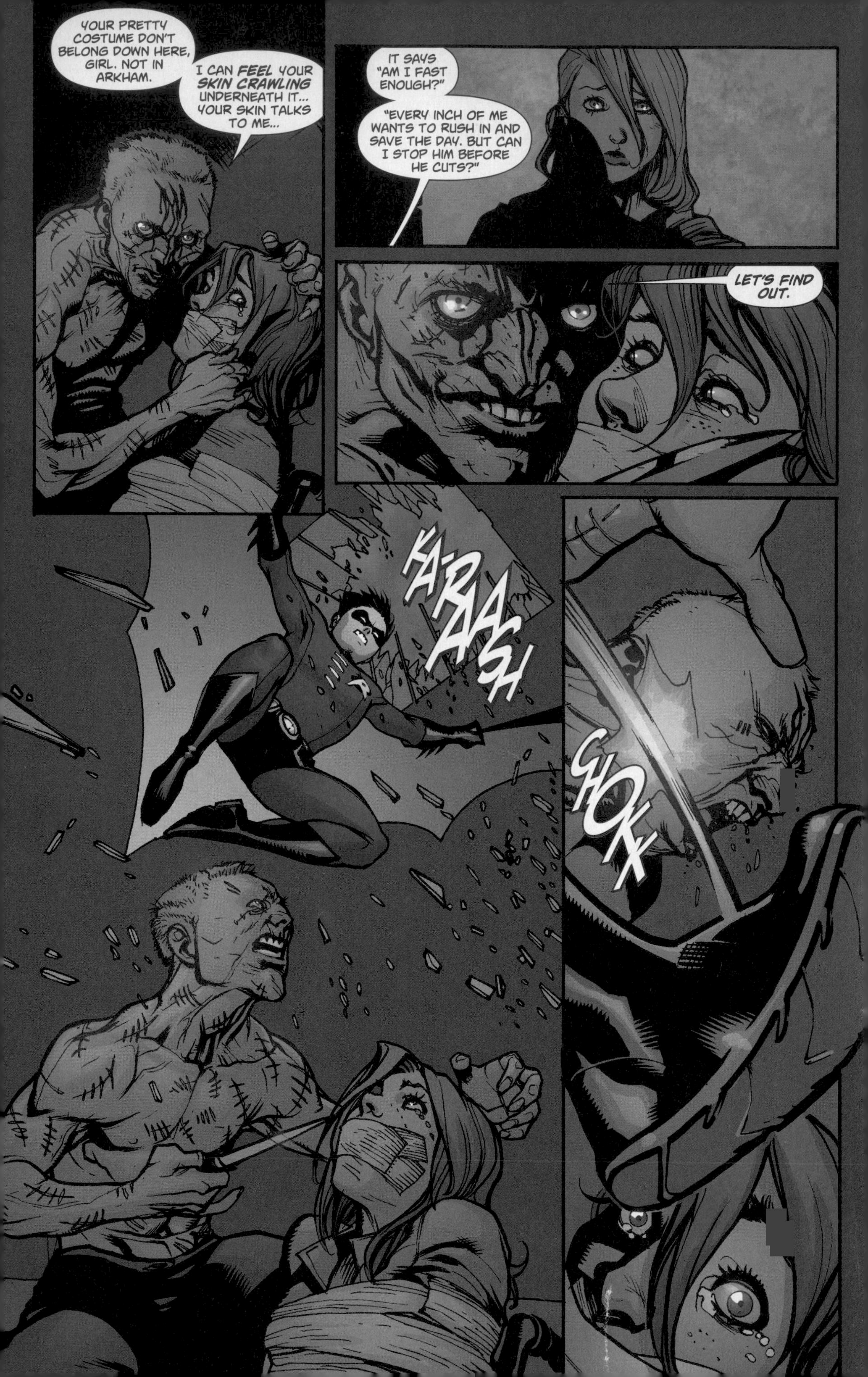
YOUR PRETTY COSTUME DON'T BELONG DOWN HERE, GIRL. NOT IN ARKHAM.
I CAN FEEL YOUR SKIN CRAWLING UNDERNEATH IT... YOUR SKIN TALKS TO ME...
IT SAYS "AM I FAST ENOUGH?"
"EVERY INCH OF ME WANTS TO RUSH IN AND SAVE THE DAY. BUT CAN I STOP HIM BEFORE HE CUTS?"
LET'S FIND OUT.
KA-RAASH
CHOKK

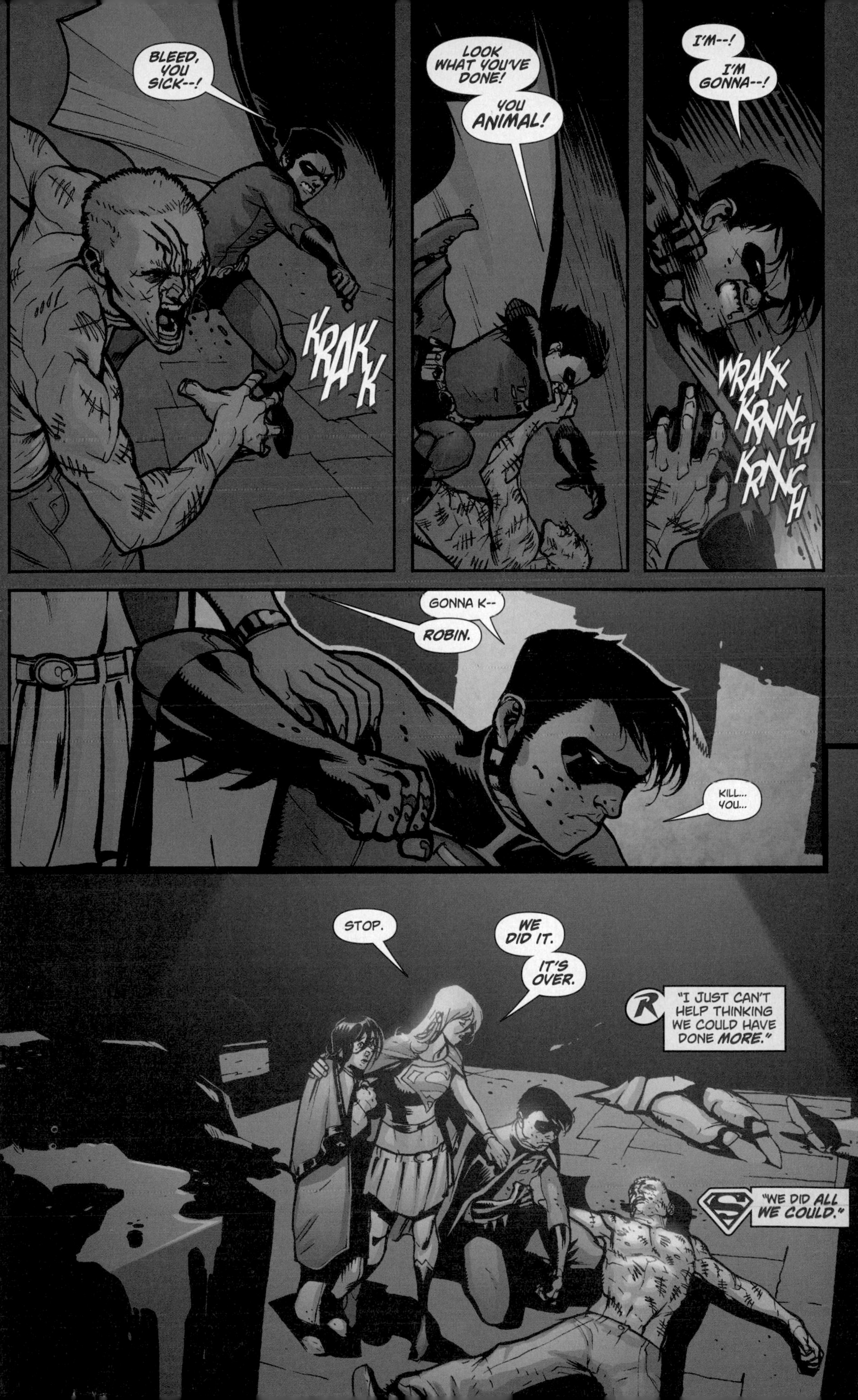
BLEED, YOU SICK--!
KRAKK
LOOK WHAT YOU'VE DONE!
YOU ANIMAL!
I'M--!
I'M GONNA--!
WRAKK
KRNNCH
KRNNCH
GONNA K--
ROBIN.
KILL... YOU...
STOP.
WE DID IT.
IT'S OVER.
"I JUST CAN'T HELP THINKING WE COULD HAVE DONE MORE."
"WE DID ALL WE COULD."

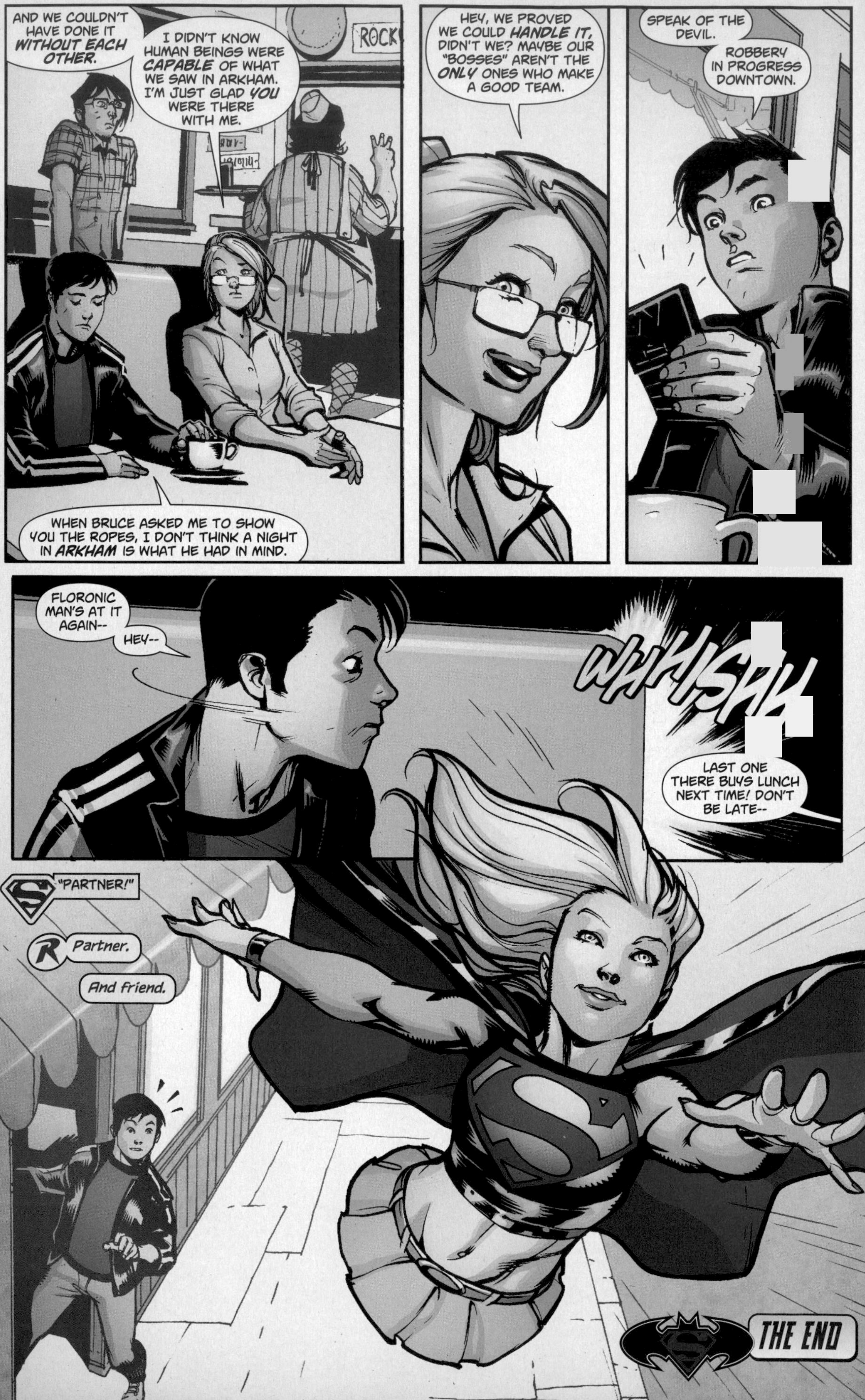

AND WE COULDN'T HAVE DONE IT WITHOUT EACH OTHER.
I DIDN'T KNOW HUMAN BEINGS WERE CAPABLE OF WHAT WE SAW IN ARKHAM. I'M JUST GLAD YOU WERE THERE WITH ME.
ROCK
WHEN BRUCE ASKED ME TO SHOW YOU THE ROPES, I DON'T THINK A NIGHT IN ARKHAM IS WHAT HE HAD IN MIND.
HEY, WE PROVED WE COULD HANDLE IT, DIDN'T WE? MAYBE OUR "BOSSES" AREN'T THE ONLY ONES WHO MAKE A GOOD TEAM.
SPEAK OF THE DEVIL.
ROBBERY IN PROGRESS DOWNTOWN.
FLORONIC MAN'S AT IT AGAIN--
HEY--
WHHISHH
LAST ONE THERE BUYS LUNCH NEXT TIME! DON'T BE LATE--
"PARTNER!"
Partner.
And friend.
THE END

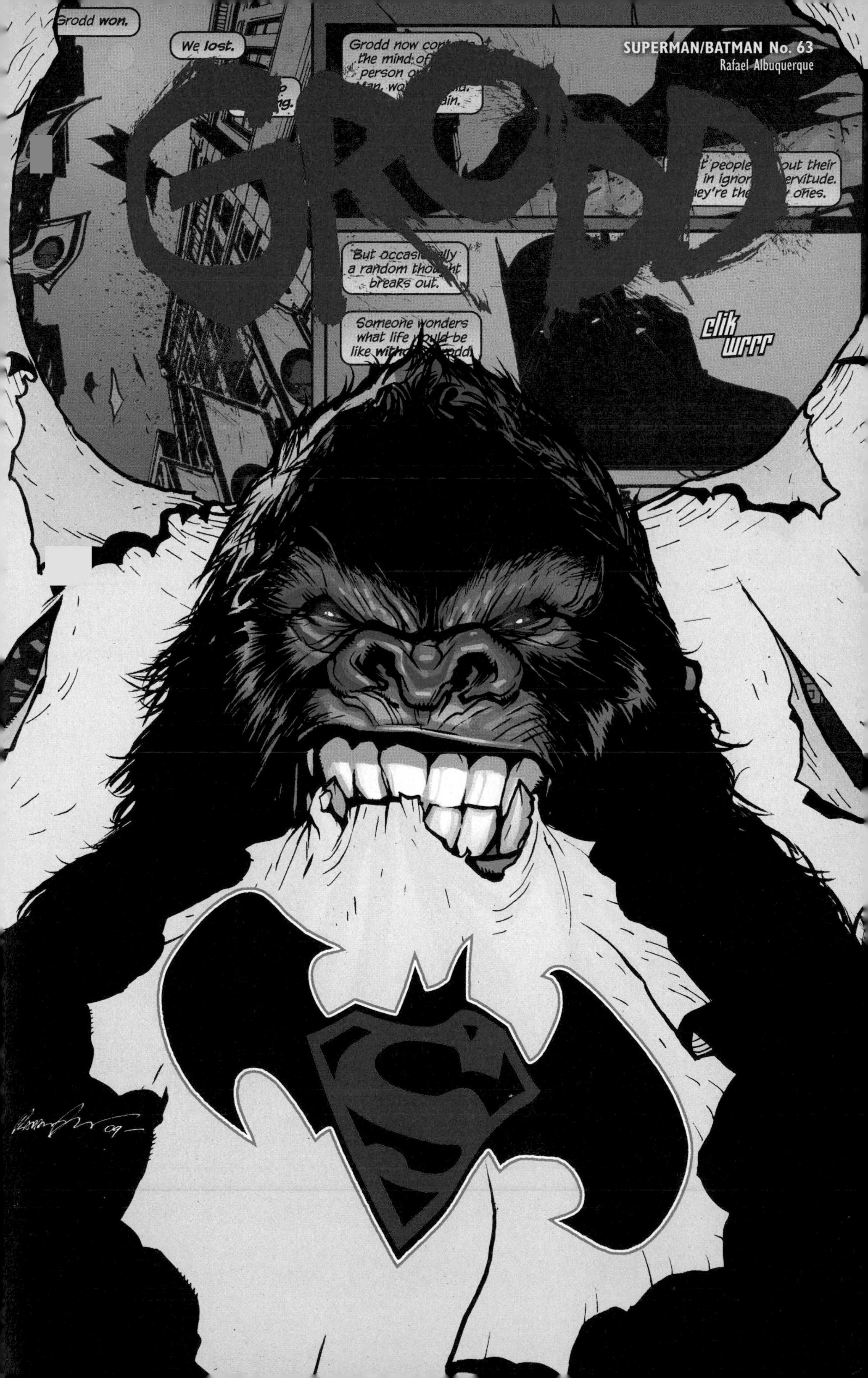
Grodd won.
We lost.
GRODD
clik
wrrr

SUPERMAN/BATMAN No. 63
Rafael Albuquerque

NIGHT & DAY

Plot: Michael Green and Mike Johnson

Dialogue: Mike Johnson

Artist: Rafael Albuquerque

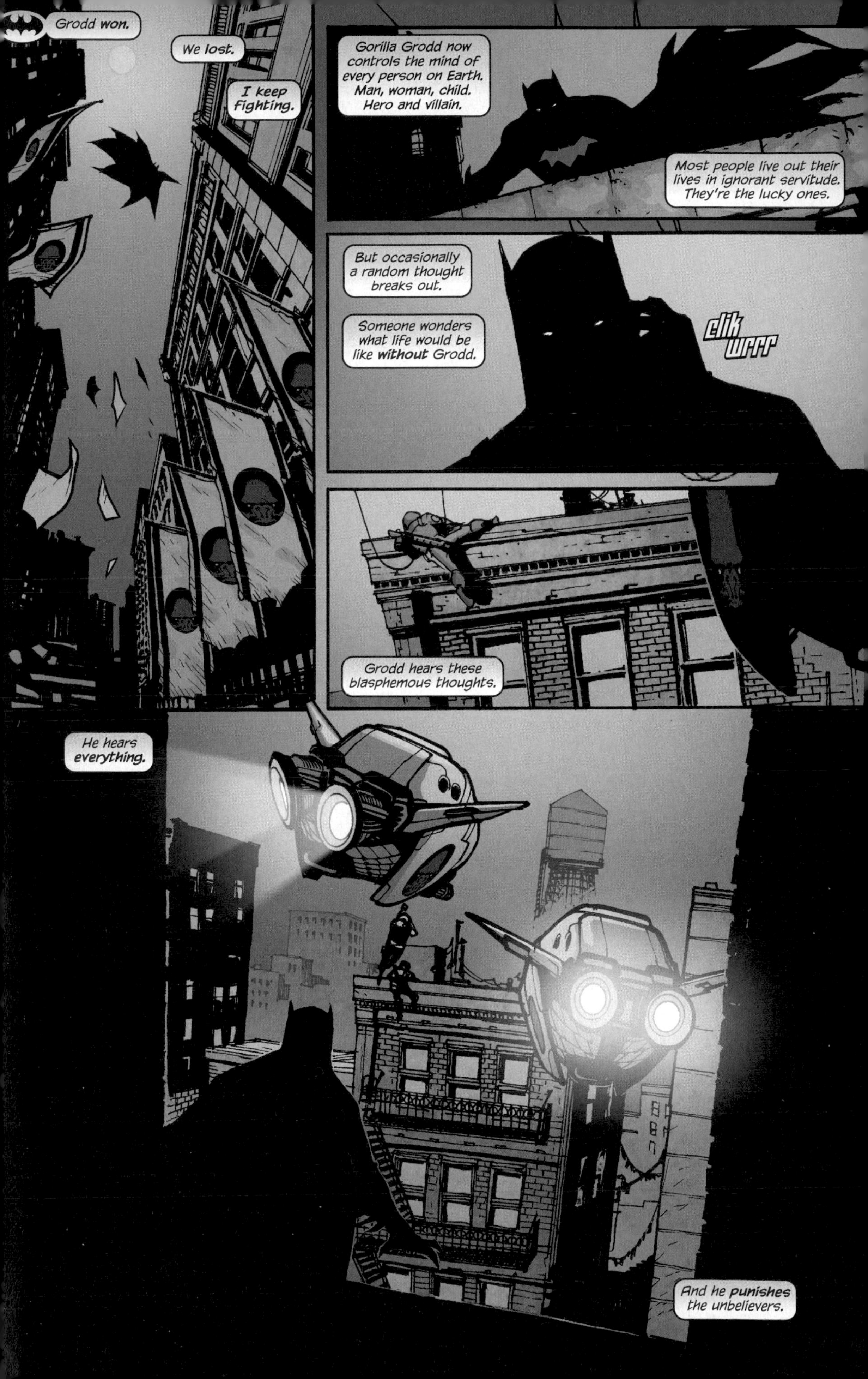

Grodd won.
We lost.
I keep fighting.
Gorilla Grodd now controls the mind of every person on Earth. Man, woman, child. Hero and villain.
Most people live out their lives in ignorant servitude. They're the lucky ones.
But occasionally a random thought breaks out.
Someone wonders what life would be like without Grodd.
clik
wrrr
Grodd hears these blasphemous thoughts.
He hears everything.
And he punishes the unbelievers.

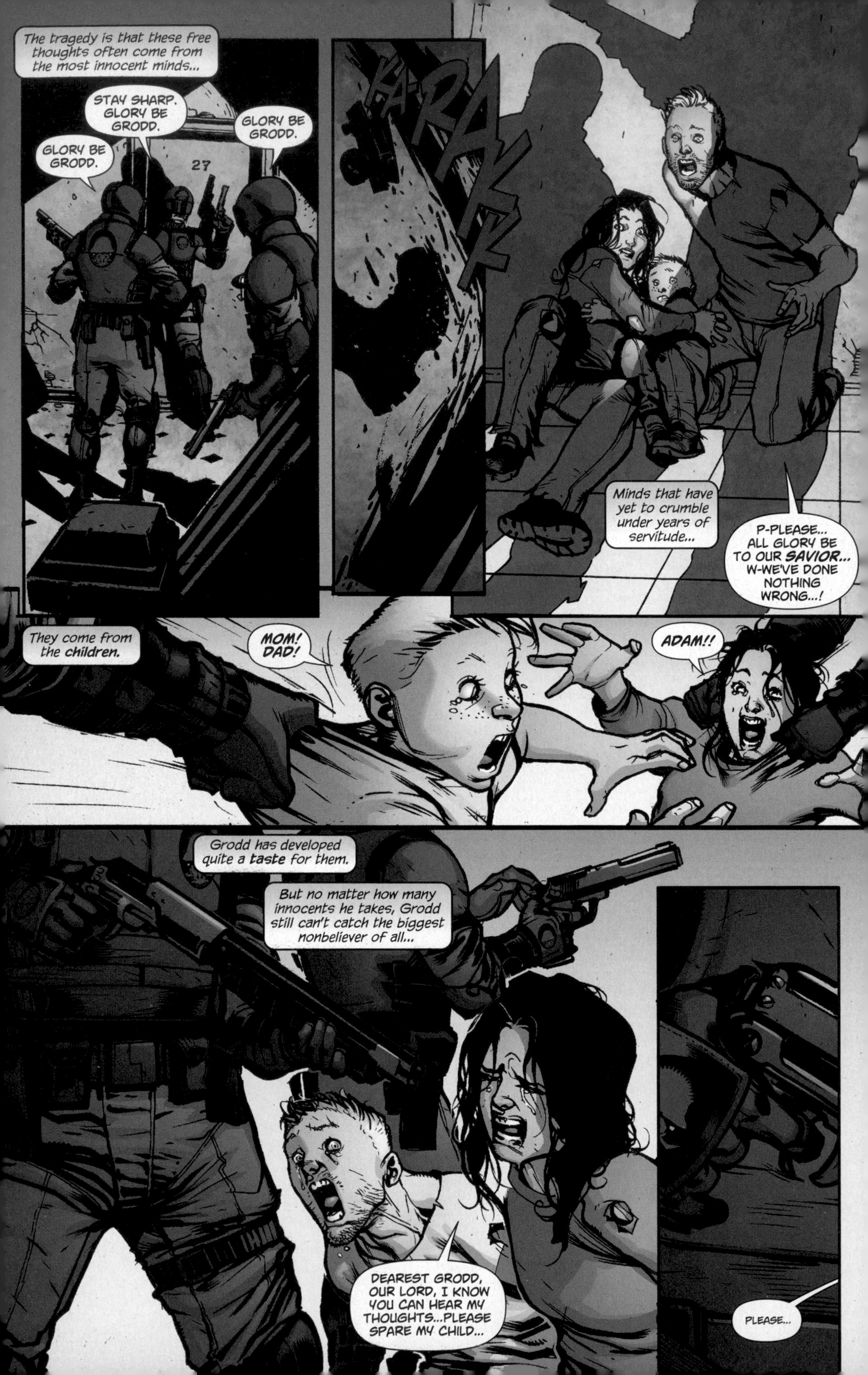

The tragedy is that these free thoughts often come from the most innocent minds...
STAY SHARP. GLORY BE GRODD.
GLORY BE GRODD.
GLORY BE GRODD.
27
KA-RAKK
Minds that have yet to crumble under years of servitude...
P-PLEASE... ALL GLORY BE TO OUR SAVIOR... W-WE'VE DONE NOTHING WRONG...!
They come from the children.
MOM! DAD!
ADAM!!
Grodd has developed quite a taste for them.
But no matter how many innocents he takes, Grodd still can't catch the biggest nonbeliever of all...
DEAREST GRODD, OUR LORD, I KNOW YOU CAN HEAR MY THOUGHTS...PLEASE SPARE MY CHILD...
PLEASE...

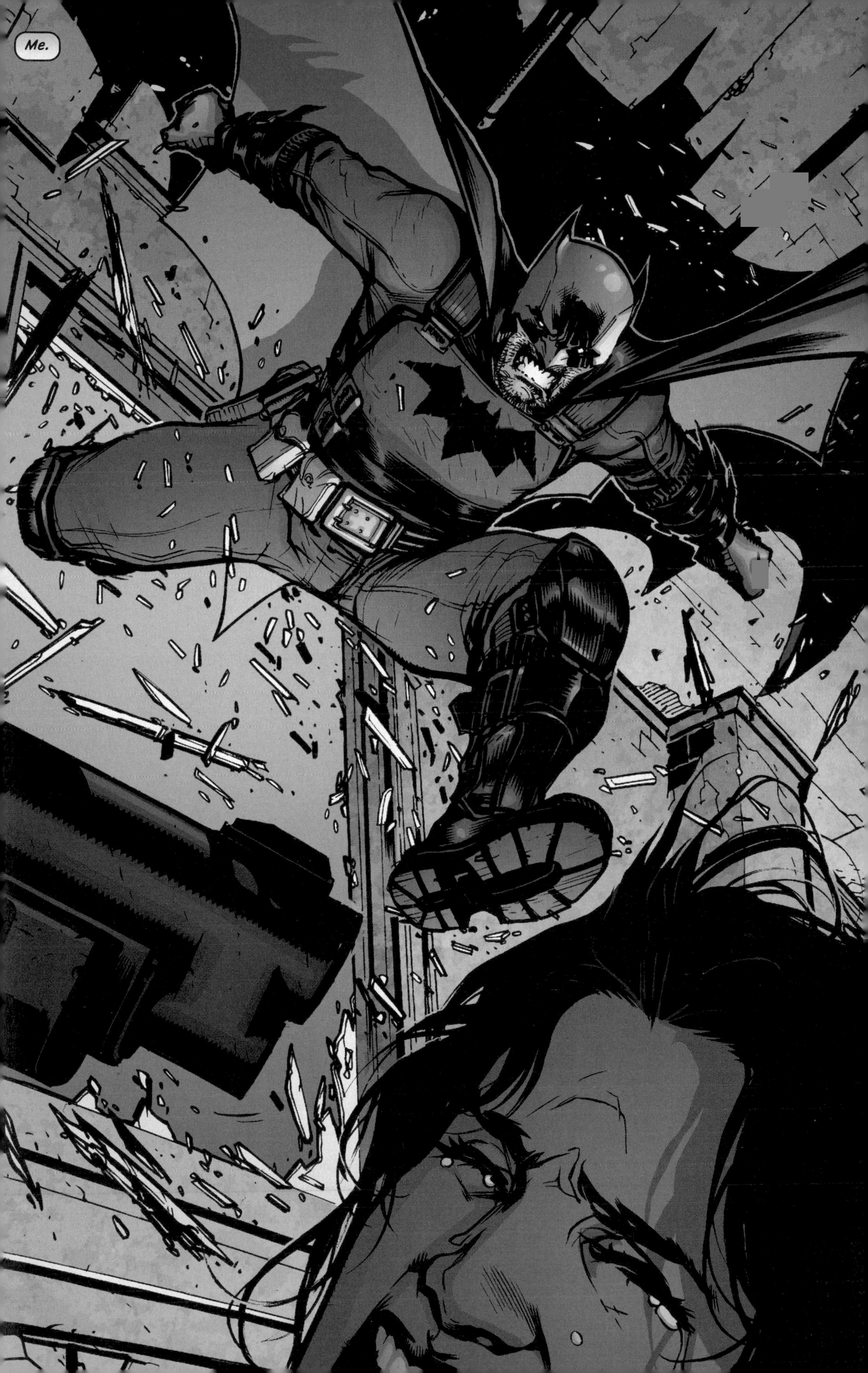
Me.

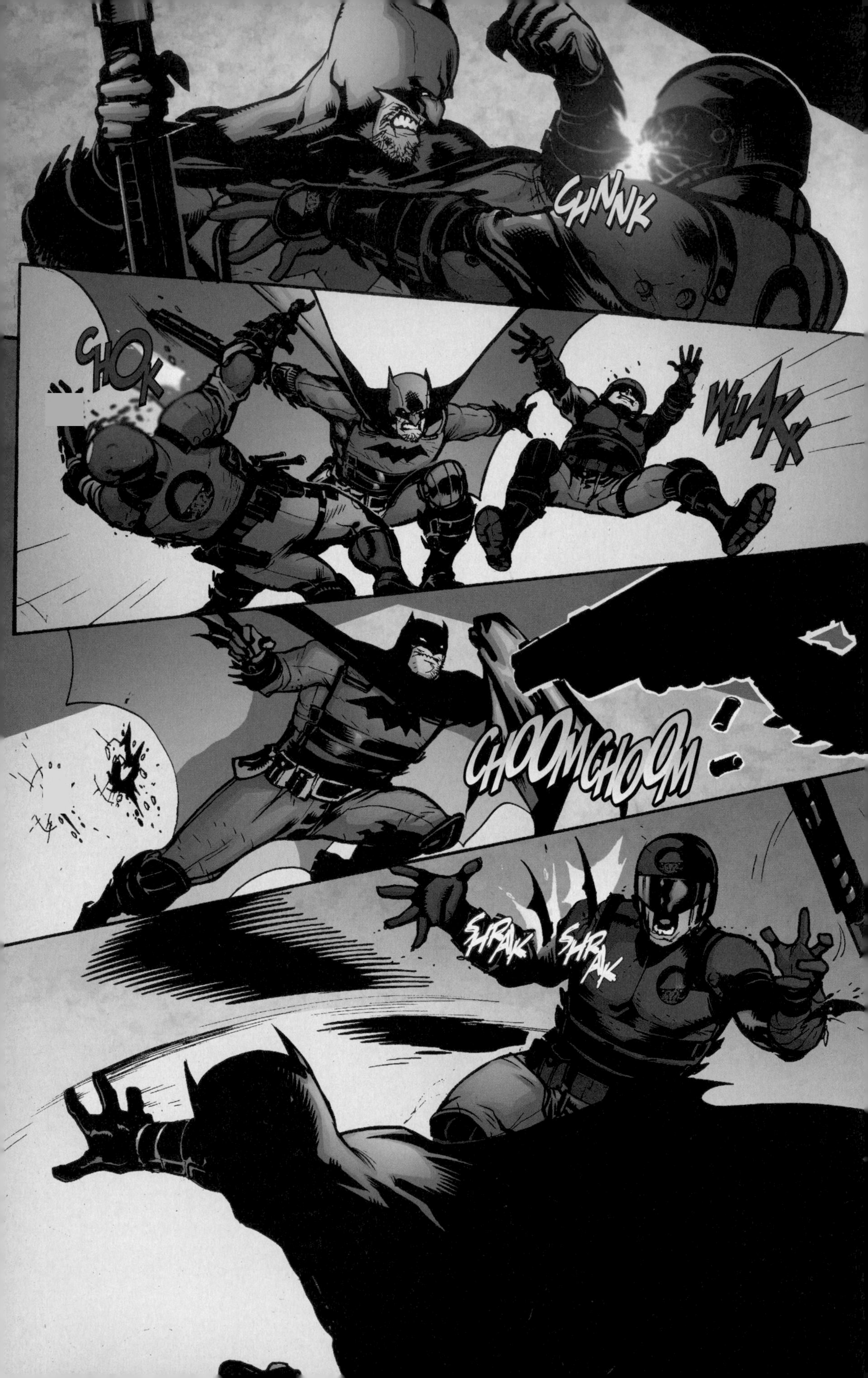
CHNNK
CHOK
WHAKK
CHOOMCHOOM
SHRAK
SHRAK

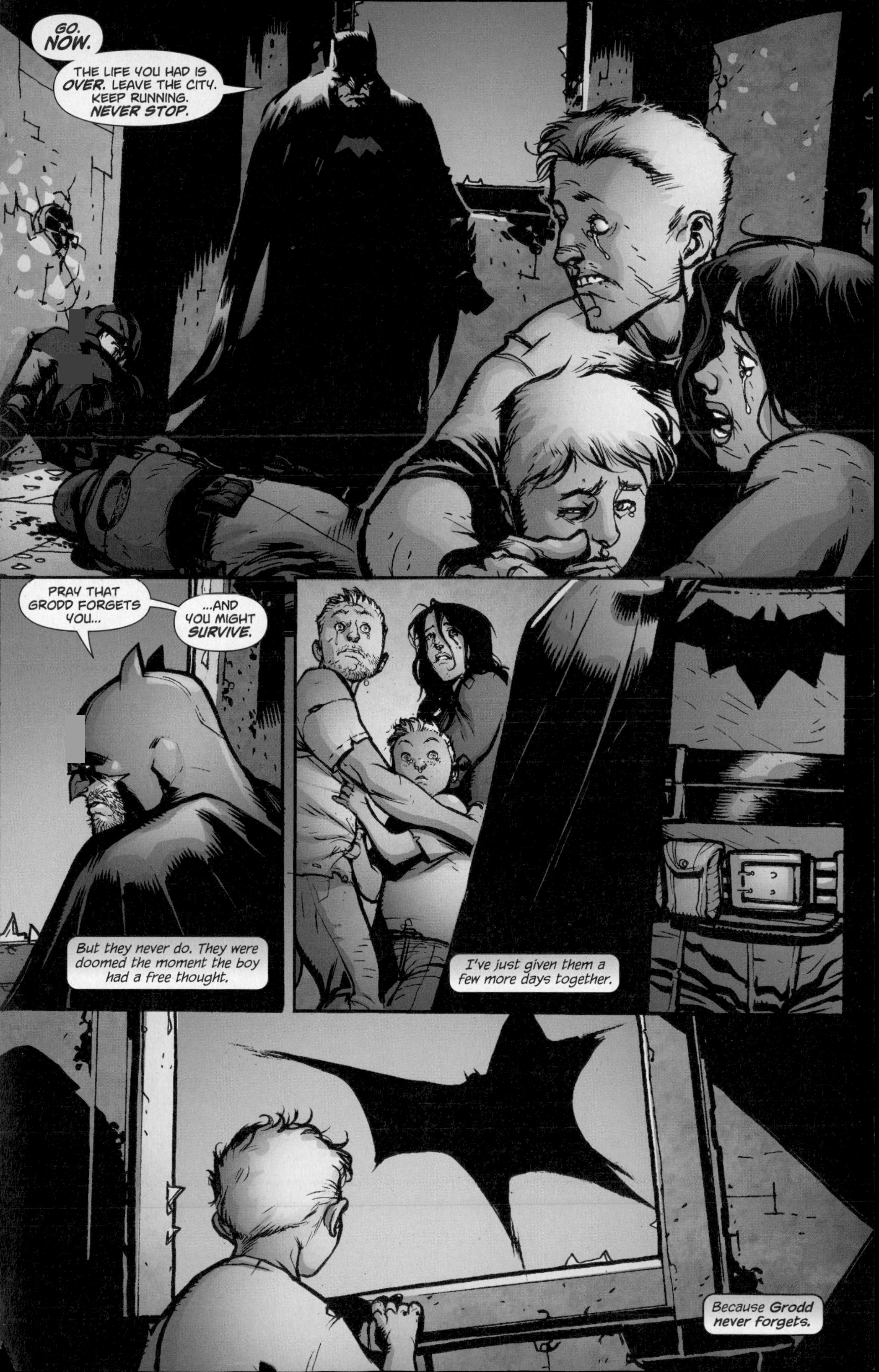
GO. NOW.
THE LIFE YOU HAD IS OVER. LEAVE THE CITY. KEEP RUNNING. NEVER STOP.
PRAY THAT GRODD FORGETS YOU...
...AND YOU MIGHT SURVIVE.
But they never do. They were doomed the moment the boy had a free thought.
I've just given them a few more days together.
Because Grodd never forgets.

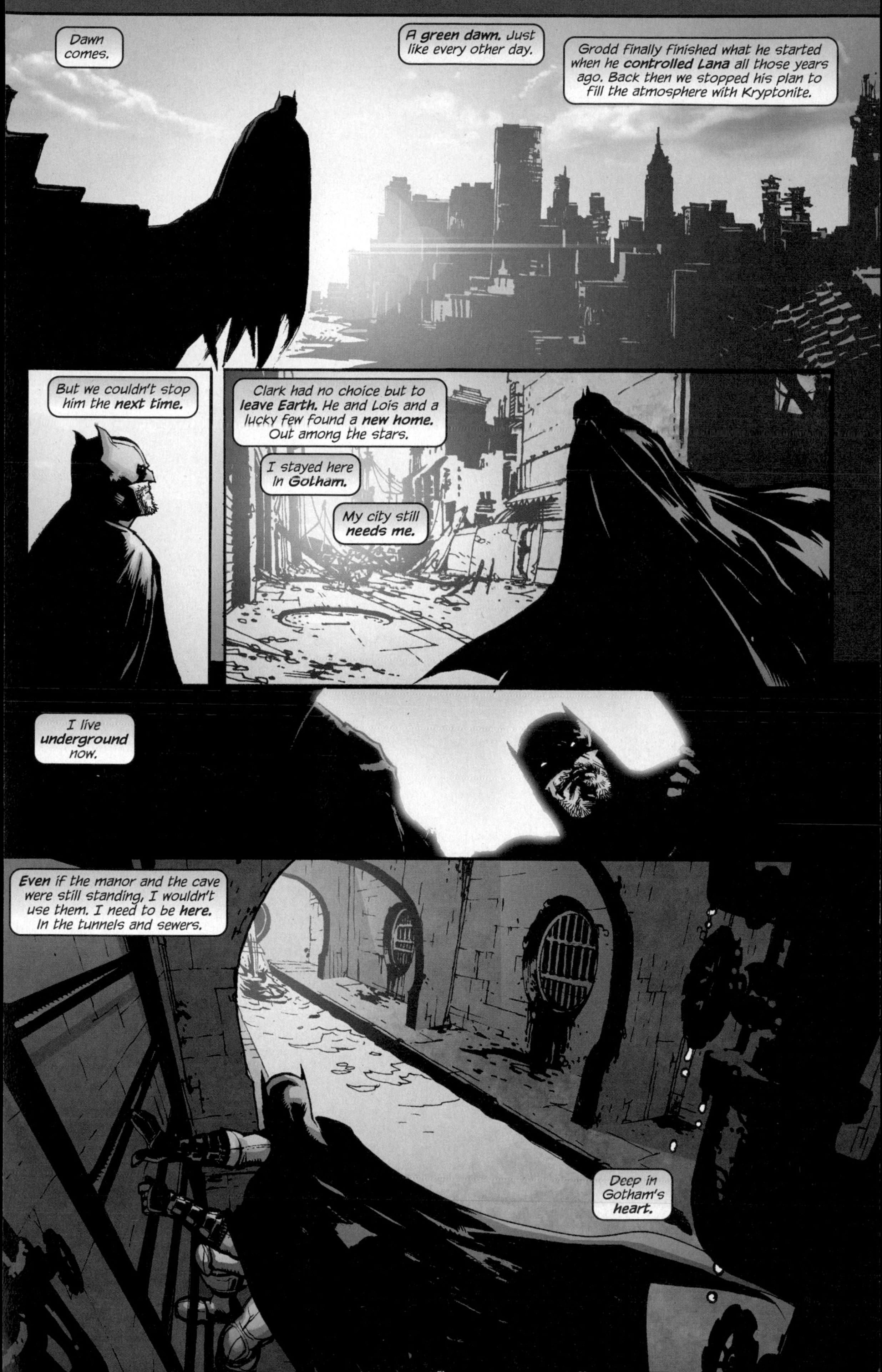
Dawn comes.
A **green dawn.** Just like every other day.
Grodd finally finished what he started when he **controlled Lana** all those years ago. Back then we stopped his plan to fill the atmosphere with Kryptonite.
But we couldn't stop him the **next time.**
Clark had no choice but to **leave Earth.** He and Lois and a lucky few found a **new home.** Out among the stars.
I stayed here in **Gotham.**
My city still **needs me.**
I live **underground** now.
Even if the manor and the cave were still standing, I wouldn't use them. I need to be **here.** In the tunnels and sewers.
Deep in Gotham's **heart.**

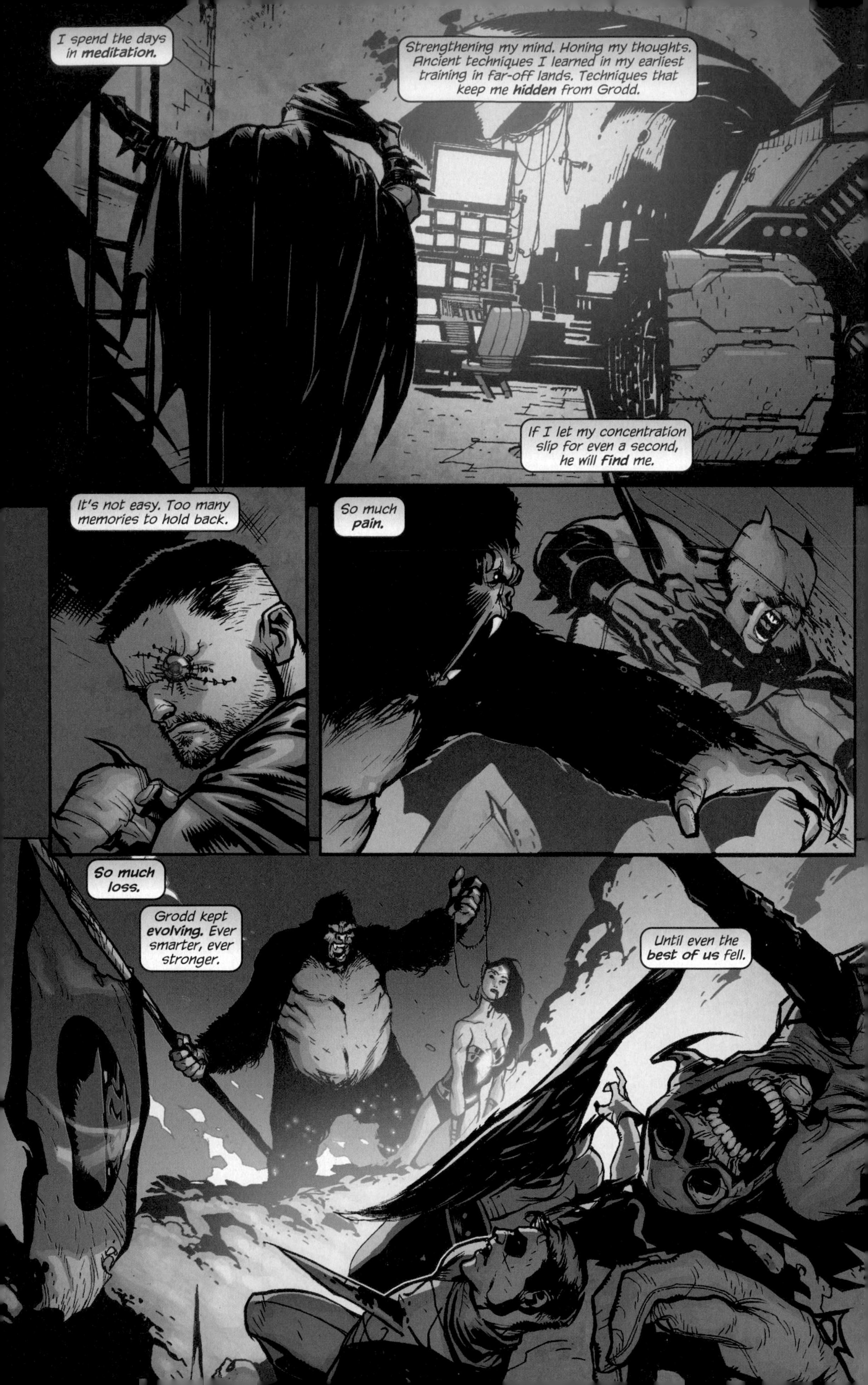
I spend the days in **meditation.**
Strengthening my mind. Honing my thoughts. Ancient techniques I learned in my earliest training in far-off lands. Techniques that keep me **hidden** from Grodd.
If I let my concentration slip for even a second, he will **find** me.
It's not easy. Too many memories to hold back.
So much **pain.**
So much loss.
Grodd kept **evolving.** Ever smarter, ever stronger.
Until even the **best of us** fell.

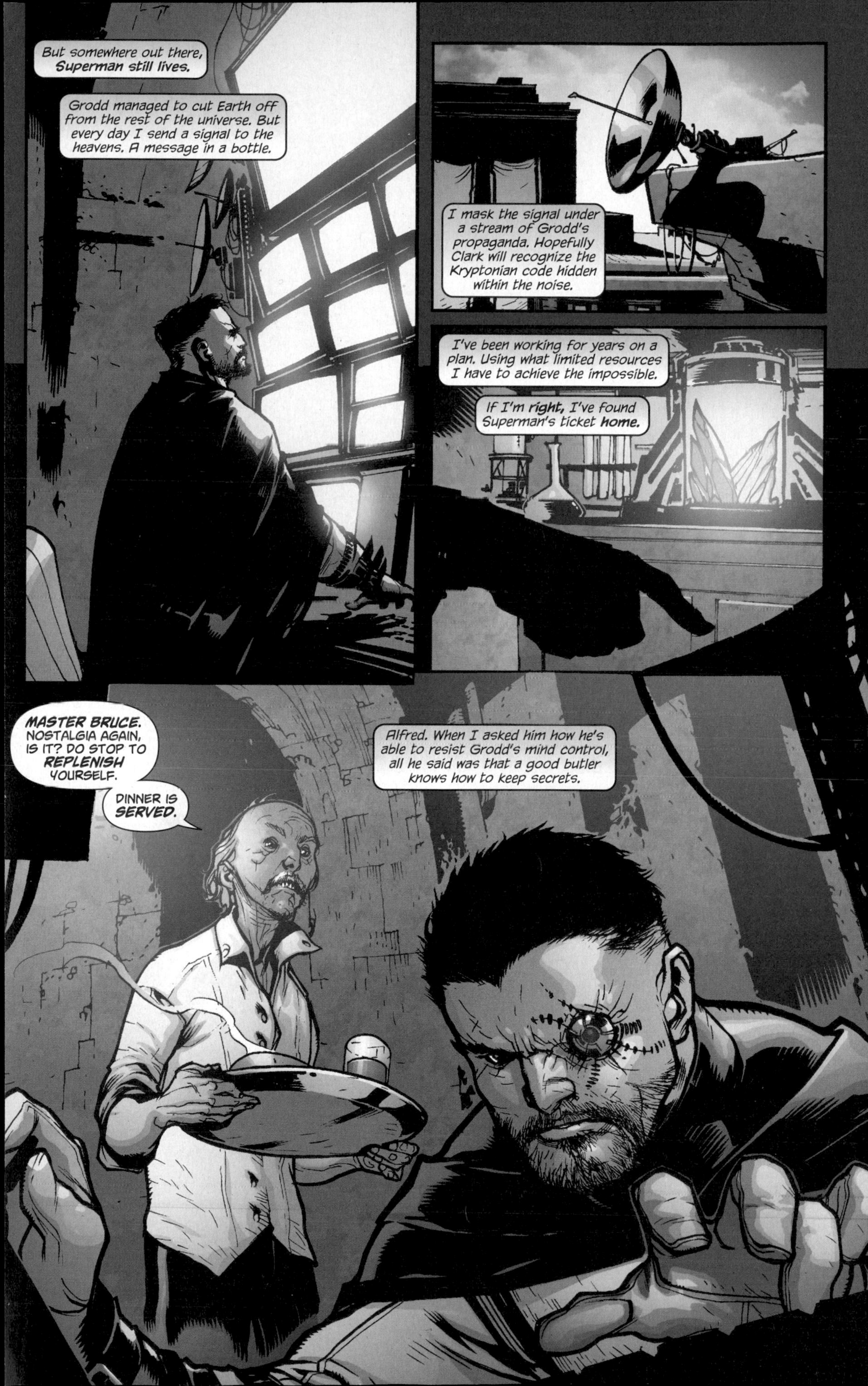
But somewhere out there, **Superman still lives.**
Grodd managed to cut Earth off from the rest of the universe. But every day I send a signal to the heavens. A message in a bottle.
I mask the signal under a stream of Grodd's propaganda. Hopefully Clark will recognize the Kryptonian code hidden within the noise.
I've been working for years on a plan. Using what limited resources I have to achieve the impossible.
If I'm **right,** I've found Superman's ticket **home.**
MASTER BRUCE. NOSTALGIA AGAIN, IS IT? DO STOP TO **REPLENISH** YOURSELF.
DINNER IS **SERVED.**
Alfred. When I asked him how he's able to resist Grodd's mind control, all he said was that a good butler knows how to keep secrets.

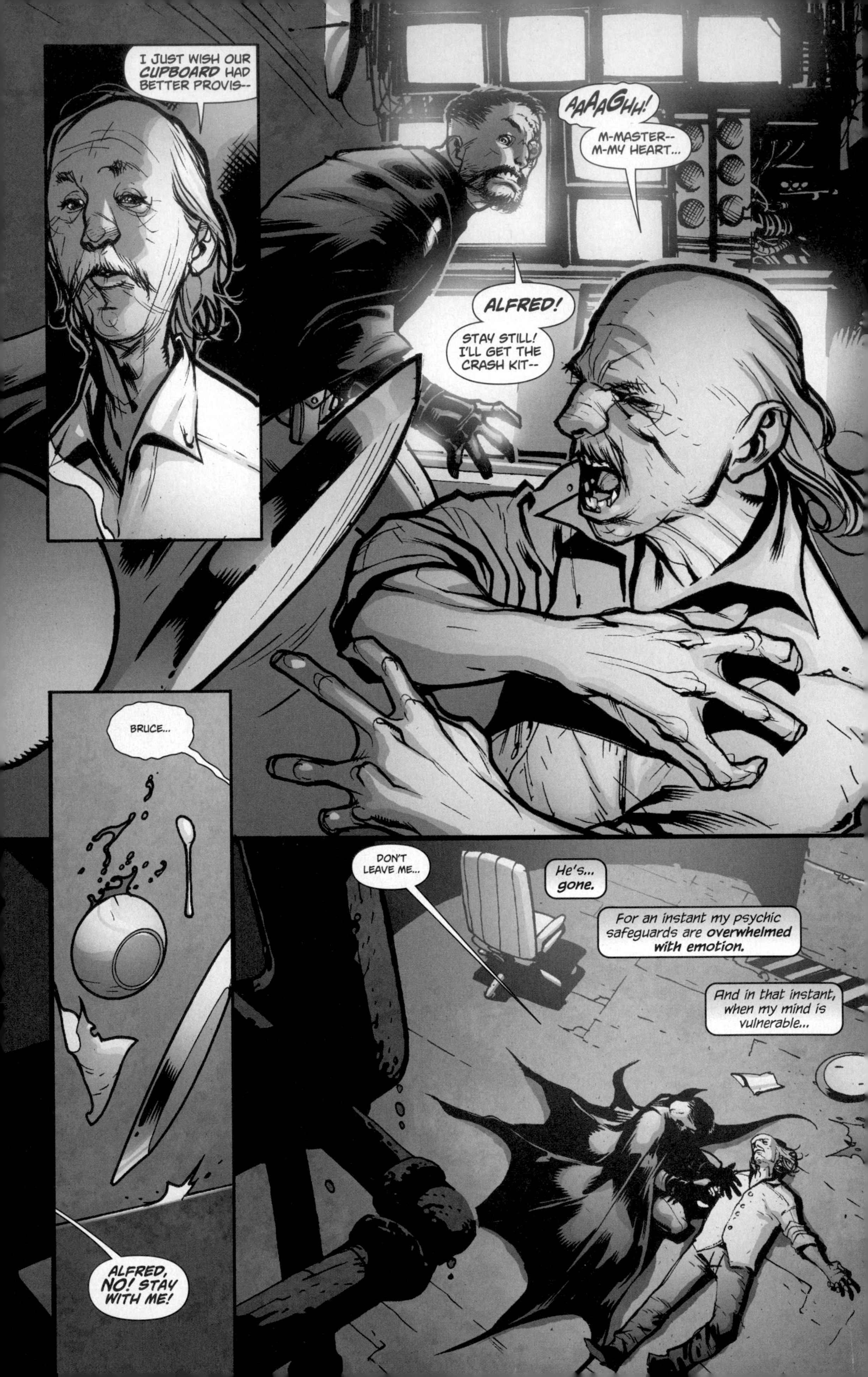
I JUST WISH OUR CUPBOARD HAD BETTER PROVIS--
AAAAGHH!
M-MASTER-- M-MY HEART...
ALFRED!
STAY STILL! I'LL GET THE CRASH KIT--
BRUCE...
ALFRED, NO! STAY WITH ME!
DON'T LEAVE ME...
He's... gone.
For an instant my psychic safeguards are overwhelmed with emotion.
And in that instant, when my mind is vulnerable...

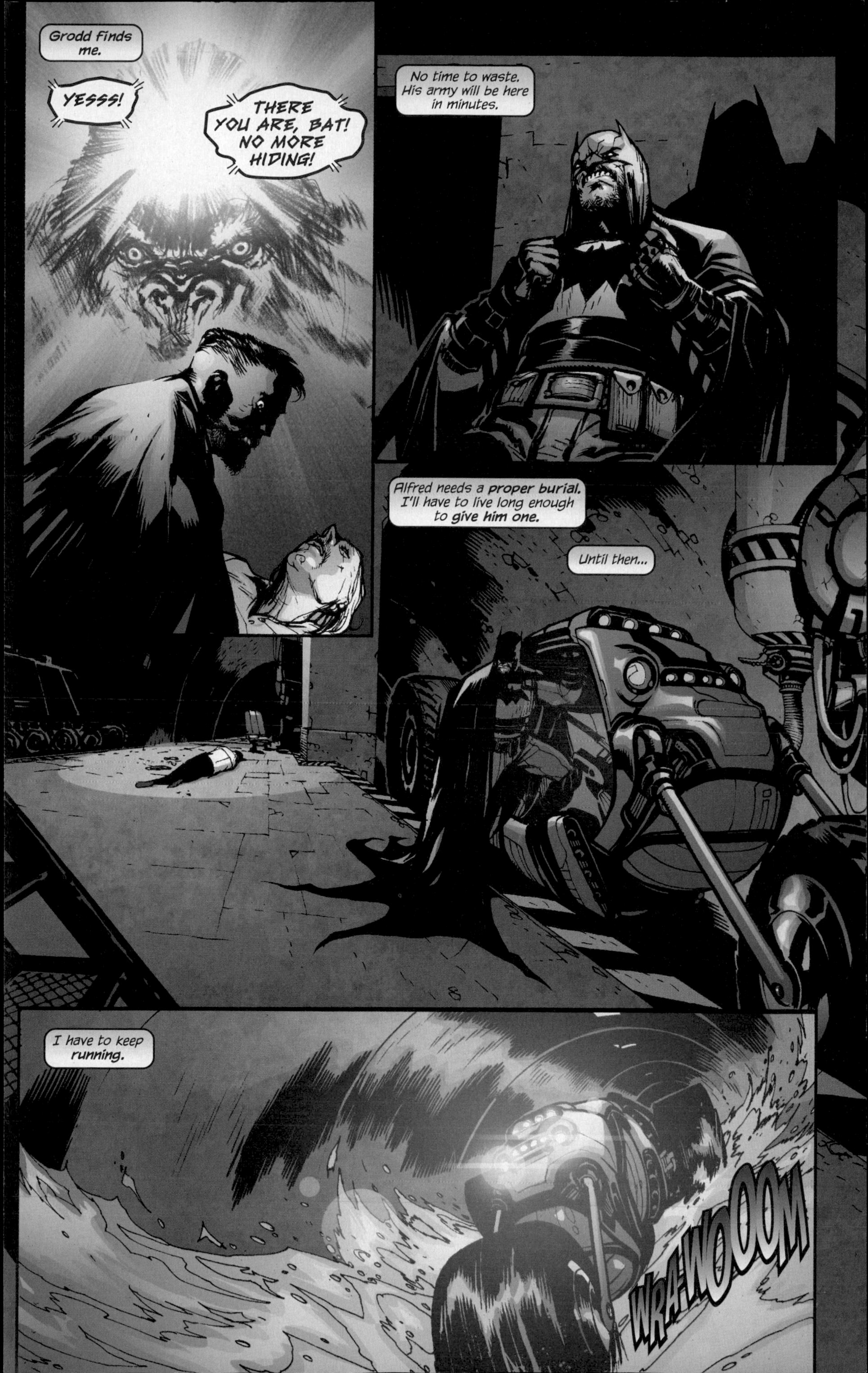

Grodd finds me.
YESSS!
THERE YOU ARE, BAT! NO MORE HIDING!
No time to waste. His army will be here in minutes.
Alfred needs a **proper burial.** I'll have to live long enough to **give him one.**
Until then...
I have to keep **running.**
WRA-WOOOM

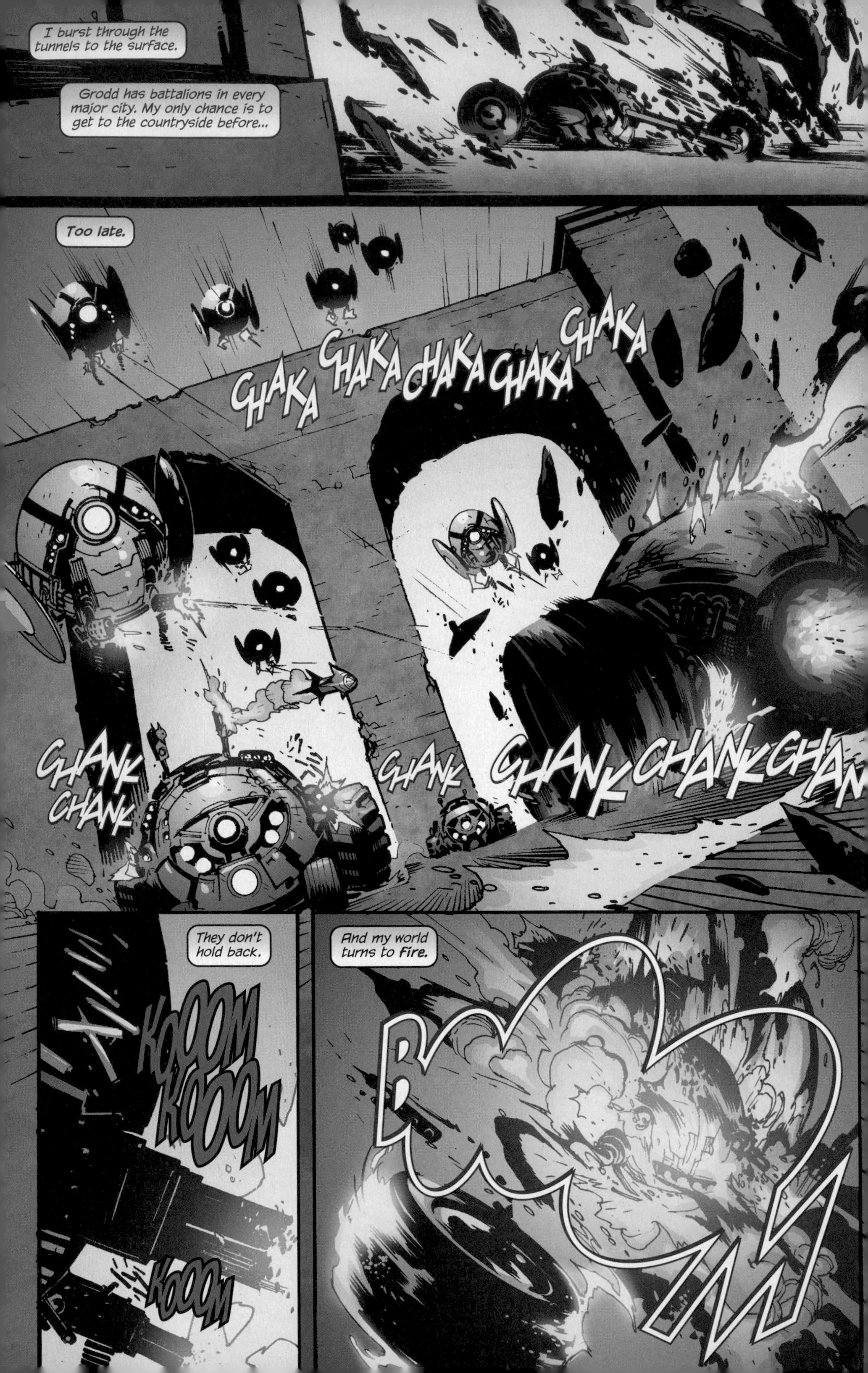

I burst through the tunnels to the surface.
Grodd has battalions in every major city. My only chance is to get to the countryside before...
Too late.
CHAKA CHAKA CHAKA CHAKA CHAKA
CHANK CHANK
CHANK
CHANK CHANK CHAN
They don't hold back.
KOOOM KOOOM
KOOOM
And my world turns to fire.
BOOM

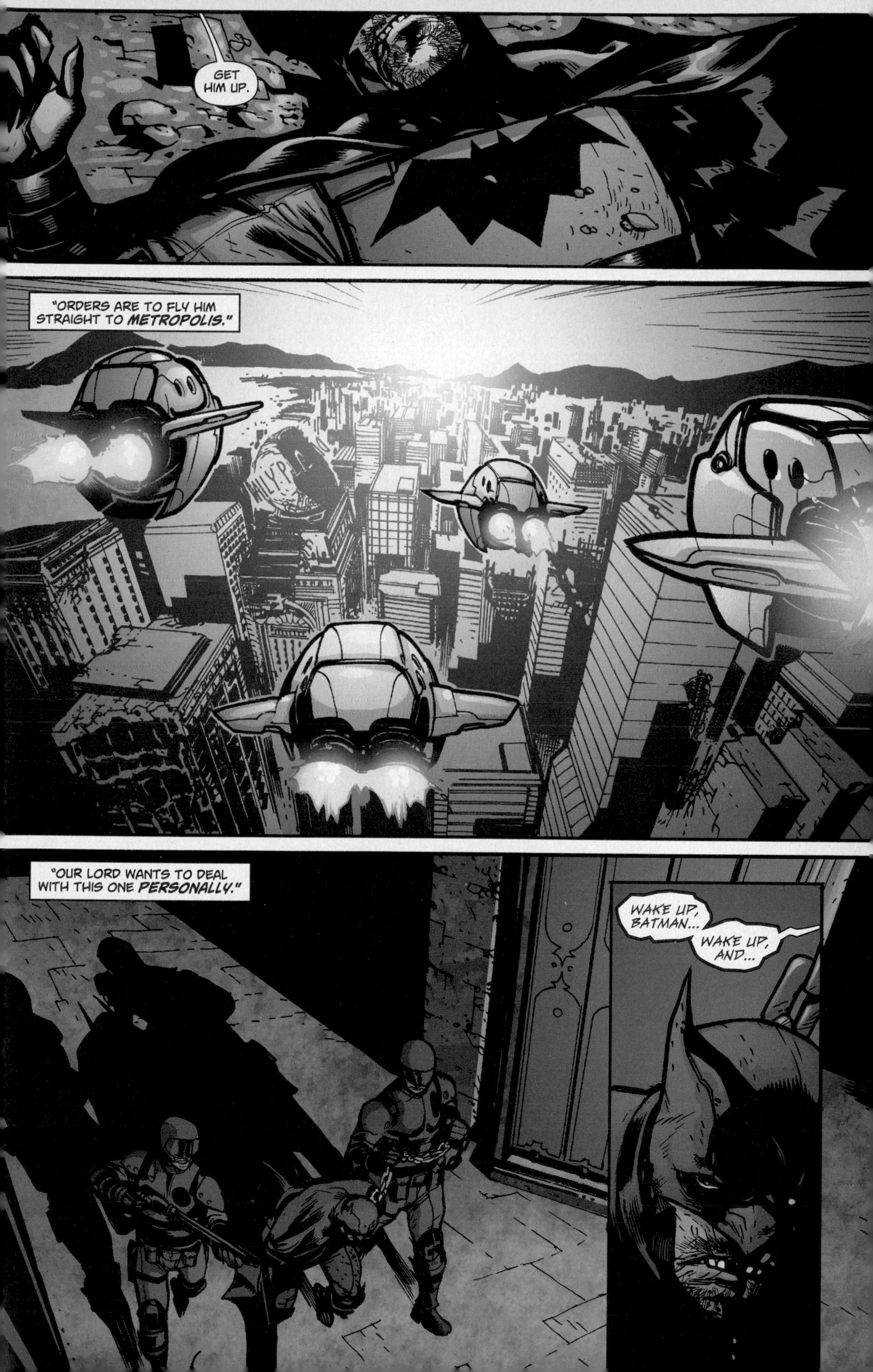

GET HIM UP.
"ORDERS ARE TO FLY HIM STRAIGHT TO METROPOLIS."
"OUR LORD WANTS TO DEAL WITH THIS ONE PERSONALLY."
WAKE UP, BATMAN...
WAKE UP, AND...

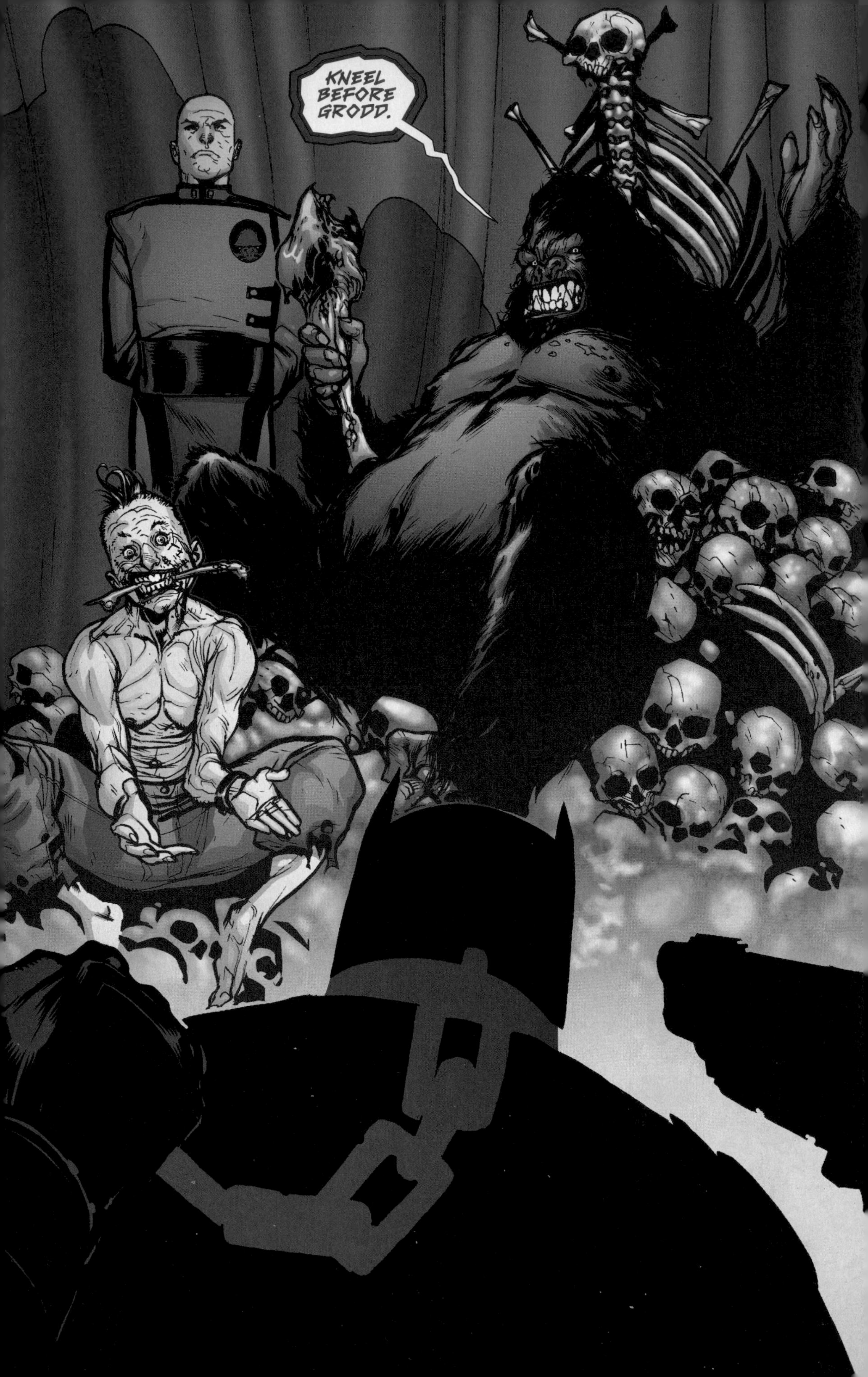
KNEEL BEFORE GRODD.

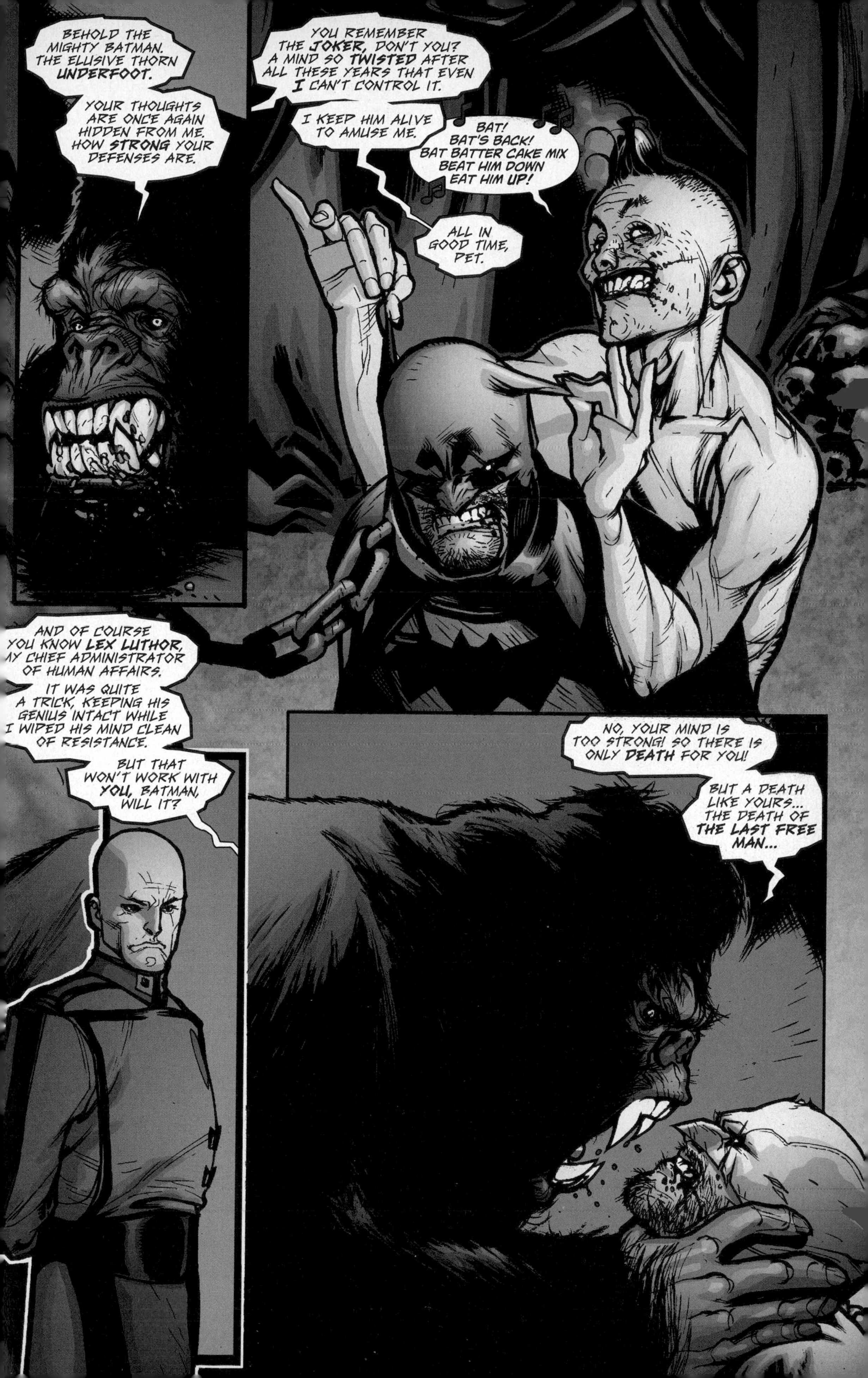
BEHOLD THE MIGHTY BATMAN. THE ELUSIVE THORN UNDERFOOT.
YOUR THOUGHTS ARE ONCE AGAIN HIDDEN FROM ME. HOW STRONG YOUR DEFENSES ARE.
YOU REMEMBER THE JOKER, DON'T YOU? A MIND SO TWISTED AFTER ALL THESE YEARS THAT EVEN I CAN'T CONTROL IT.
I KEEP HIM ALIVE TO AMUSE ME.
BAT! BAT'S BACK! BAT BATTER CAKE MIX BEAT HIM DOWN EAT HIM UP!
ALL IN GOOD TIME, PET.
AND OF COURSE YOU KNOW LEX LUTHOR, MY CHIEF ADMINISTRATOR OF HUMAN AFFAIRS.
IT WAS QUITE A TRICK, KEEPING HIS GENIUS INTACT WHILE I WIPED HIS MIND CLEAN OF RESISTANCE.
BUT THAT WON'T WORK WITH YOU, BATMAN, WILL IT?
NO, YOUR MIND IS TOO STRONG! SO THERE IS ONLY DEATH FOR YOU!
BUT A DEATH LIKE YOURS... THE DEATH OF THE LAST FREE MAN...

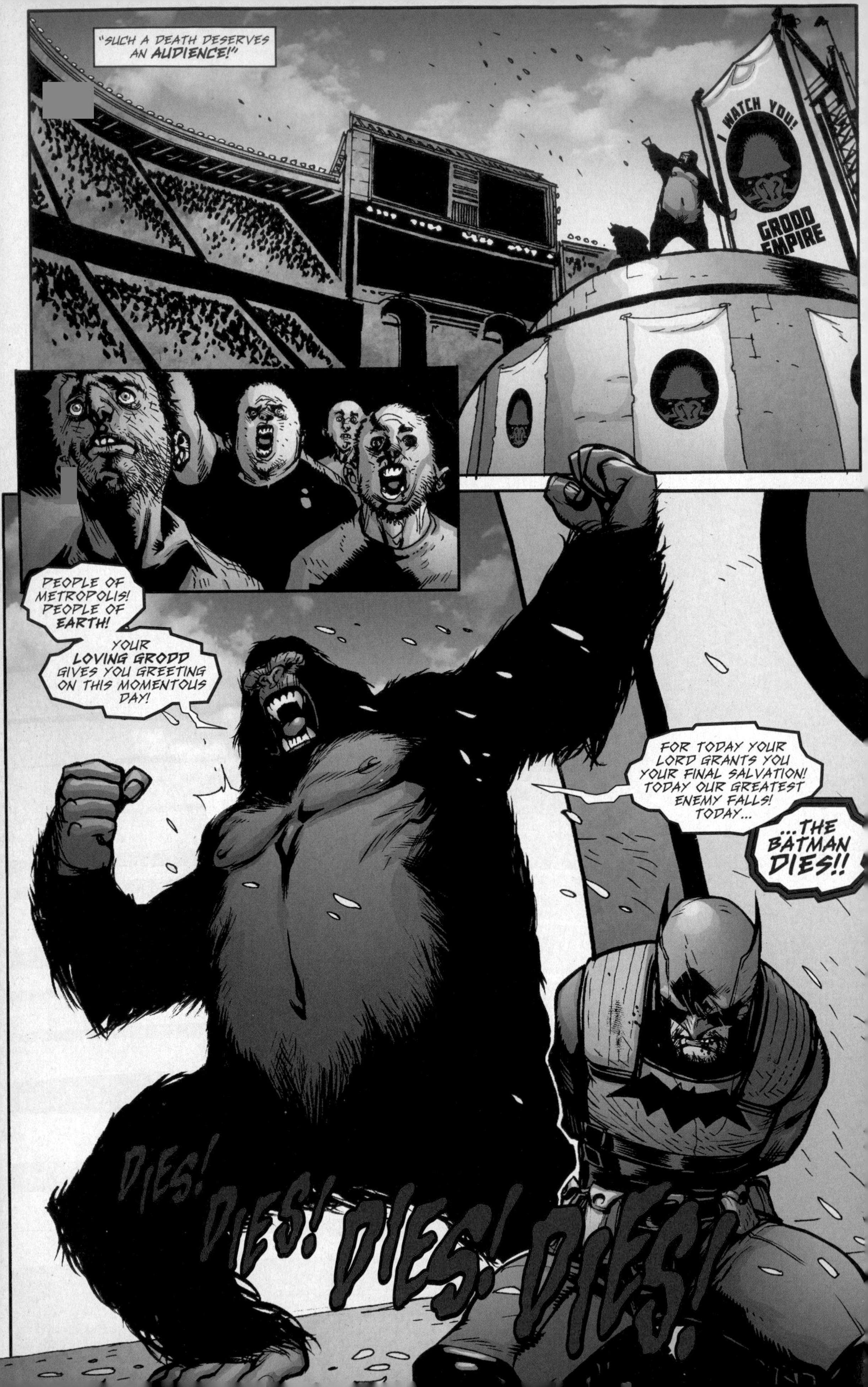
"SUCH A DEATH DESERVES AN AUDIENCE!"
I WATCH YOU!
GRODD EMPIRE
PEOPLE OF METROPOLIS! PEOPLE OF EARTH!
YOUR LOVING GRODD GIVES YOU GREETING ON THIS MOMENTOUS DAY!
FOR TODAY YOUR LORD GRANTS YOU YOUR FINAL SALVATION! TODAY OUR GREATEST ENEMY FALLS! TODAY...
...THE BATMAN DIES!!
DIES! DIES! DIES! DIES!

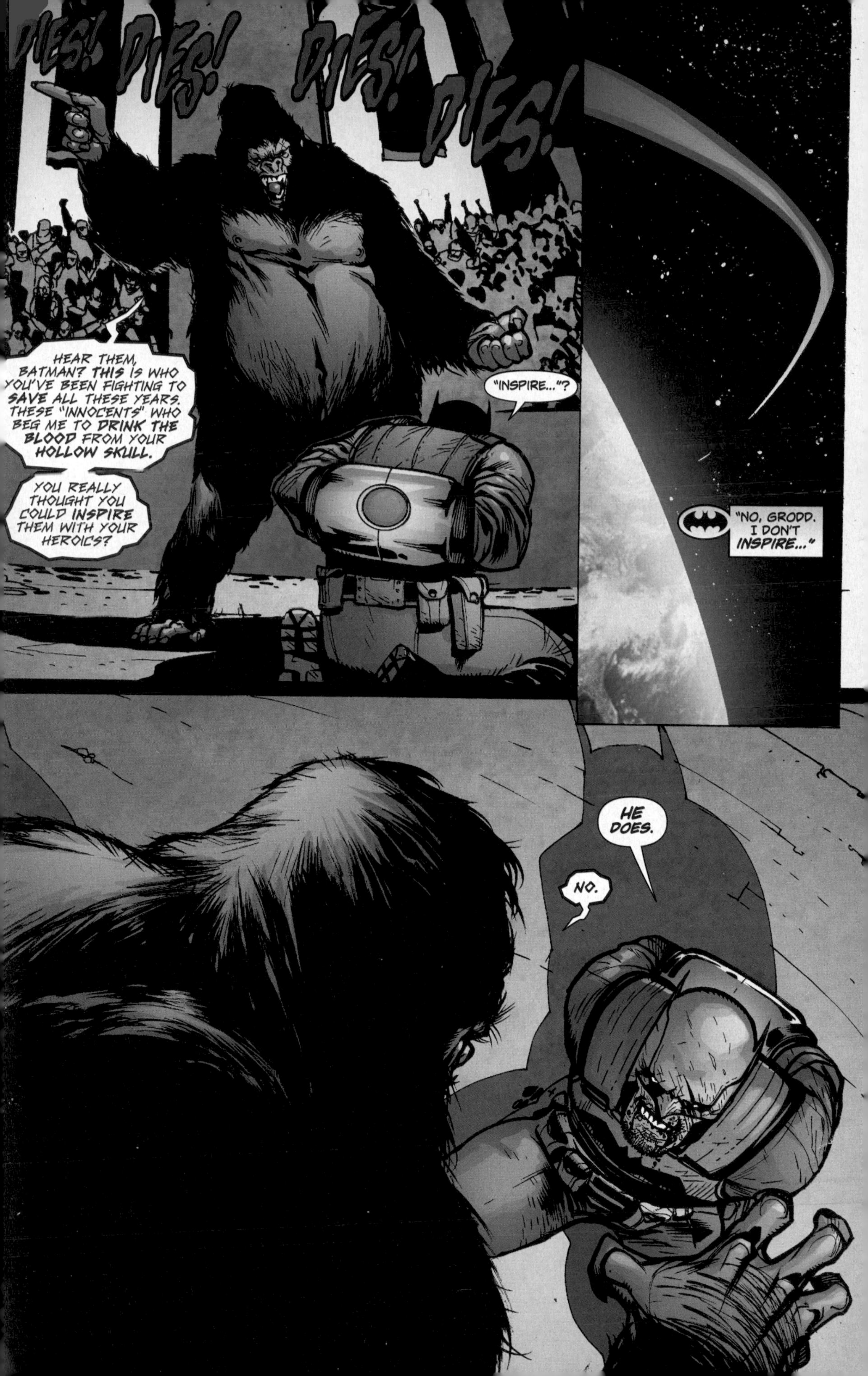
DIES! DIES! DIES! DIES!
HEAR THEM, BATMAN? THIS IS WHO YOU'VE BEEN FIGHTING TO SAVE ALL THESE YEARS. THESE "INNOCENTS" WHO BEG ME TO DRINK THE BLOOD FROM YOUR HOLLOW SKULL.
YOU REALLY THOUGHT YOU COULD INSPIRE THEM WITH YOUR HEROICS?
"INSPIRE..."?
"NO, GRODD. I DON'T INSPIRE..."
HE DOES.
NO.

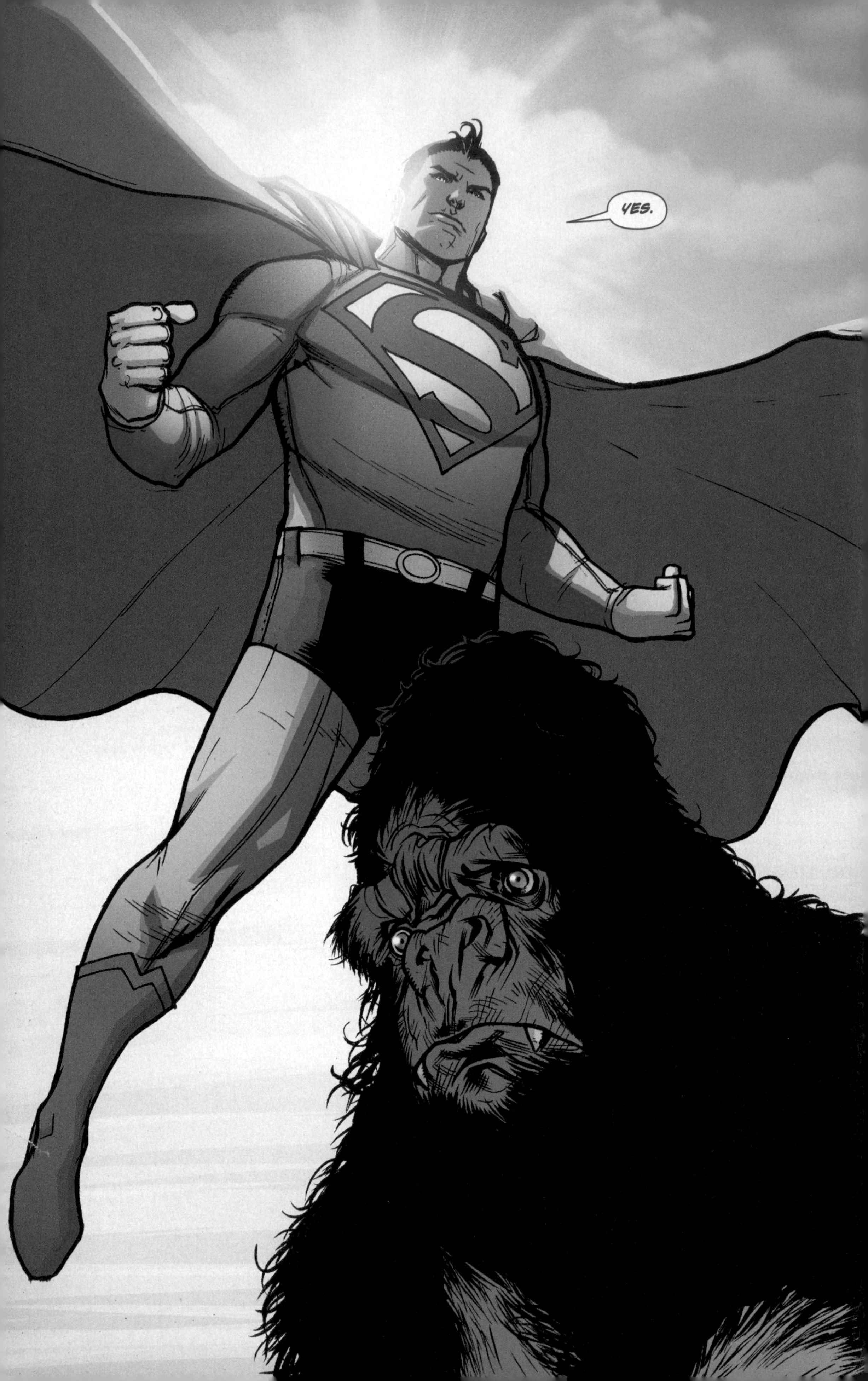
YES.

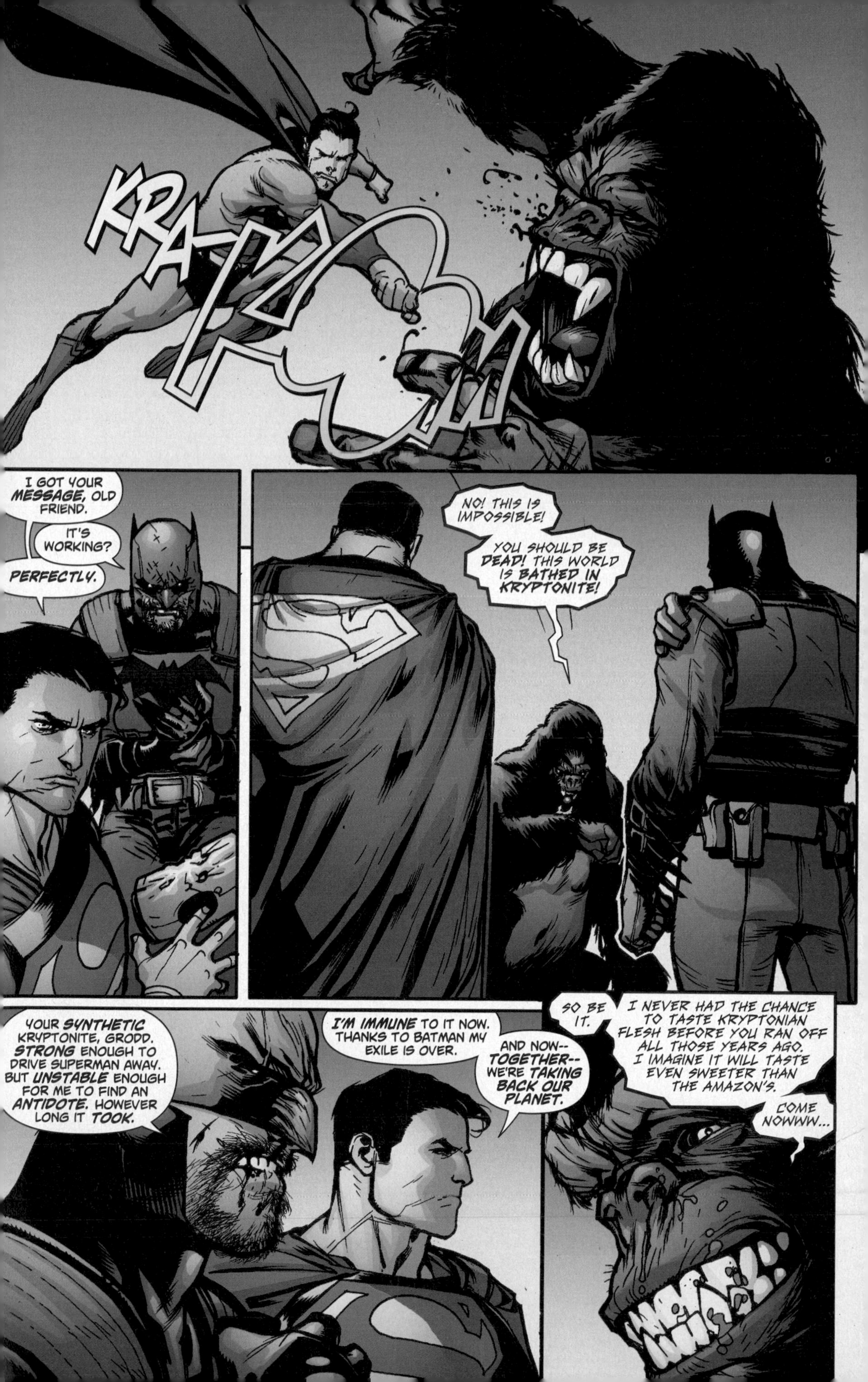
KRA-KOOM
I GOT YOUR MESSAGE, OLD FRIEND.
IT'S WORKING?
PERFECTLY.
NO! THIS IS IMPOSSIBLE!
YOU SHOULD BE DEAD! THIS WORLD IS BATHED IN KRYPTONITE!
YOUR SYNTHETIC KRYPTONITE, GRODD. STRONG ENOUGH TO DRIVE SUPERMAN AWAY. BUT UNSTABLE ENOUGH FOR ME TO FIND AN ANTIDOTE. HOWEVER LONG IT TOOK.
I'M IMMUNE TO IT NOW. THANKS TO BATMAN MY EXILE IS OVER.
AND NOW-- TOGETHER-- WE'RE TAKING BACK OUR PLANET.
SO BE IT.
I NEVER HAD THE CHANCE TO TASTE KRYPTONIAN FLESH BEFORE YOU RAN OFF ALL THOSE YEARS AGO. I IMAGINE IT WILL TASTE EVEN SWEETER THAN THE AMAZON'S.
COME NOWWW...

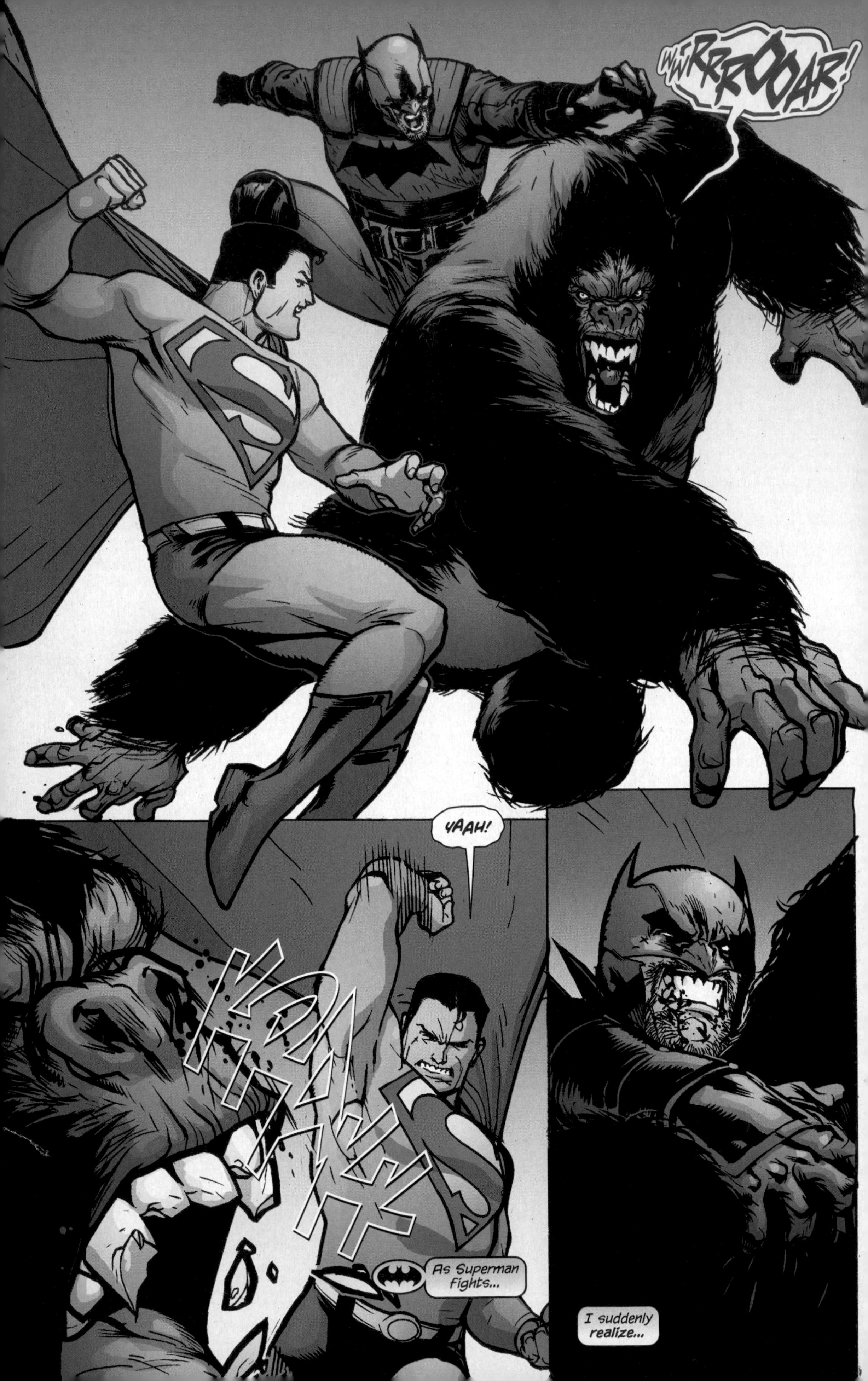

WWRRRROOAR!
YAAH!
KRAKK
As Superman fights...
I suddenly realize...

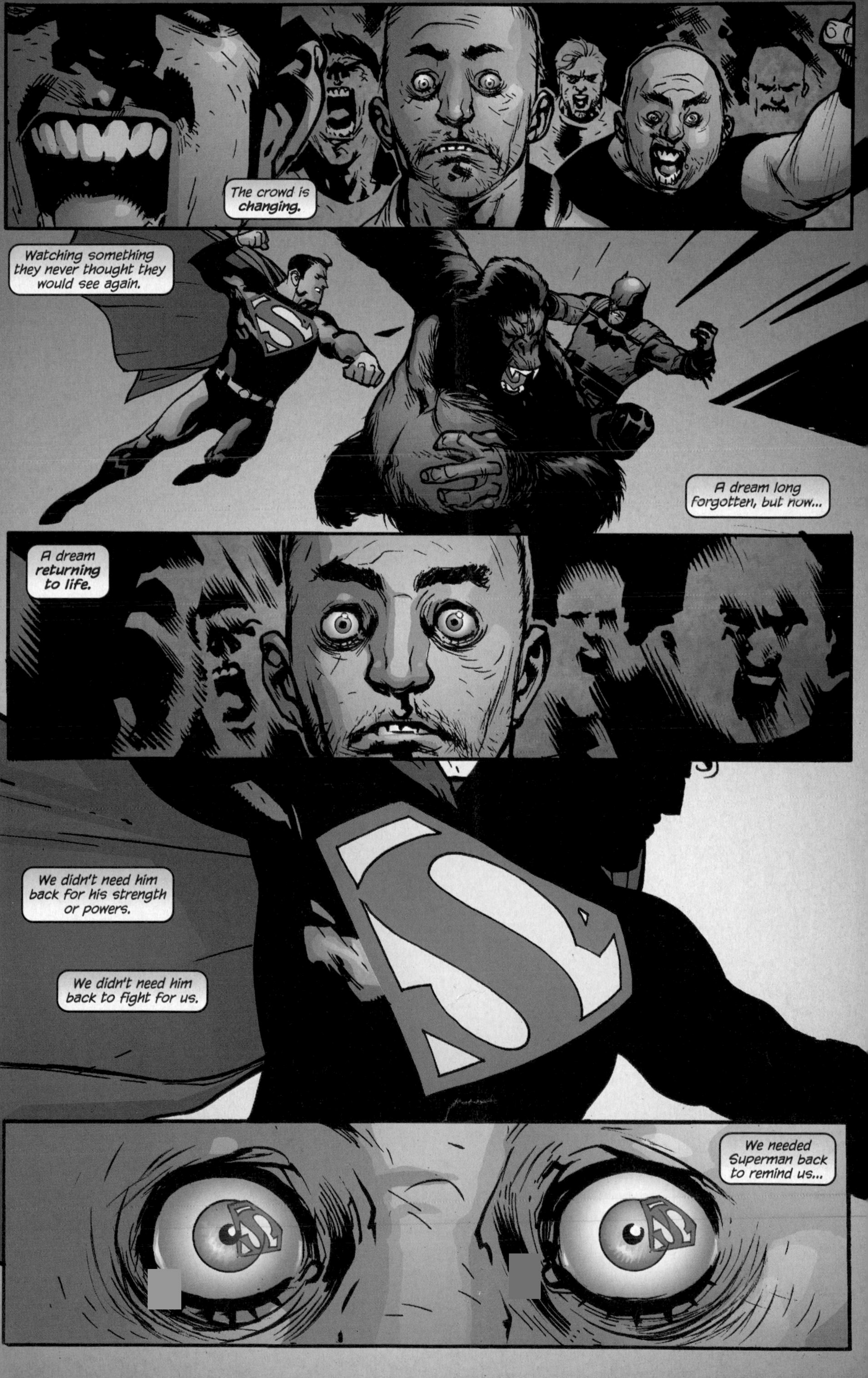
The crowd is changing.
Watching something they never thought they would see again.
A dream long forgotten, but now...
A dream returning to life.
We didn't need him back for his strength or powers.
We didn't need him back to fight for us.
We needed Superman back to remind us...

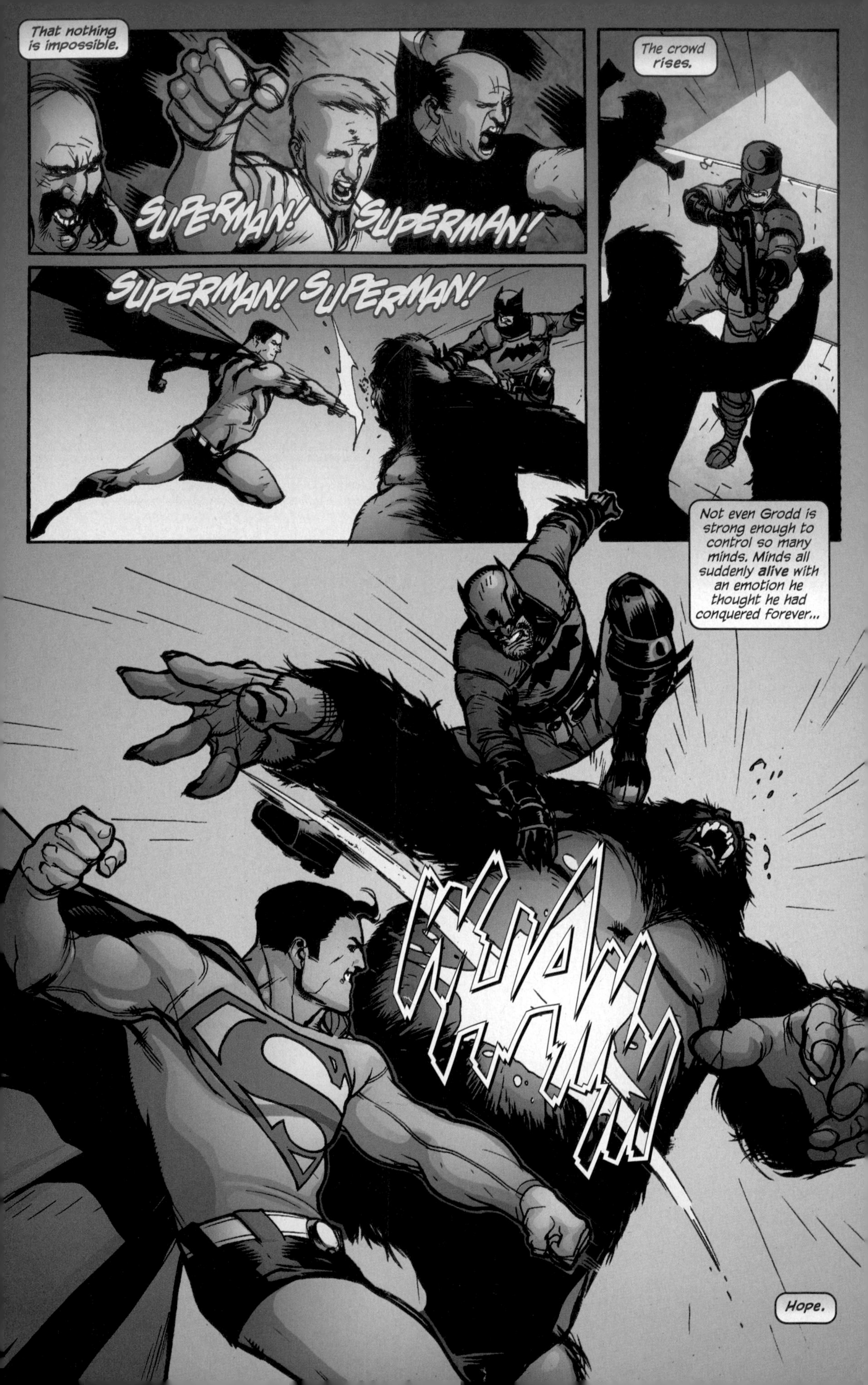
That nothing is impossible.
SUPERMAN! SUPERMAN!
The crowd rises.
SUPERMAN! SUPERMAN!
Not even Grodd is strong enough to control so many minds. Minds all suddenly alive with an emotion he thought he had conquered forever...
KWAM
Hope.

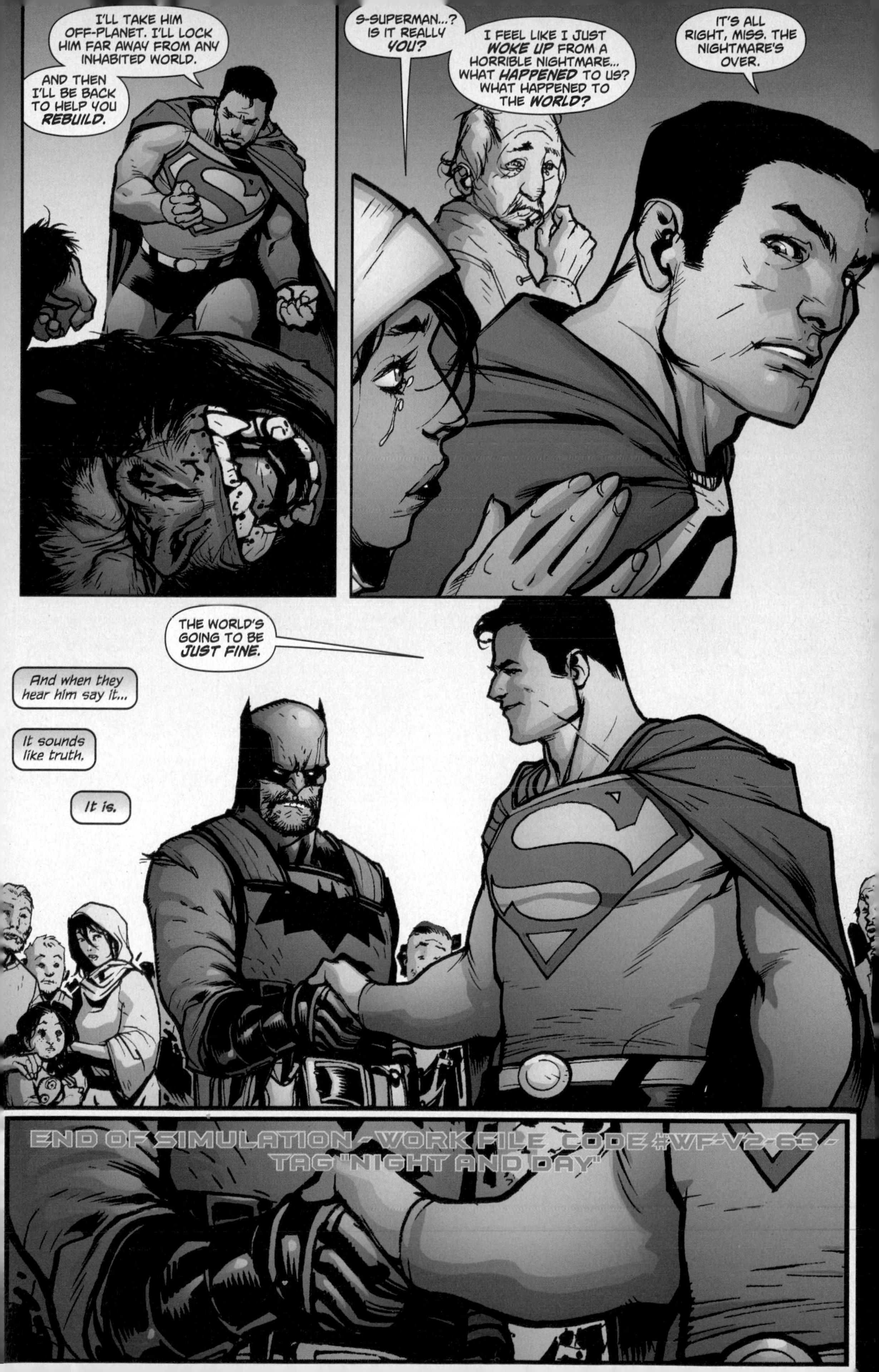
I'LL TAKE HIM OFF-PLANET. I'LL LOCK HIM FAR AWAY FROM ANY INHABITED WORLD.
AND THEN I'LL BE BACK TO HELP YOU REBUILD.
S-SUPERMAN...? IS IT REALLY YOU?
I FEEL LIKE I JUST WOKE UP FROM A HORRIBLE NIGHTMARE... WHAT HAPPENED TO US? WHAT HAPPENED TO THE WORLD?
IT'S ALL RIGHT, MISS. THE NIGHTMARE'S OVER.
THE WORLD'S GOING TO BE JUST FINE.
And when they hear him say it...
It sounds like truth.
It is.
END OF SIMULATION - WORK FILE CODE #WF-V2-63 - TAG "NIGHT AND DAY"

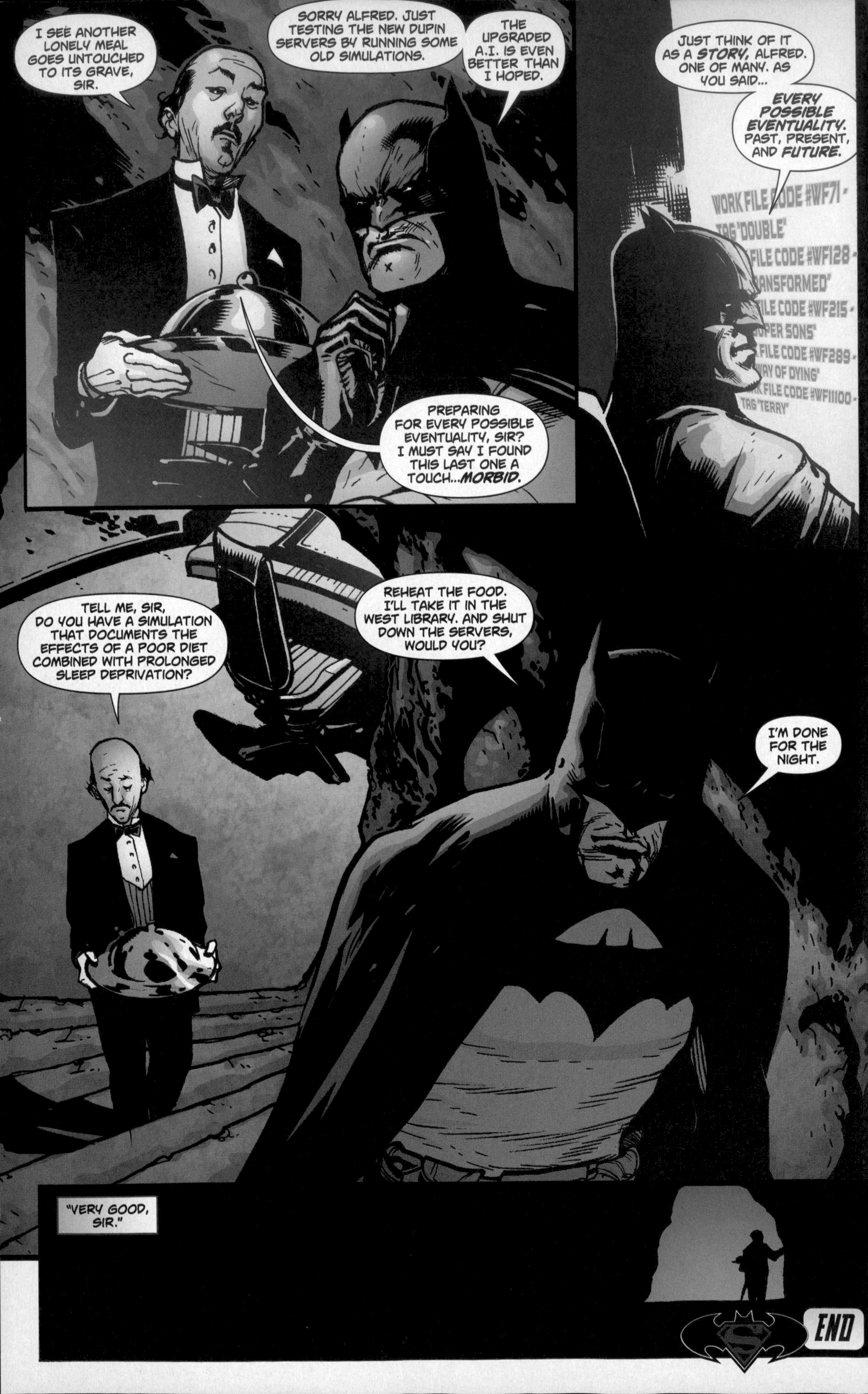
I SEE ANOTHER LONELY MEAL GOES UNTOUCHED TO ITS GRAVE, SIR.
SORRY ALFRED. JUST TESTING THE NEW DUPIN SERVERS BY RUNNING SOME OLD SIMULATIONS.
THE UPGRADED A.I. IS EVEN BETTER THAN I HOPED.
PREPARING FOR EVERY POSSIBLE EVENTUALITY, SIR? I MUST SAY I FOUND THIS LAST ONE A TOUCH...MORBID.
JUST THINK OF IT AS A STORY, ALFRED. ONE OF MANY. AS YOU SAID...
EVERY POSSIBLE EVENTUALITY. PAST, PRESENT, AND FUTURE.
WORK FILE CODE #WF71 -
TAG "DOUBLE"
FILE CODE #WF128 -
ANSFORMED"
FILE CODE #WF215 -
PER SONS"
FILE CODE #WF289 -
AY OF DYING"
FILE CODE #WF11100 -
TAG "TERRY"
TELL ME, SIR, DO YOU HAVE A SIMULATION THAT DOCUMENTS THE EFFECTS OF A POOR DIET COMBINED WITH PROLONGED SLEEP DEPRIVATION?
REHEAT THE FOOD. I'LL TAKE IT IN THE WEST LIBRARY. AND SHUT DOWN THE SERVERS, WOULD YOU?
I'M DONE FOR THE NIGHT.
"VERY GOOD, SIR."
END

SUPERMAN/BATMAN No. 65
Dustin Nguyen

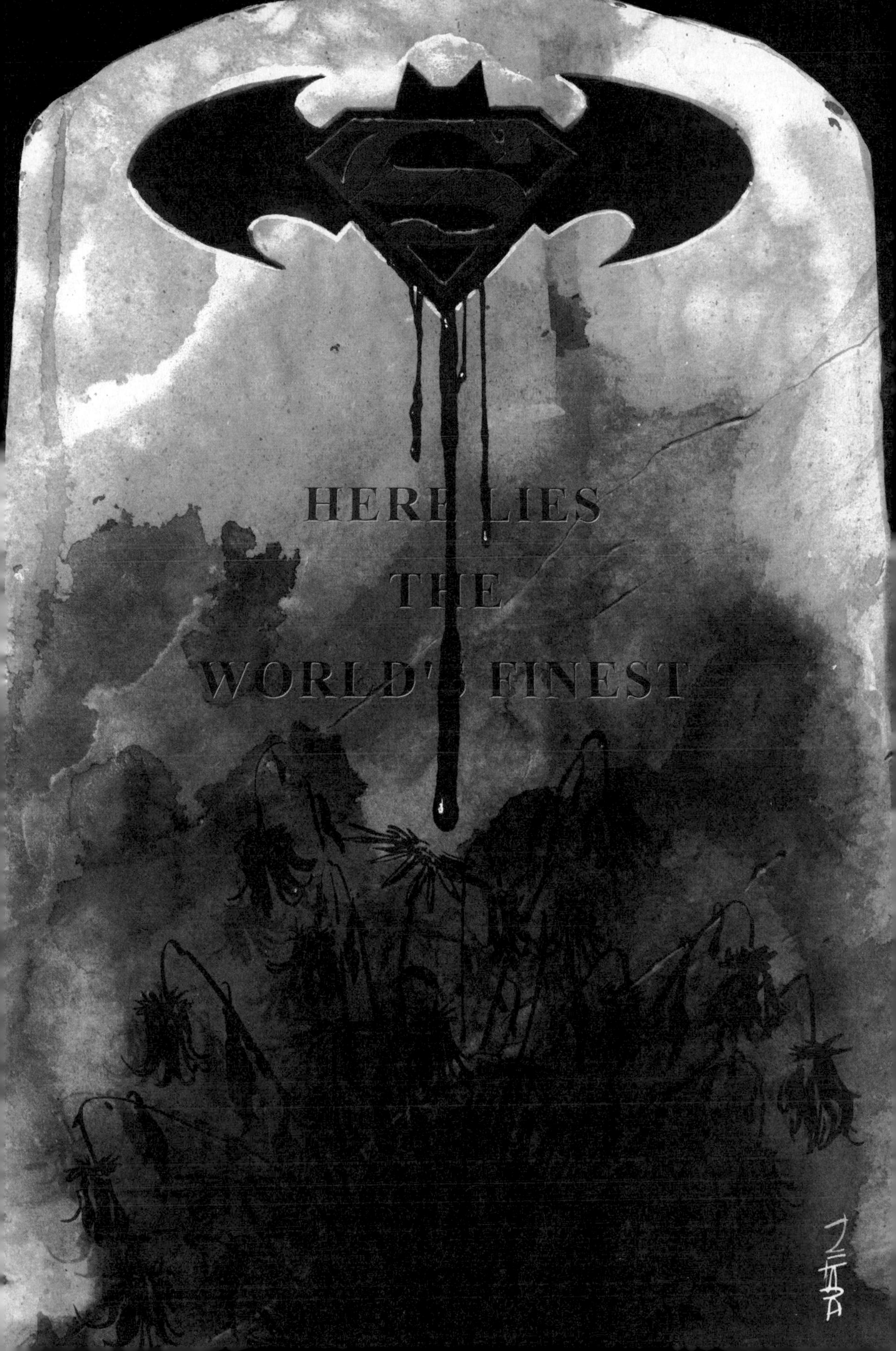

SWEET DREAMS

Writers: Peter Johnson and Matt Cherniss
Artists: Brian Stelfreeze, Brian Haberlin, Kelley Jones,
Joe Quinones, Federico Dallocchio

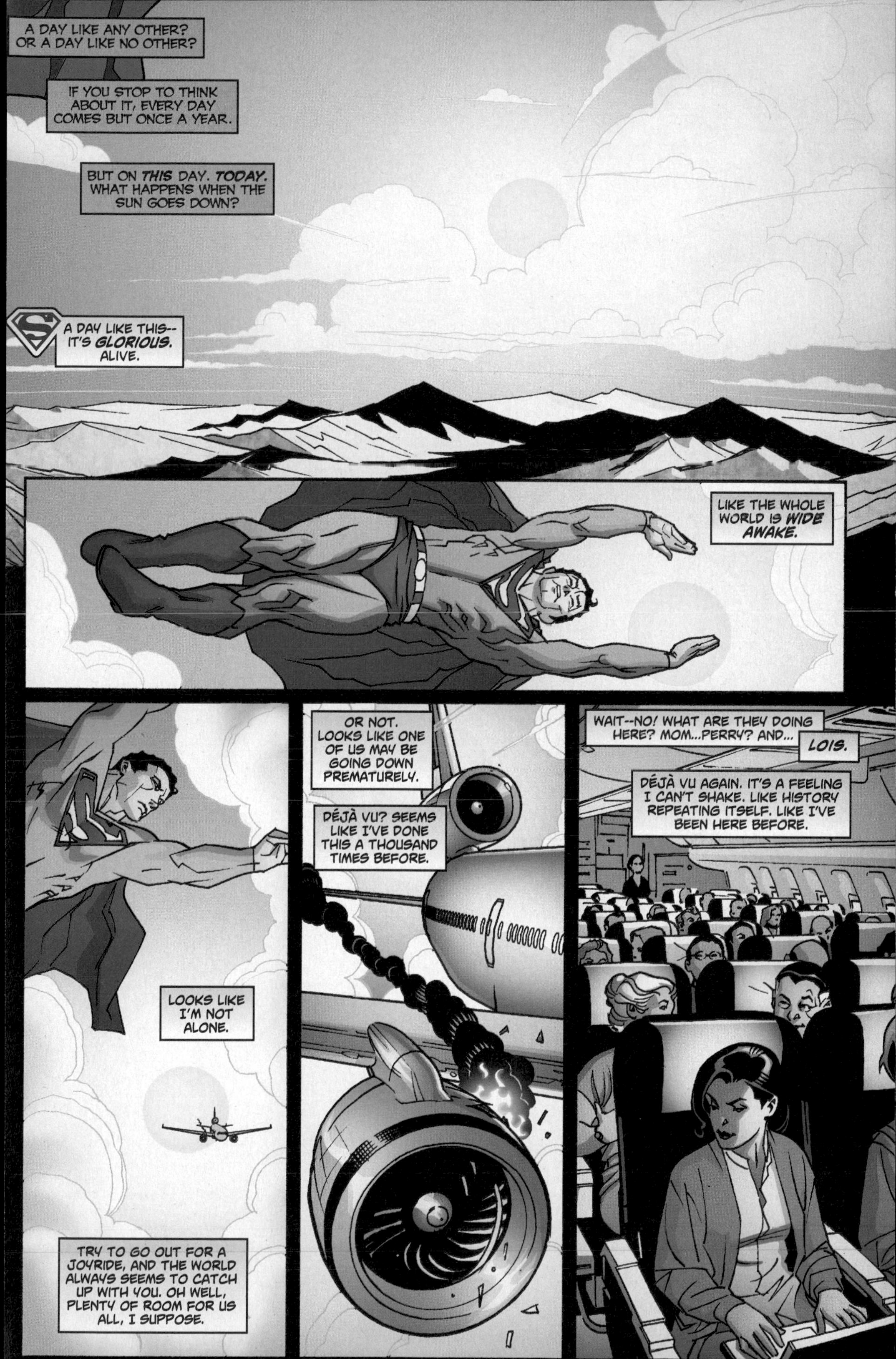

A DAY LIKE ANY OTHER? OR A DAY LIKE NO OTHER?
IF YOU STOP TO THINK ABOUT IT, EVERY DAY COMES BUT ONCE A YEAR.
BUT ON THIS DAY. TODAY. WHAT HAPPENS WHEN THE SUN GOES DOWN?
A DAY LIKE THIS-- IT'S GLORIOUS. ALIVE.
LIKE THE WHOLE WORLD IS WIDE AWAKE.
LOOKS LIKE I'M NOT ALONE.
TRY TO GO OUT FOR A JOYRIDE, AND THE WORLD ALWAYS SEEMS TO CATCH UP WITH YOU. OH WELL, PLENTY OF ROOM FOR US ALL, I SUPPOSE.
OR NOT. LOOKS LIKE ONE OF US MAY BE GOING DOWN PREMATURELY.
DÉJÀ VU? SEEMS LIKE I'VE DONE THIS A THOUSAND TIMES BEFORE.
WAIT--NO! WHAT ARE THEY DOING HERE? MOM...PERRY? AND...
LOIS.
DÉJÀ VU AGAIN. IT'S A FEELING I CAN'T SHAKE. LIKE HISTORY REPEATING ITSELF. LIKE I'VE BEEN HERE BEFORE.

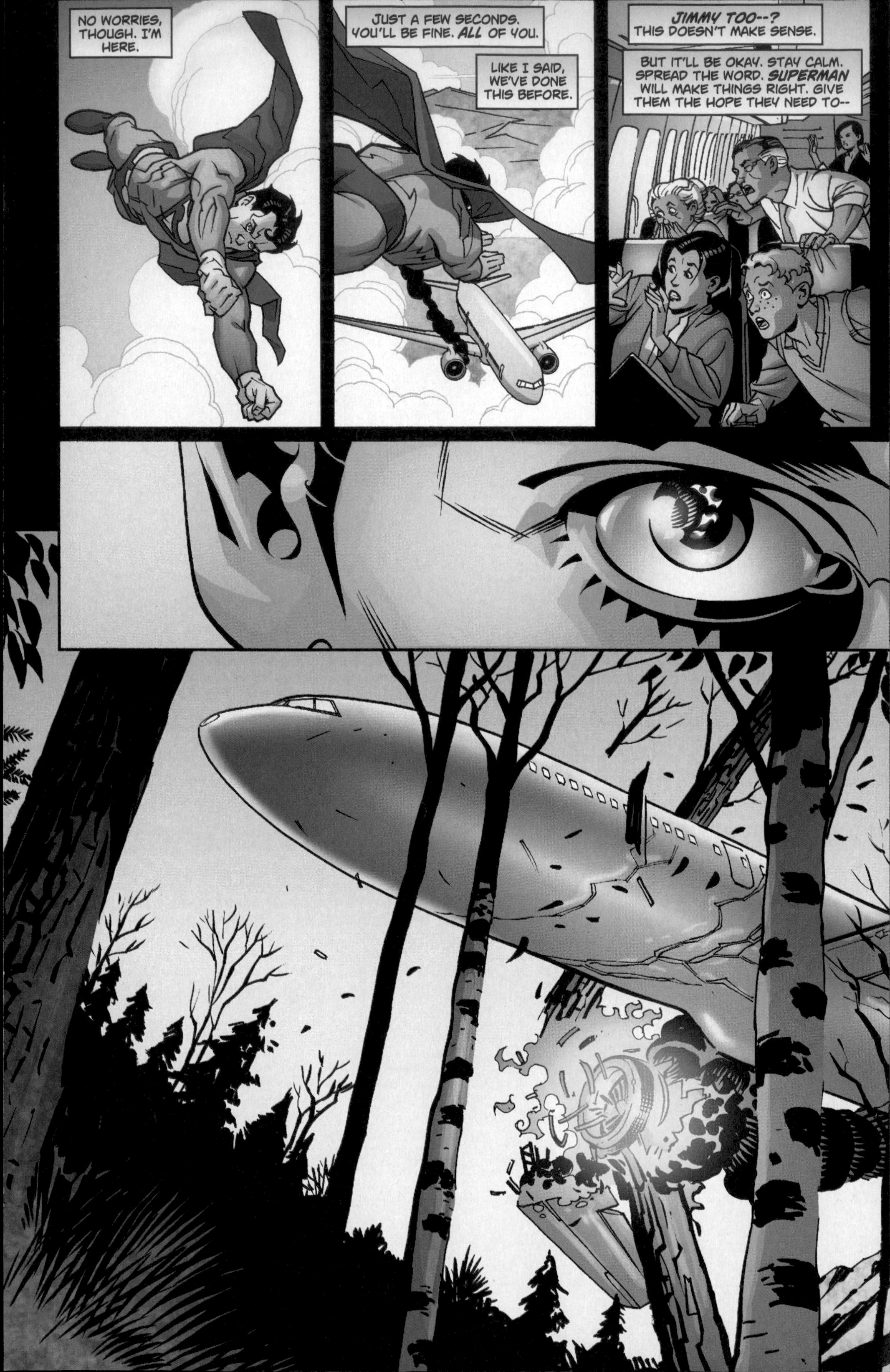
NO WORRIES, THOUGH. I'M HERE.
JUST A FEW SECONDS. YOU'LL BE FINE. ALL OF YOU.
LIKE I SAID, WE'VE DONE THIS BEFORE.
JIMMY TOO--? THIS DOESN'T MAKE SENSE.
BUT IT'LL BE OKAY. STAY CALM. SPREAD THE WORD. SUPERMAN WILL MAKE THINGS RIGHT. GIVE THEM THE HOPE THEY NEED TO--

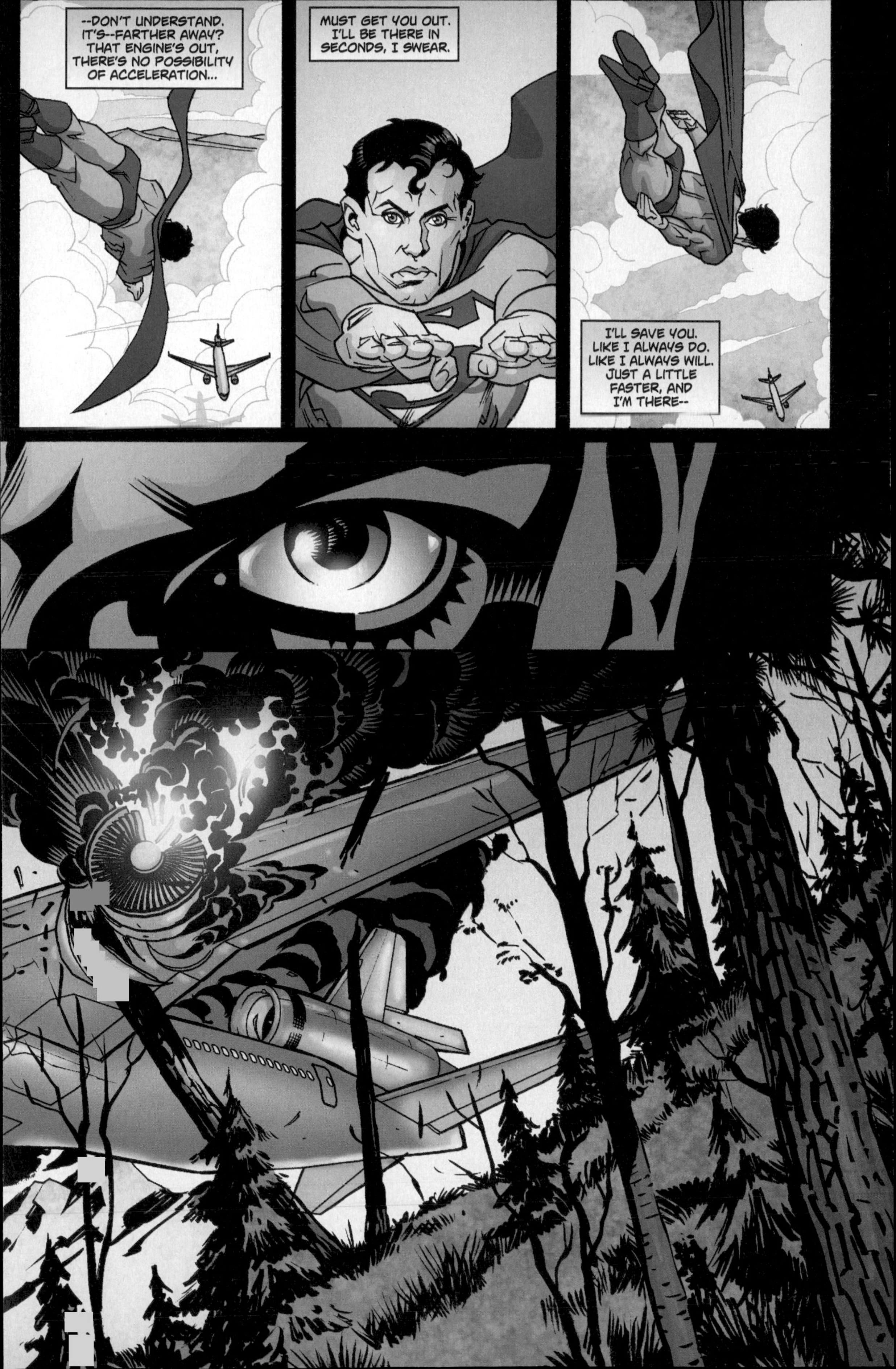
--DON'T UNDERSTAND. IT'S--FARTHER AWAY? THAT ENGINE'S OUT, THERE'S NO POSSIBILITY OF ACCELERATION...
MUST GET YOU OUT. I'LL BE THERE IN SECONDS, I SWEAR.
I'LL SAVE YOU. LIKE I ALWAYS DO. LIKE I ALWAYS WILL. JUST A LITTLE FASTER, AND I'M THERE--

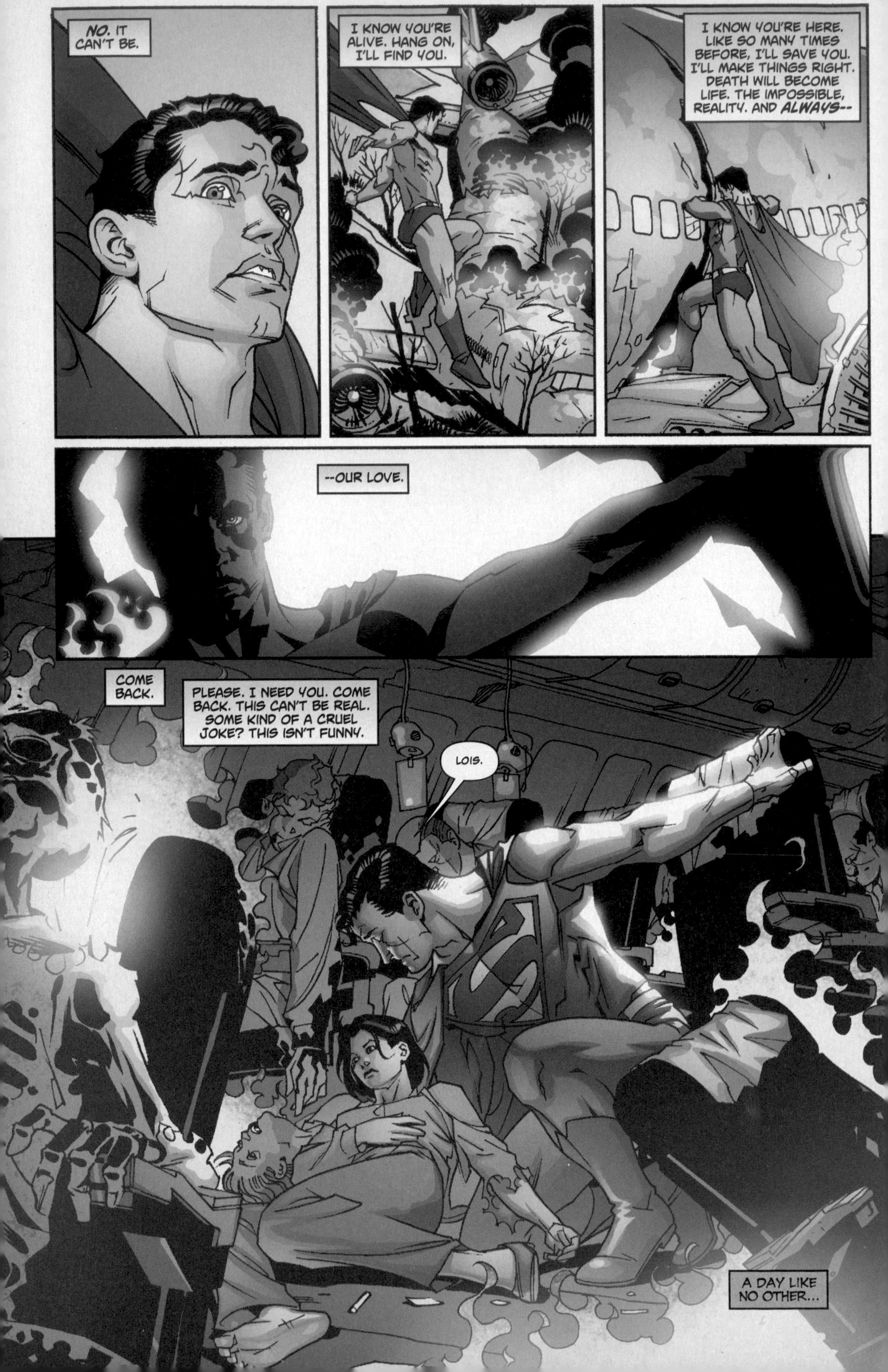
NO. IT CAN'T BE.
I KNOW YOU'RE ALIVE. HANG ON, I'LL FIND YOU.
I KNOW YOU'RE HERE. LIKE SO MANY TIMES BEFORE, I'LL SAVE YOU. I'LL MAKE THINGS RIGHT. DEATH WILL BECOME LIFE. THE IMPOSSIBLE, REALITY. AND ALWAYS--
--OUR LOVE.
COME BACK.
PLEASE. I NEED YOU. COME BACK. THIS CAN'T BE REAL. SOME KIND OF A CRUEL JOKE? THIS ISN'T FUNNY.
LOIS.
A DAY LIKE NO OTHER...

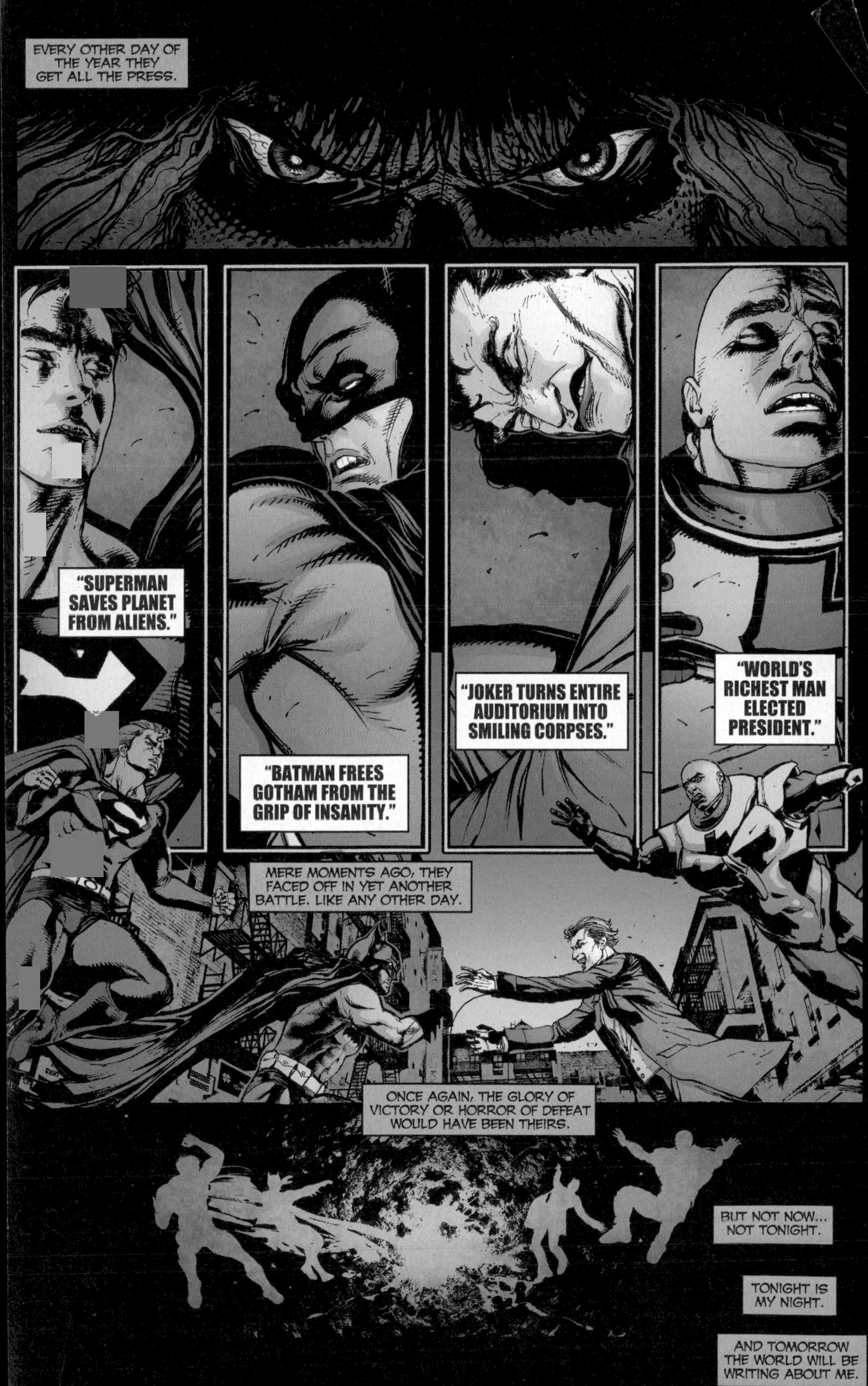
EVERY OTHER DAY OF THE YEAR THEY GET ALL THE PRESS.
"SUPERMAN SAVES PLANET FROM ALIENS."
"BATMAN FREES GOTHAM FROM THE GRIP OF INSANITY."
"JOKER TURNS ENTIRE AUDITORIUM INTO SMILING CORPSES."
"WORLD'S RICHEST MAN ELECTED PRESIDENT."
MERE MOMENTS AGO, THEY FACED OFF IN YET ANOTHER BATTLE. LIKE ANY OTHER DAY.
ONCE AGAIN, THE GLORY OF VICTORY OR HORROR OF DEFEAT WOULD HAVE BEEN THEIRS.
BUT NOT NOW... NOT TONIGHT.
TONIGHT IS MY NIGHT.
AND TOMORROW THE WORLD WILL BE WRITING ABOUT ME.

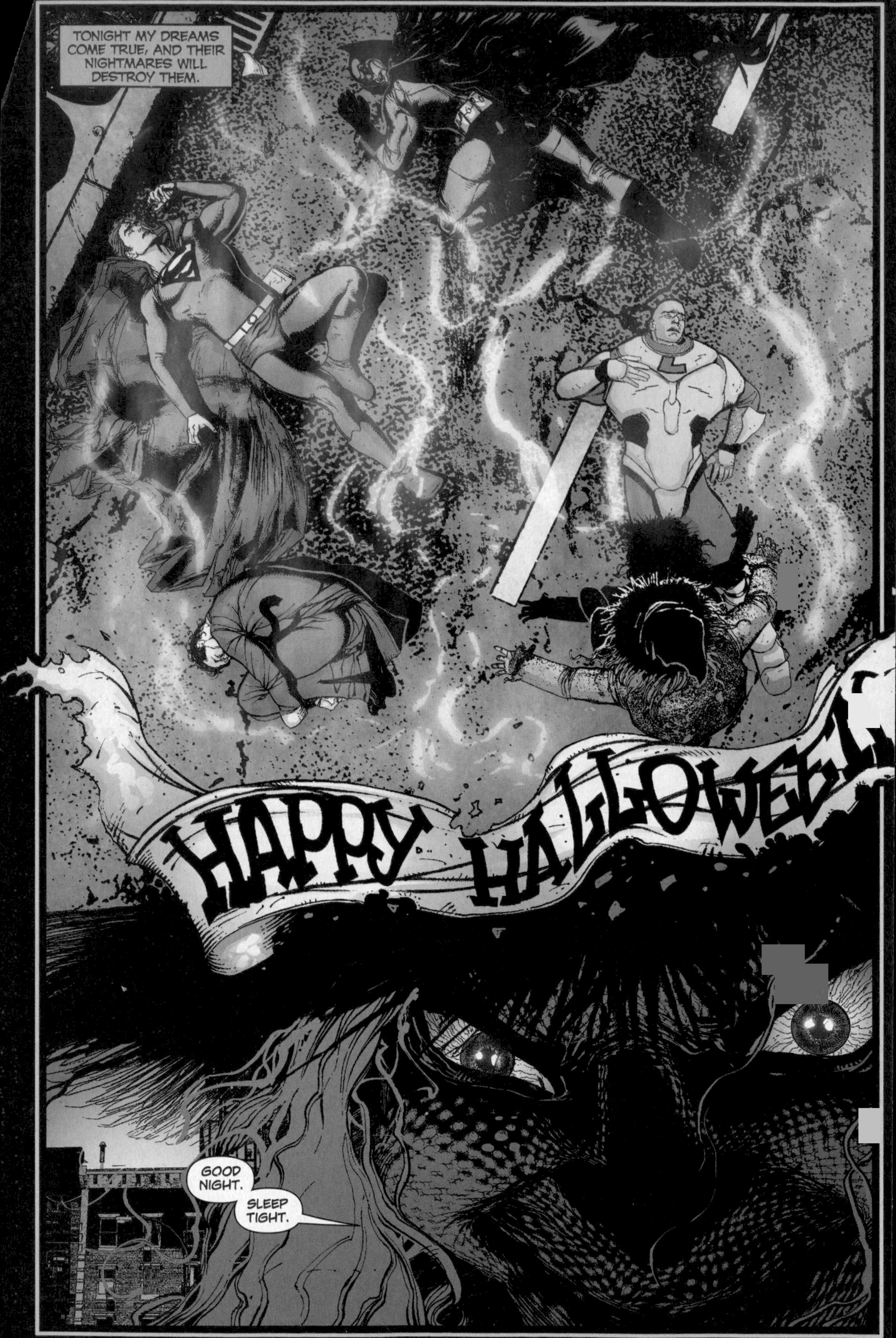
TONIGHT MY DREAMS COME TRUE, AND THEIR NIGHTMARES WILL DESTROY THEM.
HAPPY HALLOWEE
GOOD NIGHT.
SLEEP TIGHT.

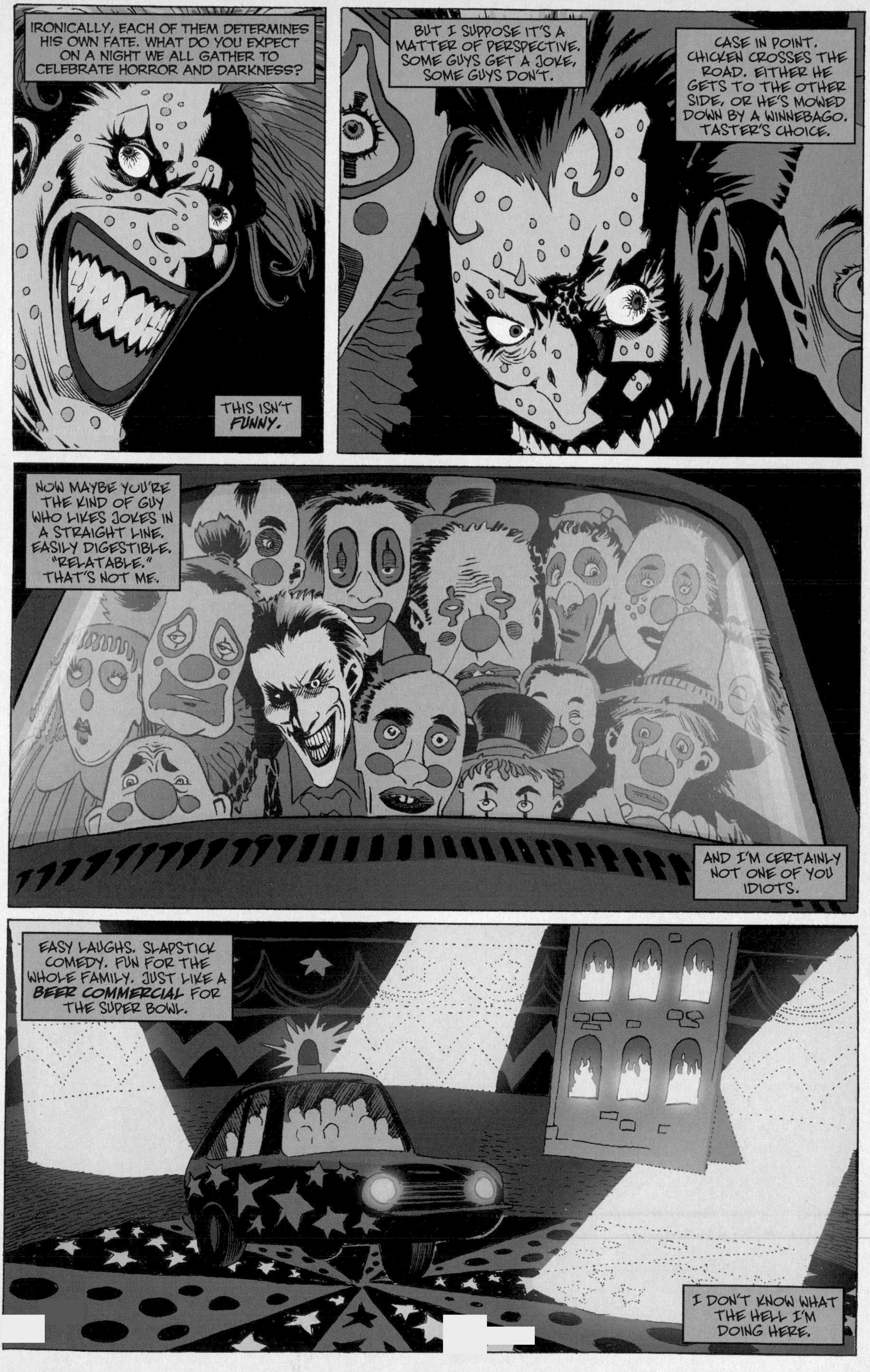
IRONICALLY, EACH OF THEM DETERMINES HIS OWN FATE. WHAT DO YOU EXPECT ON A NIGHT WE ALL GATHER TO CELEBRATE HORROR AND DARKNESS?
THIS ISN'T FUNNY.
BUT I SUPPOSE IT'S A MATTER OF PERSPECTIVE. SOME GUYS GET A JOKE, SOME GUYS DON'T.
CASE IN POINT. CHICKEN CROSSES THE ROAD. EITHER HE GETS TO THE OTHER SIDE, OR HE'S MOWED DOWN BY A WINNEBAGO. TASTER'S CHOICE.
NOW MAYBE YOU'RE THE KIND OF GUY WHO LIKES JOKES IN A STRAIGHT LINE. EASILY DIGESTIBLE. "RELATABLE." THAT'S NOT ME.
AND I'M CERTAINLY NOT ONE OF YOU IDIOTS.
EASY LAUGHS. SLAPSTICK COMEDY. FUN FOR THE WHOLE FAMILY. JUST LIKE A BEER COMMERCIAL FOR THE SUPER BOWL.
I DON'T KNOW WHAT THE HELL I'M DOING HERE.

MEANS TO AN END, I GUESS. MEANS TO AN END. KEEP TELLING MYSELF THAT. JUST LIKE A GREAT JOKE, THIS MUST BE LEADING SOMEWHERE. RIGHT?

HELP! SAVE ME!

EXCEPT THAT NO ONE IS TAKING ME SERIOUSLY.

ME. SERIOUSLY. GREAT OXYMORON.

THOUGH NONE OF THESE MORONS WOULD GET THE JOKE.

TOO BUSY WITH THEIR PIE FIGHTS.

SAME THING TOMORROW. AND THE NEXT DAY. AND THE NEXT HUNDRED.

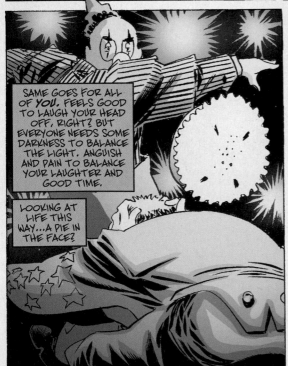

SAME GOES FOR ALL OF YOU. FEELS GOOD TO LAUGH YOUR HEAD OFF, RIGHT? BUT EVERYONE NEEDS SOME DARKNESS TO BALANCE THE LIGHT. ANGUISH AND PAIN TO BALANCE YOUR LAUGHTER AND GOOD TIME.

LOOKING AT LIFE THIS WAY...A PIE IN THE FACE?

COULD ACTUALLY HURT SOMEONE.

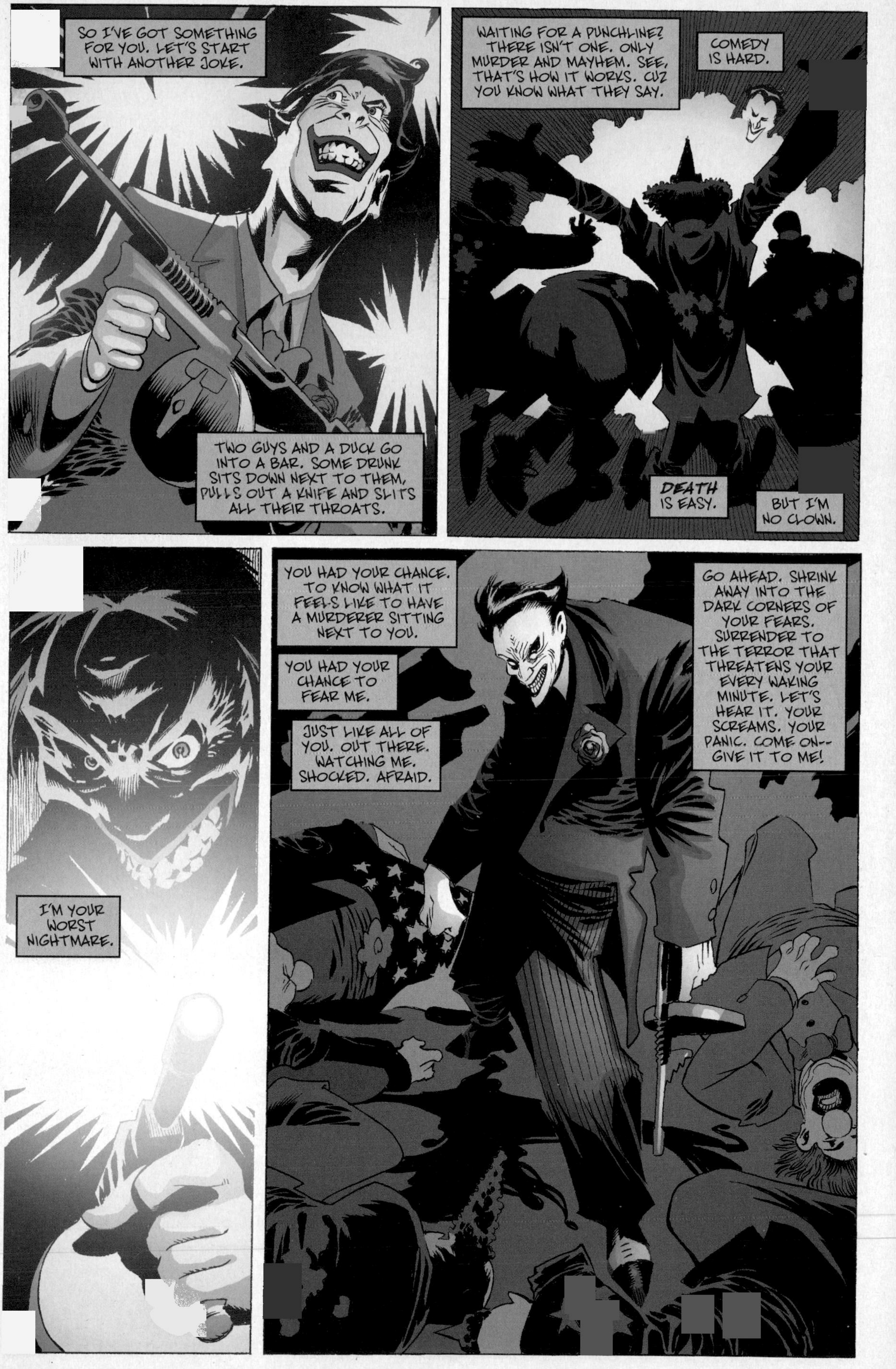
SO I'VE GOT SOMETHING FOR YOU. LET'S START WITH ANOTHER JOKE.
TWO GUYS AND A DUCK GO INTO A BAR. SOME DRUNK SITS DOWN NEXT TO THEM, PULLS OUT A KNIFE AND SLITS ALL THEIR THROATS.
WAITING FOR A PUNCHLINE? THERE ISN'T ONE. ONLY MURDER AND MAYHEM. SEE, THAT'S HOW IT WORKS. CUZ YOU KNOW WHAT THEY SAY.
COMEDY IS HARD.
DEATH IS EASY.
BUT I'M NO CLOWN.
I'M YOUR WORST NIGHTMARE.
YOU HAD YOUR CHANCE. TO KNOW WHAT IT FEELS LIKE TO HAVE A MURDERER SITTING NEXT TO YOU.
YOU HAD YOUR CHANCE TO FEAR ME.
JUST LIKE ALL OF YOU. OUT THERE. WATCHING ME. SHOCKED. AFRAID.
GO AHEAD. SHRINK AWAY INTO THE DARK CORNERS OF YOUR FEARS. SURRENDER TO THE TERROR THAT THREATENS YOUR EVERY WAKING MINUTE. LET'S HEAR IT. YOUR SCREAMS. YOUR PANIC. COME ON-- GIVE IT TO ME!

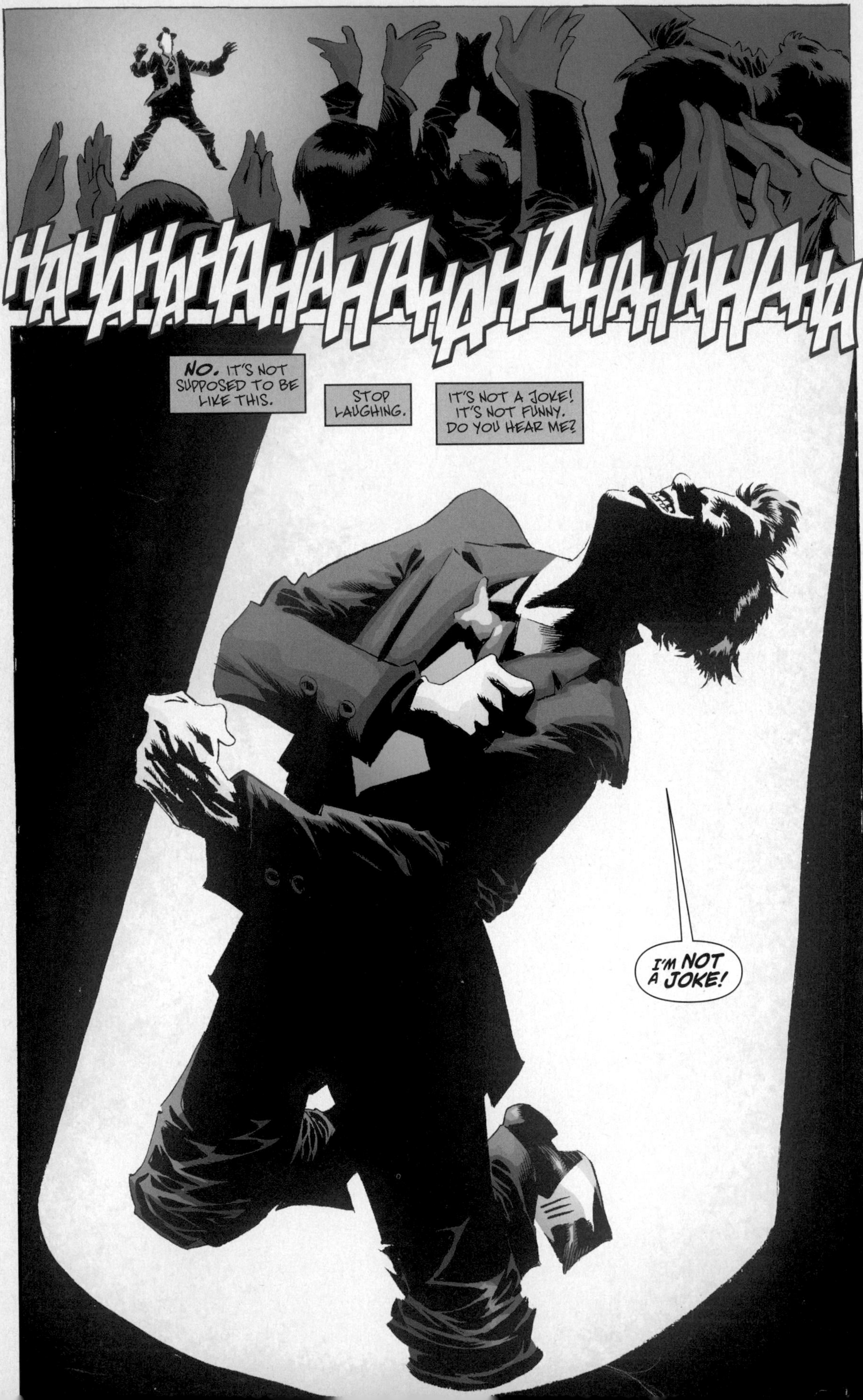
HAHAHAHAHAHAHAHAHAHAHAHAHAHAHAHA
NO. IT'S NOT SUPPOSED TO BE LIKE THIS.
STOP LAUGHING.
IT'S NOT A JOKE! IT'S NOT FUNNY. DO YOU HEAR ME?
I'M NOT A JOKE!

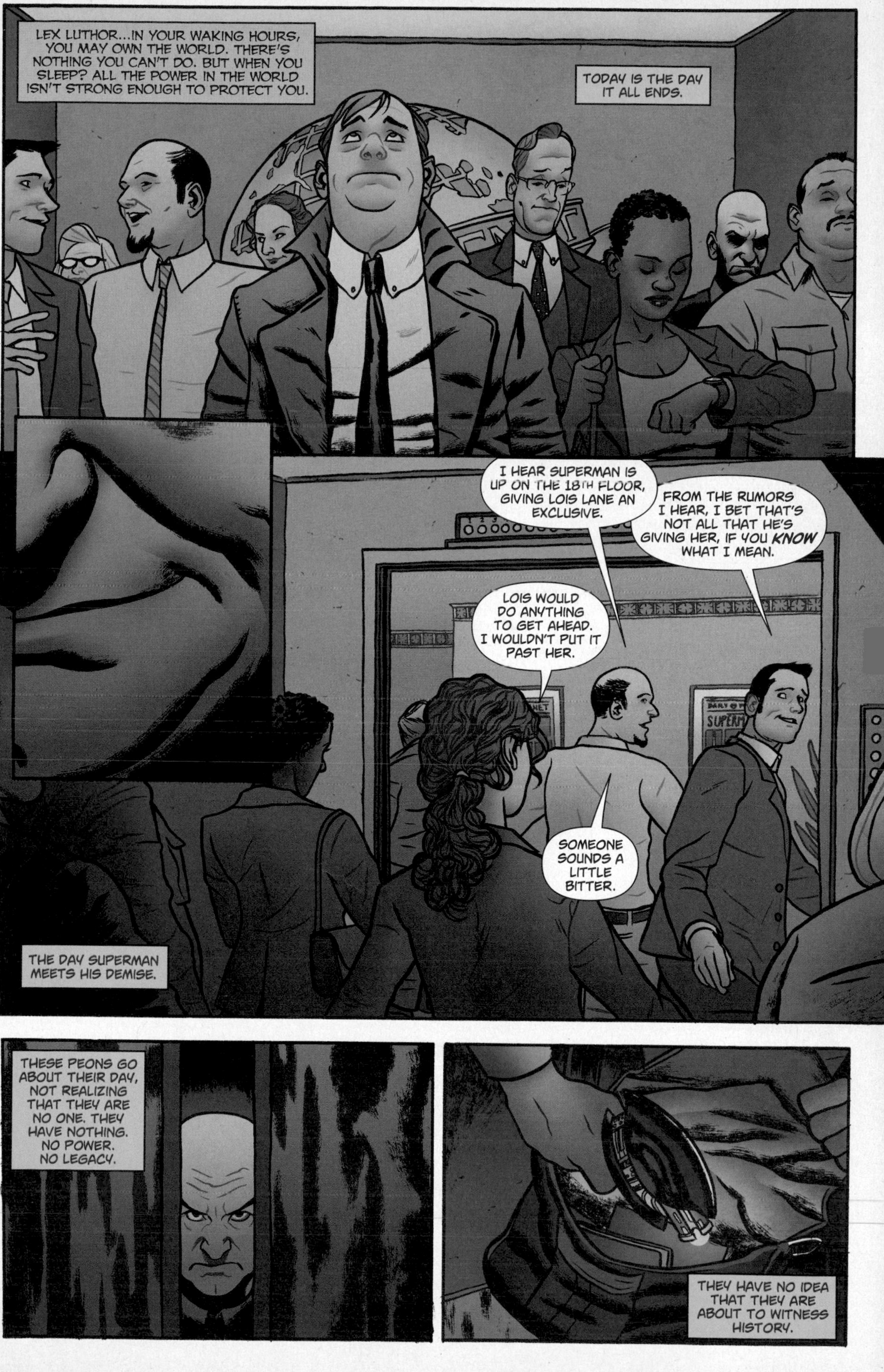
LEX LUTHOR...IN YOUR WAKING HOURS, YOU MAY OWN THE WORLD. THERE'S NOTHING YOU CAN'T DO. BUT WHEN YOU SLEEP? ALL THE POWER IN THE WORLD ISN'T STRONG ENOUGH TO PROTECT YOU.
TODAY IS THE DAY IT ALL ENDS.
I HEAR SUPERMAN IS UP ON THE 18TH FLOOR, GIVING LOIS LANE AN EXCLUSIVE.
FROM THE RUMORS I HEAR, I BET THAT'S NOT ALL THAT HE'S GIVING HER, IF YOU KNOW WHAT I MEAN.
LOIS WOULD DO ANYTHING TO GET AHEAD. I WOULDN'T PUT IT PAST HER.
SOMEONE SOUNDS A LITTLE BITTER.
THE DAY SUPERMAN MEETS HIS DEMISE.
THESE PEONS GO ABOUT THEIR DAY, NOT REALIZING THAT THEY ARE NO ONE. THEY HAVE NOTHING. NO POWER. NO LEGACY.
THEY HAVE NO IDEA THAT THEY ARE ABOUT TO WITNESS HISTORY.

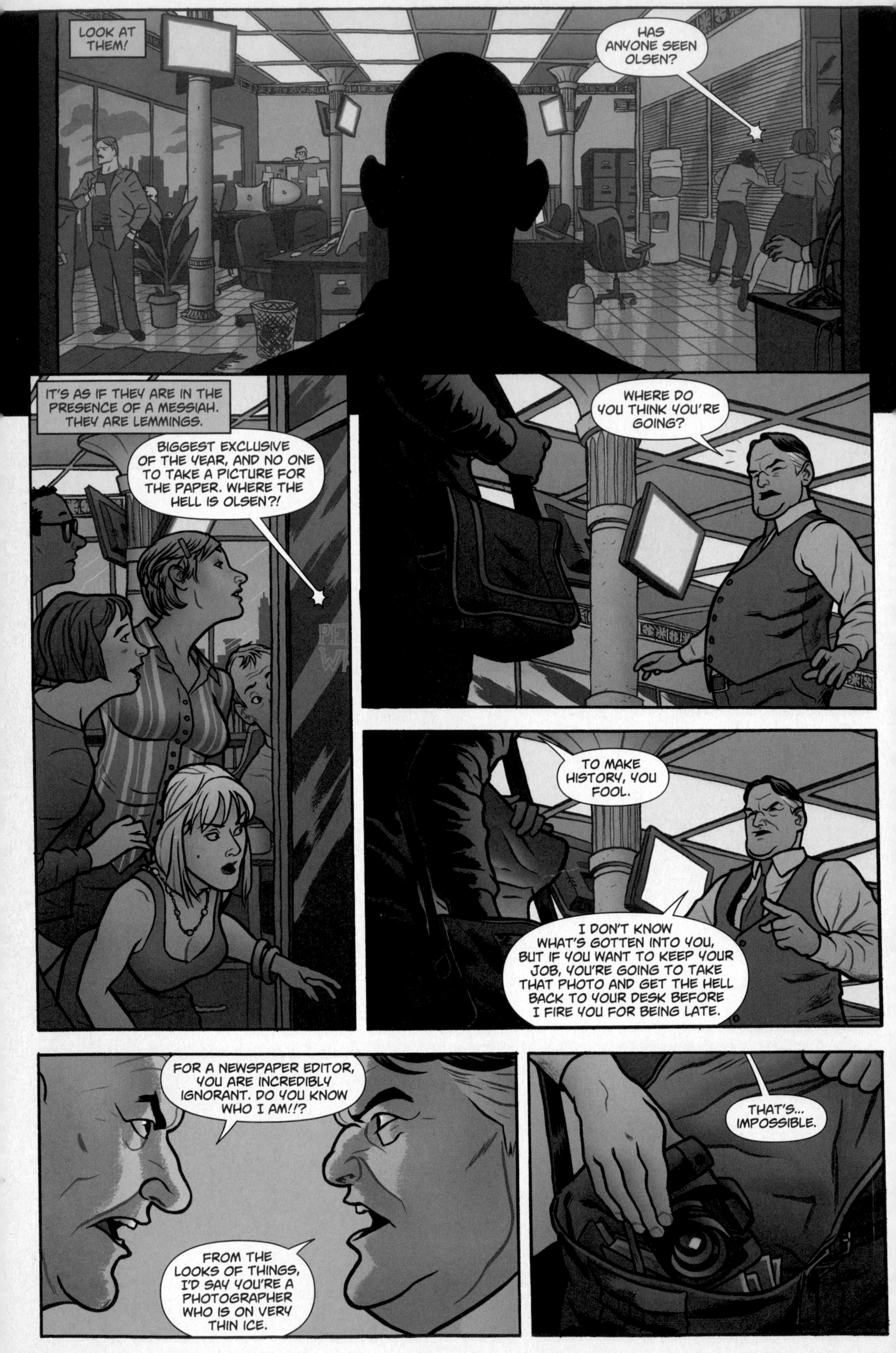
LOOK AT THEM!
HAS ANYONE SEEN OLSEN?
IT'S AS IF THEY ARE IN THE PRESENCE OF A MESSIAH. THEY ARE LEMMINGS.
BIGGEST EXCLUSIVE OF THE YEAR, AND NO ONE TO TAKE A PICTURE FOR THE PAPER. WHERE THE HELL IS OLSEN?!
WHERE DO YOU THINK YOU'RE GOING?
TO MAKE HISTORY, YOU FOOL.
I DON'T KNOW WHAT'S GOTTEN INTO YOU, BUT IF YOU WANT TO KEEP YOUR JOB, YOU'RE GOING TO TAKE THAT PHOTO AND GET THE HELL BACK TO YOUR DESK BEFORE I FIRE YOU FOR BEING LATE.
FOR A NEWSPAPER EDITOR, YOU ARE INCREDIBLY IGNORANT. DO YOU KNOW WHO I AM!!?
FROM THE LOOKS OF THINGS, I'D SAY YOU'RE A PHOTOGRAPHER WHO IS ON VERY THIN ICE.
THAT'S... IMPOSSIBLE.

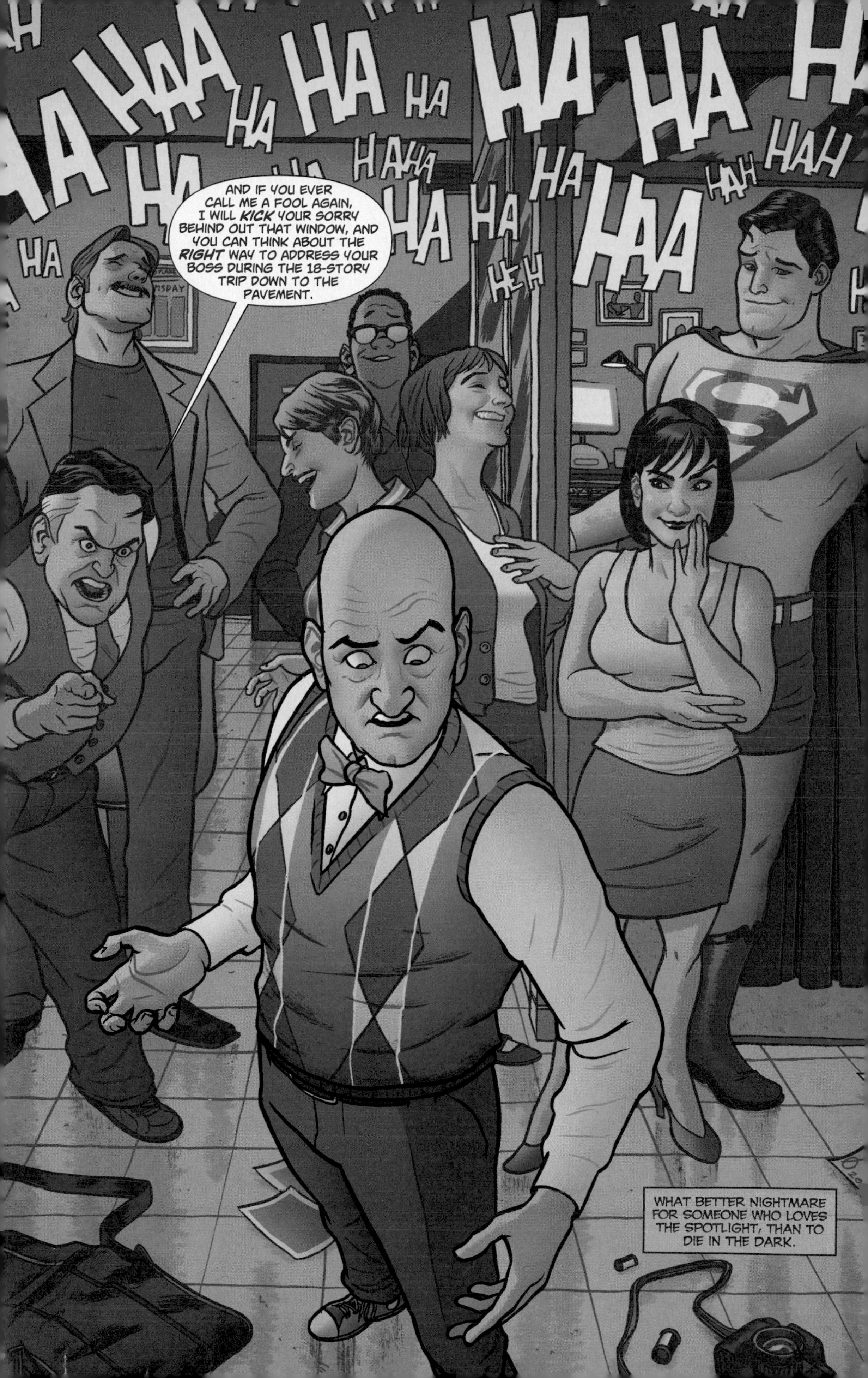
HA HA HA HA HA HA HA HA HA HA HA HA
HAHA HA HA HAH HAH HAA HEH HA
AND IF YOU EVER CALL ME A FOOL AGAIN, I WILL KICK YOUR SORRY BEHIND OUT THAT WINDOW, AND YOU CAN THINK ABOUT THE RIGHT WAY TO ADDRESS YOUR BOSS DURING THE 18-STORY TRIP DOWN TO THE PAVEMENT.
WHAT BETTER NIGHTMARE FOR SOMEONE WHO LOVES THE SPOTLIGHT, THAN TO DIE IN THE DARK.

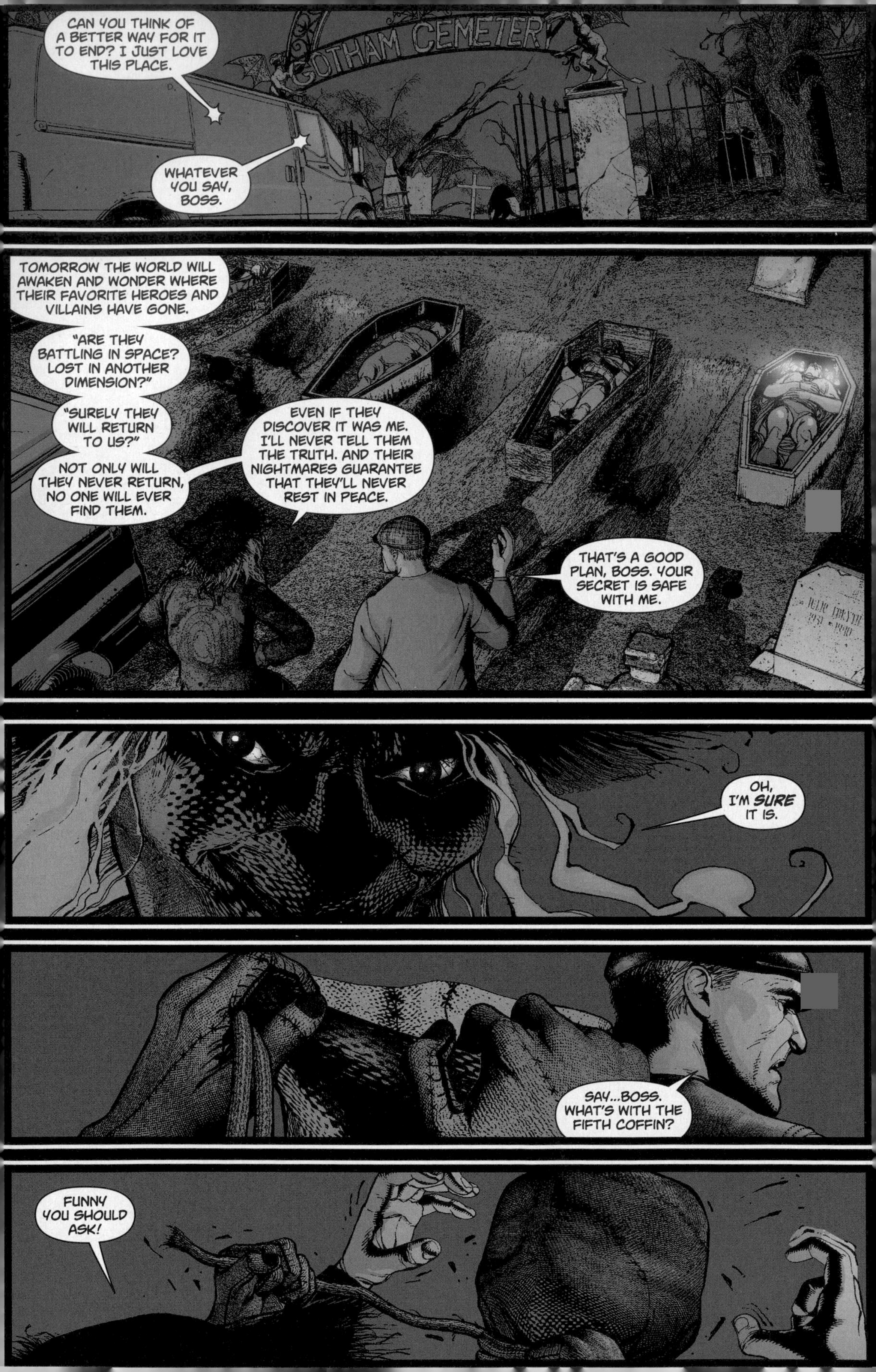
GOTHAM CEMETERY
CAN YOU THINK OF A BETTER WAY FOR IT TO END? I JUST LOVE THIS PLACE.
WHATEVER YOU SAY, BOSS.
TOMORROW THE WORLD WILL AWAKEN AND WONDER WHERE THEIR FAVORITE HEROES AND VILLAINS HAVE GONE.
"ARE THEY BATTLING IN SPACE? LOST IN ANOTHER DIMENSION?"
"SURELY THEY WILL RETURN TO US?"
NOT ONLY WILL THEY NEVER RETURN, NO ONE WILL EVER FIND THEM.
EVEN IF THEY DISCOVER IT WAS ME. I'LL NEVER TELL THEM THE TRUTH. AND THEIR NIGHTMARES GUARANTEE THAT THEY'LL NEVER REST IN PEACE.
THAT'S A GOOD PLAN, BOSS. YOUR SECRET IS SAFE WITH ME.
OH, I'M ***SURE*** IT IS.
SAY...BOSS. WHAT'S WITH THE FIFTH COFFIN?
FUNNY YOU SHOULD ASK!

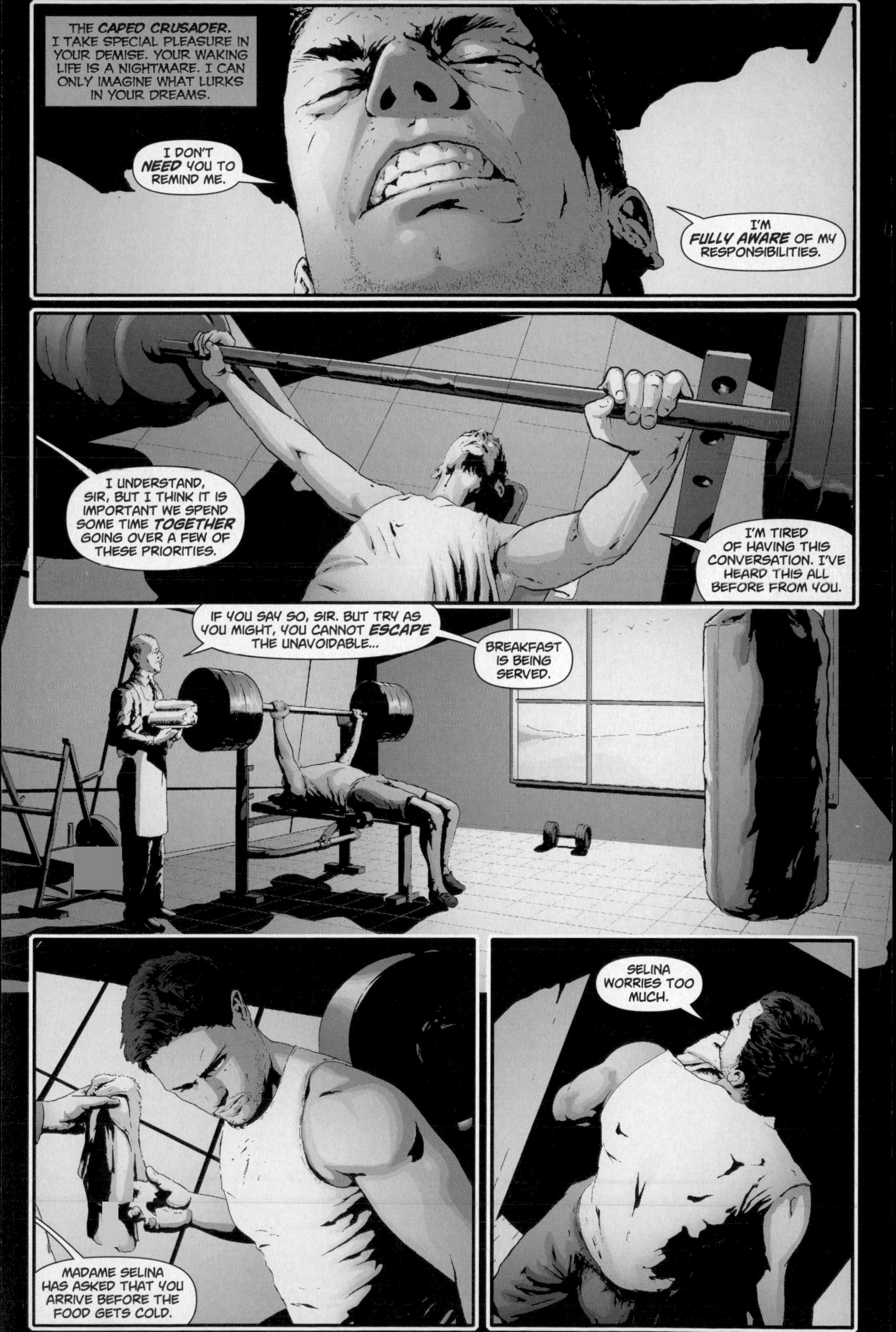
THE CAPED CRUSADER. I TAKE SPECIAL PLEASURE IN YOUR DEMISE. YOUR WAKING LIFE IS A NIGHTMARE. I CAN ONLY IMAGINE WHAT LURKS IN YOUR DREAMS.
I DON'T NEED YOU TO REMIND ME.
I'M FULLY AWARE OF MY RESPONSIBILITIES.
I UNDERSTAND, SIR, BUT I THINK IT IS IMPORTANT WE SPEND SOME TIME TOGETHER GOING OVER A FEW OF THESE PRIORITIES.
I'M TIRED OF HAVING THIS CONVERSATION. I'VE HEARD THIS ALL BEFORE FROM YOU.
IF YOU SAY SO, SIR. BUT TRY AS YOU MIGHT, YOU CANNOT ESCAPE THE UNAVOIDABLE...
BREAKFAST IS BEING SERVED.
MADAME SELINA HAS ASKED THAT YOU ARRIVE BEFORE THE FOOD GETS COLD.
SELINA WORRIES TOO MUCH.

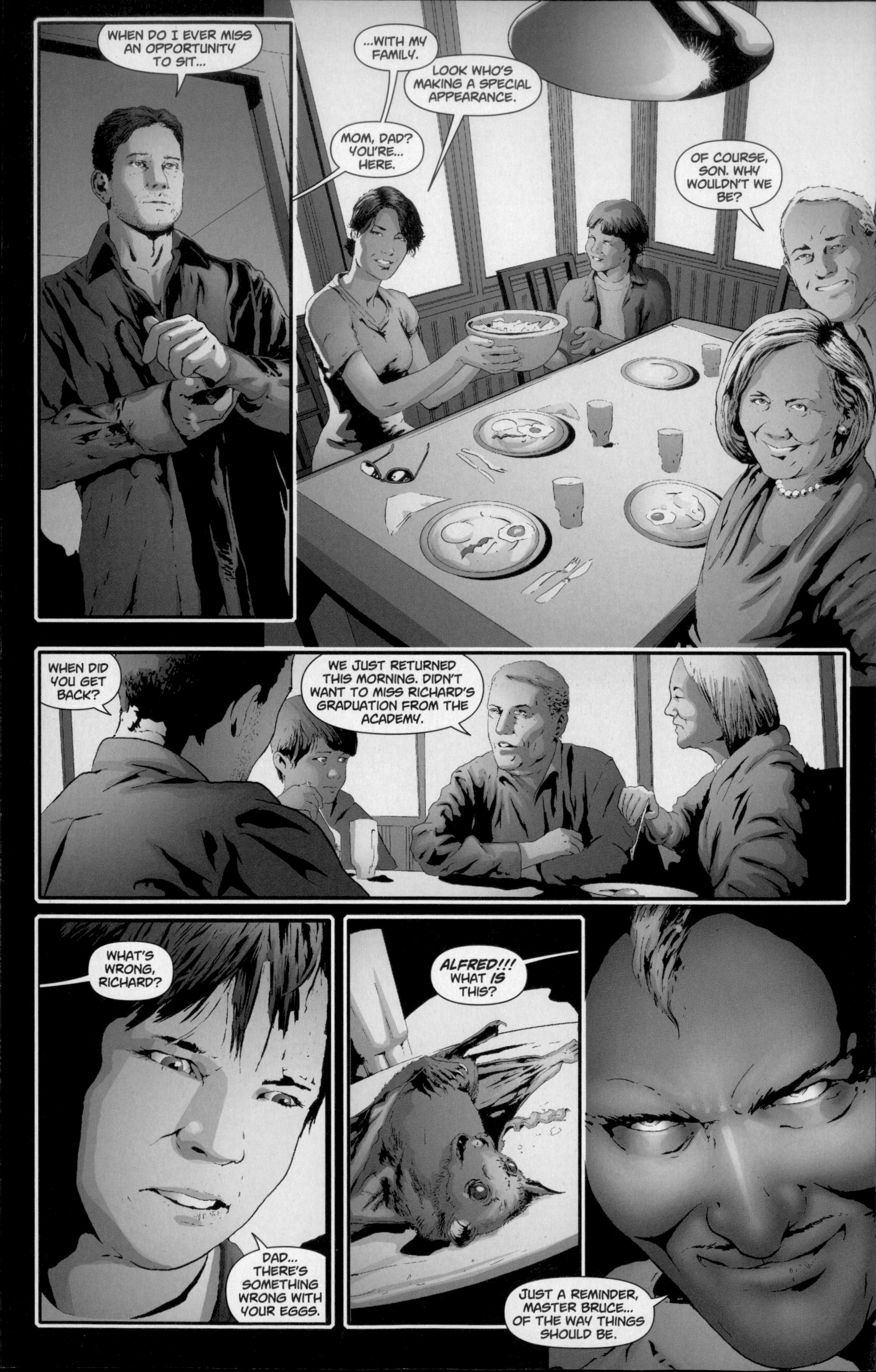
WHEN DO I EVER MISS AN OPPORTUNITY TO SIT...
...WITH MY FAMILY.
LOOK WHO'S MAKING A SPECIAL APPEARANCE.
MOM, DAD? YOU'RE... HERE.
OF COURSE, SON. WHY WOULDN'T WE BE?
WHEN DID YOU GET BACK?
WE JUST RETURNED THIS MORNING. DIDN'T WANT TO MISS RICHARD'S GRADUATION FROM THE ACADEMY.
WHAT'S WRONG, RICHARD?
DAD... THERE'S SOMETHING WRONG WITH YOUR EGGS.
ALFRED!!! WHAT IS THIS?
JUST A REMINDER, MASTER BRUCE... OF THE WAY THINGS SHOULD BE.

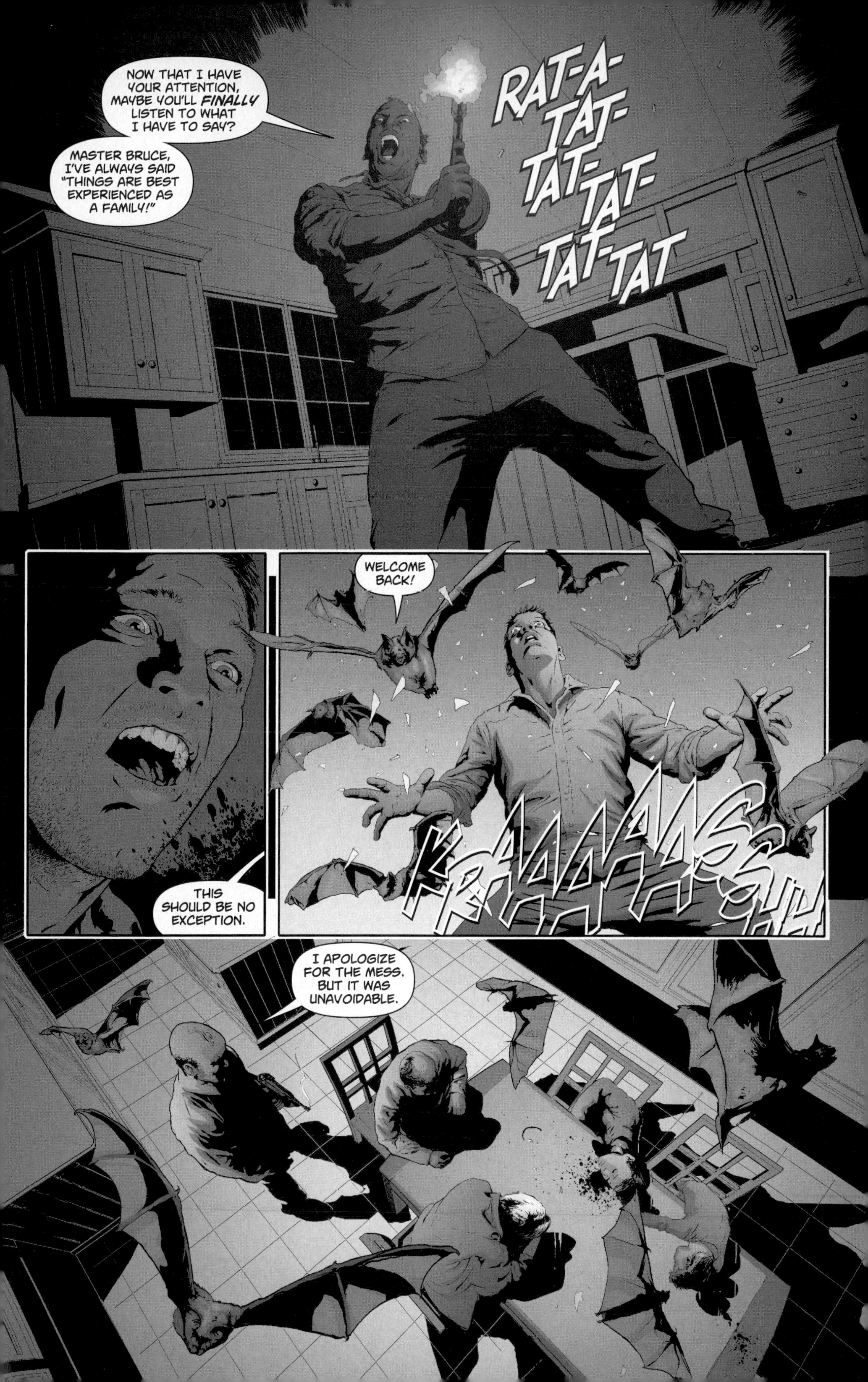
NOW THAT I HAVE YOUR ATTENTION, MAYBE YOU'LL FINALLY LISTEN TO WHAT I HAVE TO SAY?
MASTER BRUCE, I'VE ALWAYS SAID "THINGS ARE BEST EXPERIENCED AS A FAMILY!"
RAT-A-TAT-TAT-TAT-TAT-TAT
THIS SHOULD BE NO EXCEPTION.
WELCOME BACK!
I APOLOGIZE FOR THE MESS. BUT IT WAS UNAVOIDABLE.

YOU CAN'T ESCAPE IT, BRUCE. THIS IS THE WAY IT HAS TO BE.

YOU AND I, ALONE TOGETHER. IT'S OUR FATE.

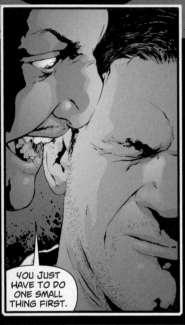

YOU JUST HAVE TO DO ONE SMALL THING FIRST.

YOU SIMPLY HAVE TO FINISH WHAT I STARTED.

YOU'VE GOT *ME* TO TAKE CARE OF YOU, MASTER BRUCE. YOU DON'T NEED *HIM*.

IT'S YOUR FAULT. IT ALWAYS *WAS*, IT ALWAYS *WILL* BE.

SON. BRUCE. PLEASE. HELP ME.

NOW'S YOUR CHANCE TO DO IT YOURSELF. NO CRIMINAL HIDING IN THE SHADOWS. NO DARKENED ALLEYWAY.

JUST YOU.

JUST YOU. ONLY YOU.

DO IT.

BLAM

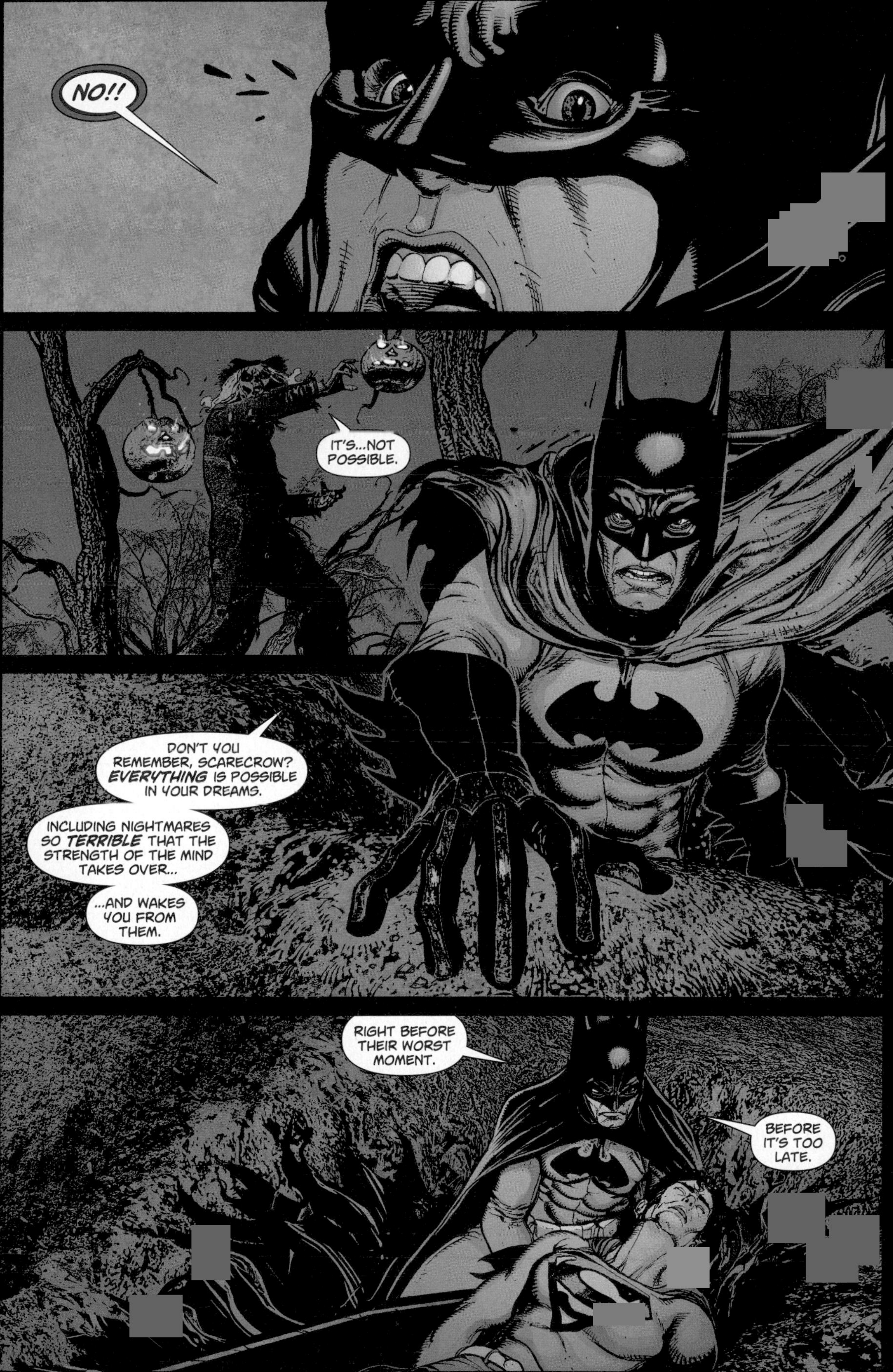
NO!!
IT'S...NOT POSSIBLE.
DON'T YOU REMEMBER, SCARECROW? EVERYTHING IS POSSIBLE IN YOUR DREAMS.
INCLUDING NIGHTMARES SO TERRIBLE THAT THE STRENGTH OF THE MIND TAKES OVER...
...AND WAKES YOU FROM THEM.
RIGHT BEFORE THEIR WORST MOMENT.
BEFORE IT'S TOO LATE.

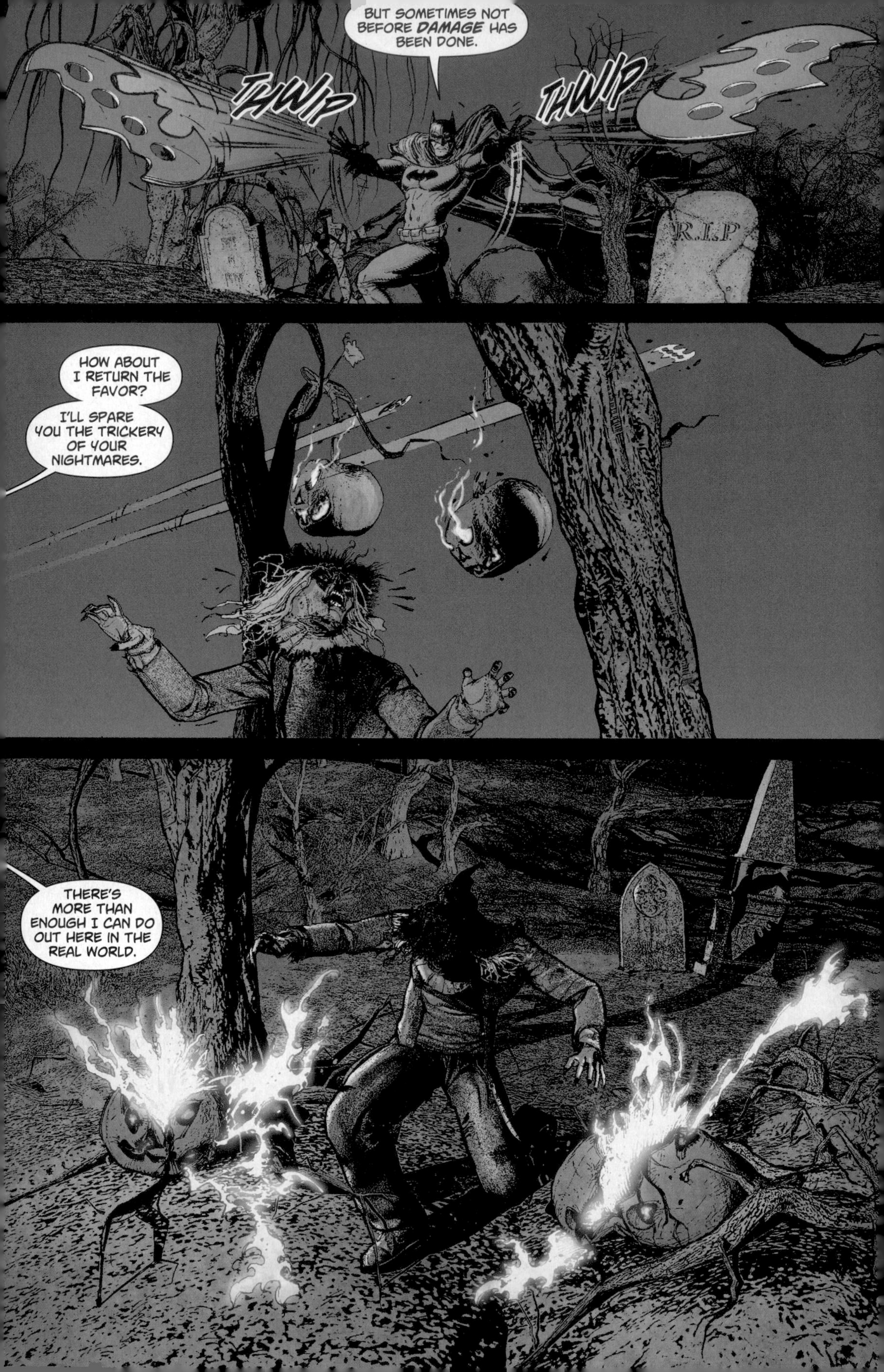
BUT SOMETIMES NOT BEFORE DAMAGE HAS BEEN DONE.
THWIP
THWIP
R.I.P.
HOW ABOUT I RETURN THE FAVOR?
I'LL SPARE YOU THE TRICKERY OF YOUR NIGHTMARES.
THERE'S MORE THAN ENOUGH I CAN DO OUT HERE IN THE REAL WORLD.

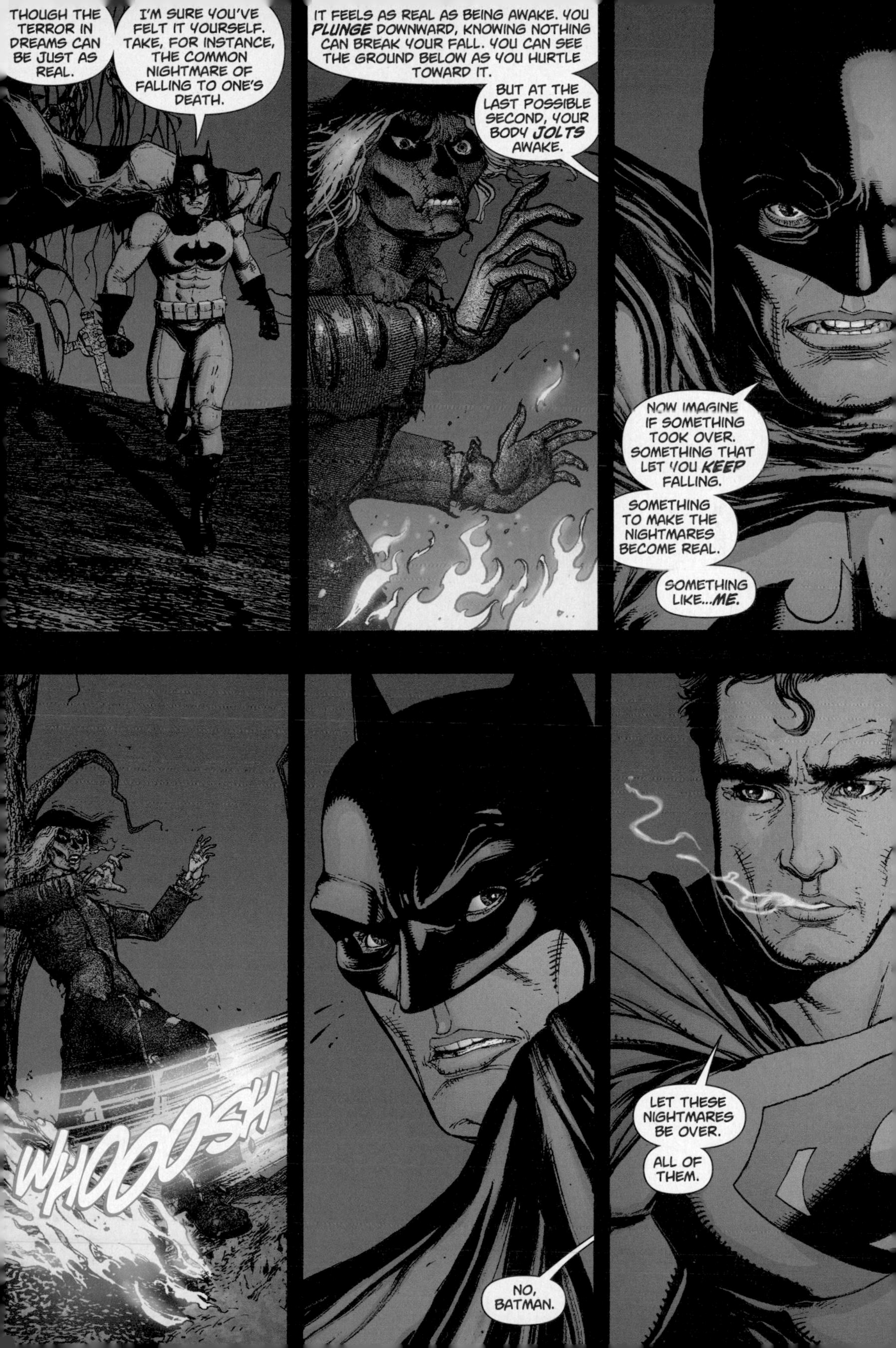
THOUGH THE TERROR IN DREAMS CAN BE JUST AS REAL.
I'M SURE YOU'VE FELT IT YOURSELF. TAKE, FOR INSTANCE, THE COMMON NIGHTMARE OF FALLING TO ONE'S DEATH.
IT FEELS AS REAL AS BEING AWAKE. YOU *PLUNGE* DOWNWARD, KNOWING NOTHING CAN BREAK YOUR FALL. YOU CAN SEE THE GROUND BELOW AS YOU HURTLE TOWARD IT.
BUT AT THE LAST POSSIBLE SECOND, YOUR BODY *JOLTS* AWAKE.
NOW IMAGINE IF SOMETHING TOOK OVER. SOMETHING THAT LET YOU *KEEP* FALLING.
SOMETHING TO MAKE THE NIGHTMARES BECOME REAL.
SOMETHING LIKE...*ME*.
WHOOOSH!
NO, BATMAN.
LET THESE NIGHTMARES BE OVER.
ALL OF THEM.

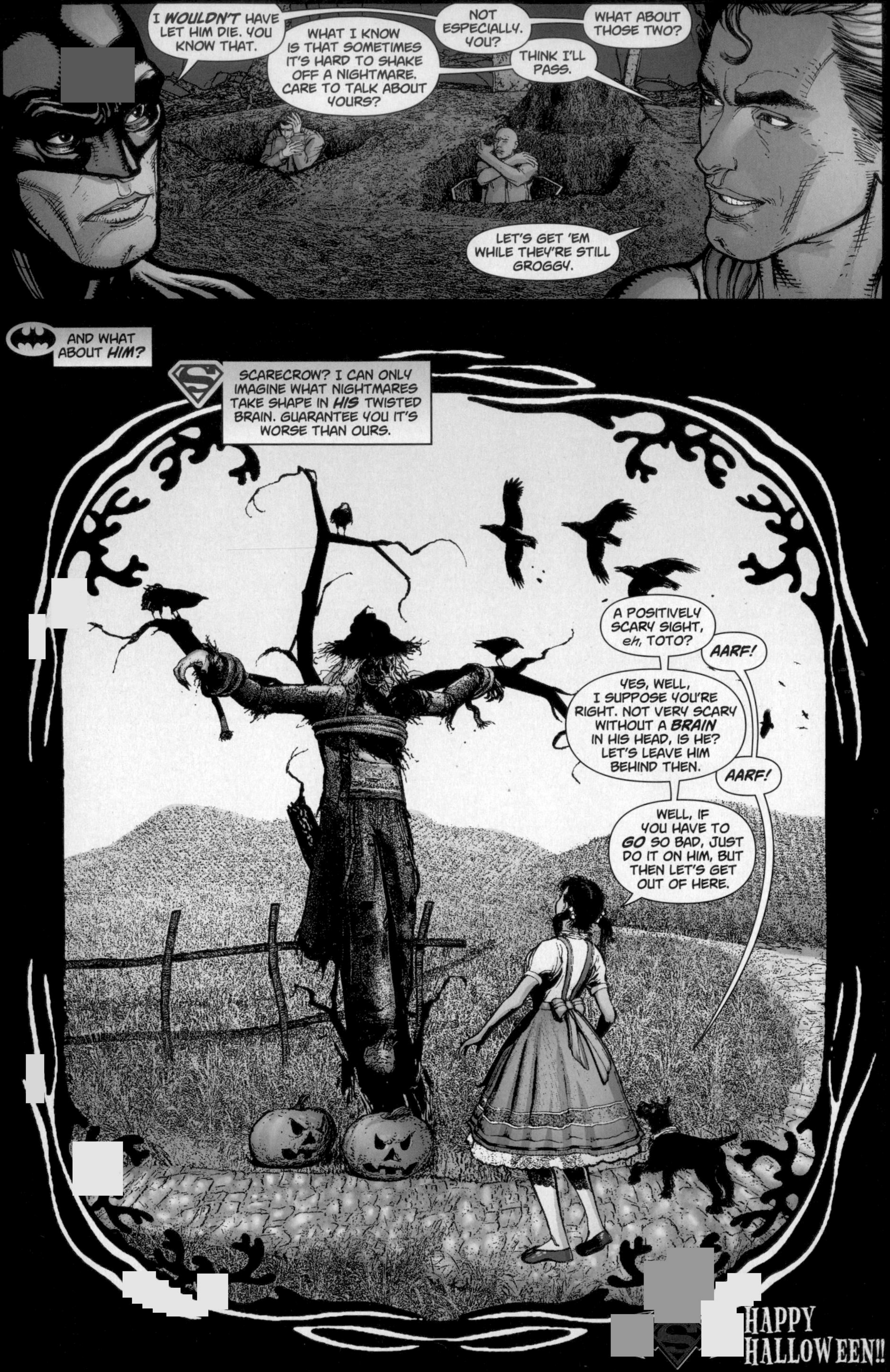
I WOULDN'T HAVE LET HIM DIE. YOU KNOW THAT.
WHAT I KNOW IS THAT SOMETIMES IT'S HARD TO SHAKE OFF A NIGHTMARE. CARE TO TALK ABOUT YOURS?
NOT ESPECIALLY. YOU?
THINK I'LL PASS.
WHAT ABOUT THOSE TWO?
LET'S GET 'EM WHILE THEY'RE STILL GROGGY.
AND WHAT ABOUT HIM?
SCARECROW? I CAN ONLY IMAGINE WHAT NIGHTMARES TAKE SHAPE IN HIS TWISTED BRAIN. GUARANTEE YOU IT'S WORSE THAN OURS.
A POSITIVELY SCARY SIGHT, eh, TOTO?
AARF!
YES, WELL, I SUPPOSE YOU'RE RIGHT. NOT VERY SCARY WITHOUT A BRAIN IN HIS HEAD, IS HE? LET'S LEAVE HIM BEHIND THEN.
AARF!
WELL, IF YOU HAVE TO GO SO BAD, JUST DO IT ON HIM, BUT THEN LET'S GET OUT OF HERE.
HAPPY HALLOWEEN!!

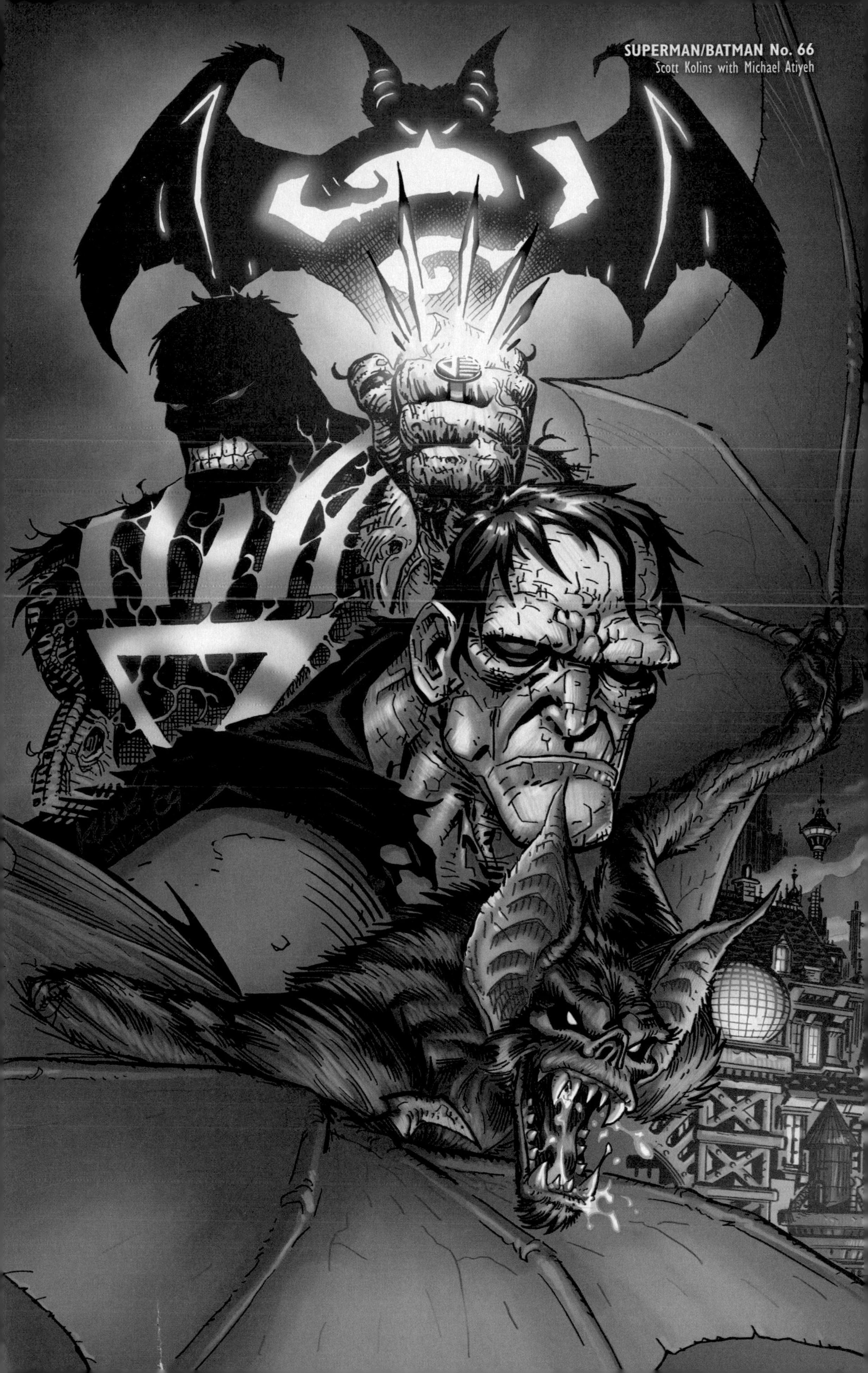

SUPERMAN/BATMAN No. 66
Scott Kolins with Michael Atiyeh

NIGHT OF THE CURE
PART ONE
Story and Art: Scott Kolins

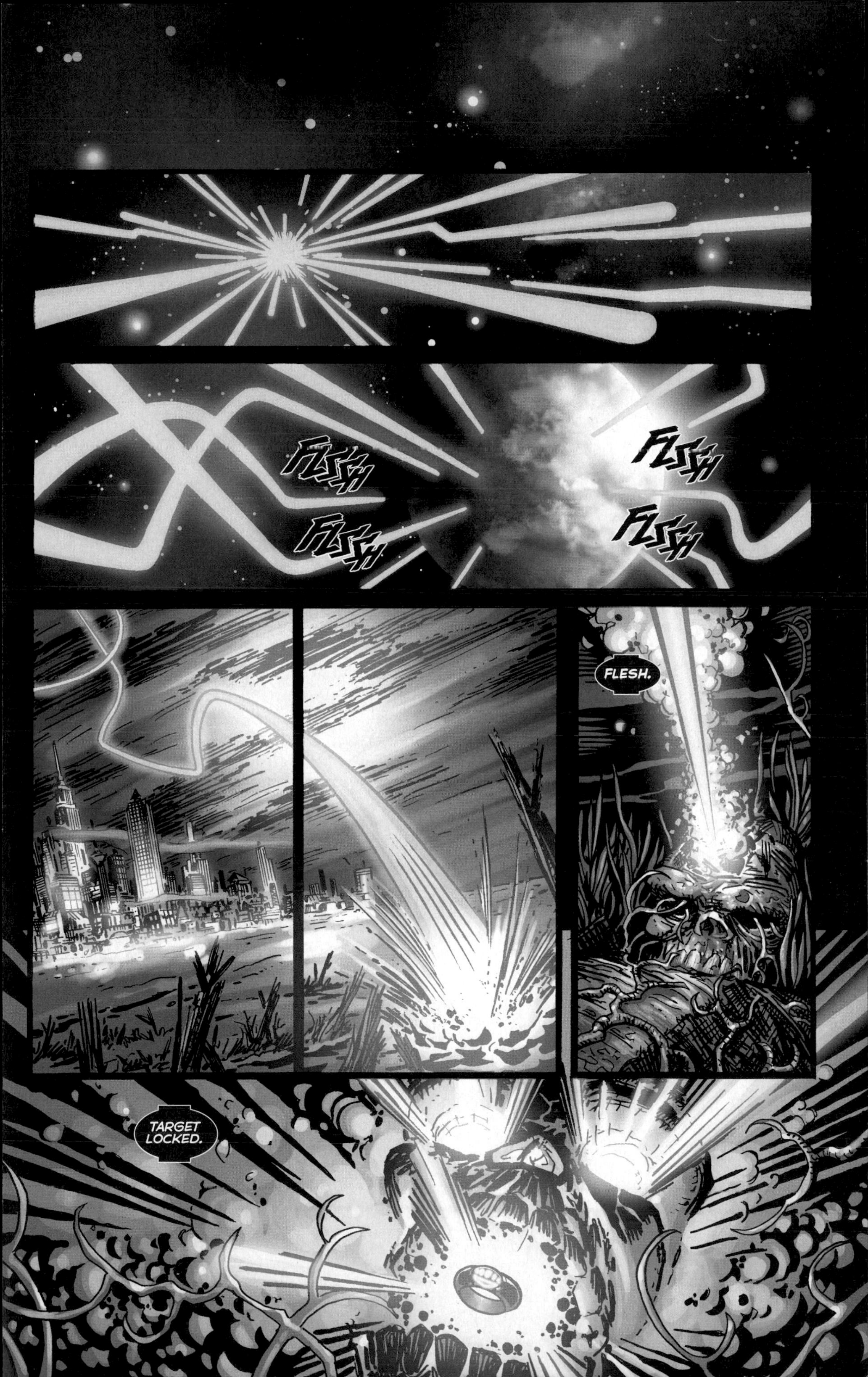
FLSSH
FLSSH
FLSSH
FLSSH
FLESH.
TARGET LOCKED.

I WAS MURDERED MANY YEARS AGO--
--AND LEFT IN A DEEP DARK HOLE FILLED WITH DEVIL'S BLOOD.
CURSED TO BECOME A MONSTER!
GROWN FROM EVIL ROOTS...
BORN
ON A
MONDAY--
--UNSTOPPABLE--
SOLOMON GRUNDY!
SOLOMON GRUNDY KILL!
DESTROYED-- DESTROYED--
GRUNDY COME BACK-- AGAIN AND AGAIN
NEVER DIE!
REGROWN!
ALWAYS ALONE--
BIZARRO-- LONELY BIZARRO.
--KILLED BY FRANKENSTEIN AND HOLY SWORD.
DIED ON A SATURD--
MEMORY DOWNLOAD COMPLETE.
SOLOMON GRUNDY OF EARTH.

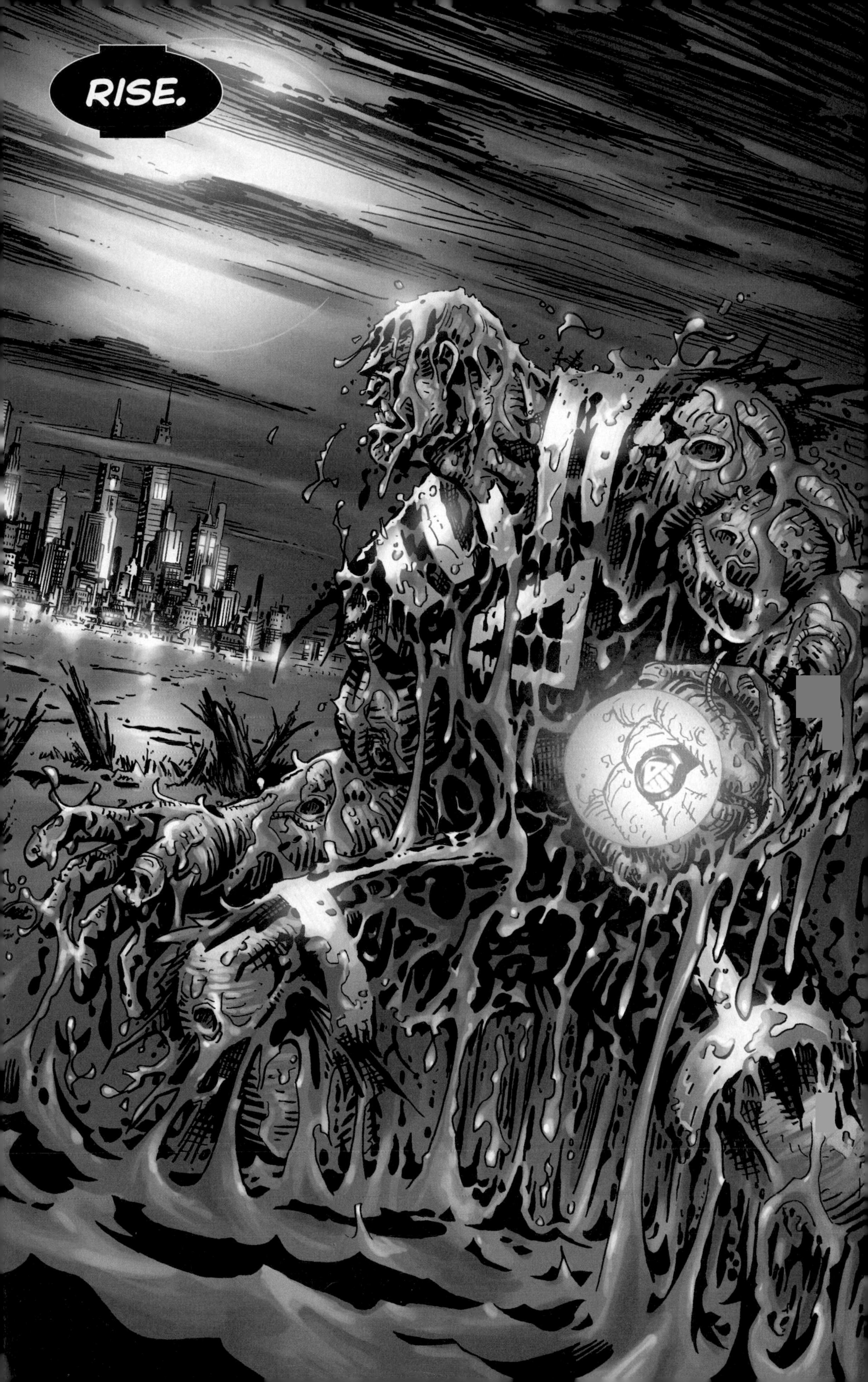
RISE.

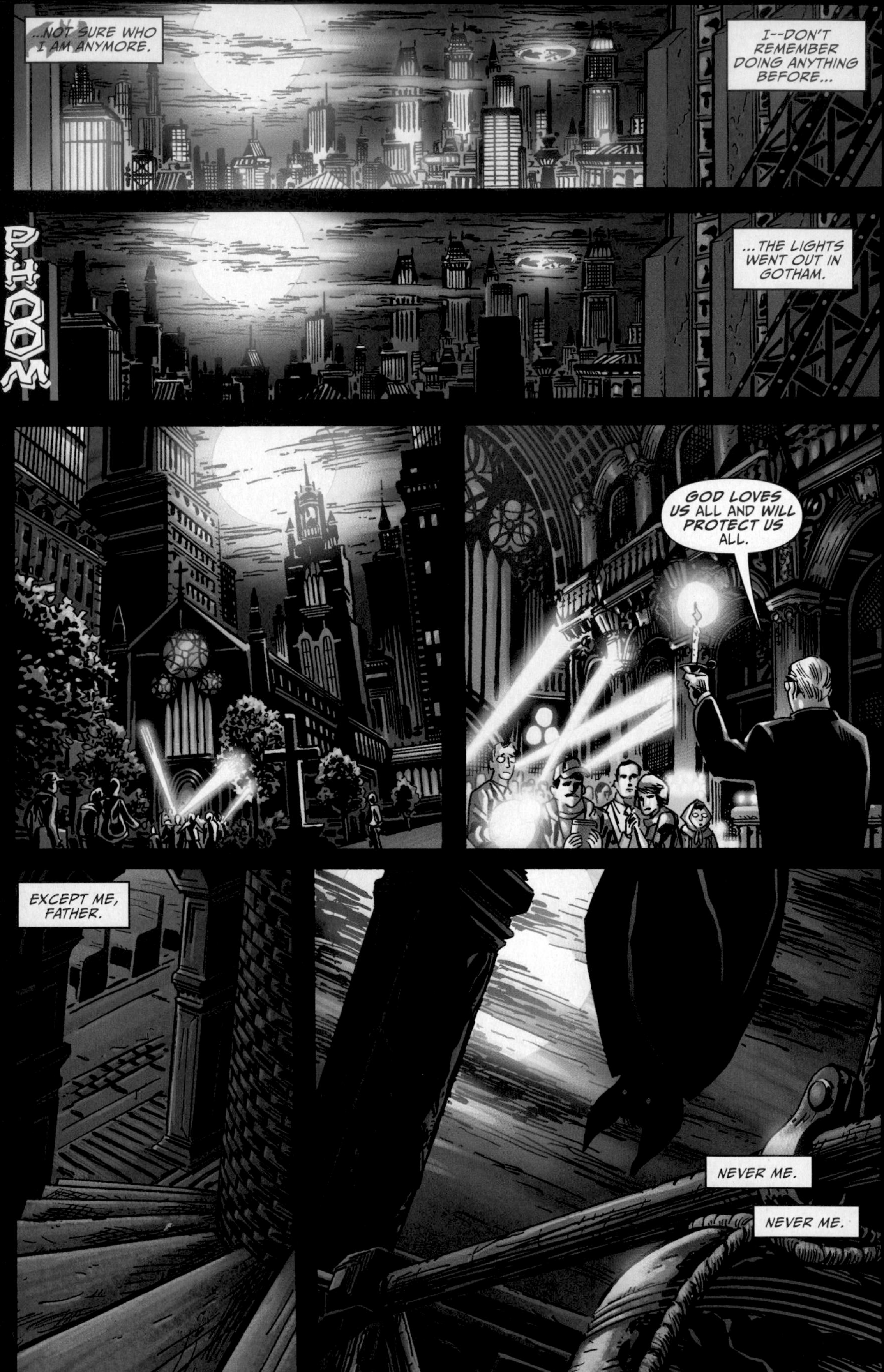
...NOT SURE WHO I AM ANYMORE.
I--DON'T REMEMBER DOING ANYTHING BEFORE...
PHOOM
...THE LIGHTS WENT OUT IN GOTHAM.
GOD LOVES US ALL AND WILL PROTECT US ALL.
EXCEPT ME, FATHER.
NEVER ME.
NEVER ME.

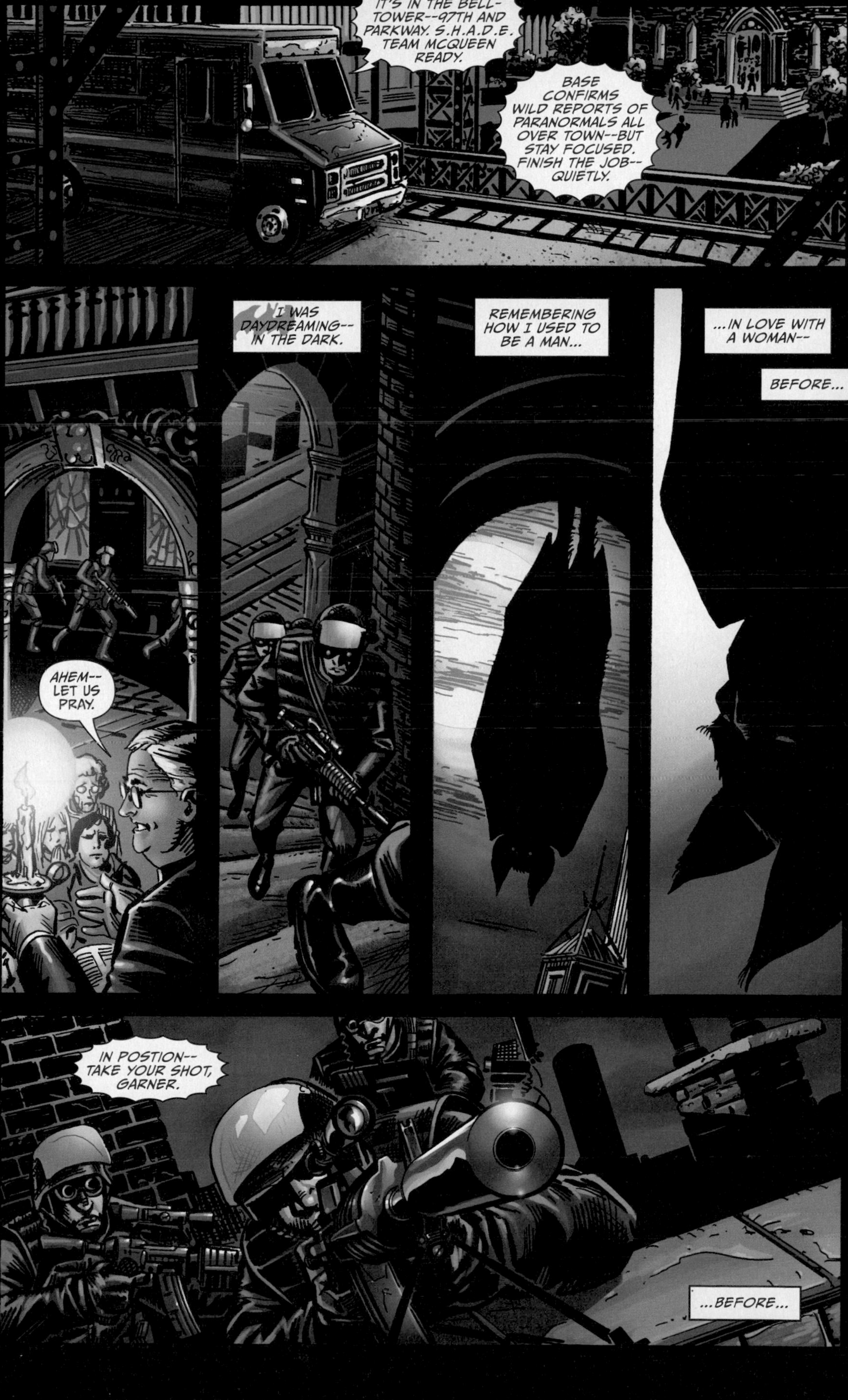
AFFIRMATIVE--IT'S IN THE BELL-TOWER--97TH AND PARKWAY. S.H.A.D.E. TEAM MCQUEEN READY.
BASE CONFIRMS WILD REPORTS OF PARANORMALS ALL OVER TOWN--BUT STAY FOCUSED. FINISH THE JOB--QUIETLY.
I WAS DAYDREAMING--IN THE DARK.
AHEM--LET US PRAY.
REMEMBERING HOW I USED TO BE A MAN...
...IN LOVE WITH A WOMAN--
BEFORE...
IN POSTION--TAKE YOUR SHOT, GARNER.
...BEFORE...

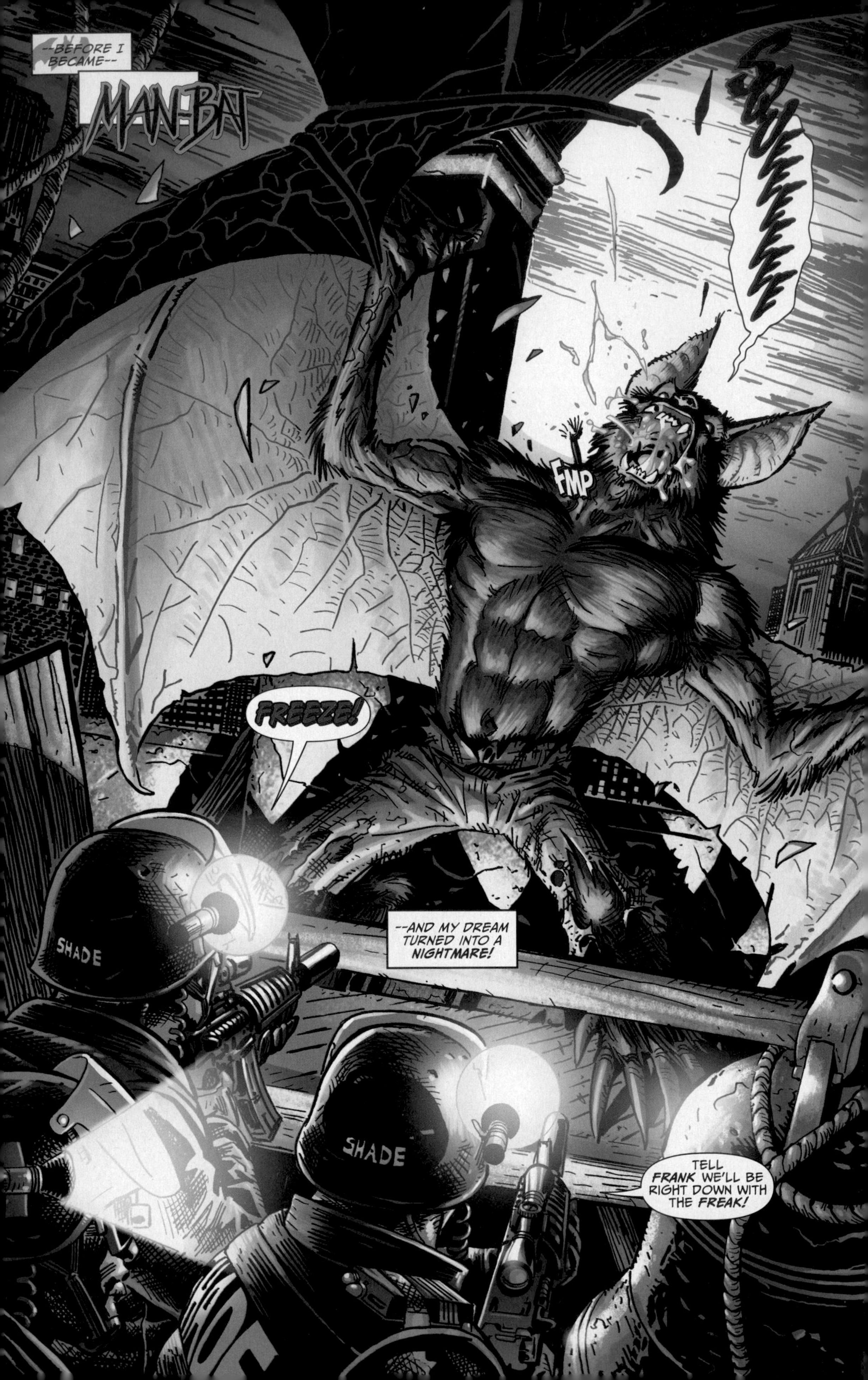
--BEFORE I BECAME--
MAN-BAT
SQUEEEEE
FMP
FREEZE!
--AND MY DREAM TURNED INTO A NIGHTMARE!
SHADE
SHADE
TELL FRANK WE'LL BE RIGHT DOWN WITH THE FREAK!

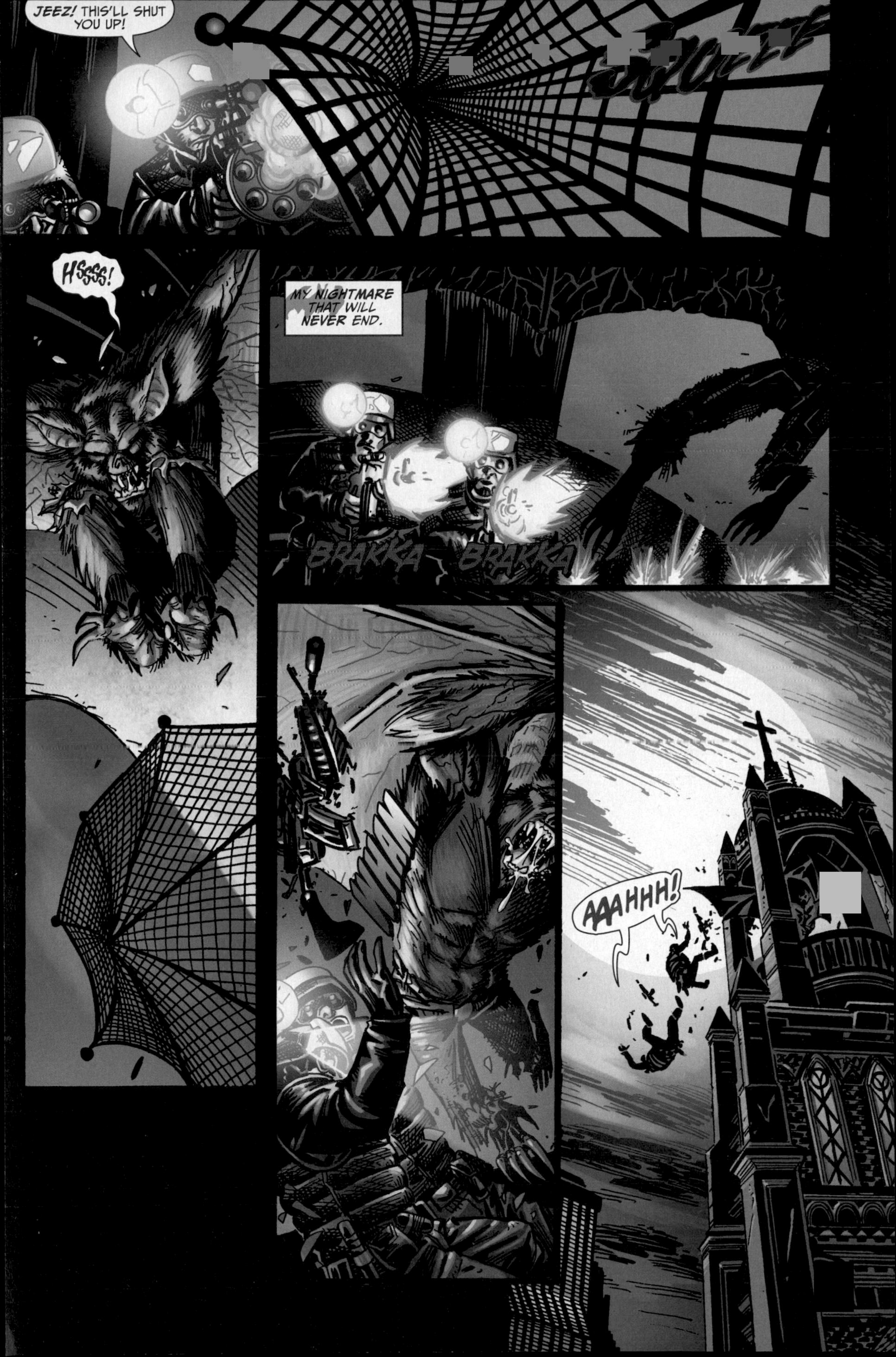
JEEZ! THIS'LL SHUT YOU UP!
HSSSS!
MY NIGHTMARE THAT WILL NEVER END.
BRAKKA
BRAKKA
AAAHHH!

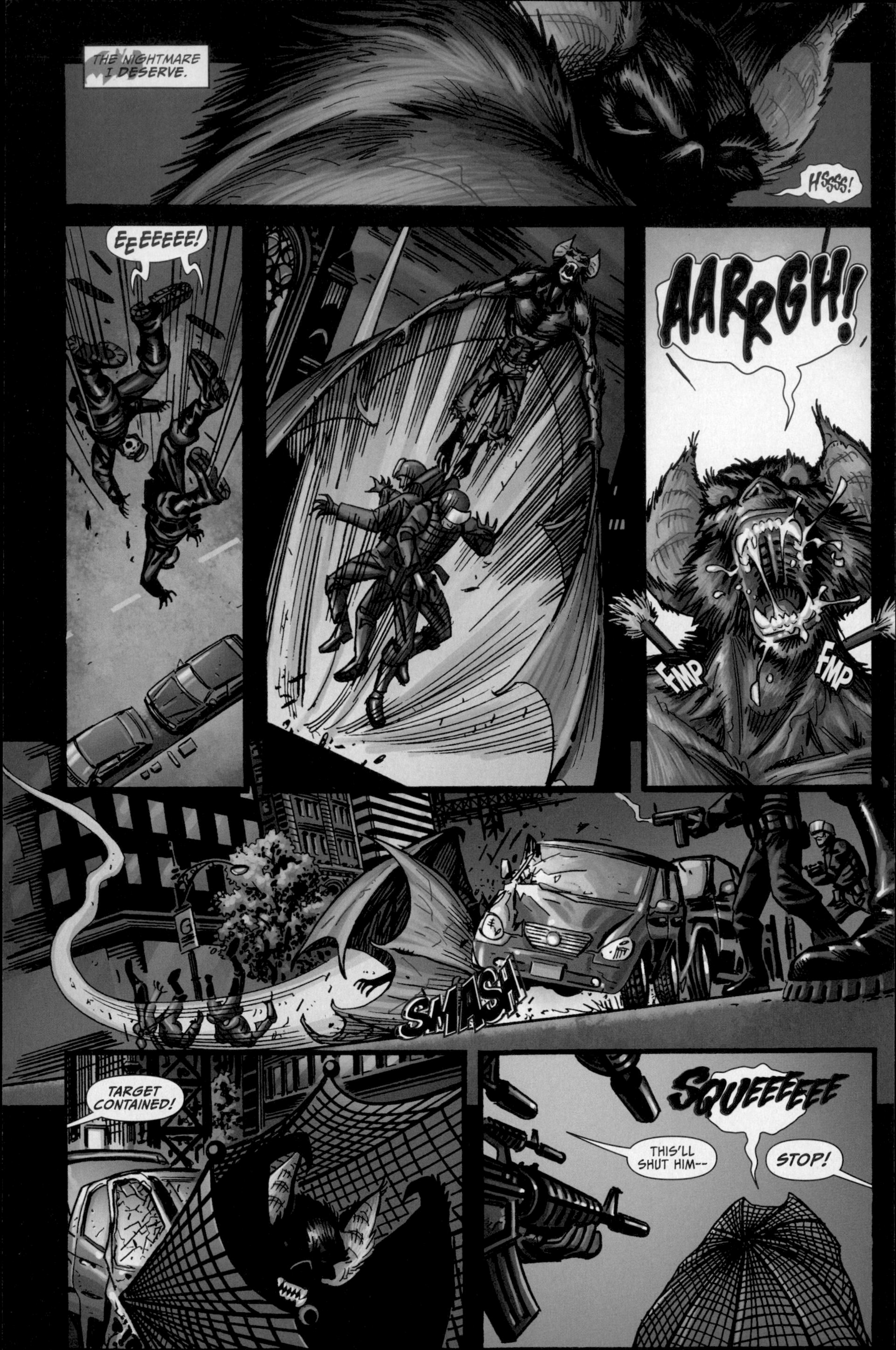
THE NIGHTMARE I DESERVE.
HSSSS!
EEEEEEE!
AARRGH!
FMP
FMP
SMASH
TARGET CONTAINED!
SQUEEEEEE
THIS'LL SHUT HIM--
STOP!

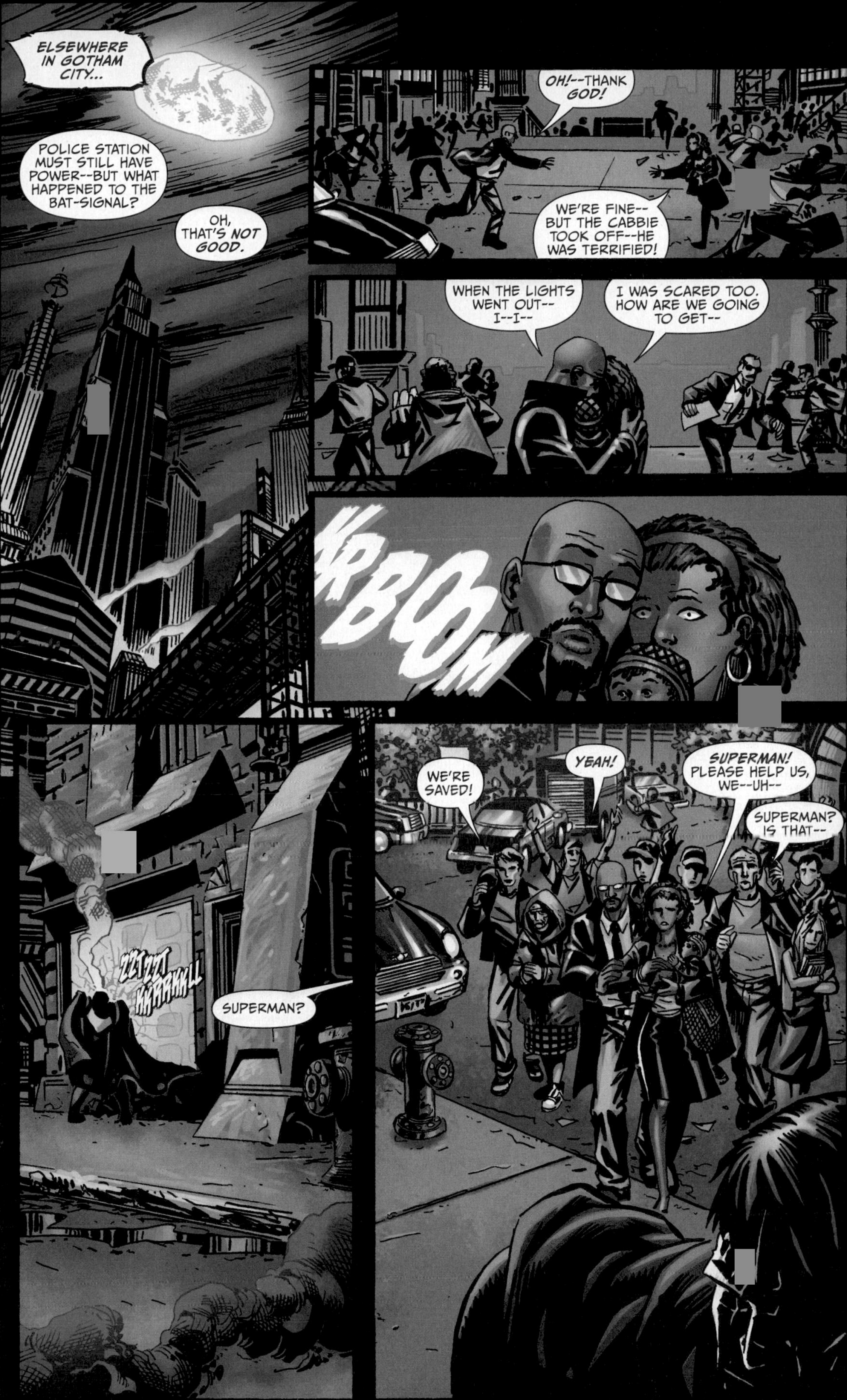

ELSEWHERE IN GOTHAM CITY...
POLICE STATION MUST STILL HAVE POWER--BUT WHAT HAPPENED TO THE BAT-SIGNAL?
OH, THAT'S NOT GOOD.
OH!--THANK GOD!
WE'RE FINE--BUT THE CABBIE TOOK OFF--HE WAS TERRIFIED!
WHEN THE LIGHTS WENT OUT--I--I--
I WAS SCARED TOO. HOW ARE WE GOING TO GET--
RBOOM
SUPERMAN?
WE'RE SAVED!
YEAH!
SUPERMAN! PLEASE HELP US, WE--UH--
SUPERMAN? IS THAT--

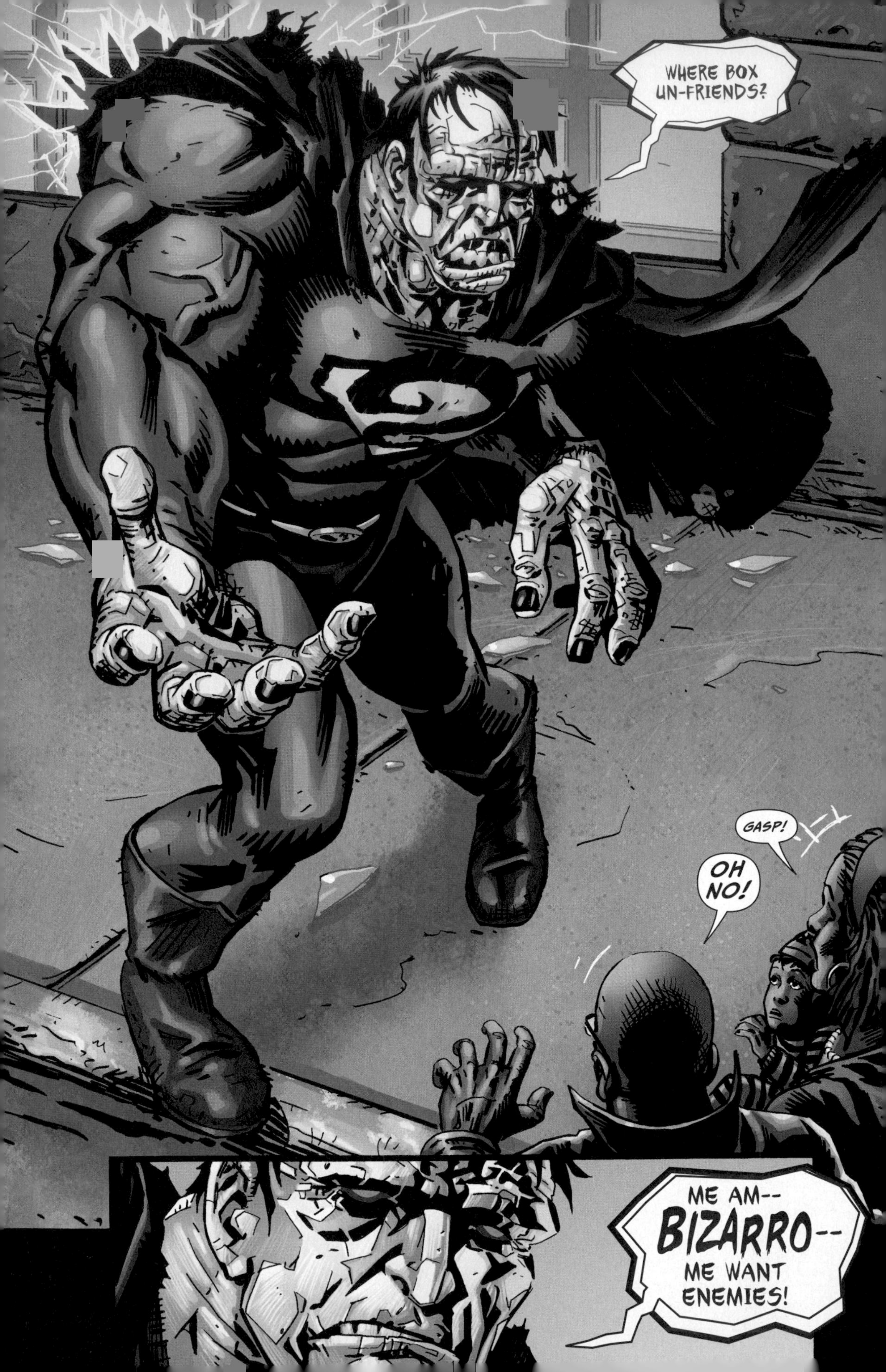
WHERE BOX UN-FRIENDS?
GASP!
OH NO!
ME AM-- BIZARRO-- ME WANT ENEMIES!

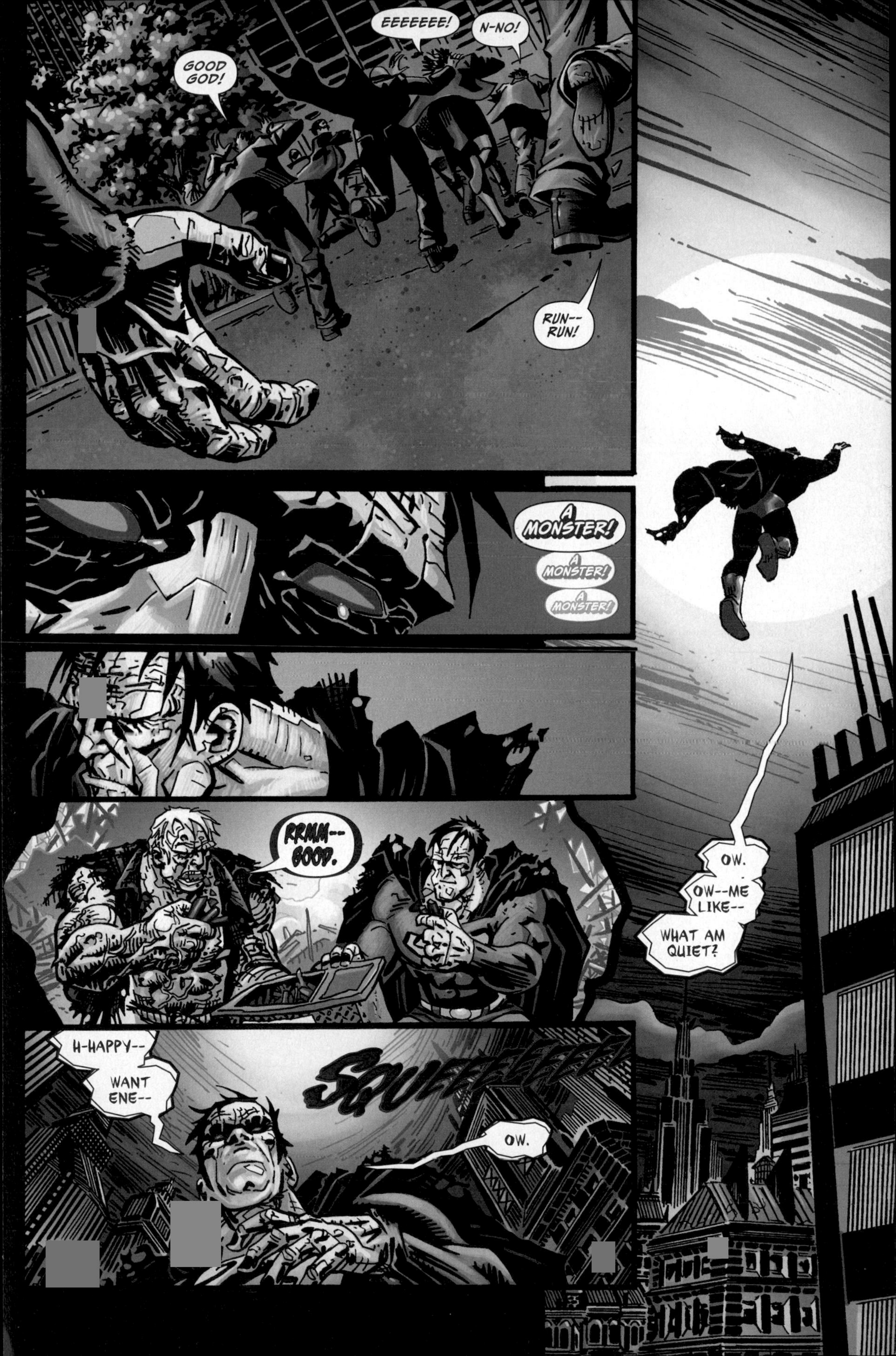
GOOD GOD!
EEEEEEE!
N-NO!
RUN--RUN!
A MONSTER!
A MONSTER!
A MONSTER!
RRMM--GOOD.
OW.
OW--ME LIKE--
WHAT AM QUIET?
H-HAPPY--
WANT ENE--
SQUEEEEEEE!
OW.

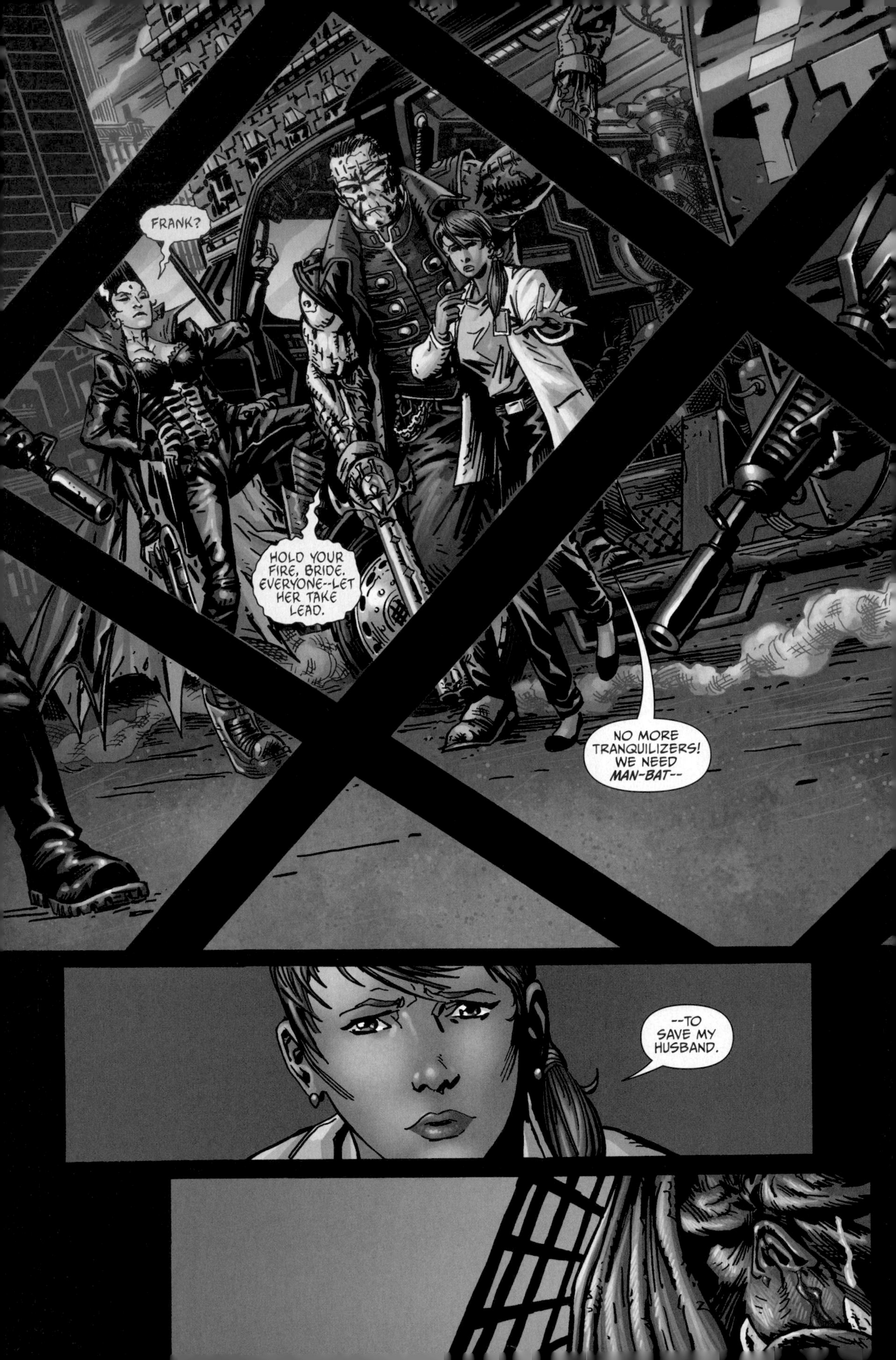
FRANK?
HOLD YOUR FIRE, BRIDE. EVERYONE--LET HER TAKE LEAD.
NO MORE TRANQUILIZERS! WE NEED MAN-BAT--
--TO SAVE MY HUSBAND.

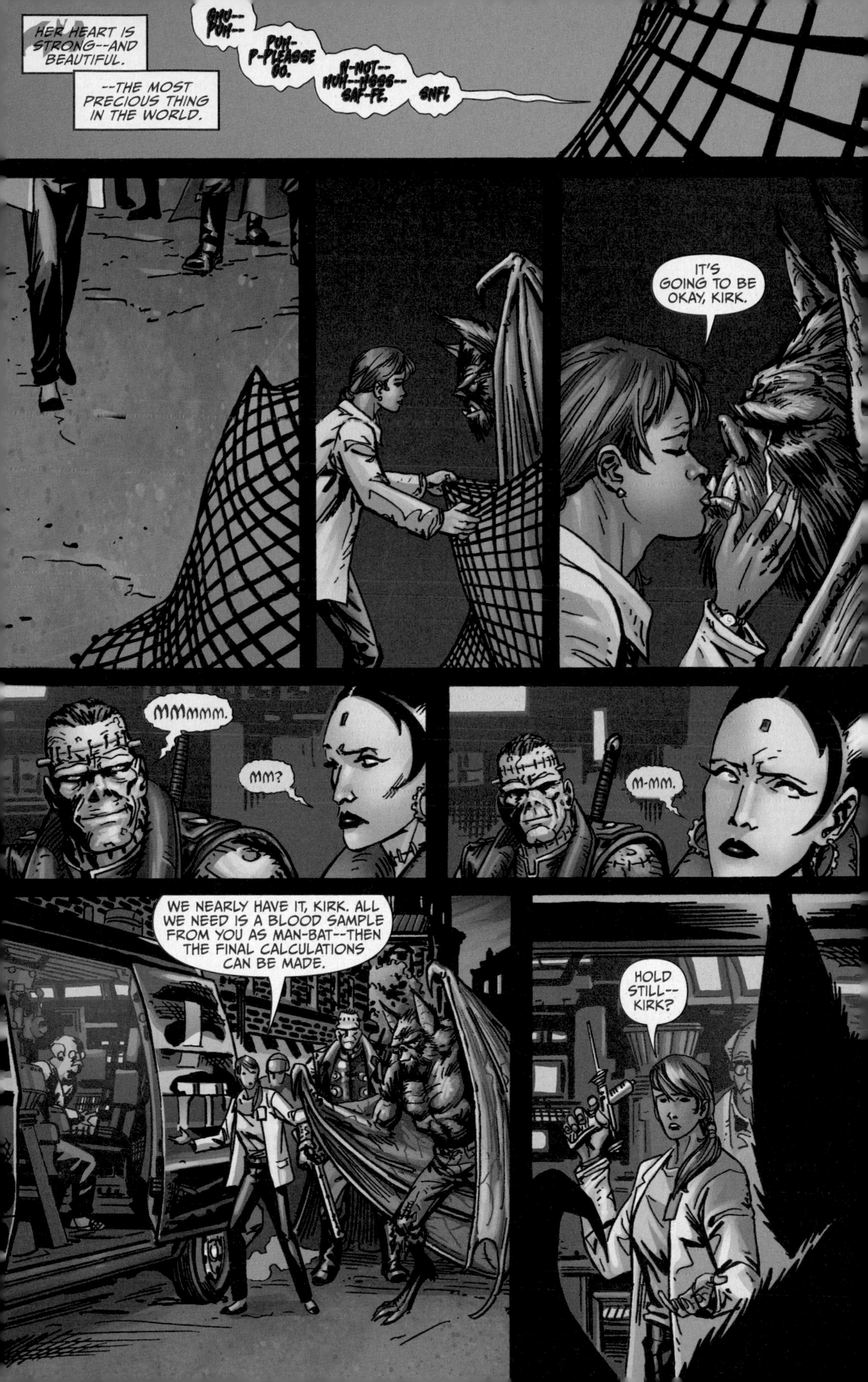
HER HEART IS STRONG--AND BEAUTIFUL.
--THE MOST PRECIOUS THING IN THE WORLD.
GHU-- PUH--
PUH-- P-PLEASSE GO.
N-NOT-- NUH--NSSS-- SAF-FE.
SNFL
IT'S GOING TO BE OKAY, KIRK.
MMmmm.
MM?
M-MM.
WE NEARLY HAVE IT, KIRK. ALL WE NEED IS A BLOOD SAMPLE FROM YOU AS MAN-BAT--THEN THE FINAL CALCULATIONS CAN BE MADE.
HOLD STILL-- KIRK?

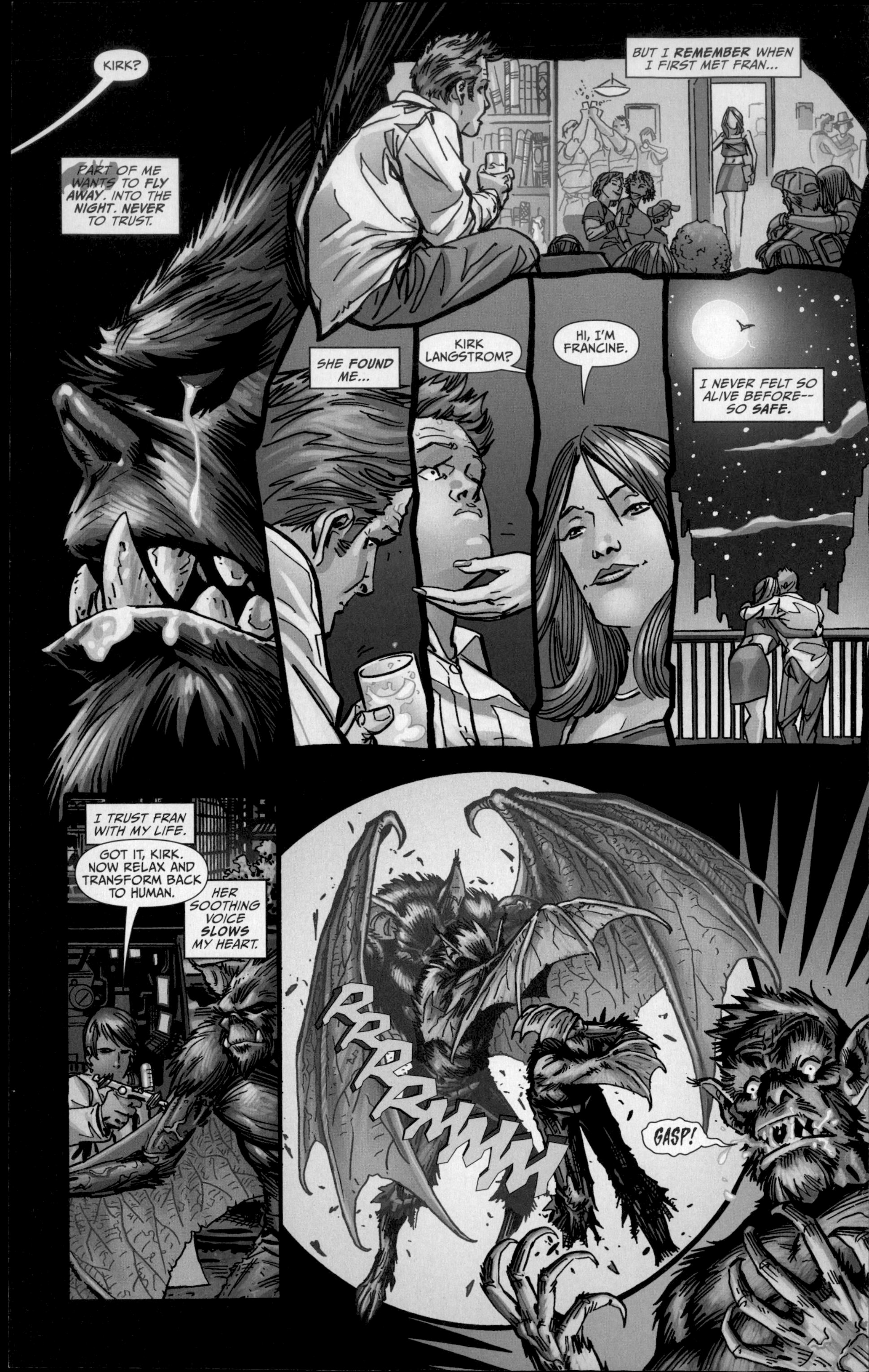

KIRK?
PART OF ME WANTS TO FLY AWAY. INTO THE NIGHT. NEVER TO TRUST.
BUT I REMEMBER WHEN I FIRST MET FRAN...
SHE FOUND ME...
KIRK LANGSTROM?
HI, I'M FRANCINE.
I NEVER FELT SO ALIVE BEFORE-- SO SAFE.
I TRUST FRAN WITH MY LIFE.
GOT IT, KIRK. NOW RELAX AND TRANSFORM BACK TO HUMAN.
HER SOOTHING VOICE SLOWS MY HEART.
RRRAWWW
GASP!

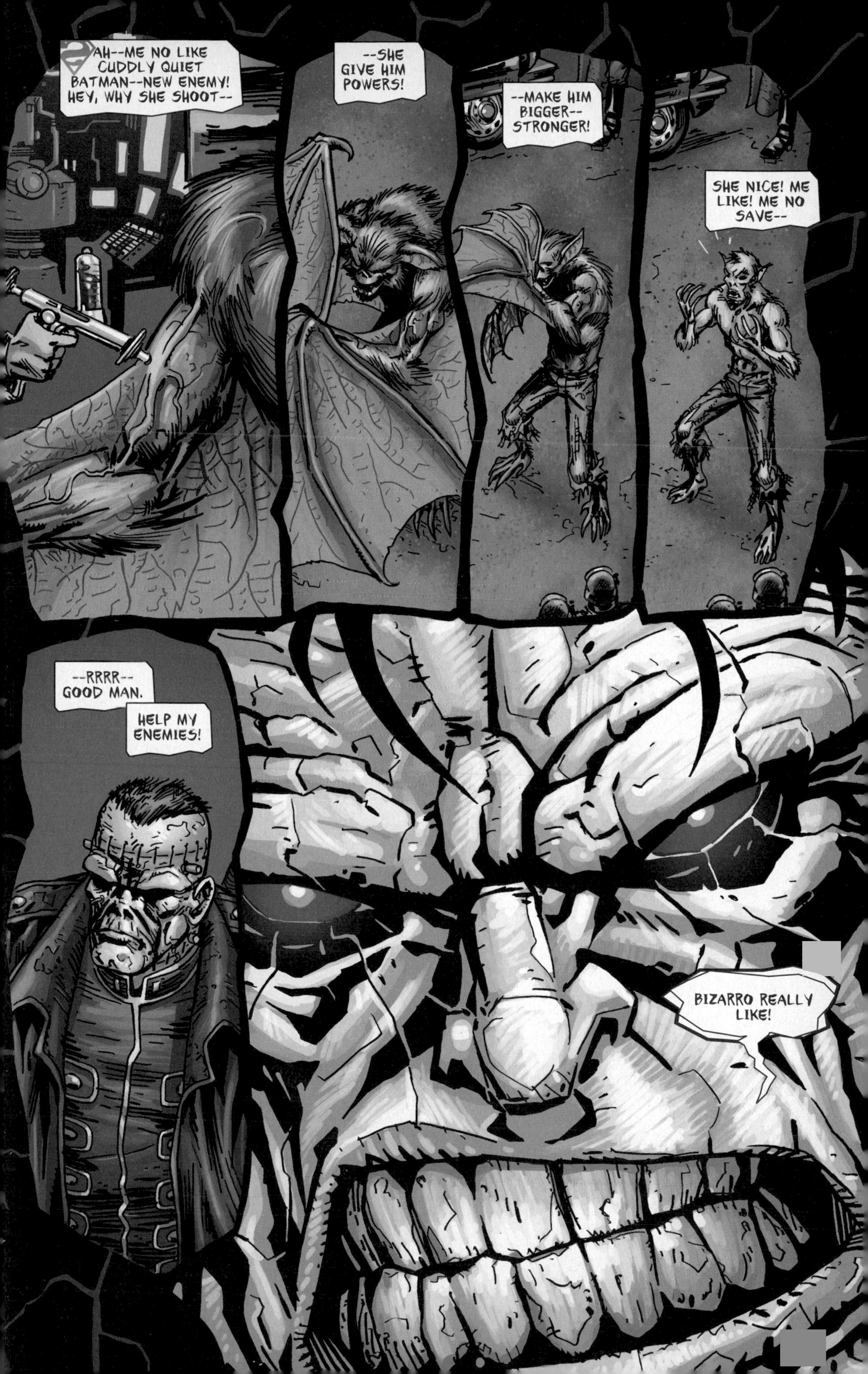
AH--ME NO LIKE CUDDLY QUIET BATMAN--NEW ENEMY! HEY, WHY SHE SHOOT--
--SHE GIVE HIM POWERS!
--MAKE HIM BIGGER--STRONGER!
SHE NICE! ME LIKE! ME NO SAVE--
--RRRR--GOOD MAN.
HELP MY ENEMIES!
BIZARRO REALLY LIKE!

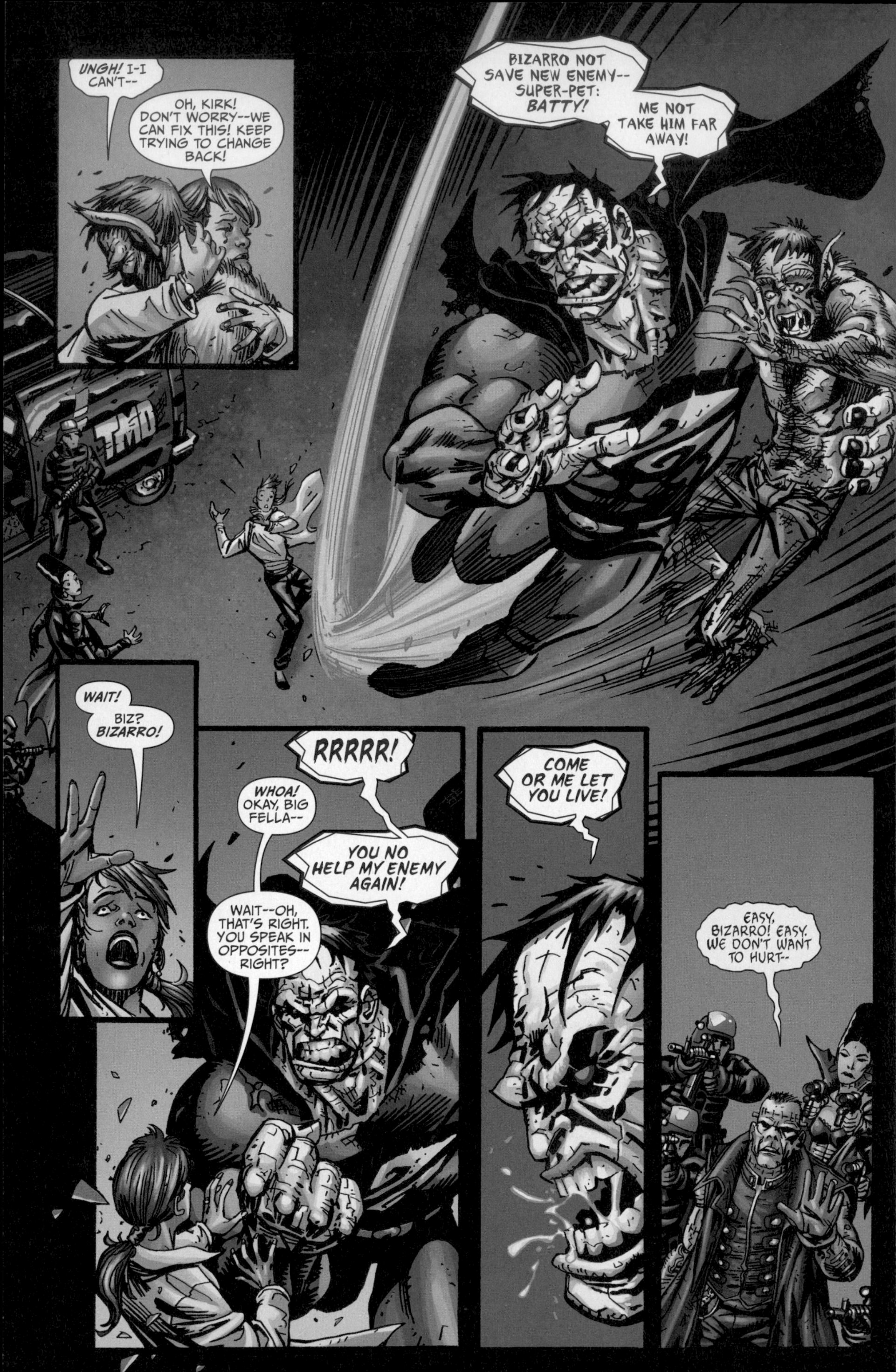
UNGH! I-I CAN'T--
OH, KIRK! DON'T WORRY--WE CAN FIX THIS! KEEP TRYING TO CHANGE BACK!
BIZARRO NOT SAVE NEW ENEMY--SUPER-PET: BATTY!
ME NOT TAKE HIM FAR AWAY!
TMD
WAIT!
BIZ? BIZARRO!
RRRRR!
WHOA! OKAY, BIG FELLA--
YOU NO HELP MY ENEMY AGAIN!
WAIT--OH, THAT'S RIGHT. YOU SPEAK IN OPPOSITES--RIGHT?
COME OR ME LET YOU LIVE!
EASY, BIZARRO! EASY. WE DON'T WANT TO HURT--

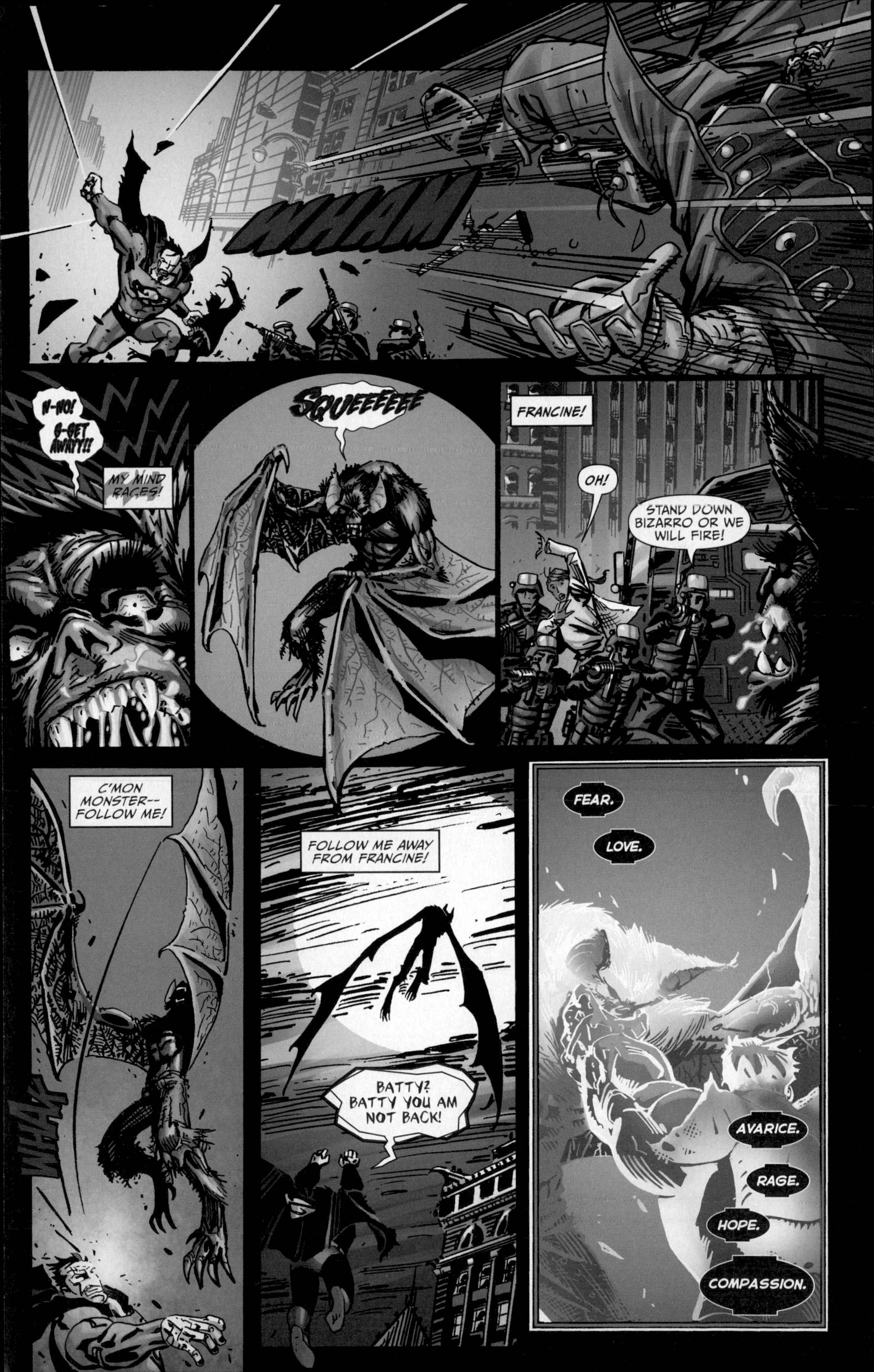
WHHAM
N-NO! G-GET AWAY!!
MY MIND RACES!
SQUEEEEEEE
FRANCINE!
OH!
STAND DOWN BIZARRO OR WE WILL FIRE!
C'MON MONSTER-- FOLLOW ME!
WHAK
FOLLOW ME AWAY FROM FRANCINE!
BATTY? BATTY YOU AM NOT BACK!
FEAR.
LOVE.
AVARICE.
RAGE.
HOPE.
COMPASSION.

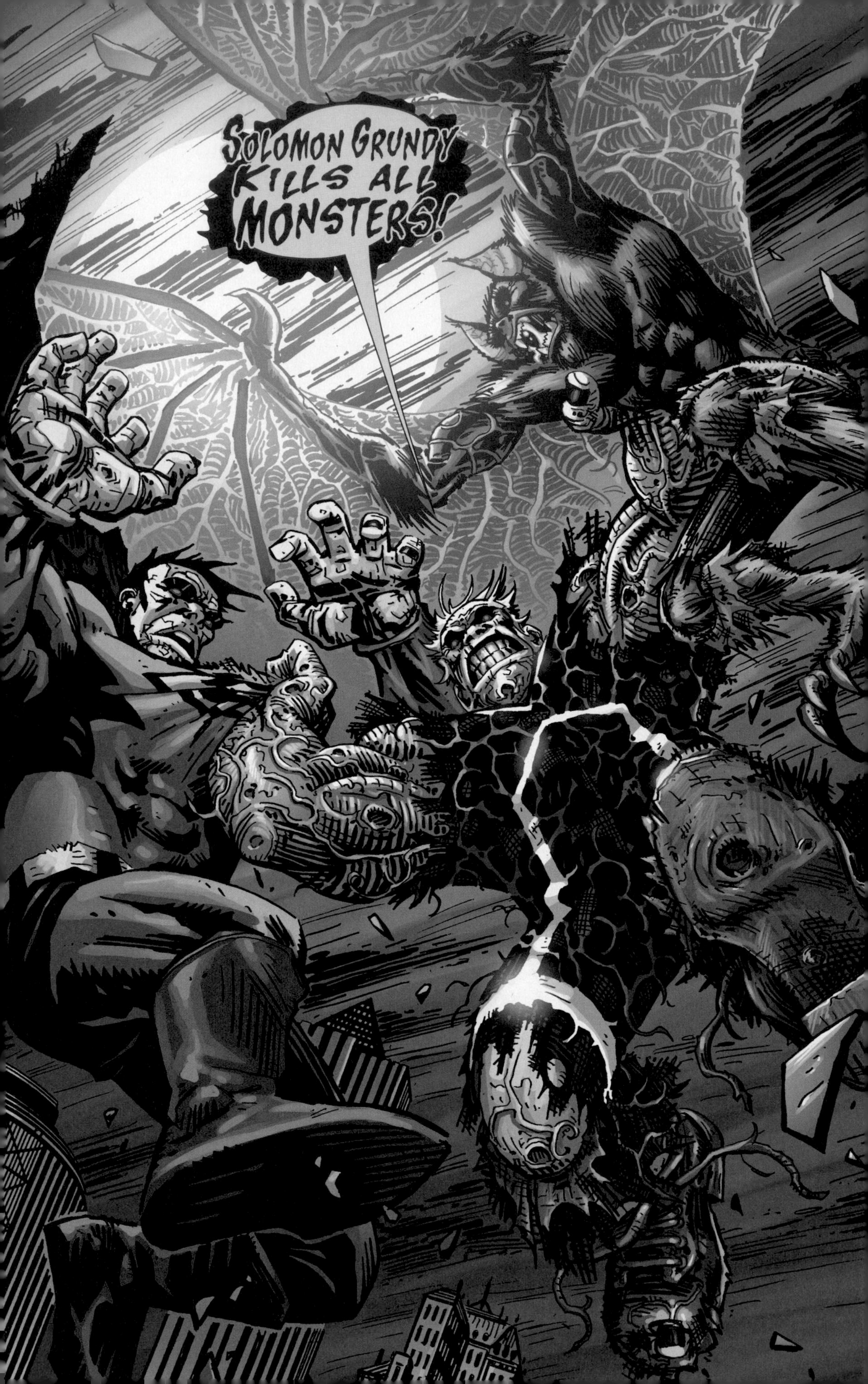
SOLOMON GRUNDY KILLS ALL MONSTERS!

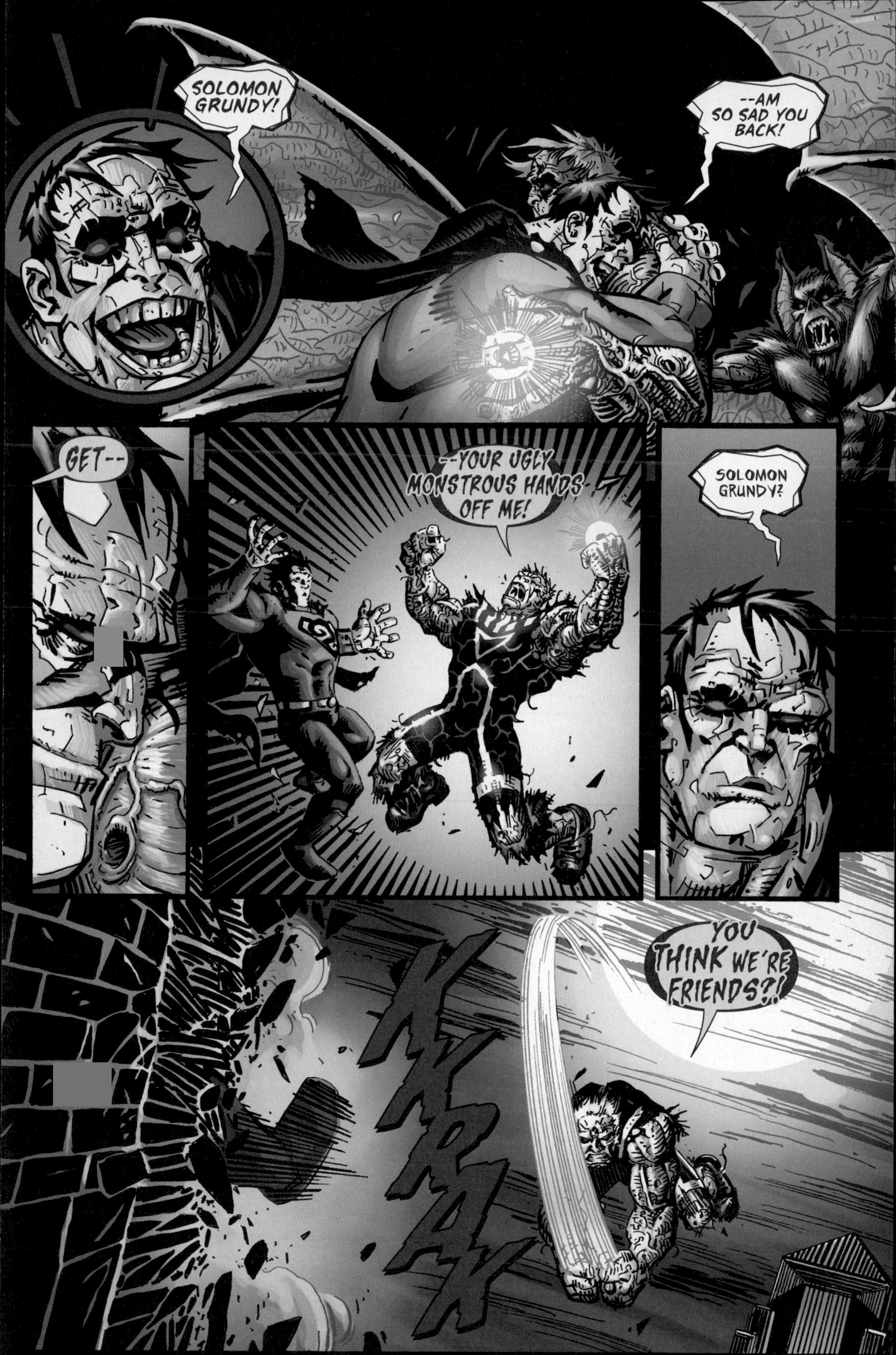
SOLOMON GRUNDY!
--AM SO SAD YOU BACK!
GET--
--YOUR UGLY MONSTROUS HANDS OFF ME!
SOLOMON GRUNDY?
YOU THINK WE'RE FRIENDS?!

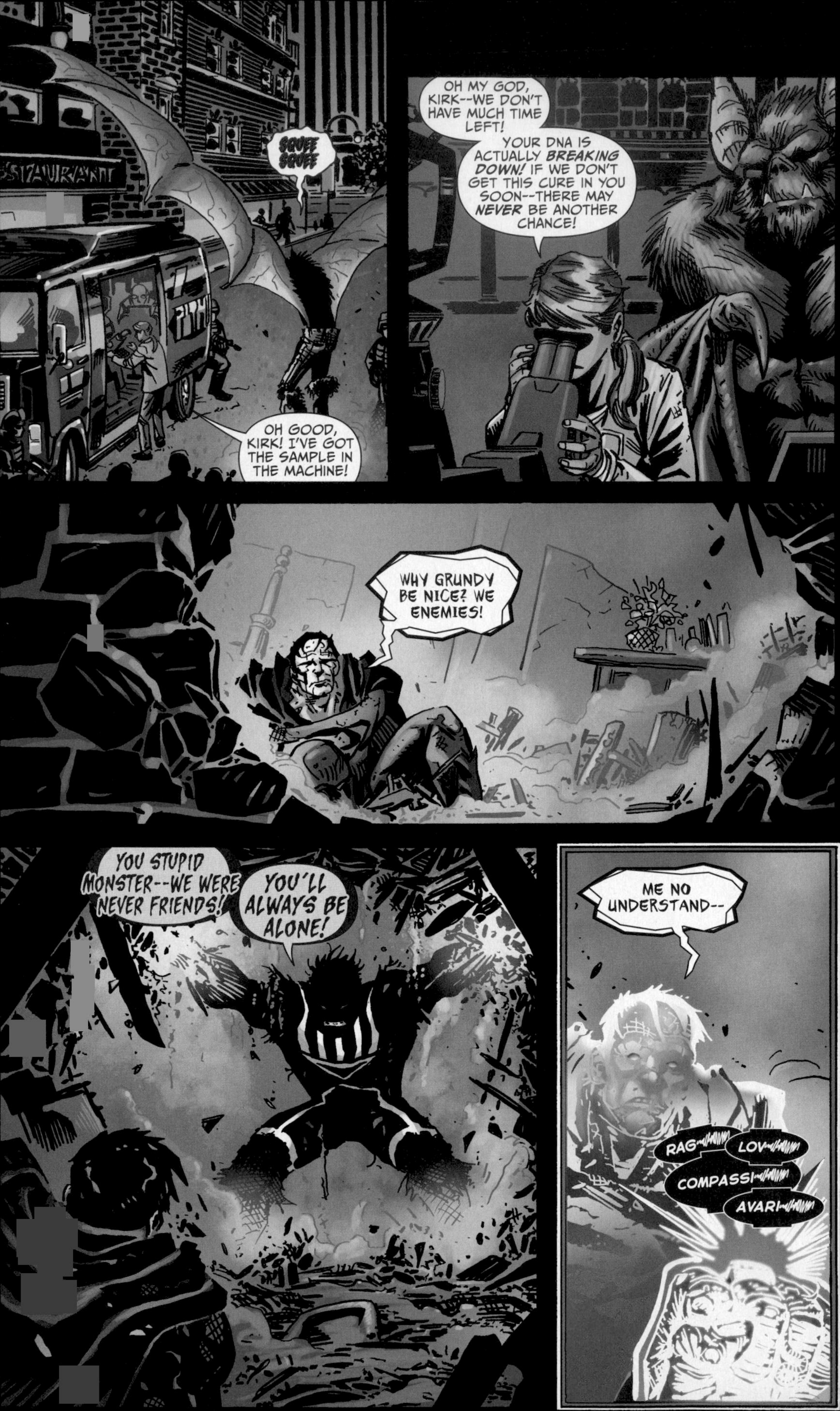
SQUEE SQUEE
OH GOOD, KIRK! I'VE GOT THE SAMPLE IN THE MACHINE!
OH MY GOD, KIRK--WE DON'T HAVE MUCH TIME LEFT!
YOUR DNA IS ACTUALLY BREAKING DOWN! IF WE DON'T GET THIS CURE IN YOU SOON--THERE MAY NEVER BE ANOTHER CHANCE!
WHY GRUNDY BE NICE? WE ENEMIES!
YOU STUPID MONSTER--WE WERE NEVER FRIENDS!
YOU'LL ALWAYS BE ALONE!
ME NO UNDERSTAND--
RAG-
LOV-
COMPASSI-
AVARI-

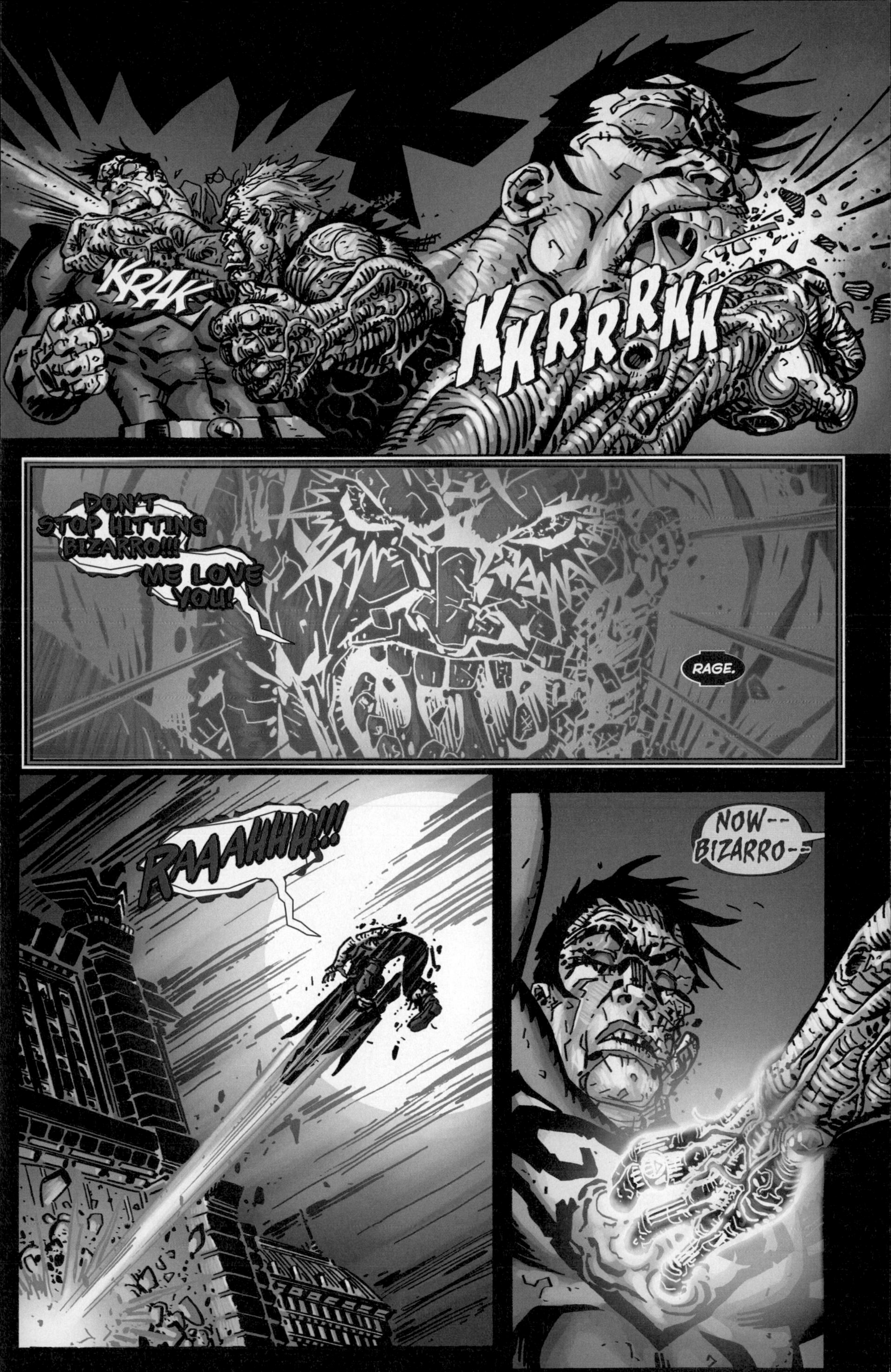
KRAK
KKRRRRKK
DON'T STOP HITTING BIZARRO!!! ME LOVE YOU!
RAGE.
RAAAHHHH!!!
NOW-- BIZARRO--

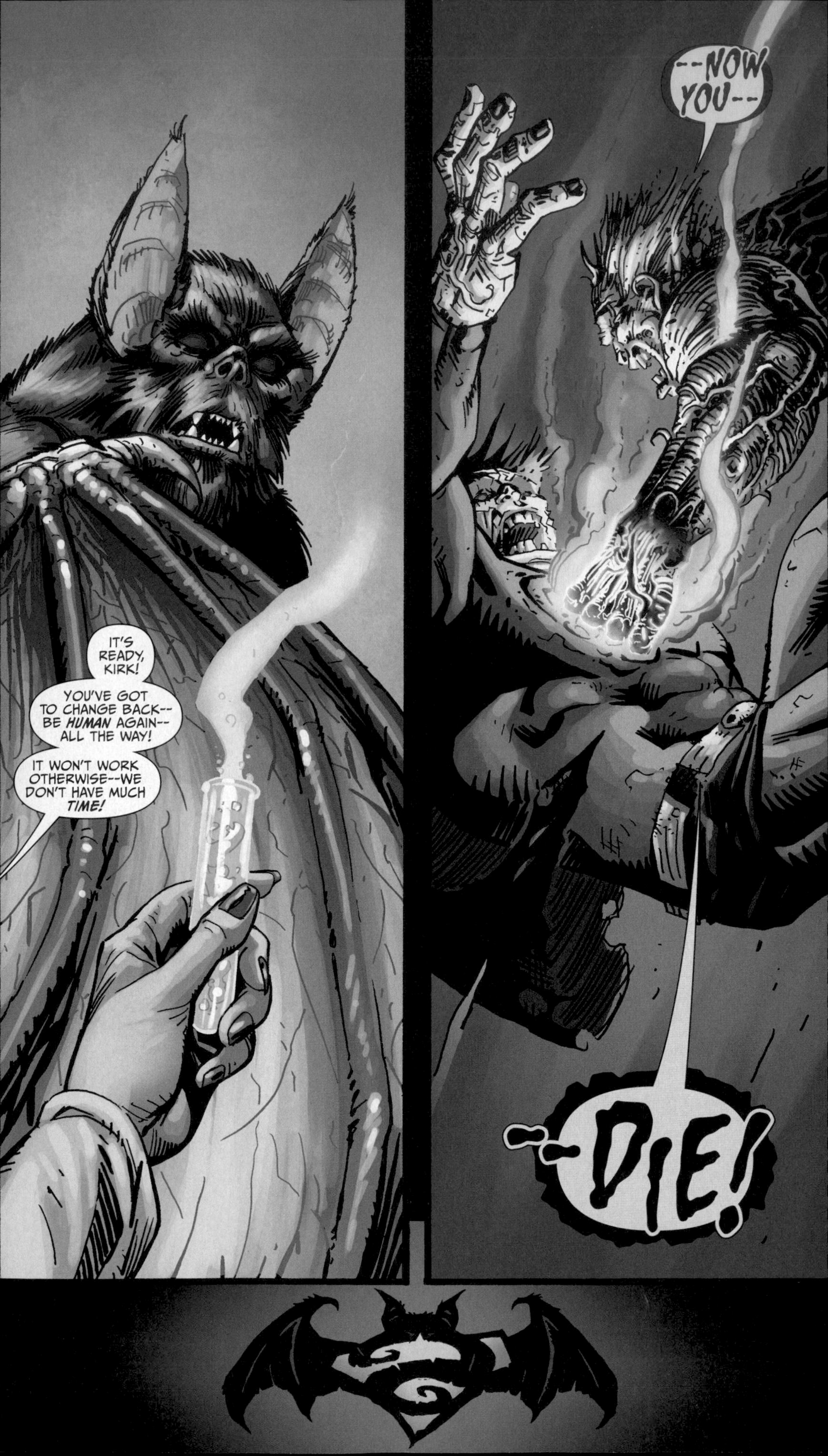
IT'S READY, KIRK!
YOU'VE GOT TO CHANGE BACK-- BE HUMAN AGAIN-- ALL THE WAY!
IT WON'T WORK OTHERWISE--WE DON'T HAVE MUCH TIME!
--NOW YOU--
--DIE!

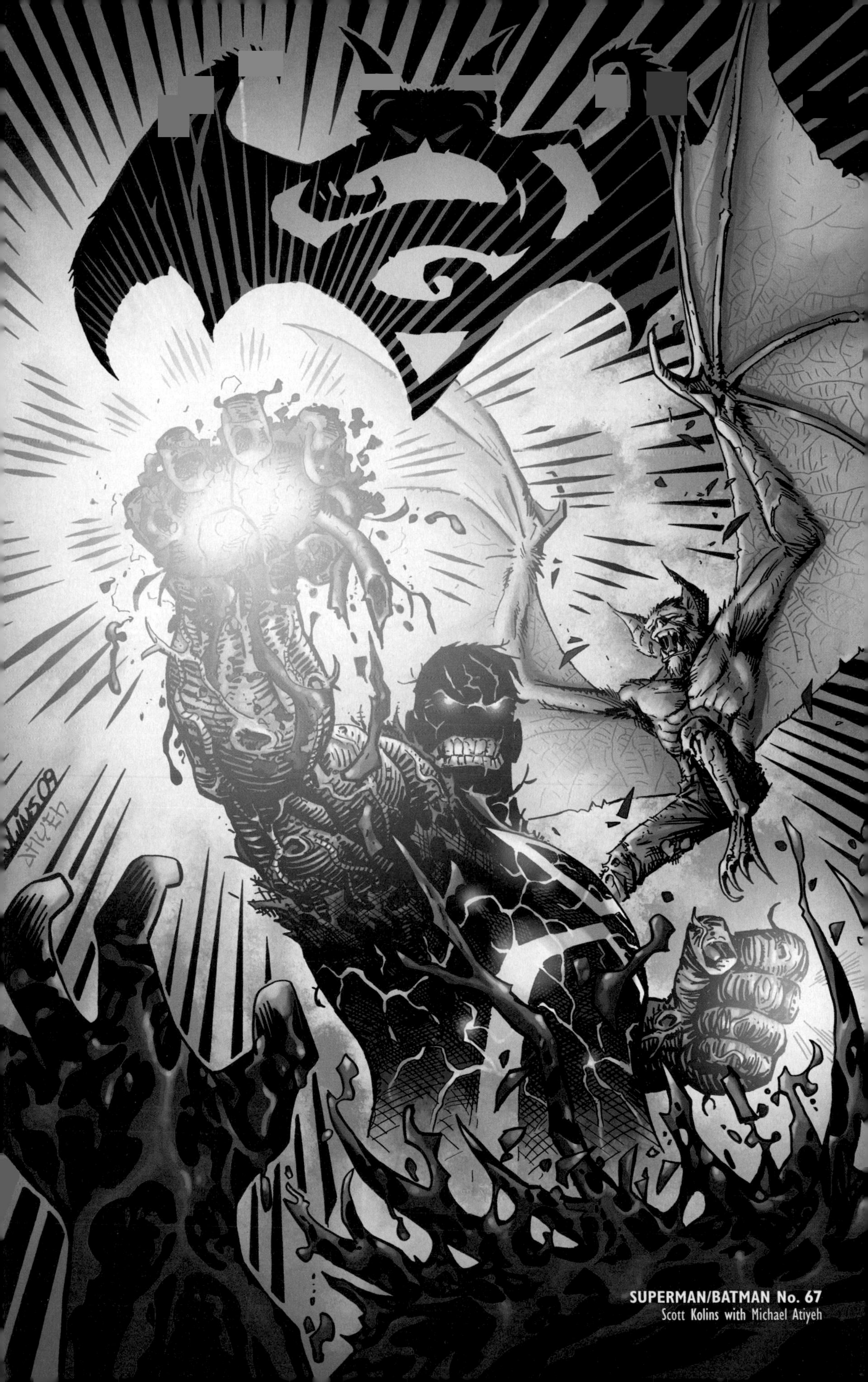

SUPERMAN/BATMAN No. 67
Scott Kolins with Michael Atiyeh

NIGHT OF THE CURE
PART TWO

Story and Art: Scott Kolins

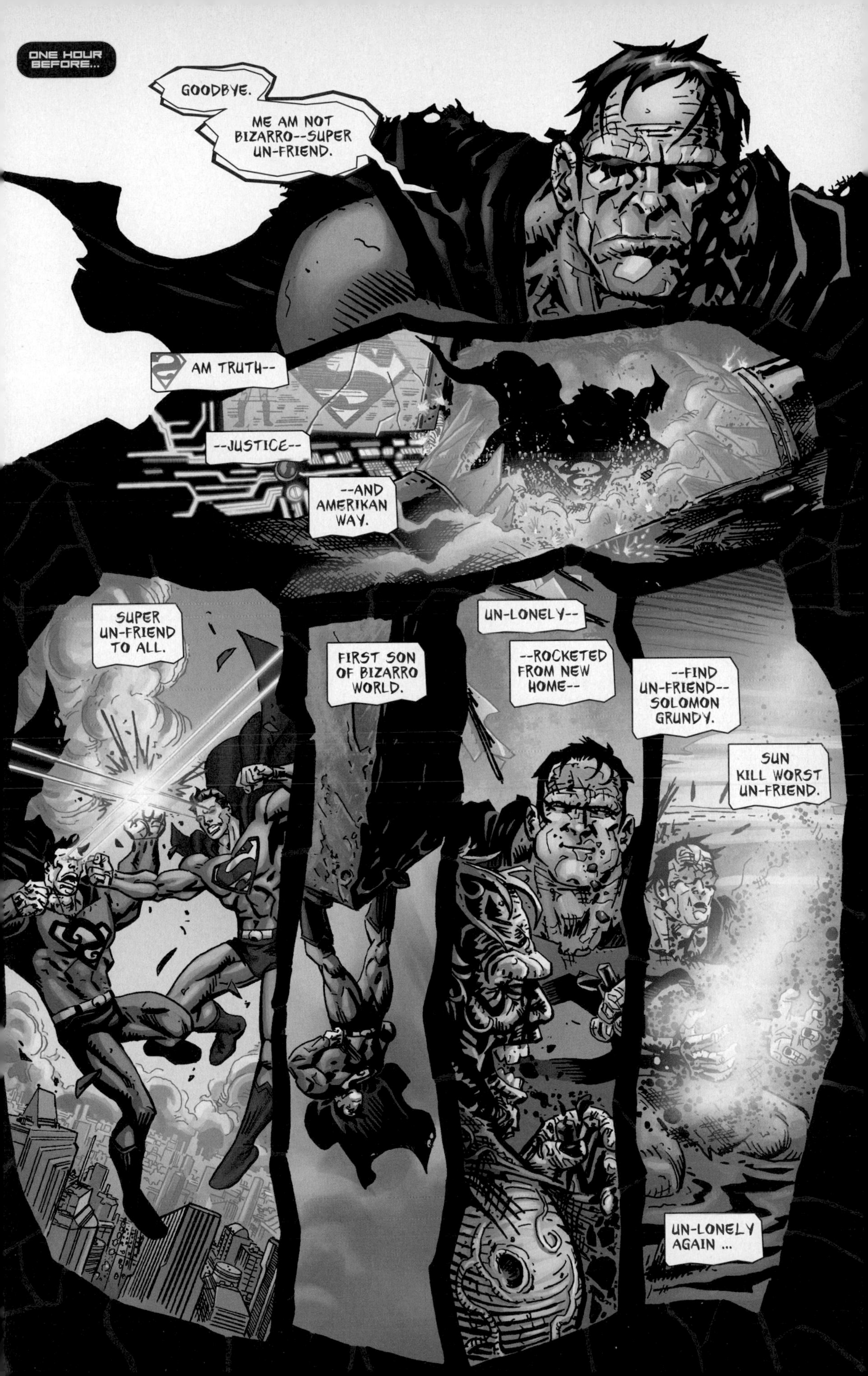
ONE HOUR BEFORE...
GOODBYE.
ME AM NOT BIZARRO--SUPER UN-FRIEND.
AM TRUTH--
--JUSTICE--
--AND AMERIKAN WAY.
SUPER UN-FRIEND TO ALL.
FIRST SON OF BIZARRO WORLD.
UN-LONELY--
--ROCKETED FROM NEW HOME--
--FIND UN-FRIEND--SOLOMON GRUNDY.
SUN KILL WORST UN-FRIEND.
UN-LONELY AGAIN ...

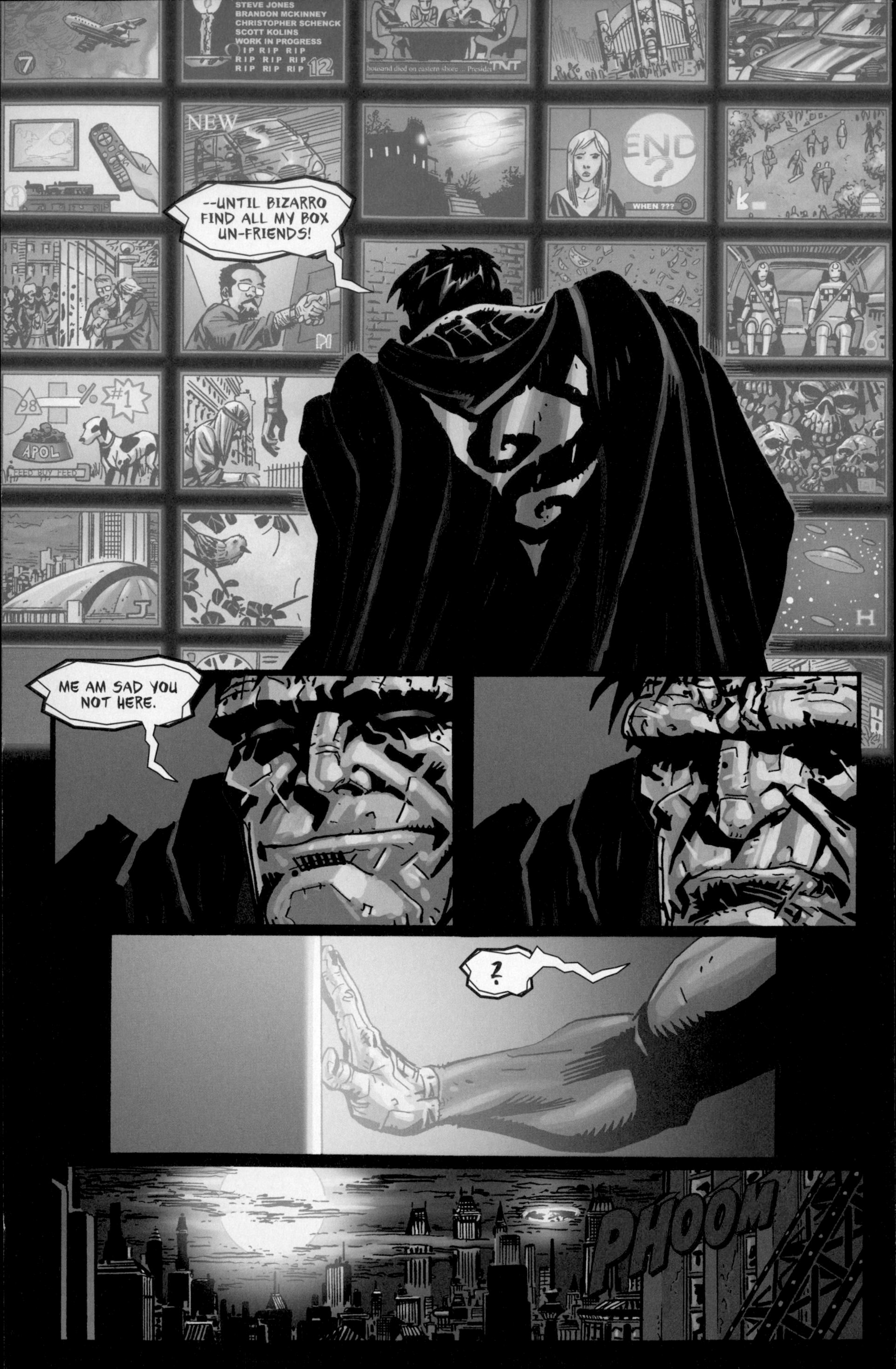

STEVE JONES
BRANDON MCKINNEY
CHRISTOPHER SCHENCK
SCOTT KOLINS
WORK IN PROGRESS
RIP RIP RIP
RIP RIP RIP
12
TNT
NEW
END ?
WHEN ???
--UNTIL BIZARRO FIND ALL MY BOX UN-FRIENDS!
#1
APOL
FEED BUY FEED
ME AM SAD YOU NOT HERE.
?
PHOOM

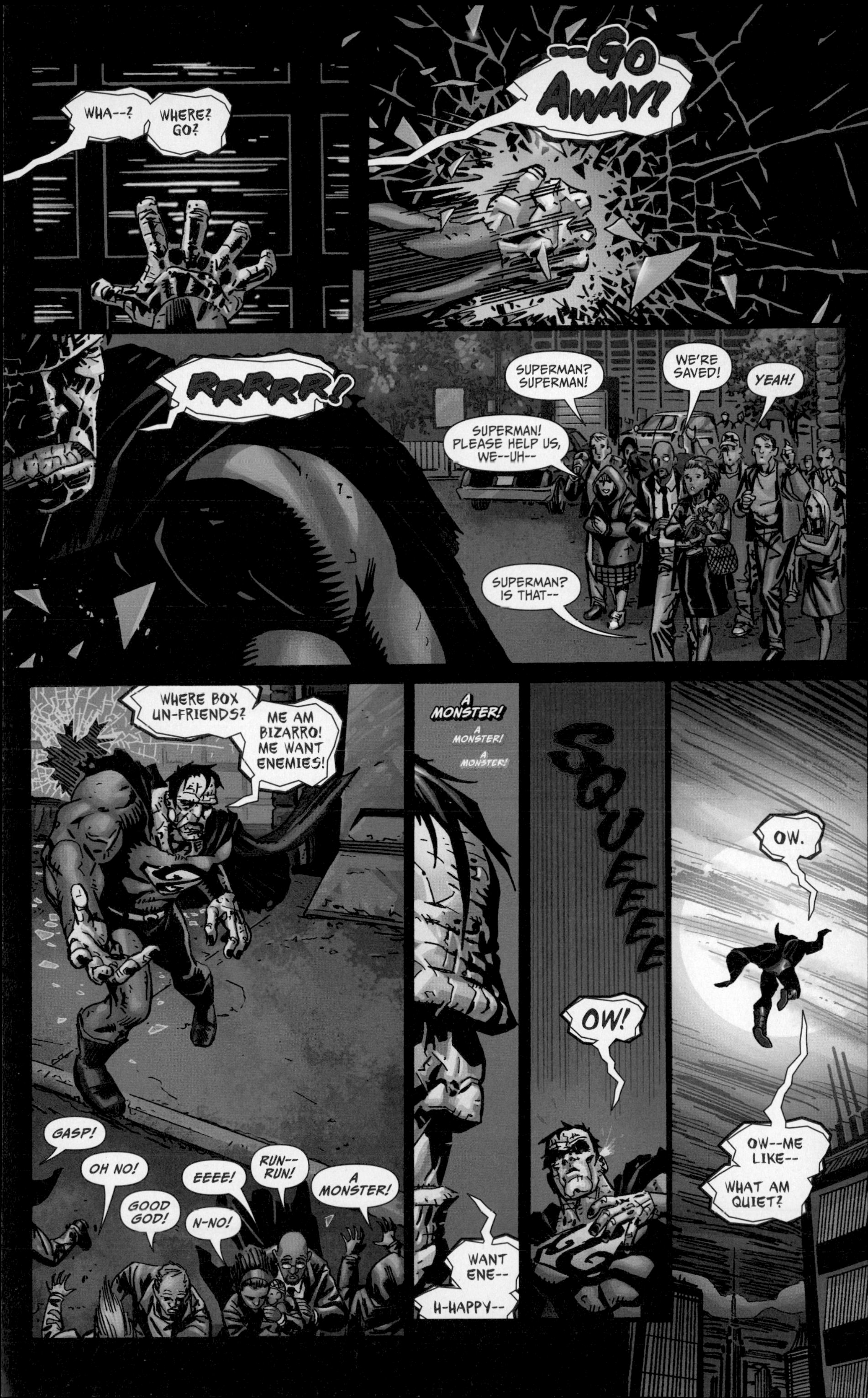
WHA--?
WHERE? GO?
--GO AWAY!
RRRRR!
SUPERMAN? SUPERMAN!
WE'RE SAVED!
YEAH!
SUPERMAN! PLEASE HELP US, WE--UH--
SUPERMAN? IS THAT--
WHERE BOX UN-FRIENDS?
ME AM BIZARRO! ME WANT ENEMIES!
GASP!
OH NO!
GOOD GOD!
EEEE!
N-NO!
RUN--RUN!
A MONSTER!
A MONSTER!
A MONSTER!
A MONSTER!
WANT ENE--
H-HAPPY--
SQUEEEEE
OW!
OW.
OW--ME LIKE--
WHAT AM QUIET?

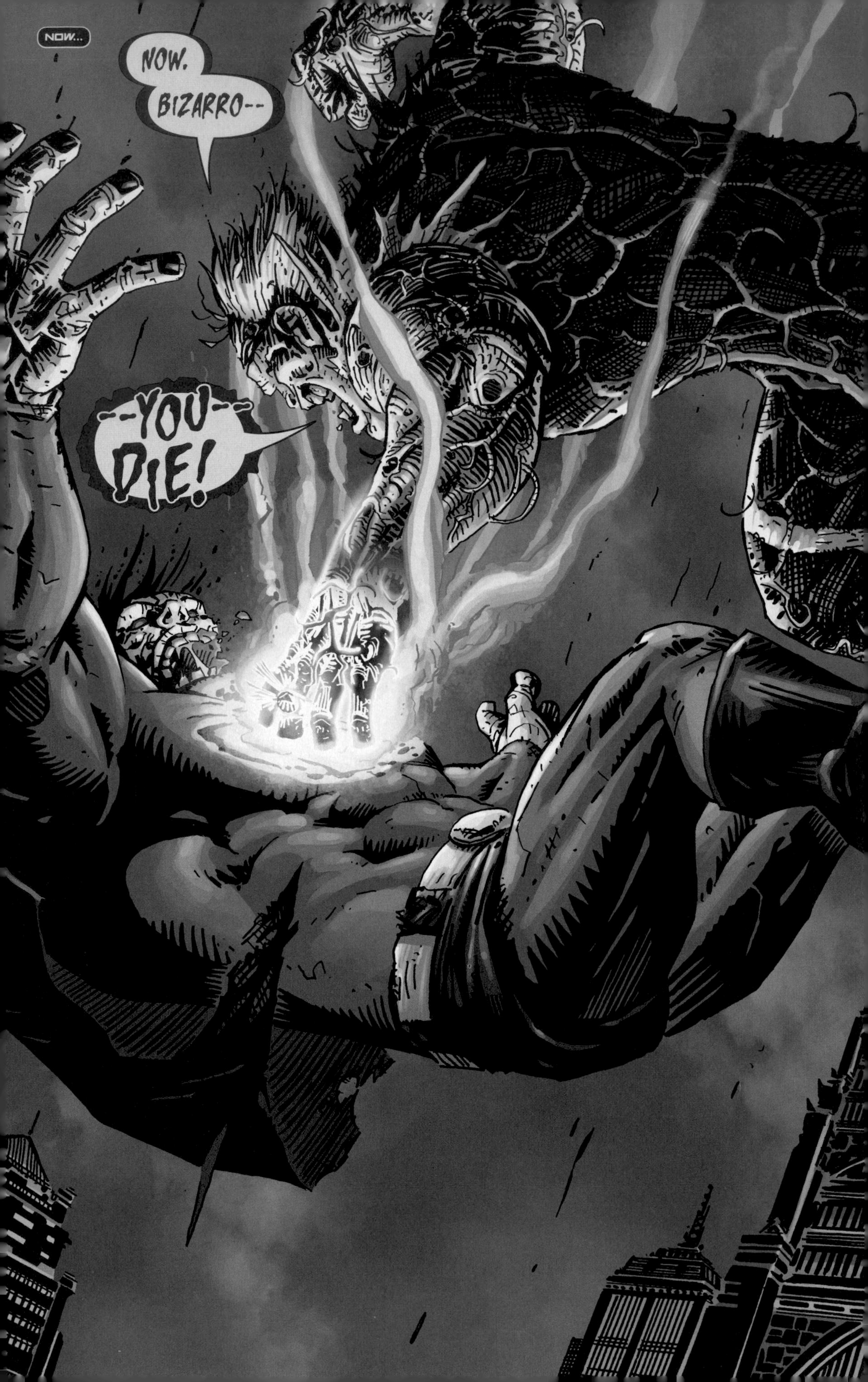
NOW...
NOW. BIZARRO--
--YOU--DIE!

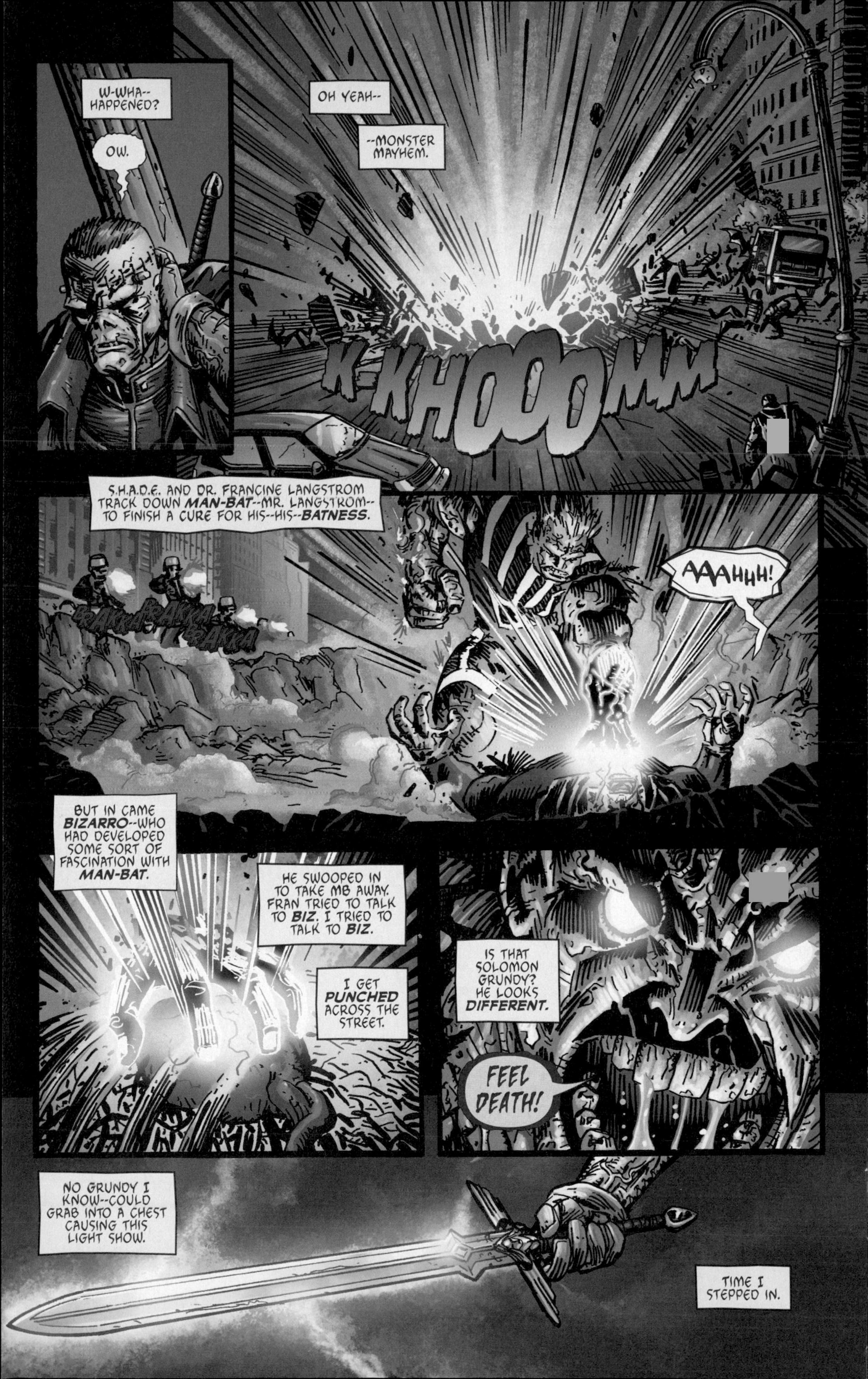
W-WHA--
HAPPENED?
OW.
OH YEAH--
--MONSTER
MAYHEM.
K-KHOOOMM
S.H.A.D.E. AND DR. FRANCINE LANGSTROM TRACK DOWN MAN-BAT--MR. LANGSTROM--TO FINISH A CURE FOR HIS--HIS--BATNESS.
BRAKKA BRAKKA BRAKKA
AAAHHH!
BUT IN CAME BIZARRO--WHO HAD DEVELOPED SOME SORT OF FASCINATION WITH MAN-BAT.
HE SWOOPED IN TO TAKE MB AWAY. FRAN TRIED TO TALK TO BIZ. I TRIED TO TALK TO BIZ.
I GET PUNCHED ACROSS THE STREET.
IS THAT SOLOMON GRUNDY? HE LOOKS DIFFERENT.
FEEL DEATH!
NO GRUNDY I KNOW--COULD GRAB INTO A CHEST CAUSING THIS LIGHT SHOW.
TIME I STEPPED IN.

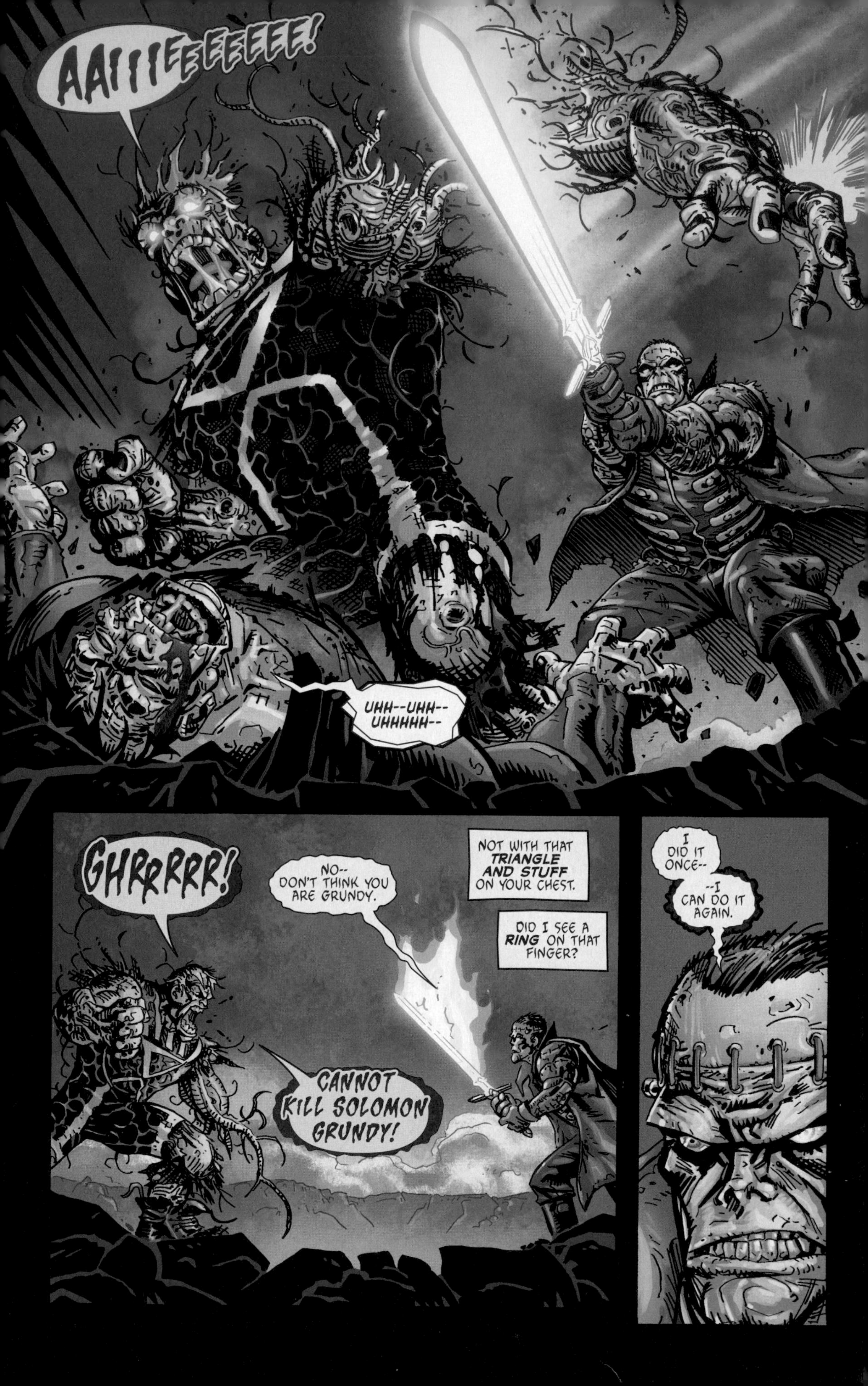
AAIIIEEEEEEE!
UHH--UHH--UHHHHH--
GHRRRRR!
NO--DON'T THINK YOU ARE GRUNDY.
CANNOT KILL SOLOMON GRUNDY!
NOT WITH THAT TRIANGLE AND STUFF ON YOUR CHEST.
DID I SEE A RING ON THAT FINGER?
I DID IT ONCE--
--I CAN DO IT AGAIN.

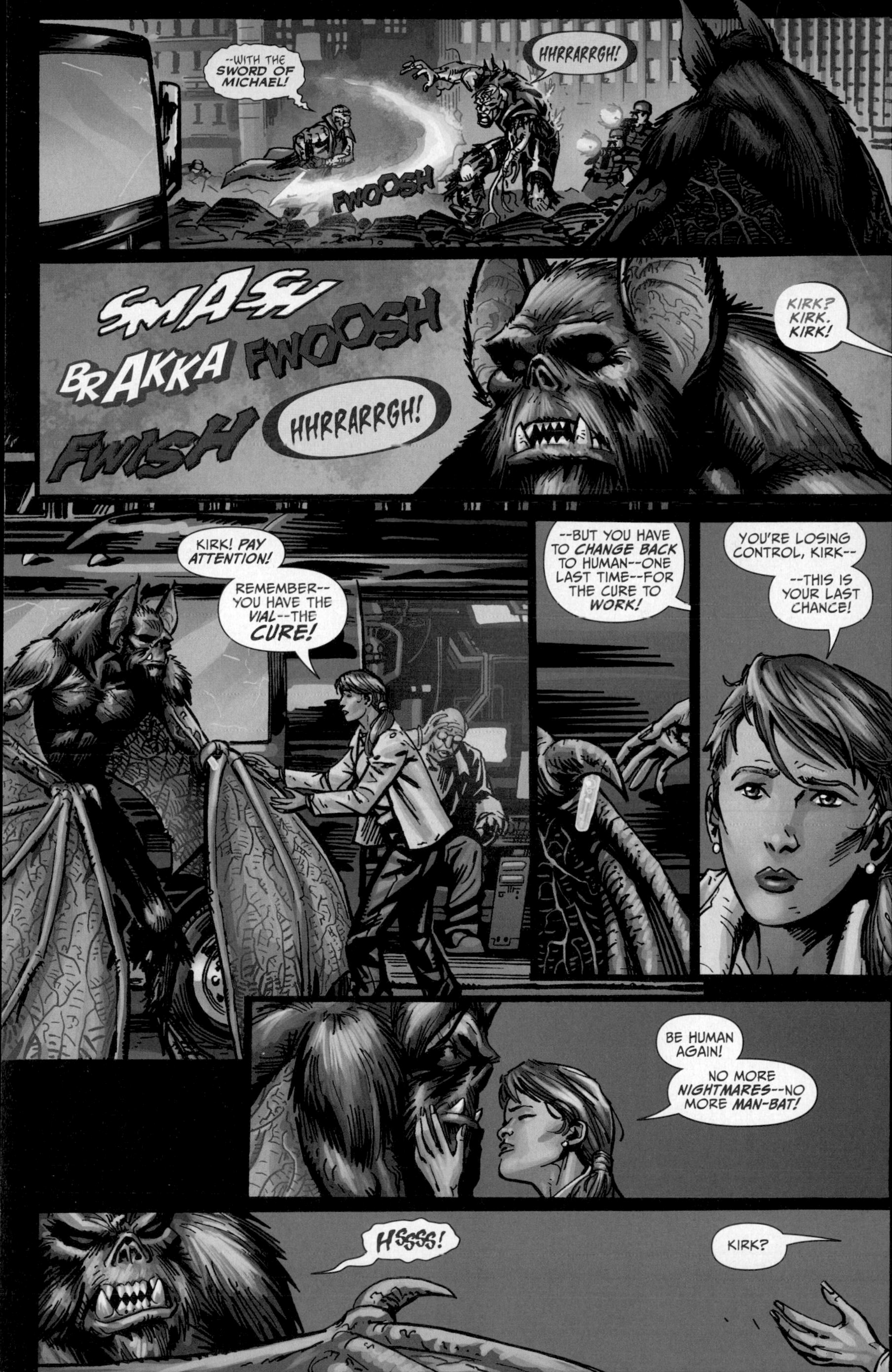
--WITH THE SWORD OF MICHAEL!
HHRRARRGH!
FWOOSH
SMASH
BRAKKA
FWOOSH
FWISH
HHRRARRGH!
KIRK? KIRK. KIRK!
KIRK! PAY ATTENTION!
REMEMBER-- YOU HAVE THE VIAL--THE CURE!
--BUT YOU HAVE TO CHANGE BACK TO HUMAN--ONE LAST TIME--FOR THE CURE TO WORK!
YOU'RE LOSING CONTROL, KIRK--
--THIS IS YOUR LAST CHANCE!
BE HUMAN AGAIN!
NO MORE NIGHTMARES--NO MORE MAN-BAT!
HSSSS!
KIRK?

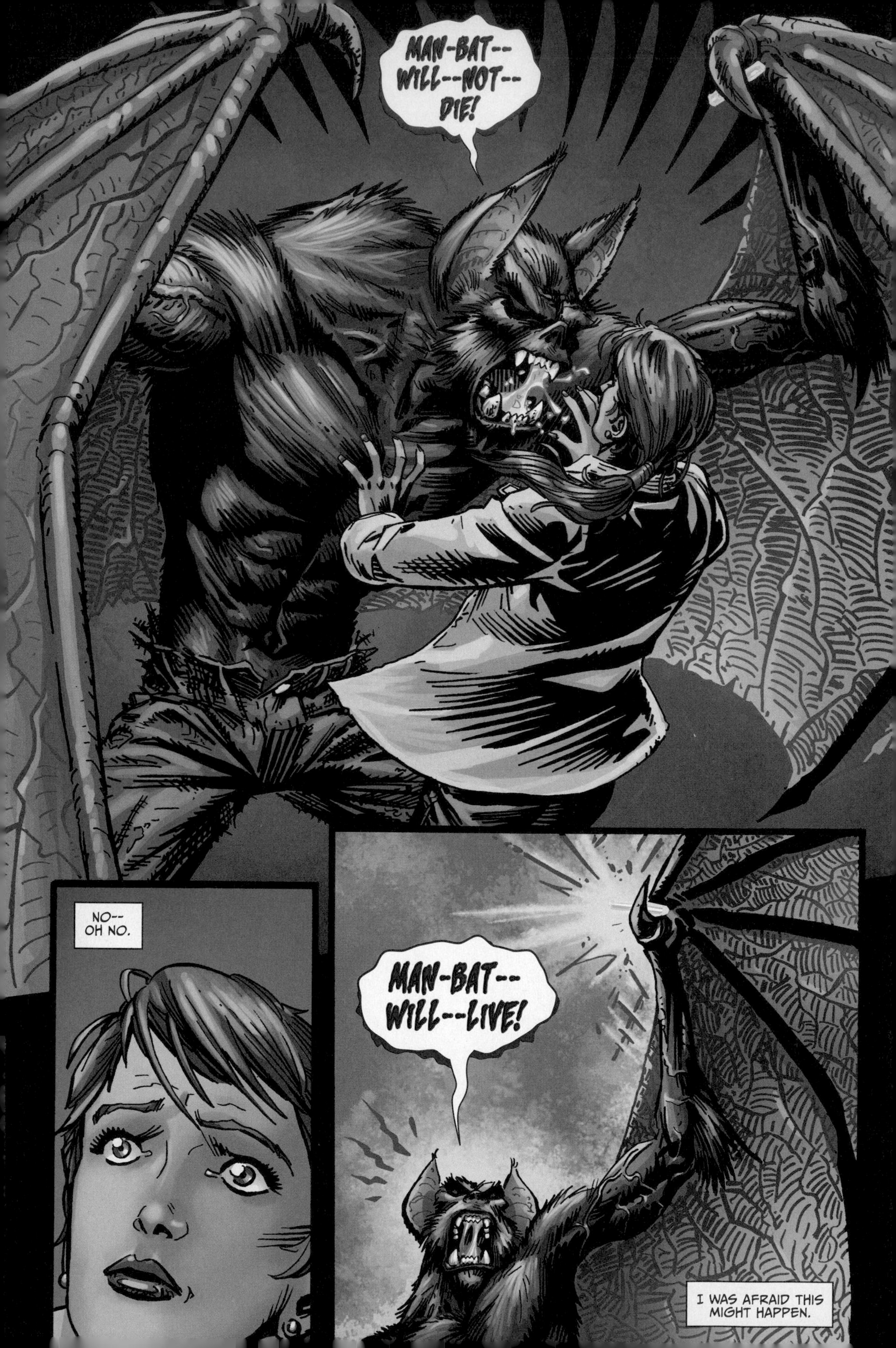
MAN-BAT--
WILL--NOT--
DIE!
NO--
OH NO.
MAN-BAT--
WILL--LIVE!
I WAS AFRAID THIS
MIGHT HAPPEN.

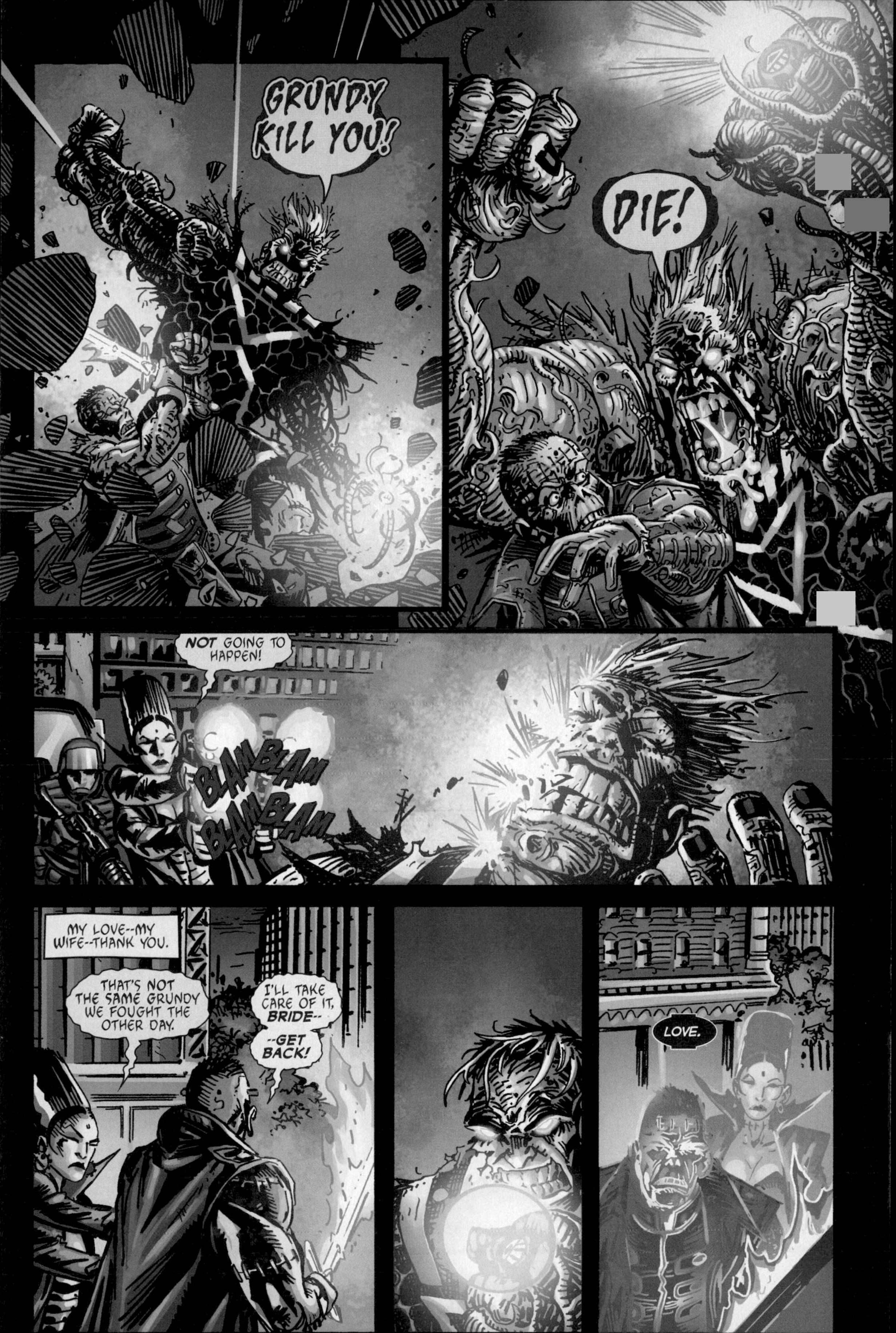
GRUNDY KILL YOU!
DIE!
NOT GOING TO HAPPEN!
BLAMBLAM BLAMBLAM
MY LOVE--MY WIFE--THANK YOU.
THAT'S NOT THE SAME GRUNDY WE FOUGHT THE OTHER DAY.
I'LL TAKE CARE OF IT, BRIDE--
--GET BACK!
LOVE.

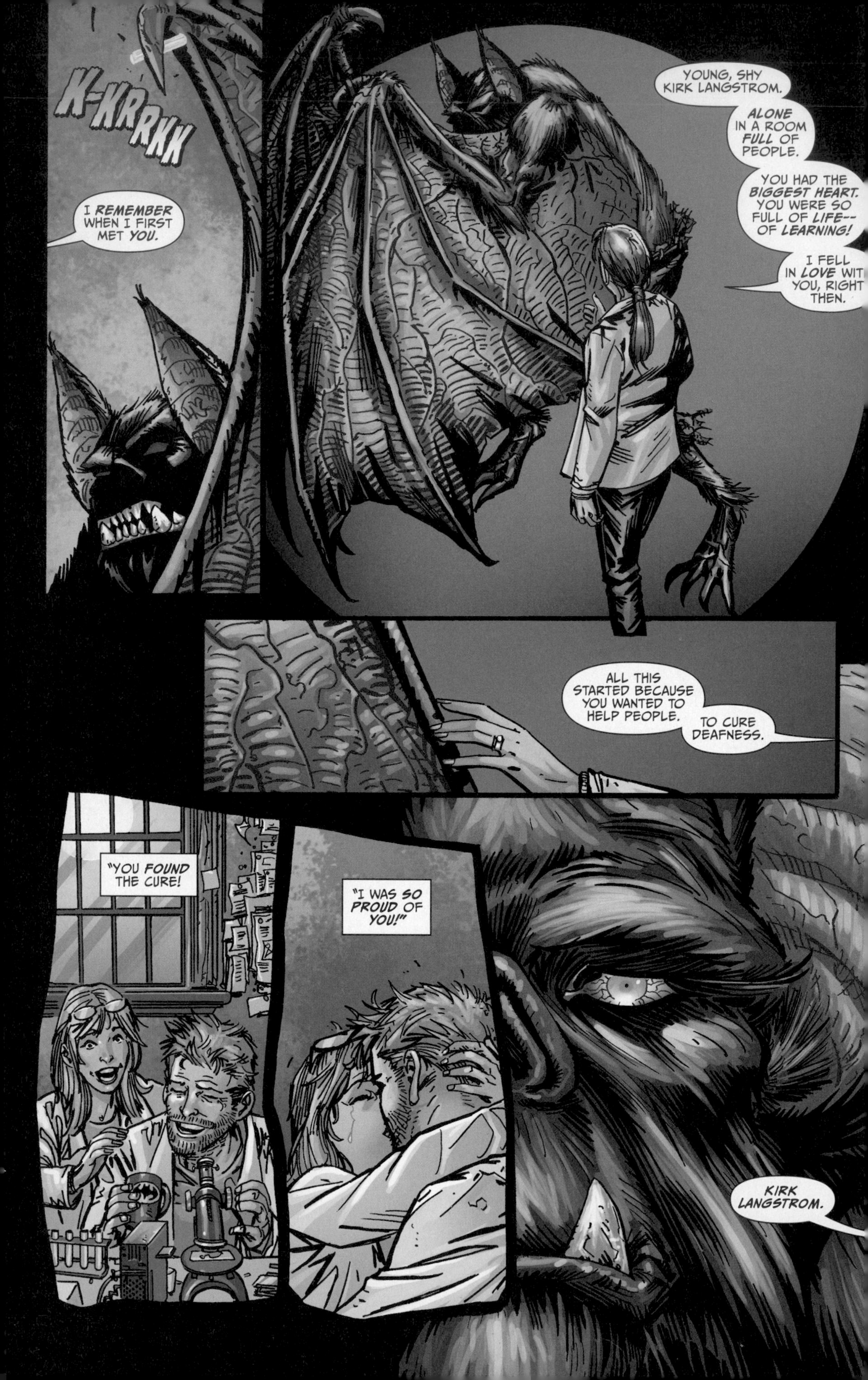
K-KRRRKK
I REMEMBER WHEN I FIRST MET YOU.
YOUNG, SHY KIRK LANGSTROM.
ALONE IN A ROOM FULL OF PEOPLE.
YOU HAD THE BIGGEST HEART. YOU WERE SO FULL OF LIFE-- OF LEARNING!
I FELL IN LOVE WIT YOU, RIGHT THEN.
ALL THIS STARTED BECAUSE YOU WANTED TO HELP PEOPLE.
TO CURE DEAFNESS.
"YOU FOUND THE CURE!
"I WAS SO PROUD OF YOU!"
KIRK LANGSTROM.

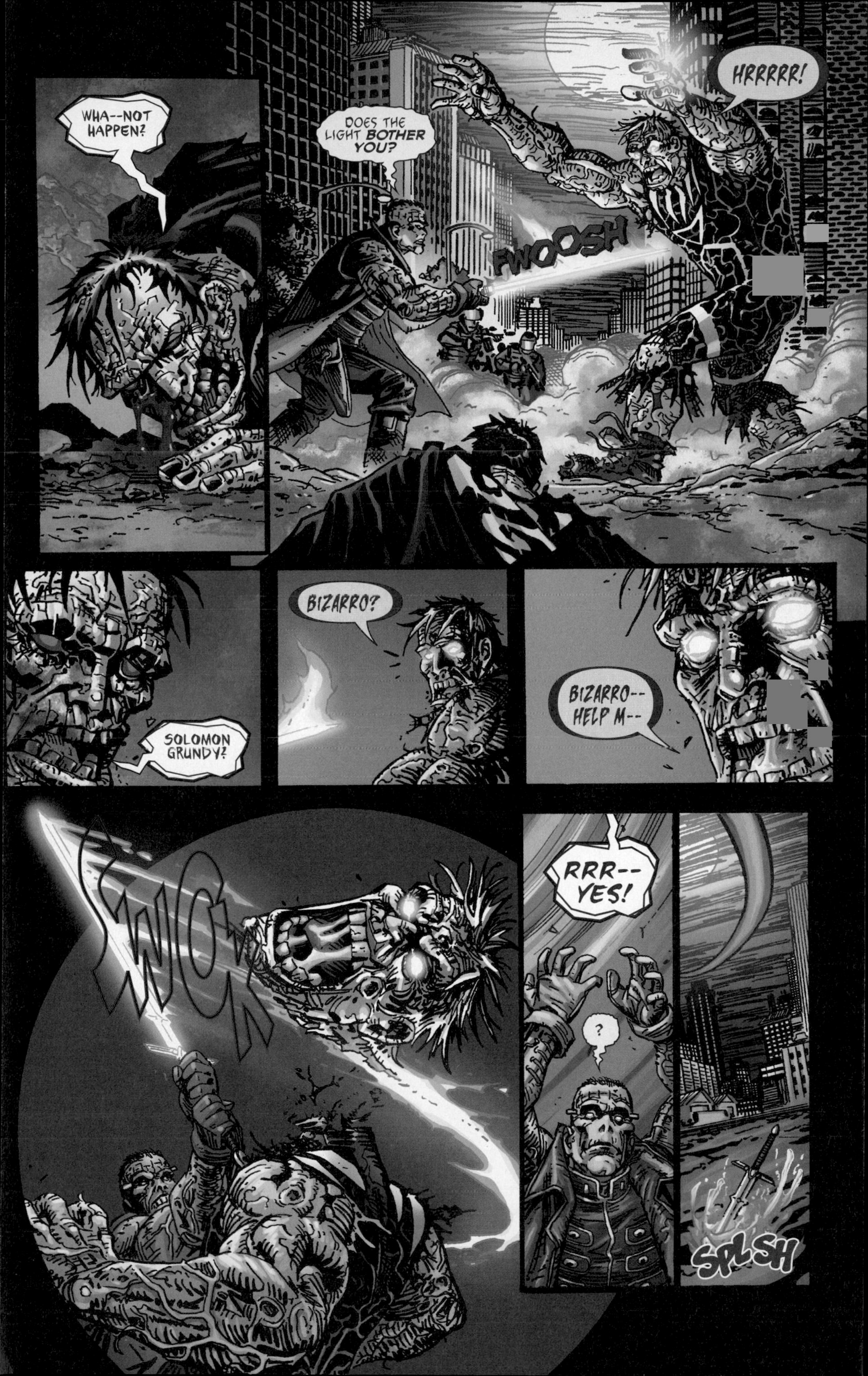
WHA--NOT HAPPEN?
DOES THE LIGHT BOTHER YOU?
HRRRRR!
FWOOSH
SOLOMON GRUNDY?
BIZARRO?
BIZARRO-- HELP M--
SWOCK
RRR-- YES!
?
SPLSH

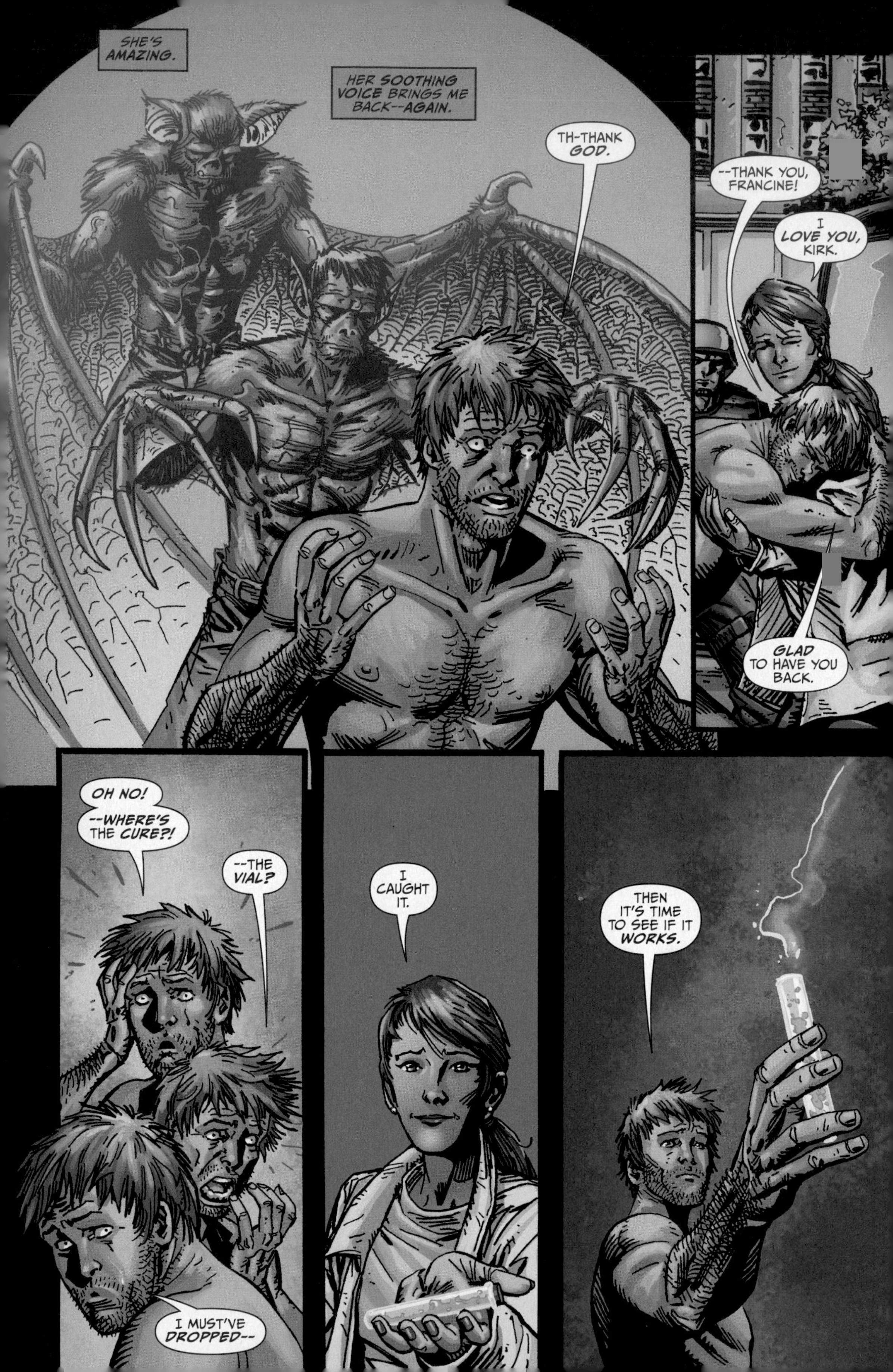
SHE'S AMAZING.
HER SOOTHING VOICE BRINGS ME BACK--AGAIN.
TH-THANK GOD.
--THANK YOU, FRANCINE!
I LOVE YOU, KIRK.
GLAD TO HAVE YOU BACK.
OH NO! --WHERE'S THE CURE?!
--THE VIAL?
I MUST'VE DROPPED--
I CAUGHT IT.
THEN IT'S TIME TO SEE IF IT WORKS.

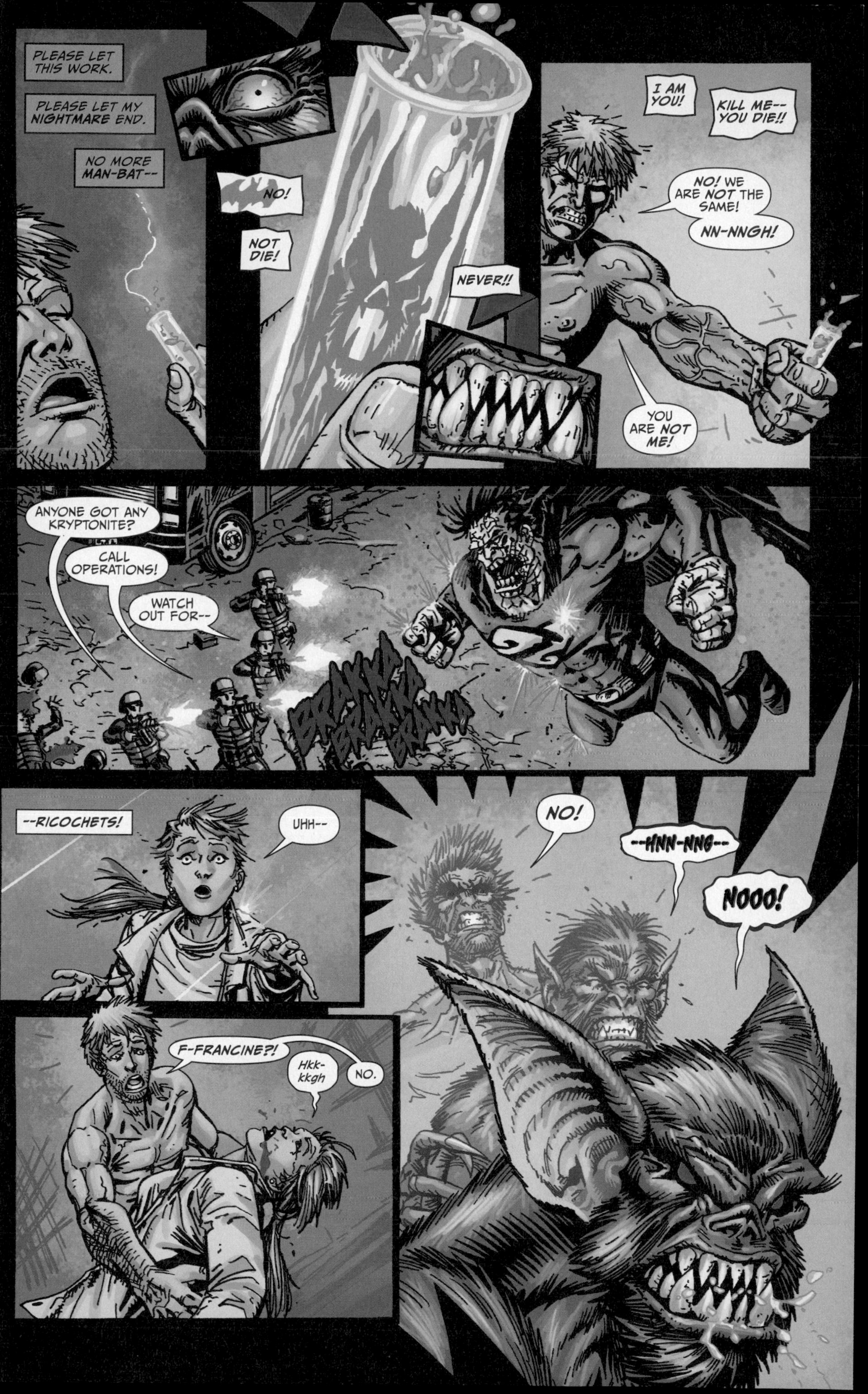
PLEASE LET THIS WORK.
PLEASE LET MY NIGHTMARE END.
NO MORE MAN-BAT--
NO!
NOT DIE!
NEVER!!
I AM YOU!
KILL ME-- YOU DIE!!
NO! WE ARE NOT THE SAME!
NN-NNGH!
YOU ARE NOT ME!
ANYONE GOT ANY KRYPTONITE?
CALL OPERATIONS!
WATCH OUT FOR--
--RICOCHETS!
UHH--
F-FRANCINE?!
Hkk-kkgh
NO.
NO!
--HNN-NNG--
NOOO!

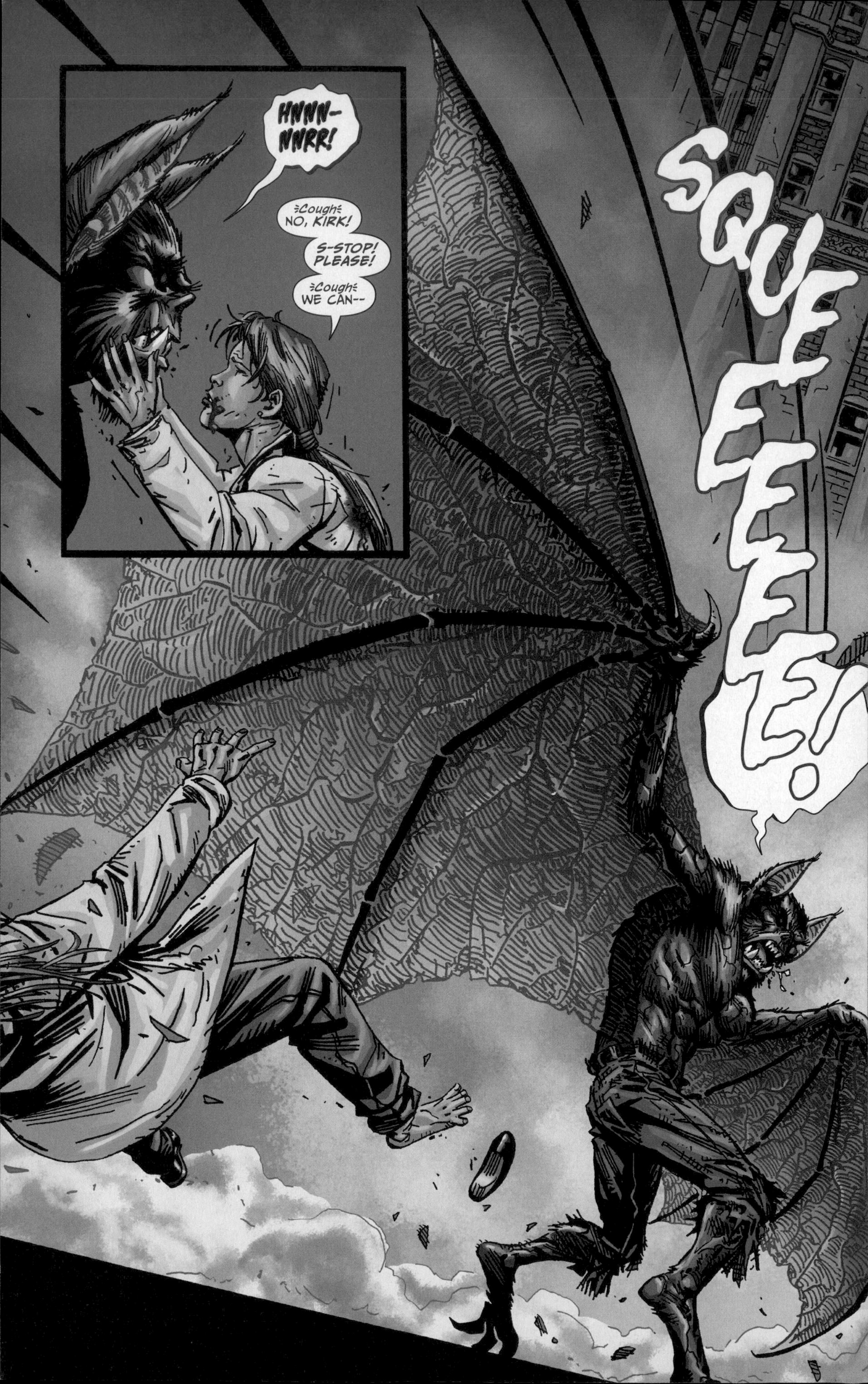

HNNN-NNRR!
Cough NO, KIRK!
S-STOP! PLEASE!
Cough WE CAN--
SQUEEEEEEE!

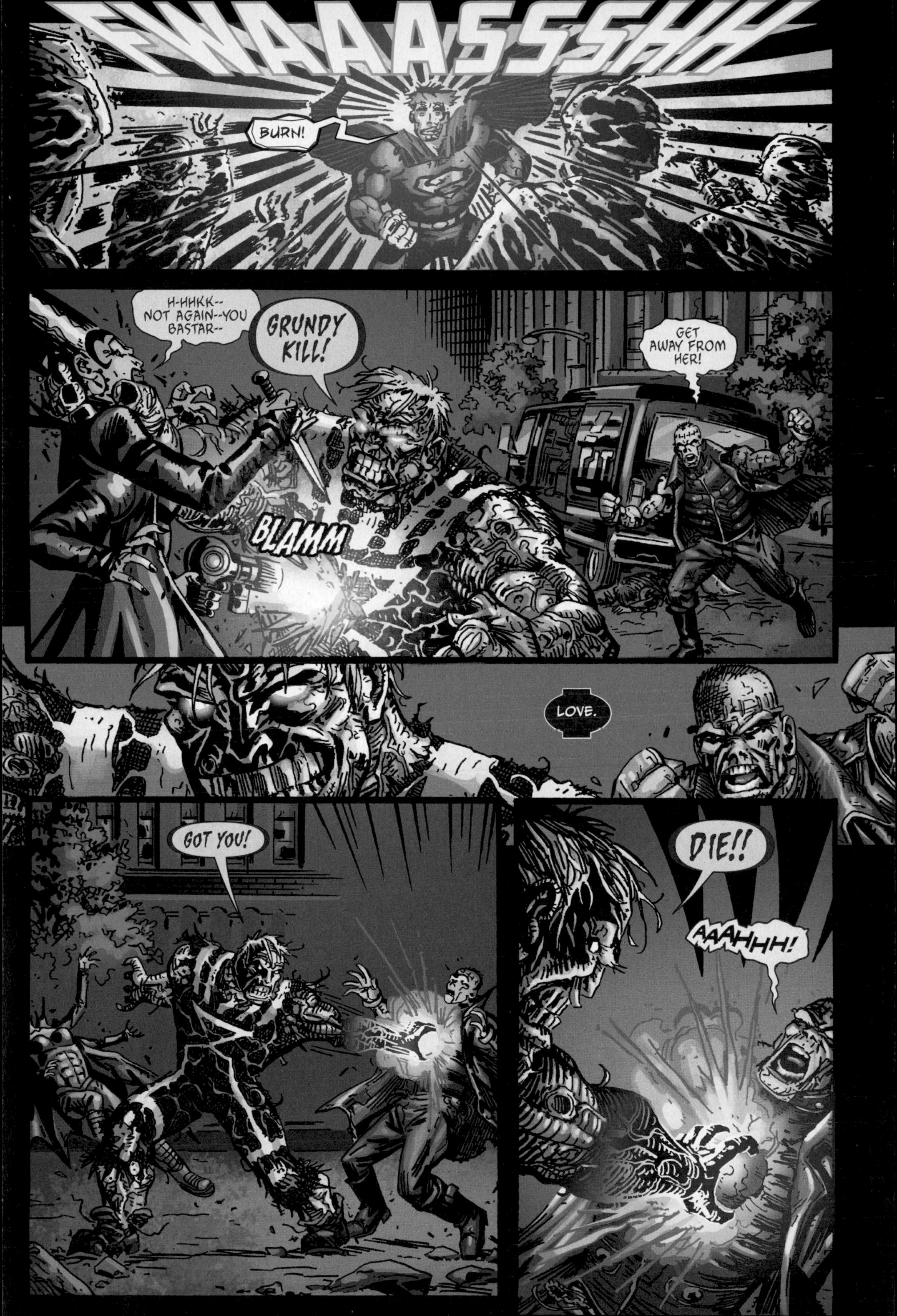
FWAAASSSHH
BURN!
H-HHKK--
NOT AGAIN--YOU
BASTAR--
GRUNDY
KILL!
BLAMM
GET
AWAY FROM
HER!
LOVE.
GOT YOU!
DIE!!
AAAHHH!

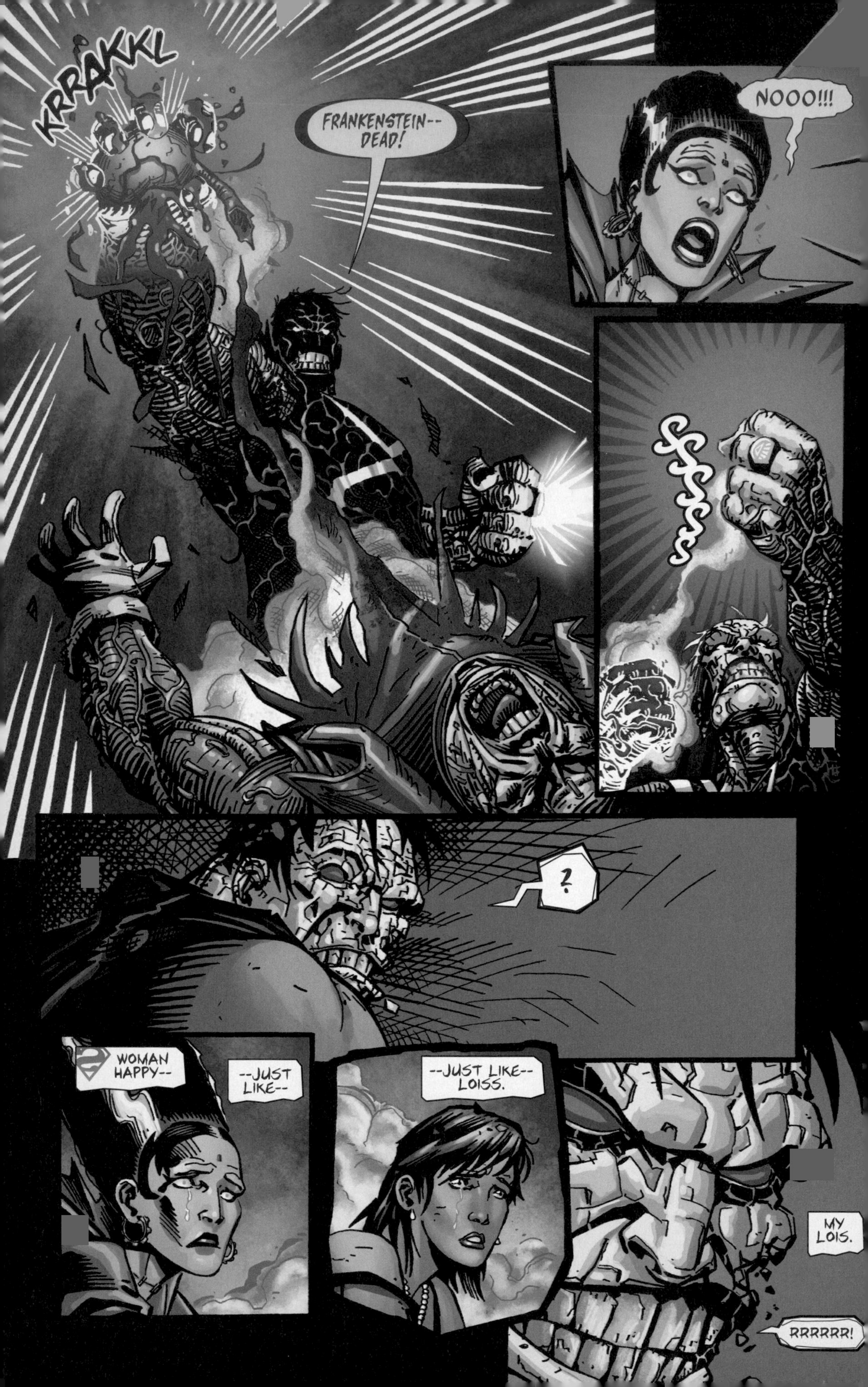
KRRAKKL
FRANKENSTEIN--DEAD!
NOOO!!!
SSSSSS
?
WOMAN HAPPY--
--JUST LIKE--
--JUST LIKE--LOISS.
MY LOIS.
RRRRRR!

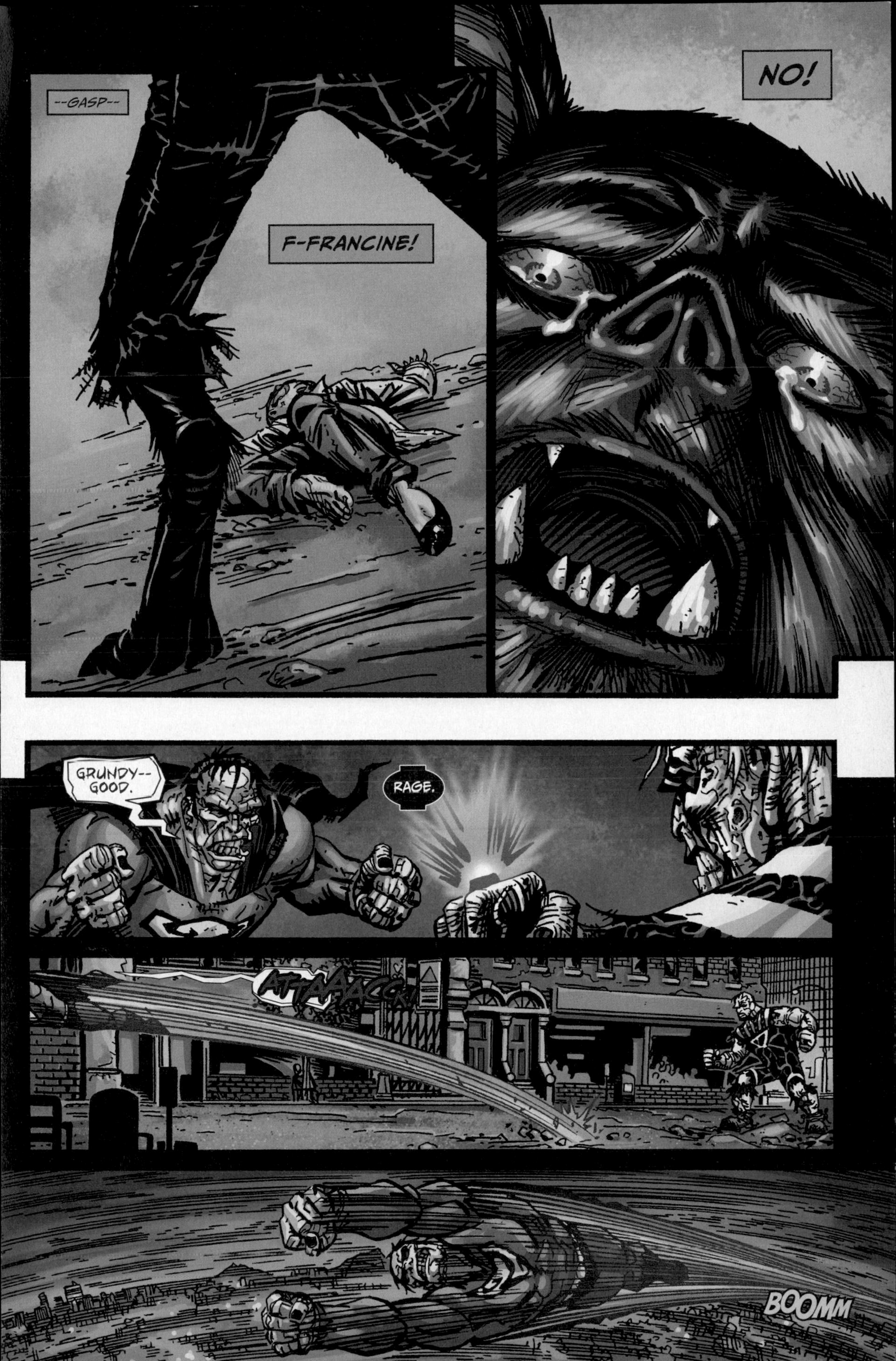
--GASP--
F-FRANCINE!
NO!
GRUNDY-- GOOD.
RAGE.
BOOMM

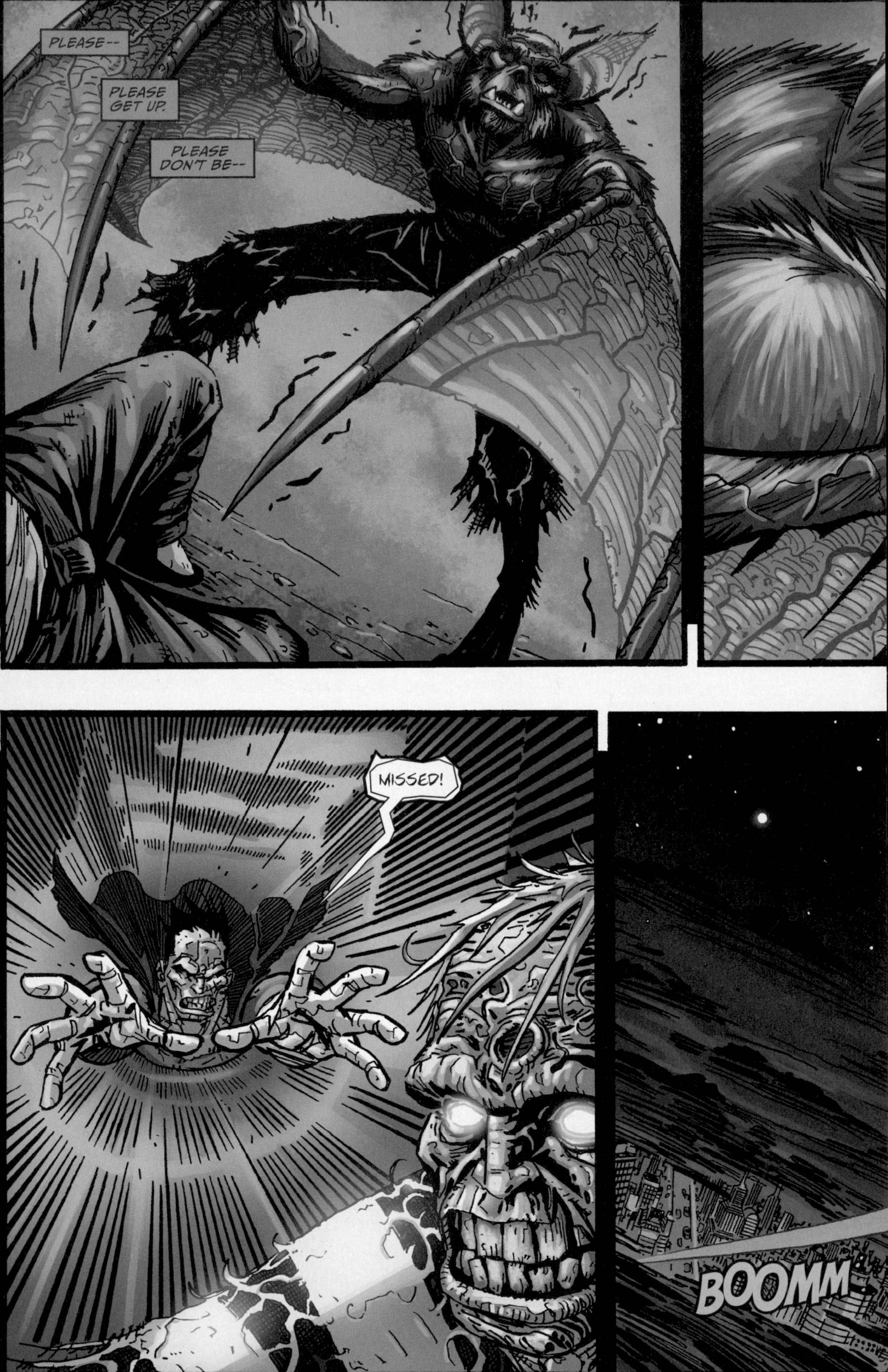
PLEASE--
PLEASE GET UP.
PLEASE DON'T BE--
MISSED!
BOOMM

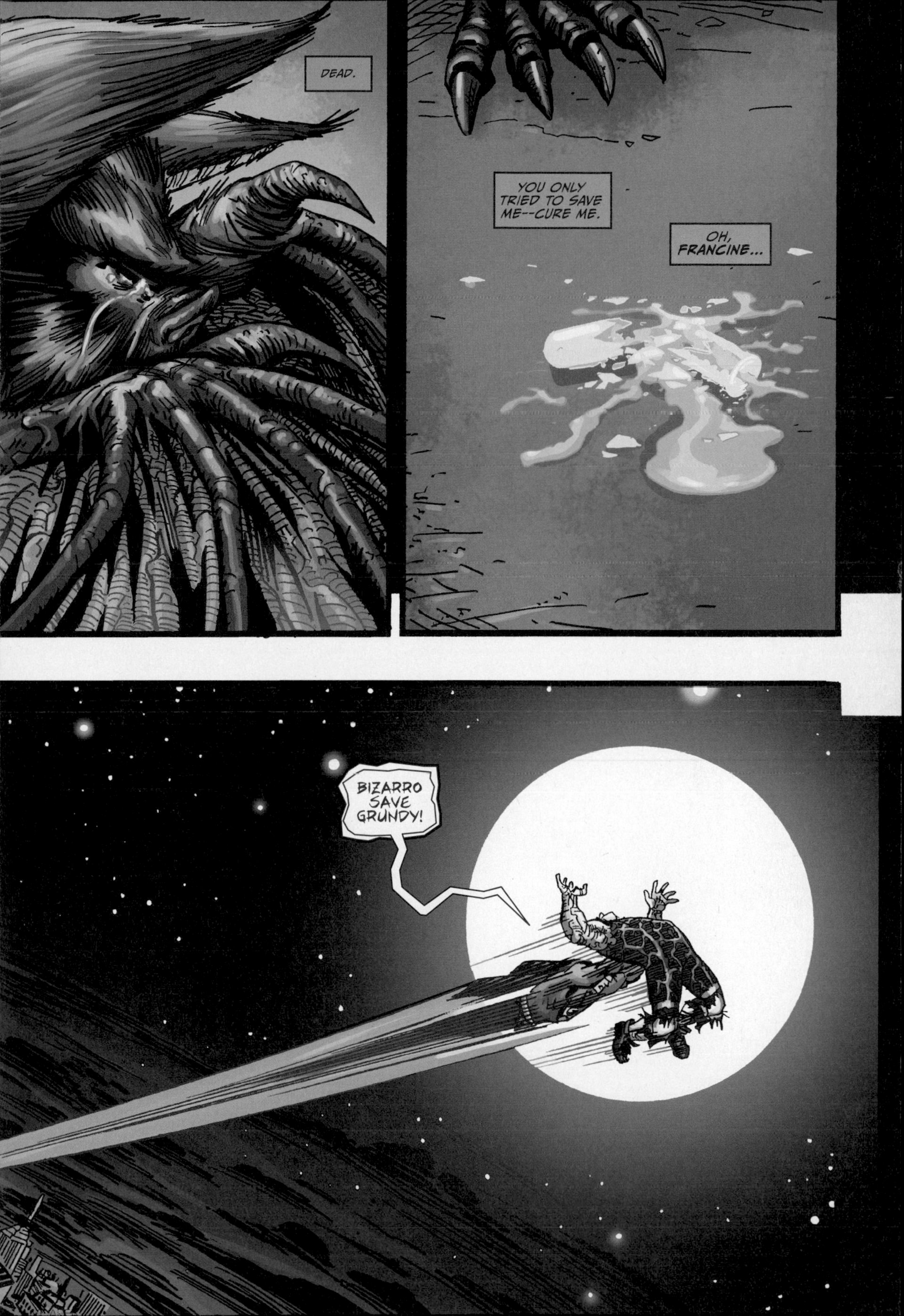
DEAD.
YOU ONLY TRIED TO SAVE ME--CURE ME.
OH, FRANCINE...
BIZARRO SAVE GRUNDY!

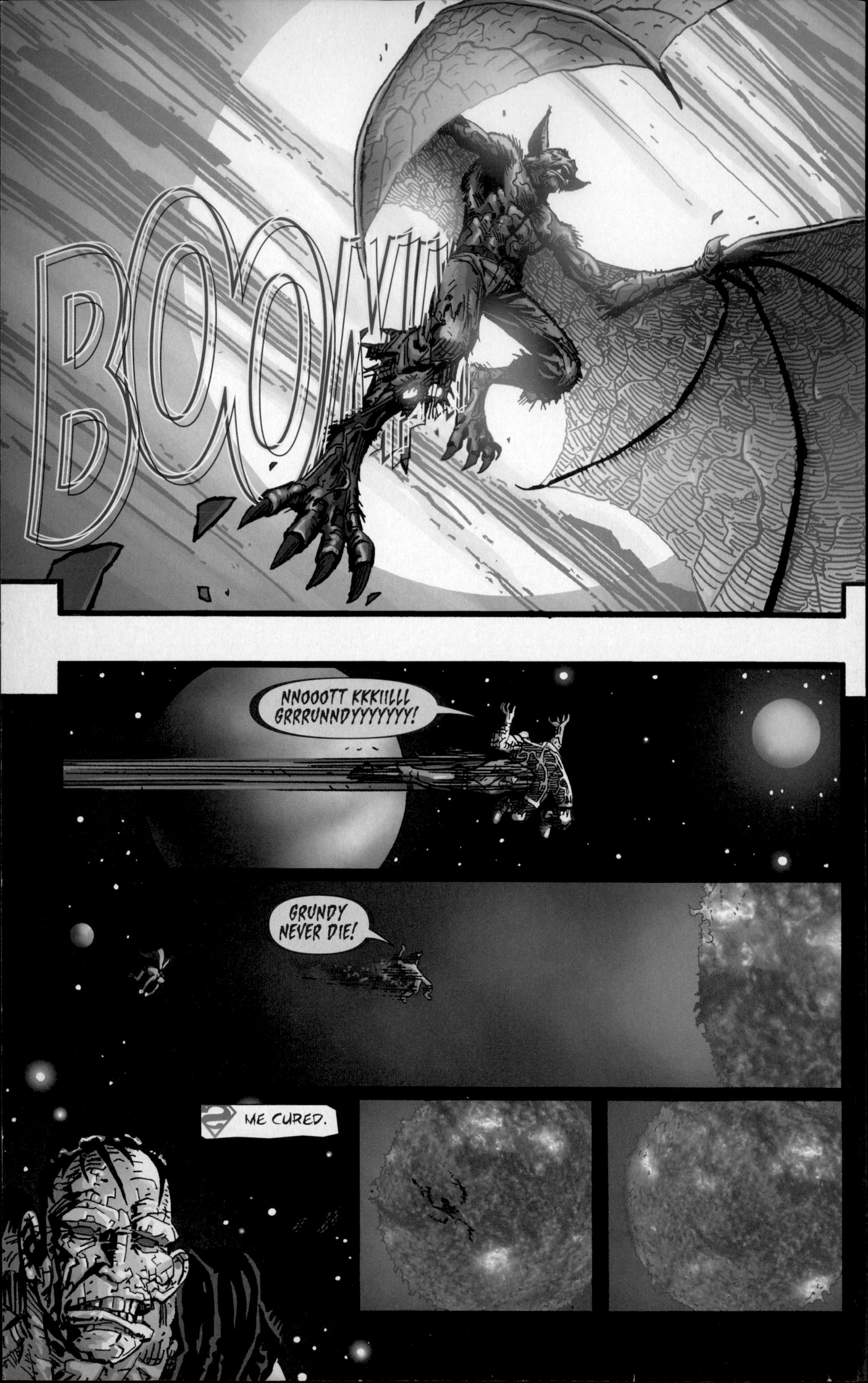
BOOOM
NNOOOTT KKKIILLL GRRRUNNDYYYYYYY!
GRUNDY NEVER DIE!
ME CURED.

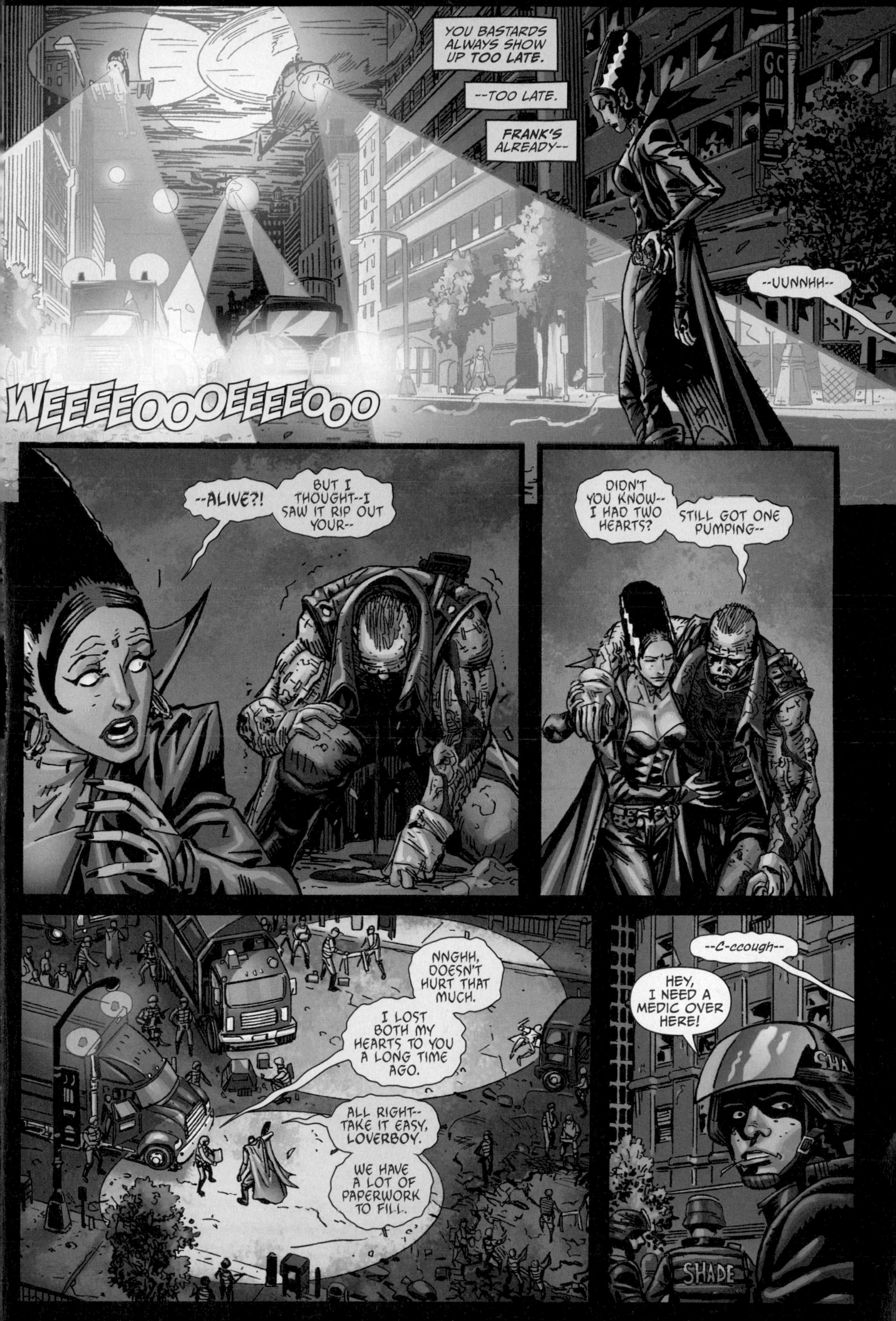

YOU BASTARDS ALWAYS SHOW UP TOO LATE.
--TOO LATE.
FRANK'S ALREADY--
--UUNNHH--
WEEEEOOOEEEEOoo
--ALIVE?!
BUT I THOUGHT--I SAW IT RIP OUT YOUR--
DIDN'T YOU KNOW--I HAD TWO HEARTS?
STILL GOT ONE PUMPING--
NNGHH, DOESN'T HURT THAT MUCH.
I LOST BOTH MY HEARTS TO YOU A LONG TIME AGO.
ALL RIGHT--TAKE IT EASY, LOVERBOY.
WE HAVE A LOT OF PAPERWORK TO FILL.
--C-ccough--
HEY, I NEED A MEDIC OVER HERE!
SHADE

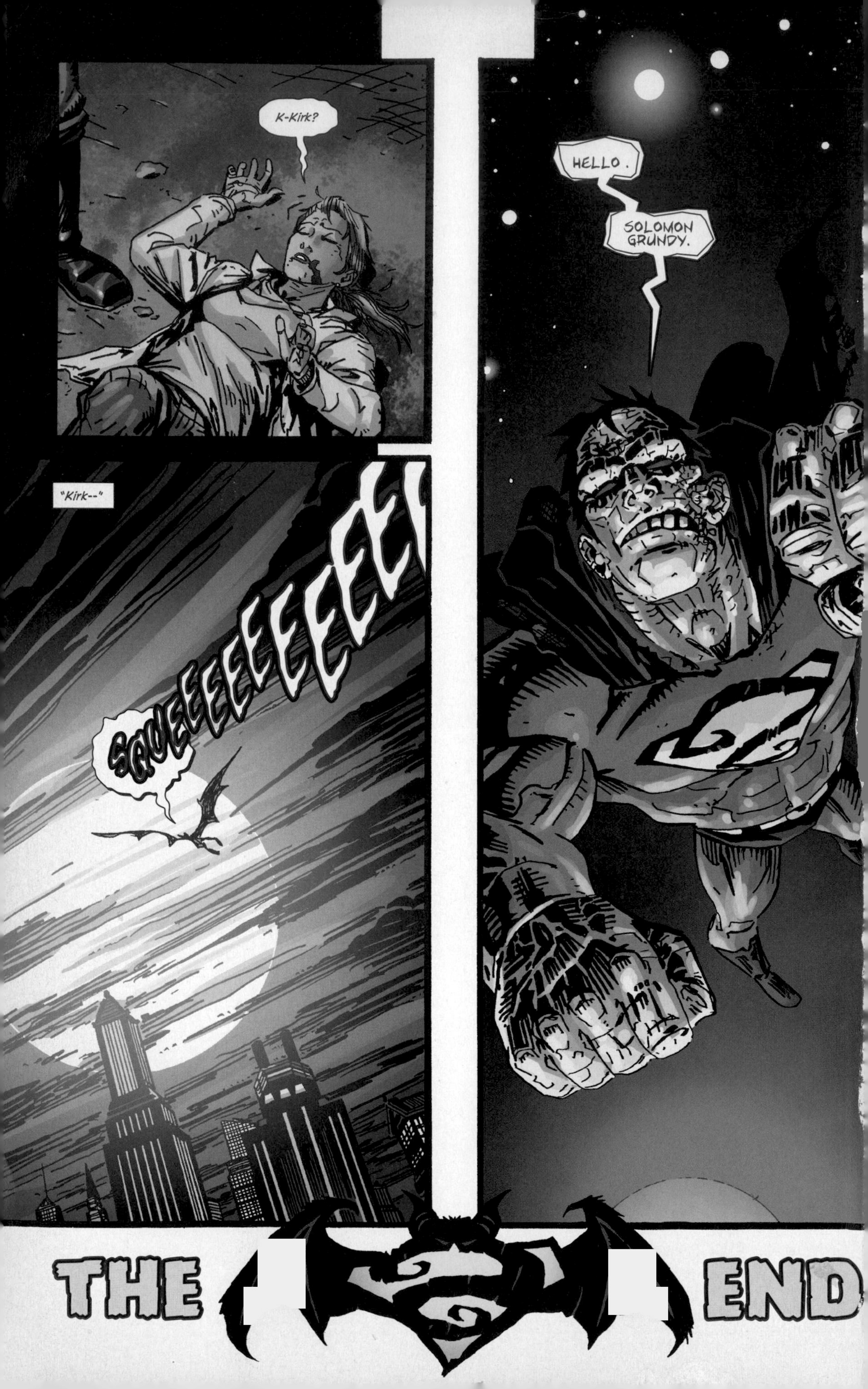
K-Kirk?
"Kirk--"
SQUEEEEEEEEEEE
HELLO.
SOLOMON GRUNDY.
THE END